Corporate Social Responsibility, Human Rights and the Law

D1423490

Routledge research in corporate law

Corporate Social Responsibility, Human Rights and the Law

Multinational corporations in developing countries

Olufemi Amao

Routledge
Taylor & Francis Group

LONDON AND NEW YORK

First published 2011
by Routledge
2 Park Square, Milton Park, Abingdon, Oxon OX14 4RN

Simultaneously published in the USA and Canada
by Routledge
711 Third Avenue, New York, NY 10017

Routledge is an imprint of the Taylor & Francis Group, an informa business

First issued in paperback 2013

British Library Cataloguing in Publication Data
A catalogue record for this book is available from the British Library

Library of Congress Cataloging in Publication Data
Amao, Olufemi.
  Corporate social responsibility, human rights and the law:
  multinational corporations in developing countries / Olufemi
  Amao.
  p. cm. – (Routledge research in corporate law)
  1. International business enterprises–Law and legislation–
  Developing countries. 2. Corporate governance–Law and
  legislation–Social aspects. 3. Social responsibility of business–
  Developing countries. I. Title.
  K1322.A96 2011
  346'.065091724–dc22
  2011003143

ISBN: 978-0-415-59785-2 (hbk)
ISBN: 978-0-203-81555-7 (ebk)

Typeset in Baskerville
by Wearset Ltd, Boldon, Tyne and Wear

To Anne-Marie

With 606 oilfields, the Niger delta supplies 40 per cent of all the crude the United States imports and is the world capital of oil pollution. Life expectancy in its rural communities, half of which have no access to clean water, has fallen to little more than 40 years over the past two generations. Locals blame the oil that pollutes their land and can scarcely believe the contrast with the steps taken by BP and the US government to try to stop the Gulf oil leak and to protect the Louisiana shoreline from pollution.

John Vidal, "Nigeria's Agony Dwarfs the Gulf Oil Spill. The US and Europe Ignore It" *Observer*, Sunday 30 May 2010

Plainly, companies must be profitable as well as socially responsible,... CSR is no longer optional.

Gideon Spanier, "Corporate Responsibility is No Longer Optional" *Evening Standard*, 15 June 2010

Perhaps no place on earth has been as battered by oil, experts say, leaving residents here astonished at the nonstop attention paid to the gusher half a world away in the Gulf of Mexico. It was only a few weeks ago, they say, that a burst pipe belonging to Royal Dutch Shell in the mangroves was finally shut after flowing for two months: now nothing living moves in a black-and-brown world once teeming with shrimp and crab.

Adam Nossiter, "Far from Gulf, A Spill Scourge Decades Old" *New York Times*, 16 June 2010

Of course you need a profit ... but it is a by-product, a hallmark of success. It is not the be all and end all. It is not the raison d'être of business. What is the purpose of business? Friedman says the social responsibility of business is to make a profit but that will no longer do. Plain common sense will tell you that cannot do. Plain common sense will tell you that you have to have a sustainable business model. You have to inevitably go back to the considerable things that go beyond simply saying that it is the social responsibility of business to make a profit.

Stephen Green, HSBC Chairman, Telegraph website, 7 July 2010

Contents

Foreword

In the past decades, it has become widely accepted that the multinational corporations (MNCs) have a massive economic and social impact on the developing countries and moreover, that this impact is not always beneficial to the developing world. In spite of this, the link between the concept of corporate social responsibility (CSR) – gradually making its way into the public and corporate consciousness – and human rights law remains to a certain extent a practical, if not a conceptual, challenge. In his book, Dr Olufemi Amao addresses the difficult interface between CSR and the law from the perspective of the consequences that the limitations of this interface have in the developing countries.

Rather than taking a traditional legalistic or corporate management path, Dr Amao breaks new ground by addressing the critical confluence between CSR and the legal discourse and in particular between CSR and the human rights legal discourse. The relationship between CSR and the law is presented against the backdrop of a comprehensive historical analysis of the evolution of the MNCs and of the initial challenging attempts to control them at international level. The innovation of his approach lies in anchoring firmly his analysis into the human rights debate in the context of the developing countries. Moreover, he advances and argues for a concept of international corporate agency and personality that could become instrumental in addressing some of the legal inconsistencies found in the normative overlap between CSR and human rights. These features make the volume theoretically solid while, at the same time, concrete and intelligible for readers coming from a variety of disciplinary backgrounds.

The originality of Dr Amao's arguments makes this a valuable contribution as a clear overview of the CSR normative challenges and as an innovative framework for regulating global corporations and for conceptualising MNCs as social, political, economic and legal actors that could potentially serve a broader set of stakeholders. He confronts economic and legal models of MNC agency with the crude social and economic realities of the developing countries, offering a valuable insight into the international and regional CSR mechanisms as well as into the judicial and regulatory mechanisms in the United States, Europe and Africa. In this way, Dr Amao offers tools both for analysis and practical change.

A systematic study of corporate social responsibility in the human rights context, this work commands attention from scholars and practitioners alike. It represents a substantial contribution to the debate in the field of CSR, of unique value to those who seek to understand the relationship between CSR and the human rights law in a globalising world.

Aurora Voiculescu
London, December 2010

Table of cases

International Tribunals/Courts

World Trade Organization

International Labour Organization

European Court of Human Rights/European Court of Justice

Inter-American Court of Human Rights

United Kingdom

United States of America

African Commission on Human and Peoples' Rights

Nigeria

South Africa

Acknowledgements

I thank Professor Irene Lynch Fannon who agreed to supervise my research upon which this book is based, supported my application for funding and guided the writing of my PhD thesis with her expertise. This work has benefitted greatly from her excellent mentorship and insightful comments. Many thanks also to my second supervisor, Dr Ursula Kilkelly. Her kind and generous expertise has influenced this work greatly. I am much obliged to Professor John Mee who was instrumental in my going to UCC to do my research. I thank Professor Caroline Fennell for giving me the opportunity to undertake the research and also to acquire teaching experience in the university. I thank Dr Siobhan Mullally for her support and encouragement. I also thank all the other members of staff at University College Cork for their support. I gratefully acknowledge University College Cork's funding of my research through the President's PhD Scholarship Scheme and the Department of Law for giving me additional funding under the Department of Law Postgraduate Research Scholarship Scheme.

I am grateful to Dr Aurora Voiculescu for her help and also to Professor Blainad Clarke.

I thank my friends and colleagues Juan Pablo Cortes Diéguez, Onder Bakircioglu, Stephen Onakuse, Sinéad Ring, Joe McGrath, John McNally, Aderinsayo Adewumi, Olufemi Omoniyi, Bola Olaiya and Edet Essien. I also thank my friend and wife, Anne-Marie Quirke to whom this book is dedicated.

Many thanks to my parents, Mary and Elkanah Amao who set the ball rolling and my brothers Dele, Segun, Bosun and Yemi for their support and encouragement.

Finally, my appreciation to the invisible hand without whom (I believe) nothing is possible.

Olufemi O. Amao
London, October, 2010.

Abbreviations

ACP	African, Caribbean and Pacific states
ACrtHPR	African Court on Human and Peoples' Rights
ATCA	Alien Torts Act
AU	African Union
BIAC	Business Industry Advisory Council
CAMA	Companies and Allied Matters Act
CARIFORUM	Caribbean Forum of African, Caribbean and Pacific States
CBI	Confederation of British Industry
CCP	Common Commercial Policy
CEDAW	Convention on the Elimination of All Forms of Discrimination against Women
CERCA	Comprehensive Environmental Response, Compensation and Liability Act
CESR	Centre for Economic and Social Rights
CIME	Committee on International Investment and Multinational Enterprises
CRC	Convention on the Rights of the Child
CSR	Corporate social responsibility
EBA	Everything but arms
EC Treaty	Treaty Establishing the European Community
ECA	Export credit agency
ECHR	European Convention on Human Rights
ECJ	European Court of Justice
ECtHR	European Court of Human Rights
EFCC	Economic and Financial Crime Commission
EMAS	Eco-management and audit scheme
EPA	Economic Partnership Agreement
Farben	IG Farbenindustrie AG
FTA	Free-trade area
GATT	General Agreement on Tariffs and Trade
GSP	Generalised System of Preferences
IACtHR	Inter-American Court of Human Rights

IC	International company
ICC	International Chamber of Commerce
ICCPR	International Covenant on Civil and Political Rights
ICEM	International Federation of Chemical, Energy, Mine and General Workers' Unions
ICERD	International Convention on the Elimination of All Forms of Racial Discrimination
ICESCR	International Covenant on Economic, Social and Cultural Rights
ICPC	Independent Corrupt Practices Commission
ILC	International Law Commission
ILO	International Labour Organization
IOE	International Organisation of Employers
LDC	Least developed country
MNC	Multinational corporation
MNE	Multinational enterprise
NCP	National Contact Point
NDLEA	National Drug Law Enforcement Agency
NGO	Non-governmental organisation
NLERS	Non-legally enforceable rules and standards
NNOC	Nigerian National Oil Corporation
NNPC	Nigerian National Petroleum Corporation
NRE	Nouvelles Regulations Economiques
NUPENG	National Union of Petroleum and Natural Gas Workers
OAS	Organization of American States
OAU	Organisation of African Unity
OECD	Organisation for Economic Cooperation and Development
PENGASSAN	Petroleum and Natural Gas Senior Association of Nigeria
PTA	Preferential Trade Arrangement
SE	Societas Europaea
SEA	Single European Act
SERAC	Social and Economic Rights Action Centre
SIA	Sustainability Impact Assessment
SPDC	Shell Petroleum Development Corporation
TA	Treaty of Amsterdam
TDCA	Trade Development and Cooperation Agreement
TEU	Treaty of the European Union
TNC	Transnational corporation
UDHR	Universal Declaration of Human Rights
UNCLOS	United Nations Convention of the Law of the Sea
UNCTC	United Nations Centre on Transnational Corporations
UNDP	United Nations Development Programme
UNEP	United Nations Environmental Programme
UNGC	United Nations' Global Compact

USCIB	United States Council for International Business
VCLT	Vienna Convention on the Law of Treaties
WBCSD	World Business Council for Sustainable Development
WTO	World Trade Organization
ZANU (PF)	Zimbabwe African National Union Patriotic Front

Introduction

Multinational corporations (MNCs) operate in what has been described as "a vacuum between ineffective national laws and non-existent or unenforceable international law".[1] National laws have proved inadequate in the governance of MNCs because of territorial limitations. Under international law the MNC is barely recognised and generally not directly bound by international law.[2] Attempts to fill the vacuum in which MNCs operate have resorted to soft laws and/or self-regulation.[3] To date these approaches have not yielded satisfactory results. For their part, many MNCs have adopted corporate social responsibility (CSR) strategy to fill the vacuum. This strategy generally lacks formal state power of sanction and instead seeks normative authority from international law.[4] Significantly, human rights issues are increasingly incorporated in companies' CSR strategies. Human rights issues are included, for example, in corporate assessments mentioning human rights compliance, sustainability reports touting compliance with international human rights standards and corporate codes of conduct. The CSR philosophy is convenient for corporations as the approach shifts focus away from regulation. According to Buhmann, the emerging concept of CSR and its relationship to law and

---

1 R. Fowler, "International Standards for Transnational Corporations" (1995) 25 *Environmental Law* 1, 3. See also C.D. Wallace, *The Multinational Enterprise and Legal Control: Host State Sovereignty in an Era of Economic Globalization* (The Hague: Martinus Nijhoff Publishers, 2002), 11; P. Muchlinski noted the argument that MNCs appear to be powers unto themselves. See P.T. Muchlinski, *Multinational Enterprises and the Law* (second edition, Oxford: Oxford University Press, 2007), 3.

2 See D. Kinley and J. Tadaki, "From Talk to Walk: The Emergence of Human Rights Responsibilities for Corporations at International Law" (2003–2004) *Virginia Journal of International Law* 931, 935; I. Bantekas, "Corporate Social Responsibility in International Law" (2004) 22 *Boston University International Law Journal* 309, 310.

3 D. French, "International Rhetoric and the Real Global Agenda" in R. Brownsend, ed., *Global Justice and the Quest for Justice Vol. 4 Human Rights* (Oxford and Portland, OR: Hart Publishing, 2004), 121, 131.

4 T. McInerney, "Putting Regulation before Responsibility: Towards Binding Norms of Corporate Social Responsibility" (2007) 40 *Cornell International Law Journal* 172.

legal standards has had limited attention paid to it by legal academics.[5] This may not be surprising as the predominant view of CSR that it consists of "ethical, voluntary, non-enforceable rules"[6] would seem to have placed the concept outside the ambit of the law as law is generally known, especially from a positivist perspective.[7] According to Dine, since corporate initiatives are voluntary they are liable to capture by the public relations department of companies. She further opines that "it is likely that a great deal of energy will be spent to little effect. The participants have 'a feel good' factor which deflects them from the more important structural issues causing the problems".[8]

However, in the last two decades an increasing number of legal scholars have expressed interest in analysing the implications of the concept of CSR for law and how the law can engage with CSR.[9] This is particularly important because, as this book argues, the whole idea of CSR started with the legal debate in the 1930s about the social responsibility of business. A major flaw with these attempts, which this book aims to correct, is the obsessive focus on the laws of developed countries and international regulation with little examination of the legal framework in developing

---

5   K. Buhmann, "Corporate Social Responsibility: What Role for Law? Some Aspects of Law and CSR" (2006) 6 (2) *Corporate Governance* 188.

6   R. Mullerat, "The Global Responsibility of Business" in Ramon Mullerat, ed., *Corporate Social Responsibility: The Corporate Governance of the 21st Century* (The Netherlands: Kluwer Law International and International Bar Association, 2005), 3.

7   According to Parkinson, CSR refers

> To behaviour that involves voluntarily sacrificing profits, either by incurring additional costs in the course of the company's production processes, or by making transfers to non-shareholder groups out of the surplus thereby generated, in the belief that such behaviour will have consequences superior to those flowing from a policy of pure profit maximization.
>
> (J.E. Parkinson, *Corporate Power and Responsibility: Issues in the Theory of Company* (Clarendon, Oxford, 1993), 260–261)

8   J. Dine, *Companies, International Trade and Human Rights* (Cambridge: Cambridge University Press, 2005), 44–45, 229.

9   See for example, P.T. Muchlinski, "Human Rights and Multinationals: Is there a Problem?" (2001) 77 (1) *International Affairs* 31; Dine (note 8); C.M. Dickerson, "How Do Norms and Empathy Affect Corporation Law and Corporate Behaviour? Human Rights: The Emerging Norm of Corporate Social Responsibility" (2001–2002) 76 *Tulane Law Review* 1431; L.E. Mitchell and T.A. Gabaldon, "If I Only Had a Heart: Or, How Can We Identify a Corporate Morality" (2001–2002) 76 *Tulane Law Review* 1645; C.A. Harwell Wells, "The Cycles of Corporate Social Responsibility: An Historical Retrospective for the Twenty-First Century" (2002) 52 *Kansas Law Review* 77; D. McBarnet, A. Voiculescu and T. Campbell, eds., *The New Corporate Accountability: Corporate Social Responsibility and the Law* (Cambridge: Cambridge University Press, 2007); Buhmann (note 5); J.A. Zerk, *Multinationals and Corporate Social Responsibility: Limitations and Opportunities in International Law* (Cambridge: Cambridge University Press, 2006); Bantekas (note 2).

countries which are at the frontline of issues raised in the CSR discourse in the MNCs context.[10]

This book thus seeks to achieve a number of aims. First it will show the difference between CSR as practised today and the law. Second, the book will refocus the corporate responsibility debate from the focus on international regulation to domestic jurisdictions and explore how the international forum can effectively complement and support domestic jurisdictions. The discourse has hitherto been patronising to domestic jurisdictions, especially in developing states, instead of engaging with them. Third, the book will argue that there is a need to employ the law effectively in this area.

It is posited in this book that the emergence of CSR philosophy signifies a paradigm shift which would challenge different field of study especially the law. It has been suggested that:

> Major corporations ... are in the throes of a paradigm shift of historic proportion. We are currently in the process of rethinking the true purpose of the corporation; its relationship with society and its stakeholders, and the standards by which its performance should be judged.[11]

The question is how should the law respond to these developments? There are suggestions of a theoretical reconceptualisation of what regulation is and how it could work with the concept of CSR. The identifiable suggestions are: the meta-regulatory approach as advanced by Parker[12] and the reflexive law theory approach.[13] These approaches, as this book will show,

---

10 Prof. Larry Cata Backer in a recent unpublished article also noted this huge lacuna in the CSR debate from the legal perspective. See L.C. Backer, "Extraterritoriality and Corporate Social Responsibility: Governing Corporations, Governing Developing States" (2008) 26 (2) *Berkeley Journal of International Law* 503.

11 I. Wilson, "The New Rules Ethics, Social Responsibility and Institutional Change in the Corporation: The New Social Contract" (2005) 3 (1) *On The Horizon* 20; see also K Greenfield, "Reclaiming Corporate Law in a Gilded Age" (2008) 2 (1) *Harvard Law and Policy Review* 1.

12 See C. Parker, "Meta-Regulation: Legal Accountability for Corporate Social Responsibility?" in McBarnet *et al.* (note 9), 207–240.

13 C. Barnard, S. Deakin and R. Hobbs "Reflexive Law, Corporate Social Responsibility and the Evolution of Labour Standards: The Case of Working Time" (2004) ESRC Centre for Business Research, University of Cambridge Working Paper no. 294; R. Rogowski and T. Wilthagen *Reflexive Labour Law* (The Netherlands: Kluwer Law and Taxation Publishers 1994); G. Teubner "Global Bukowina: Legal Pluralism in the World Society" in G. Teubner (ed.) *Global Law Without a State* (Brookfield: Dartmouth, 1997), 3. S. Wheeler, *Corporations and the Third Way* (Oxford and Portland, OR: Hart Publishing, 2002); O. Semotiuk, "Sally Wheeler, *Corporations and the Third Way*. Oxford: Hart Publishing, 2002, 178 pp., £22 (hbk)" 2003 (12) *Social and Legal Studies* 562.

are not without their criticisms and drawbacks. Other approaches rooted in positive law have looked at possibilities in international law,[14] international human rights law[15] and company law.[16] In respect of company law, Dine points out that "the corporate social responsibility movement rarely addresses the fundamental issue of the design of companies ... because of this, it is much less effective than it otherwise would be".[17] In making the case for a company law approach she goes further by arguing that at the heart of the capitalist system and the free market economy lies company law. According to her, "it is through the medium of companies that wealth is created. More than this, the way in which companies are regulated says a great deal about the values that each society and the global community gives preference to".[18] In a similar vein, Greenfield contends that corporate law can do more than it is presently doing if it moves away from its traditional focus on managers and shareholders.[19] Arguing from the US perspective, he advocates, for example, the adoption of stakeholder governance which can be achieved by widening the fiduciary duties of management and by the provision of mechanism for non-shareholder stakeholders to elect representatives to the board of the company.[20]

In his text on company law from the UK perspective, Parkinson attempted to analyse CSR from a corporate law angle.[21] One of the two themes of his book is the need for a redistribution of corporate wealth to take into account other stakeholders apart from shareholders. Parkinson contends that public companies with publicly listed shares should be reclassified as "social enterprises".[22] He argues that the suggestion that "companies should be classified as social enterprises is designed to challenge the prevalent view that companies are private and that legal regulation of companies should concentrate on encouraging corporate managers to maximize profits".[23] According to Parkinson, the reclassification is necessary in order to allow states to intervene to safeguard the interests of the public and ensure compliance with "publicly acceptable ethical standards".[24] He notes correctly that the then framework of English

---

14 Zerk (note 9).
15 M. Addo (ed.), *Human Rights Standards and the Responsibility of Transnational Corporations* (The Hague: Kluwer Law International, 1999), N. Jagers, *Corporate Human Rights Obligations: in Search of Accountability* (Antwerp: Intersentia, 2002); Greenfield (note 11), 1.
16 Dine (note 8); Parkinson (note 7); Australian Government, Corporations and Markets Advisory Committee, The Social Responsibility of Corporations Report, 2006.
17 Dine (note 8), 45.
18 Ibid., 47.
19 Greenfield (note 11), 1.
20 Ibid., 23–24.
21 Parkinson (note 7).
22 Ibid., 4.
23 C. Bradley, "Review: Corporate Power and Control in the 1990S: The Transnational Dimension" (1995) 15 (2) *Oxford Journal of Legal Studies* 269, 270.
24 Parkinson (note 7), 4.

company law constrained the ability to act in a socially responsible manner. Parkinson considers the extent to which corporate managers should be allowed to pursue social responsibility. He makes two alternative suggestions. The first suggestion is derived from business ethics and management and relies on managerial voluntarism. According to him:

> In establishing a legal framework for responsible behaviour the controversial substantive issues can be avoided by approaching responsibility as a "process concept", that is, a concept concerned with the characteristics of the corporate decision-making process and not with particular outcomes. Social responsibility as a process concept thus takes responsibility to be an attribute of decision-making processes rather than as involving compliance with a set of specific standards for guiding conducts.[25]

The second alternative, which he admits is an ambitious process, is to make the company "more responsive to the interests of affected groups by increasing the ability of those groups to shape corporate conduct".[26] He suggests increasing inward flow of information in order to understand the effects of business operations on third parties,[27] extending fiduciary duties to include the interests of certain non-shareholder groups,[28] extending mandatory disclosure to cover social and environmental reporting, external auditing,[29] mandatory consultation with affected stakeholders[30] and altering the composition of the board.[31]

Thus the underlying question for law rests on the role of the corporation in society and whether corporations should be regulated merely as private actors/private property or also as public actors.

25 Ibid., 345.
26 Ibid., 346.
27 Ibid., 367.
28 Ibid., 369.
29 Ibid., 382.
30 Ibid., 383.
31 Ibid., 387.

1 Multinational corporations, states and international regulation

Historical background

Introduction

This chapter is an historical introduction to the role of multinational corporations (MNCs), states and the international regulation of MNCs. The chapter starts with a consideration of the meaning of the concept "multinational corporations". The chapter goes on to examine the relationship between MNCs and states and the concerns about MNCs involvement in the abuse of human rights. The chapter explores the role of corporations in the slave trade, the colonial enterprise and the Second World War. It further examines the relationship between MNCs and the countries of the South after independence.

What are "multinational corporations"?

Different nomenclatures have been used to describe MNCs over the years. Apart from "multinational corporation (MNC)", the concept has variously been referred to as "transnational corporation (TNC)" and "multinational enterprise (MNE)". The different names have been used in attempts to encapsulate the nature of MNCs in an appropriate definition. In practice today, these names are used interchangeably and it will serve no useful purpose to distinguish between them. Since there is no legal instrument ascribing a definition to MNCs, defining the concept may not be possible with any degree of accuracy.[1] Muchlinski therefore suggests that it may be helpful to show how MNEs[2] differ from uninational companies (a

---

1 P.T. Muchlinski, *Multinational Enterprises and the Law* (second edition, Oxford: Oxford University Press, 2007) 7.
2 Muchlinski (note 1) uses the term "multinational enterprises". The term was adopted in the Organisation for Economic Cooperation and Development (OECD) Guidelines which states that multinational enterprises

> Usually comprise companies or other entities established in more than one country and so linked that they may co-ordinate their operations in various ways. While one or more of these entities may be able to exercise a significant influence over the activities of others, their degree of autonomy within the enterprise may vary widely from one multinational enterprise to another. Ownership may be private, state or mixed.
> (OECD, Guidelines for Multinational Enterprises (Paris: OECD, 2000))

company incorporated and domiciled in only one country). In the first place, MNCs operate their assets and control their use across national borders unlike uninational companies whose operations remain within national borders. The organisational structure of an MNC is such that it allows managerial control to reach across national frontiers despite the different national identities of the various operating units within the group. MNCs also have a distinct competitive advantage with their ability to trade across borders not only in respect of finished products but also in factor inputs, such as technical knowhow and managerial skills, between affiliates and third parties.[3] Other legal commentators have also tried to define the concept. Wallace describes a "multinational enterprise" as: "an aggregate of corporate entities, each having its own juridical identity and national origin, but each in some way interconnected by a system of centralised management and control, normally, exercised from the seat of primary ownership".[4] Kamminga describes an MNC as "a legal person that owns or controls production, distribution or service, facilities outside the country it is based".[5] According to Dine, "multinational and transnational companies do not exist as an entity defined or recognised by law. They are made up of complex structures of individual companies with an enormous variety of interrelationships".[6] In an attempt to ascribe a legal definition to MNCs, the moribund, United Nation's Norms on Responsibility of Transnational Corporations and other Business Enterprises with regard to Human Rights[7] provides in its paragraph 20 that

> The term "transnational corporation" refers to an economic entity operating in more than one country or a cluster of economic entities operating in two or more countries – whatever their legal form, whether in their home country or country of activity, and whether taken individually or collectively.

The distinctive features of MNCs have led commentators to recognise the challenges posed by their operations to the traditional legal framework.

---

3 Muchlinski (note 1), 8.
4 C.D. Wallace, *The Multinational Enterprise and Legal Control: Host State Sovereignty in an Era of Economic Globalization* (The Hague: Martinus Nijhoff Publishers, 2002), 9.
5 M.T. Kamminga, "Holding Multinational Corporations Accountable for Human Rights Abuses: A Challenge for the EC" in P. Alston, ed., *The EU and Human Rights* (Oxford: Oxford University Press, 1999), 553.
6 J. Dine, *Companies, International Trade and Human Rights* (Cambridge: Cambridge University Press, 2005), 48.
7 Norms on the Responsibilities of Transnational Corporations and Other Business Enterprises with Regard to Human Rights, UN Doc. E/CN.4/Sub.2/2003/12/Rev.2 (2003). Approved 13 August 2003, by UN Sub-Commission on the Promotion and Protection of Human Rights resolution 2003/16, UN Doc. E/CN.4/Sub.2/2003/L.11 at 52 (2003). The document is discussed in detail later in this chapter.

Muchlinski observes that the features of MNCs permit them to affect international allocation of productive resources, and consequently create distinct problems in the development of economic policy in the states where they operate.[8] According to Jagers:

> The common feature of these large and often rather opaque corporations is that they operate across national borders. Operating in many different countries places these corporations outside the effective supervision of domestic and international law, which can result in a deficiency.[9]

For the purpose of this book the term MNC is used to describe *companies with foreign origin/seat that operate in one or more countries through affiliates or subsidiaries and have production or marketing facilities in these other countries.*

Multinational corporations and states

The modern history of most developing countries would be incomplete without an examination of the role of foreign MNCs in the emergence of the states. Foreign MNCs played a pivotal role in exposing many parts of the world and uncovering their wealth. Corporations were instrumental to the development and advancement of nation states in Africa and Asia and it is therefore not surprising that they have emerged as the driver of globalisation in the modern era.[10] While their operations have been largely beneficial in the case of developed countries, the same cannot be said of the experience in the developing countries of the South.

Explaining the relationship between the states of the North and MNCs: the mercantilist origin of the multinational corporation

The modern capitalist system and the predecessor of the modern day MNC were established during the period generally described as the "mercantilist" period. The mercantile system was in operation for more than 200 years between the sixteenth and eighteenth centuries. The mercantile system was dominant for so long because it was beneficial to rent seeking merchants and governments.[11] Central to the mercantile system is the belief that governments should advance the goal of maintaining a positive

---

8 Muchlinski (note 1), 8.
9 N. Jagers, *Corporate Human Rights Obligations: In Search of Accountability* (Antwerp: Intersentia, 2002), 11.
10 Wallace (note 4), 9.
11 R.B. Ekelund and R.D. Tollison, *Mercantilism as a Rent-Seeking Society: Economic Regulation in Historical Perspective* (College Station, Texas: Texas A&M University Press, 1981).

balance of trade with other nations by assuming a protectionist role in the economy. To achieve this end, governments enforced monopolies, banned foreign competitions and subjected workers to poor conditions of service for the benefit of merchants. To the mercantilist, trade was a zero sum game with each participant taking advantage of the other in a ruthless competition.[12] Most of the companies that could arguably be regarded as the predecessors of modern day MNCs such as the East India Company, Hudson's Bay Company and the African Company were established and became big players during this period.[13] It has been suggested that mercantilism provides a meaningful interpretation of the relationship between MNCs and government.[14]

Today some of the ideas of the mercantile system can be perceived in the relationship between developed countries and MNCs based on their territories. In their study of MNCs, Ruigrock and van Tulder found that "virtually all of the world's largest core firms have experienced a decisive influence from government policies and/or trade barriers on their strategy and competitive position", second that "at least 20 companies in the 1993 Fortune 100 would not have survived at all as independent companies, if they had not been saved by their respective governments" and third, that government intervention had been the rule rather than the exception in the past two centuries and "has played a key role in the development and diffusion of many product and process innovations – particularly in aerospace, electronics, modern agriculture, materials technologies, energy, and transportation technology".[15] Chomsky points out other areas such as the Internet and the World Wide Web and in the earlier days, textiles, steel and energy industries where government intervention on behalf of MNCs has been the decisive factor in their emergence as powerful entities.[16] The 2008/2009 financial crisis and the intervention of governments is also a manifestation of this relationship. The British government's support for BP in the face of scathing criticisms of the company for the Gulf of Mexico oil spill disaster in 2010 also exemplify the strong bond between states and MNCs.

12 R. Gilpin, "The Political Economy of the Multinational Corporation: Three Contrasting Perspectives" (1976) 70 (1) *American Political Science Review*, 184.

13 J. Micklethwait and A. Wooldridge, *The Company* (London: Phoenix, 2005) 25. See also W. Cragg, "Human Rights Globalization and the Modern Shareholder Owned Corporations" in T. Campbell and S. Miller, *Human Rights and the Moral Responsibilities of Corporate and Public Sector Organizations* (The Netherlands: Kluwer Academic Publishers, 2004) 105,112.

14 Gilpin (note 12), 189.

15 W. Ruigrok and R. van Tulder, *The Logic of International Restructuring* (London: Routledge, 1995), 221–222: 217.

16 N. Chomsky, *Profit over People: Neoliberalism and Global Order* (New York: Seven Stories, 1999), 38.

This is not, however, to argue that there is a formal conspiracy between MNCs and governments but that structures are devised to protect and support them by their home governments. Gilpin, explaining the relationship between states and MNCs says from an American perspective that:

> While these political and corporate elites have interests in common, they also have divergent interests. At the same time, therefore, that public officials attempt to utilize corporate power to advance perceived national objectives, the corporate executives seek to maximize their freedom from *all* government restrictions and to utilize national power for corporate advantage. But generally, in the relationship between American business and government the activities of the corporation are seen by public officials to advance the larger security and economic interests of the nation.[17]

The synergy between the state and corporations has enhanced corporate power and, as shall be shown in this book, corporate ability to interfere with human rights.

Corporations and the transatlantic slave trade

The earliest form of corporate abuse of human rights in the countries of the South (including Africa) can be traced to the slave trade period. Though the corporation did not exist then in the form it does today, companies of the slave trade era are very similar in the manner of their operations to the modern day corporate form. Carlos and Nicholas correctly argue that the early sixteenth- and seventeenth-century companies such as the English and Dutch East India companies, the Muscovy Company, the Hudson's Bay Company and the Royal African Company meet the criteria of modern day multinational corporations.[18] In their article, which emphasises the transaction cost and theory of the firm, the authors argue that the defining character of modern business enterprise similar to early MNCs is a hierarchy of salaried managers who make decisions on production, distribution and prices. The managers of the early MNCs grappled with how to make decisions in the context of trading overseas and similar challenges are faced by the managers of modern MNCs. The search for an organisational structure capable of accommodating global trade is a common feature of early and modern MNCs. In the same vein, Levitt argues that because of their structures, the present day MNCs are similar in character to the trading corporations of the mercantile era.[19] Gilpin asserts that "the

---

17 Gilpin (note 12) 190.
18 A.M. Carlos and S. Nicholas, "Giants of Earlier Capitalism: The Chartered Trading Companies as Multinational Corporations" (1988) 62 *Business History Review* 398.
19 K. Levitt, *Silent Surrender: The American Economic Empire in Canada* (New York: Liveright Press, 1970). Levitt's view was also discussed by Gilpin (note 12).

giant American corporations which comprise most of the world's multinationals are the descendants of the East India Company and the other mercantile enterprises that dominated the world economy in the seventeenth and eighteenth centuries".[20] The significance of the slave trade for corporations is that it set the stage for the rise to prominence of corporations which had huge implications for the economic well-being of nation states. From this period, corporations leveraged their powers to bargain with governments and gradually extricate themselves from state control. States of the North also recognised the economic potential of corporations in international trade and thus grew protective of the corporation.

The pioneers of the slave trade were Portuguese traders who arrived in Africa in the fifteenth century.[21] They were followed by the Spanish and later other European nations, namely the Dutch, the French and the English. Generally speaking, the Portuguese dominated the trade before 1640 and after 1807, with the British displacing them in the intervening period. The French, Dutch, Spanish, Danish and US slave traders were small players by comparison, though at particular times some of these national groups did assume importance.[22] The slave trade gradually increased as the demand for slave labourers grew in the burgeoning economies of Europe. The prosperity of the trade in England encouraged merchants to form joint stock companies and petition the monarch for royal charters to enable them deal in slaves in particular areas of Africa. Monarchs issued royal charters to companies for trade overseas.

The Royal African Company (originally known as the Company of Royal Adventurers Trading to Africa), formed in England in 1672, was the most famous of the slave trading companies. Thanks to its influential promoters,[23] the company was so powerful that it was given a monopoly over English slave trade by its charter and actually monopolised the trade in West Africa for 26 years. It established trading posts on the West African coast and it was responsible for seizing any rival English ships that were dealing in slaves in the region. In return for trade monopoly the company was expected to protect English interests in Africa by building and maintaining forts on the African coast. The company played a major role in the success of the British Caribbean sugar plantation created around this period as it supplied much needed slave labour to the labour intensive enterprise. It is interesting to

---

20 Gilpin (note 12).

21 H. Thomas, *The Slave Trade: The History of the Atlantic Slave Trade, 1440–1870* (London: Papermac, 1998), 22.

22 D. Eltis, "The Volume and Structure of the Transatlantic Slave Trade: A Reassessment" (2001) 58 (1) *William and Mary Quarterly* 17.

23 The trustees and officers of the company included James, Duke of York (later James II), Sir Benjamin Bathurst (whose name used to denote the city now known as Banjul in the Gambia), Edward Colston (a Bristol-born philanthropist, Humphrey Morrice, who founded the Bank of England in 1694) and the philosopher John Locke. See Thomas (note 21), 201.

note that corporations yearning for deregulation and free trade in international trade first emerged in the slave trade era in England. Merchants from Liverpool and Bristol, together with the support of politicians, successfully campaigned to end the monopoly of the Royal African Company. In 1698 other traders were allowed to freely participate in the trade subject to the payment of a certain percentage of the value of their cargoes to the Royal African Company for the maintenance of its forts.

One of the most important consequences of the slave trade was the development of new forms of economic and social power. Companies grew wealthy and prosperous through slave trading and other slave related activities in Africa and other parts of the world. Many of the companies that grew rich from the transatlantic slave trade reinvested their wealth in other sectors of the economy. A growing number of big corporations in countries of the North have been linked with the transatlantic slave trade. Some of the corporations include the following known names: Aetna (insurance), AIG (insurance), J.P. Morgan Chase (financial services), Lloyd's of London (insurance), New York Life (insurance), Brown Bros. Harriman (investment bank), Lehman Bros. (investment bank), Norfolk Southern (railroad), CSX (railroad), Union Pacific (railroad), Canadian National (railroad), WestPoint Stevens (textiles), FleetBoston (bank) and Deutsche Banc Alex. Brown (bank).[24]

Corporate colonialism

Corporate colonialism has been used to describe corporate involvement in the colonial enterprise. The role of the corporation as a powerful force, which started its ascendancy during the slave trade, became more pronounced in the days of colonialism. According to Ottaway, governments found it cheaper to extend their political and commercial powers by giving charters to corporations in designated areas and requiring them in turn to maintain order in those areas.[25] It must be noted though, that these corporations were private commercial undertakings – they were neither state owned nor ordinarily subsidised or guaranteed by states. However, Staley notes that the "subtle line of State control existed in the form of personal unions between the directors of the companies and the nation's governing class".[26] These chartered companies (sometimes called privileged or sovereign companies) had the authority to govern and to trade in the territories under their jurisdiction. They had the authority to

---

24 J. Cox, "Corporations Challenged by Reparations Activists" *USA Today*, 21 February 2002.
25 M. Ottaway, "Reluctant Missionaries" (2001) 125 *Foreign Policy* 44; J Braithwaite and P. Drahos, *Global Business Regulation* (Cambridge: Cambridge University Press, 2000), 533.
26 E. Staley, *War and the Private Investor* (New York: Double Day, Doran & Company Inc, 1935).

make currencies, conclude treaties, build forts, lay out roads, have policing systems, levy duties and taxes and make war.[27]

The corporation became very useful in this regard because the original purpose of allowing the use of the corporate form was to serve the public interest and accomplish public good by performing tasks that individual citizens or governments could not.[28] As Grossman and Adams observe, in England, English kings chartered many companies such as the East India Company, the Hudson's Bay Company and many American colonies to enable them control property and commerce.[29] This assertion is buttressed by the fact that in colonies where the companies operated, English kings appointed the governors, judges, provided soldiers, dictated tax rates, investment types, production modes, labour regulation and controlled markets.[30]

An important point to note is that in its earlier forms, the corporation was subjected to more state control than modern corporations. This situation enabled the state to dictate its direction of the growth. Perhaps the most important control retained by the state over the corporate form was the ability to limit the duration of any charter granted and to revoke it when the state felt necessary.[31] For example the original charter granted to the East India Company was for a period of 15 years and under the condition that, "if not found to be advantageous to the country, it might be annulled at any time under a notice of two years; if advantageous, it might, if desired by the company, be renewed for 15 years".[32]

Presumably, in consequence of the role played by British corporations in the colonisation of the United States, early corporations in the United States were subjected to more state control under charter than British corporations. From the beginning the task of chartering corporations was assigned to the legislature. The charters granted were few and were granted for a specific purpose and for a limited number of years. Manufacturing charters in Maryland, for example, were restricted to 40 years, mining to 50 years and most others to 30 years.[33] In Pennsylvania, the

---

27 J. Braithwaite and P. Drahos, "Globalisation of Corporate Regulation and Corporate Citizenship" in F. MacMillan ed., *International Corporate Law Annual Vol. 2 2002* (Oxford and Portland, OR: Hart Publishing, 2003) 8; P.J. Spiro, "New Players on the International Stage" (1997) 2 *Hofstra Law and Policy Symposium* 19, 28.

28 J. Kirkbride, S. Letza, X. Sun and C. Smallman, "The Boundaries of Governance in the Post-Modern World" (2008) 59 (2) *Northern Ireland Legal Quarterly* 161, 162. R. Estes, *The Tyranny of the Bottom Line: Why Corporations Make Good People Do Bad Things* (San Francisco: Berret-Khoehler Publishers, 1996) 21.

29 R.L. Grossman and F.T. Adams, *Taking Care of Business: Citizenship and the Charter of Incorporation* (Cambridge, MA: Charter Ink, 1993), 5.

30 Ibid.

31 F. Evans, "The Evolution of the English Joint Stock Limited Trading Company" (1908) 8 (5) *Columbia Law Review* 339.

32 Ibid.

33 Grossman and Adams (note 29).

manufacturing charter was limited to 20 years.[34] Most corporations were
chartered to build turnpikes, canals and bridges. The legislature set down
rules for each business and retained the power to revoke the charters
issued.[35] Many corporations' charters were actually revoked at some point.
For example, in 1884, the charter of the Standard Oil Trust of New York
was revoked. Also in 1890, the North River refining corporation lost its
charter in New York. Many banks in Pennsylvania had their charters
revoked and many oil, sugar and whiskey companies had their charters
revoked in Michigan, Ohio and New York.[36]

The significance of this use of the early forms of the corporation is that
the corporate form was employed as a viable tool for the colonialists'
expansionist project. The colonialists found the company very useful for
three main reasons. First, the company did not have the kind of responsibility that was placed on government. The company could experiment
and take risks, which governments could not engage in and if a company's
operation ran into any kind of trouble that would embarrass the government, the government could easily disown the company. Second, governments found it easier to circumvent oppositions to the colonial project by
the use of the company. The company was not shackled with the bureaucracy and parliamentary control to which the government was subject. Thus
it was more malleable to changing circumstances and could take more
drastic steps to achieve its aim than governments could. Third, it could
run on a cheaper budget by defraying part of its costs by trading.[37]

The East India Company and corporate colonialism

The East India Company, usually described as the world's first MNC, and
the Dutch East India Company are the two most significant colonial

---

34 Ibid.
35 Ibid.
36 K. Lasn, "Grounding the Corporation" article originally published in the *Ecologist Maga-
zine* (May 1999) reproduced in K. Lasn, *Culture Jam: The Uncooling of America* (New York:
Harper Collins, 1999), 157. See also J. Balkan *The Corporation* (London: Constable, 2005),
156–158.
37 Staley (note 26). In assessing the role of the company in the colonial enterprise, Ratner
states that

European companies became the principal agents for the economic exploitation of
the colonial territory. That support gave enterprises and individuals access to the
wealth of the colonies on extraordinarily favourable terms. Local communities
received few economic benefits for their work and had no basis to complain. The
colonial legacy included swaths of African farmland owned by whites, African mineral
wealth controlled by Europeans, and significant petroleum sources in the Middle
East granted to Western oil companies.

(S.R. Ratner, "Corporations and Human Rights: A Theory of Legal Responsibility"
(2001) 111 *Yale Law Journal* 443, 453)

corporations.[38] The East India Company operated for more than two centuries and had a wide-ranging economic, political and cultural influence. The charter establishing the company granted it many exclusive privileges, which primarily included the monopoly of the Indian trade and the power to prohibit others from trading in the area except by its licence.[39] According to Osgood:

> In the case of the East India Company trade is expressly stated to be the object; and although the power to buy, hold or dispose of land is given, the exercise of that right is wholly subordinated to purposes of traffic. Governmental powers, save in the very limited form necessitated by the character of the grant, were not bestowed.[40]

However, the charter of the corporation was periodically renewed and in 1661 the company's powers were extended to include the power to make peace or war. The company was thus transformed from a commercial trading venture to one with governmental powers. It ruled India until the company's dissolution in 1858. According to Roukis, "the idea of corporations possessing security forces and actively carrying out military operations is best exemplified by the history of the British East India Company".[41] In aid of its military and governmental operations the company administered an effective information gathering system, ran spies and conducted diplomacy. The British government used the corporation as a front in committing questionable acts of imperialism in India. As far back as the nineteenth century, the company had been accused of corporate greed, the ruination of traditional ways of life, share-price bubbles and western imperialism.[42] In its business activities, the company engaged in bribery and extortion of local merchants. It paid "protection money" to the British government and local powers.[43] The British government's economy at this time was heavily intertwined with that of the

---

38 J. Micklethwait and A. Wooldridge *The Company: A Short History of a Revolutionary Idea* (London: Phoenix, 2003), 29–36: Braithwaite and Drahos (note 25), 533.

39 MERIP (Middle East Research and Information Project) Reports, no. 36 (April, 1975), 3–4.

40 H.L. Osgood, "The Corporation as a Form of Colonial Government" (1896) *Political Science Quarterly* 259, 264.

41 G.S. Roukis, "The British East India Company 1600–1858: A Model of Transition Management for the Modern Global Corporation" (2004) 23 (10) *Journal of Management Development* 938.

42 N. Robins, "The World's First Multinational" *New Statesman* (London, 13 December 2004), N. Robins, *The Corporation That Changed the World: How the East India Company Shaped the Modern Multinational* (London: Pluto Press, 2006).

43 K. Marx, "The East India Company, Its History and Results" *New York Daily Tribune* (11 July 1853).

company as the government borrowed money from the company on favourable terms in return for the monopoly it granted the company.[44]

The Royal Niger Company, Nigeria and corporate colonialism

Just as in India, the British company, the Royal Niger Company facilitated the effective colonisation of Nigeria by the British government. As in the case of India trade did not follow the flag (government) but the flag followed the trade into Nigeria.[45] In 1879, an official of the British Royal Engineers, George Goldie Taubman, amalgamated all the British traders interested in trade in parts of the area now known as Nigeria to form a new venture which was initially called the United African Company, then later the National African Company and eventually the Royal Niger Company. The company had a monopoly of trade in the area but had no power of administration. The next step Goldie took was to seek political authority for the company. In order to receive a royal charter for that purpose, Goldie made illiterate traditional rulers sign unconscionable treaties, which ceded their "sovereignty", their land and their natural resources to the company.[46] The company received its royal charter in 1886. According to Staley, the company was the only one of the British chartered companies of that era that proved a paying investment for its stockholders as it declared a regular yearly dividend of between 6 and 6.5 per cent.[47] Goldie's successes as a monopoly trader were achieved by looting, murder and destruction of towns and villages.[48] Though the company eventually lost its charter in 1899, it paved the way for effective colonial administration in the country. According to Sir Michael Hicks

---

44 P.D. Curtin, *Cross Cultural Trade in World History* (Cambridge: Cambridge University Press, 1984), 149–152; in summarising the conduct of the company in India, Robins says that,

> Like the modern multinational, it was eager to avoid the mere interplay of supply and demand. It jealously guarded its chartered monopoly of imports from Asia. But it also wanted to control the sources of supply by breaking the power of local rulers in India and eliminating competition so that it could force down its purchase prices. By controlling both ends of the chain, the company could buy cheap and sell dear. This means organising coups against local rulers and placing puppets on the throne. By the middle of the 18th century, the company was deliberately breaching the terms of its commercial concessions in Bengal by trading in prohibited domestic goods and selling its duty free passes to local merchants. Combining economic muscle with extended bribery and the deployment of its small but effective private army, the company engineered a series of "revolutions" that gave it territorial as well as economic control.

(See Robins, 2004 (note 42))

45 A.F. Mockler-Ferryman, "British Nigeria" (1902) 1 *Journal of Royal African Society* 160.
46 Ibid.
47 Staley (note 26).
48 I. Okonta and O. Douglas, *Where Vultures Feast* (London: Verso, 2003), 13.

Beach, a former British chancellor of the exchequer, within the region of Nigeria

> Three different kinds of British Administration were established. First there was the colony of Lagos under the control of the Colonial Office; secondly there was the Niger Coast protectorate under the Foreign Office; and thirdly there was the Royal Niger Company subject only, as far as Her Majesty's Government were concerned to ... very slight control.[49]

This brief discussion of the role of the corporation in the slave trade and the colonial enterprise serves to underscore the growing capacity of the corporation from as early as the fifteenth century to interfere with human liberty in the course of trade and the privileges and protections afforded to the corporations because of the importance of their operations to their home state's economic well-being.

Multinational corporations in the Second World War

The next part of this chapter discusses another historical landmark that demonstrates the growing power of MNCs – the Second World War. This book is moving in this direction because issues relating to corporate responsibility featured, albeit indirectly, in the trials following the Second World War. In the cases discussed here, the tribunals were not concerned with the issue of corporate veil under corporate law in holding the alter ego of companies responsible for the acts of companies.

Corporations, the Holocaust and the Second World War industrialist cases

Human rights abuses by corporations during the Second World War took different dimensions and involved big corporations from so many parts of the North that it is difficult to comprehend how the founders of the global human rights system overlooked their threat to human rights. Stephen has suggested that corporations utilised their enormous power to mask their operations during this period.[50] This is, debatable however; as we shall see presently, the atrocities committed through corporations came to light, to some extent, at the Nuremberg trials following the Second World War. According to Stephen, the number of domestic German corporations

49 Quoted in F.W. Taylor "The Word 'Nigeria'" (1939) 38 *Journal of the Royal African Society* 154, 154.
50 B. Stephens, "The Amorality of Profit: Transnational Corporations and Human Rights" (2002) 20 *Berkeley Journal of International Law* 45; See also S. Chesterman, "Oil and Water: Regulating the Behaviour of Multinational Corporations through Law" (2004) 36 *International Law and Politics* 307, 323–325.

estimated to have benefited from the slave labour of eight to ten million people may be up to thousands.[51] However, it was not only domestic German corporations that benefited, the collaboration of MNCs such as IBM, Ford, Siemens, Volkswagen, Daimler-Benz and BMW are well documented.[52] Many of these corporations had no inhibition using slave labour in their operations. The relationship with the Nazi government and for some companies, the use of cheap slave labour, provided vast profits which assisted them in acquiring the enormous power that they have today.

It is significant to note that despite the huge involvement of corporations in Nazi Germany, no corporation was brought to trial after the Second World War. However, four cases involving trials of German industrialists established the culpability of corporations in the war crimes and crimes against humanity committed in Nazi Germany. *United States* v. *Krauch* (the Farben Case)[53] was the first time an international court attempted to impose liability on a group of persons who were collectively in charge of a company for crimes, or complicity in crimes committed during times of war.[54] The 24 defendants were all directors or officers of the German conglomerate, IG Farbenindustrie AG (Farben); 13 of the defendants were found guilty of the commission of offences of spoliation or employment of slave labour, while five of them were held criminally liable for plunder. In this case, the court recognised corporate responsibility stating as follows:

> With reference to the charges in the present indictment concerning Farben's activities in Poland, Norway, Alsace-Lorraine, and France, we find that the proofs establish beyond a reasonable doubt that offences against property as defined in Control Council Law no. 10 were committed by Farben ... The actions of Farben and its representatives, under these circumstances, cannot be differentiated from acts of plunder or pillage committed by officers, soldiers or public officials of the German Reich.[55]

In the *Zyklon B*[56] case tried by British military court, the owner of a firm (Tesch and Stabenow) and his deputy were convicted for the manufacturing

51 Stephens (note 50).
52 See E. Black, *IBM and the Holocaust* (London: Time Warner, 2002); M. Wallace, *The American Axis: Henry Ford, Charles Lindbergh and the Rise of the Third Reich* (New York: St. Martin's Press, 2003); United Nations Conference on Trade and Development, 2003, *FDI Policies for Development: National and International Perspectives*; World Investment Report 2003 (Geneva: UNCTAD, 2003).
53 Trials of War Criminals before the Nuremberg Tribunals Vols 6–9 (1950–1953).
54 "Business and International Crimes: Assessing the Liability of Business Entities for Grave Violations of International Law" (A Joint Project of the International Peace Academy and Fafo; Report 467, 2004).
55 Ibid.
56 1 Law Reports of War Criminals 93 (1997) (Brit Mil. Ct. 1946).

(by their company) of Zyklon B agent used in the gas chambers during the war. The court was of the opinion that even though Zyklon B was not designed to kill humans, the company should have known what the Nazis intended to use the gas for. The activities which were the subject matter of the case were those of the company though eventually the owner of the company and his deputy, the alter ego of the company, were made to pay for the crimes of the company.

In *United States* v. *Alfred Krupp*,[57] Alfred Krupp was indicted along with 11 officers of the Krupp firm. They were prosecuted for commission of war crimes and crimes against humanity with respect to plunder and spoliation of civilian property and factories in occupied territories and also the deportation of and use of prisoners of war and concentration camp inmates as forced labourers in various Krupp factories during the war. Of the 12 defendants, 11 were convicted and sentenced by the US Military Tribunal. The tribunal recognised the firm's complicity in the allegations and it stated that:

> There are a number of other such examples, which make it clear to us that the initiative for the acquisition of properties, machines, and materials in the occupied countries was that of the Krupp firm and that it utilized Reich government and Reich agencies whenever necessary to accomplish its purposes.[58]

In *United States* v. *Flick*,[59] Friedrich Flick, a prominent steel industrialist was convicted of war crimes and crimes against humanity because he had knowledge of and approved of certain unlawful activities of his deputy Bernhard Weiss. Flick was also convicted of spoliation and plunders of occupied territories and of taking control of a French cement plant in Lorraine in 1940.

The four cases mentioned above were brought under a special law promulgated by the Allied powers, the Control Council Law no. 10, which established a uniform basis for the prosecution of war criminals and other similar offences except those dealt with by the International Military Tribunal. It must be noted that the law did not make any direct reference to corporations, which may explain why corporations were not directly brought before the courts. However, in trying the leaders of industries for various crimes, the court had occasion to pronounce on the culpability of corporations in the crimes committed. The courts in these cases used the various activities of the companies as a starting point in determining the guilt of individuals based on their knowledge and participation. According

57 Trials of War Criminals before the Nuremberg Tribunals Vols 6–9 (1950–1953).
58 Ibid.
59 Ibid.

to Ratner, the focus on the role of the firms in these cases "shows an acceptance that the corporations themselves had duties that they had breached".[60]
These duties were nevertheless not taken into consideration in the drafting
of early human rights norms. Also worth noting is the ignoring of corporate
veil under corporate law in the adjudication of these cases.

Multinational corporations and the nascent states of the South after independence: changing roles

After corporations were divested of involvement in colonialism most of
them went back to commercial activities. For example, the Royal Niger
Company, after the British authorities revoked its royal charter, changed
its name to Niger Company Ltd and went back to trading as a commercial
concern in Nigeria. However, the corporations operated in an extremely
favourable environment facilitated by the colonial administrations. Many
companies that are dominant in economic activities in the South today
secured that advantage during the period of colonialism. According to
Frynas *et al.*, the preferential treatment given to Shell in Nigeria by the
British colonial authorities, for example, gave the company a first mover
advantage and a virtual monopoly which has ensured the company's dominance in the oil industry in Nigeria to date.[61]

A major change in the relationship between MNCs and host countries
came with the attainment of independence by countries of the South. The
nascent states of the South, realising the gap between their new states and
the countries of the North arising from the previous colonial relationship
sought a new structuring of the economic relationship between the North
and the South. Parts of the demands of the countries of the South were
that MNCs should be made more accountable for their actions and that
the new states should have the exclusive right to exercise sovereignty over
their natural resources.[62] This became more important because of the
involvement of MNCs in the destabilisation of countries and violations of
human rights in countries such as Guatemala, Chile and South Africa.[63]

---

60 Ratner (note 37).
61 J.G. Frynas, M.P. Beck and K. Mellahi, "Maintaining Corporate Dominance after Decolo-
    nization: The 'First Mover Advantage' of Shell-BP in Nigeria" (2000) 27 (85) *Review of
    African Political Economy* 407: R. Brown, "The Relationship between the State and the Mul-
    tinational Corporation in the Exploitation of Resources" (1984) 33 (1) *International and
    Comparative Law Quarterly* 218.
62 R. Browne, "Delinkage – Response of a Spurned Lover or a Rational Part for Africa?"
    (1984) 27 *Howard Law Journal* 937.
63 On Guatemala and MNCs see S. Schlesinger and S. Kinzer *Bitter Fruit: The Story of the
    American Coup in Guatemala: Expanded Edition* (Cambridge: Harvard University, 1990), 65;
    M. Gibney, "United States' Responsibility for Gross Levels of Human Rights Violations in
    Guatemala from 1954 to 1996" (1997–1998) 7 *Journal of Transnational Law and Policy* 77,
    80. On Chile and MNCs see M.E. Winston, "Review of Human Rights and International

The countries of the South perceived foreign MNCs as agents of the North in the economic and political domination of the South and thus agitated for a redefinition of the ties between the North and the South.[64]

In order to redress the imbalance, countries of the South resorted to significant expropriation of foreign investments in their territories.[65] In the period following the Second World War, US and British investors suffered expropriation and nationalisation of their MNCs in Algeria, Argentina, Bolivia, Brazil, Burma, Ceylon, India, Indonesia, Iran, Iraq, Libya, Nigeria, Peru, Somalia, South Yemen, Sudan, Syria, Tanzania, Uganda and the United Arab Republic.[66] As Truitt suggests, the acts of the new states in this regard were attempts by them to shed the last vestige of colonialism and attain some measure of social justice in their dealings with MNCs.[67] By this strategy, the states of the South tried to renegotiate their economic and legal relationships with the MNCs. They also tried to put a check on the powers of MNCs through the drafting and adoption of a multinational code of conduct for MNCs at the international level. However, as we shall see in the next chapter, the attempt at drafting a code of conduct for MNCs failed.

These trends were, however, reversed as the countries of the South discovered, to their dismay that their economic well-being was bound up with foreign direct investments from the North. The Cold War and the battle for allies between the West and the East had aided the South in its quest for development. The rivalry had ensured a steady stream of economic aid from either side of the iron curtain, which had helped the new states stay afloat.[68] The end of the Cold War changed the dynamics as the flow of aid slowed down. Coupled with this was the ending of international banks loans to the new states, which also came to an end in the same period in many countries due to the inability of these states to service their debts.

Ironically, the only avenue opened to the South was in foreign investment. International institutions, policy makers and economists advised the states of the South that international trade and free trade were the

---

Political Economy in Third World Nations: Multinational Corporations, Foreign Aids, and Repression, by William H. Meyer" (1999) 21 (3) *Human Rights Quarterly* 824; R.J. Barnet and R.E. Muller, *Global Reach: The Power of Multinational Corporations* (New York: Simon and Schuster, 1974 On South Africa and MNCs see G.W. Seidman, "Monitoring Multinationals: Lessons from the Anti-Apartheid Era" (2003) 31 (3) *Politics and Society* 381; M.B. Meznar; D. Nigh; C. Kwok, "Effects of Announcements of Withdrawal from South Africa on Stockholder Wealth" (1994) 37 (6) *Academy of Management Journal* 1633.

64 Ratner (note 37).
65 Ibid.
66 J.F. Truitt, "Expropriation of Foreign Investment: Summary of the Post World War II Experience of American and British Investors in the Less Developed Countries" (1970) 1 *Journal of International Business Studies* 21.
67 Ibid.
68 Ratner (note 37).

solutions to underdevelopment in the South. The countries of the South were presented with only one option: to push a free market development model which essentially meant opening up their economies to accommodate MNCs. The balance of power shifted to foreign MNCs yet again because they could provide foreign investment. Furthermore, development aid, loans and other international incentives were conditional upon free trade and investments in the South. Countries of the South had to adjust domestic laws to make them more attractive to MNCs and sometimes even turn a blind eye to the violations of domestic laws.[69] MNCs and their home states had the upper hand and thus set the terms of the relationship with the South through various contracts and agreements.

Summary

The discussion in this chapter situated this book within its historical global context. The chapter showed the relationship between MNCs and states. The relationship which can be traced back to the mercantilist period has continued to influence state responses to corporate abuse of their privileges and power. Reviewing the participation of the corporate form in the eighteenth-century slave trade, colonialism and the Second World War atrocities, the chapter showed how the culture of corporate abuse has developed over the years.

---

69 Ibid.

2 Major attempts at the international level to control multinational corporations

This chapter surveys various attempts at the international level to develop a framework for the control of MNCs. In this respect, the chapter discusses the Universal Declaration of Human Rights and the European Convention on Human Rights and their applicability to MNCs. Furthermore, the chapter discusses various international initiatives to control MNCs including the International Labour Organisation's Tripartite Declaration of Principles Concerning Multinational Enterprises and Social Policy, the United Nations Centre on Transnational Corporations, the OECD Guidelines for Multinational Enterprises, the United Nation's Global Compact, the Norms on Responsibility of Transnational Corporations and other Business Enterprises with regard to Human Rights (the Norms) and the work of the special representative of the UN secretary general on the issue of human rights and MNCs and other business enterprises. The chapter ends with a brief discussion of developments in international environmental law regulation and MNCs.

MNCs and international law

With increasing realisation of the capacity of MNCs to abuse their powers and violate human rights standards, there developed a significant interest in regulating their activities at the international level.[1] The recourse to the international forum is due to the perceived weaknesses in the ability of host states to address the phenomenon of MNCs with their multi-jurisdictional status and their extensive powers relative to that of the state. Furthermore, the nature of MNCs and their ability to operate on an international basis led academics, legal experts and politicians to look to international law to develop a viable framework for the control of MNCs.

---

1 D. French, "International Rhetoric and the Real Global Agenda" in Roger Brownsword ed., *Global Governance and the Quest for Justice Vol. 4 Human Rights* (Oxford and Portland, OR: Hart Publishing, 2004) 121, 130; L. Cata Backer, "The Autonomous Global Corporation: On the Role of Organizational Law beyond Asset Partitioning and Legal Personality" (2006) 14 (3) *Tulsa Law Review* 541, 558.

Much has been written about the ambiguous relationship between MNCs and international law.[2] This book will not repeat what has been written in this regard. The book, however, notes that the focus on international law has proved so far to be unsuccessful. International law is made by states and is ordinarily binding on states. Under the classic conception of international law, MNCs are neither participant in international law-making nor are they subject of international law. That aside, even as regards states, who are direct participants and subjects of international law, it has proved difficult to ensure adequate compliance with international law. Some states pick and choose which international laws to observe and when it is convenient to do so. Powerful states violate international law at will because of the weak enforceability of its norms. The question then is how international law can address MNCs given the situation.

Zerk argues that international law has the potential of responding to the challenges posed by MNCs.[3] Zerk argues that the soft law tradition at the international level has the potential to develop into hard law. She argues that states are capable of developing a regulatory framework based on the experience from the soft law experience. She argues that existing soft law instruments have the potential to help create new customary international obligations. Zerk further argues that while it is problematic to negotiate an overarching treaty on CSR, devising international regimes to tackle specific CSR issues might be more feasible. She buttresses her point with reference to some CSR-related treaty-based regimes that have been facilitated mainly by home states of MNCs to underscore her point that given the political will, international law could be employed to control MNCs. She predicts the emergence of new international institutions to promote and enforce CSR standards of MNCs.

However, the limitations of international law have led to the failure at the international level to find a workable framework for corporate responsibility. While it is agreed that there are potentials in international law, it is argued that the potentials are only practical as complement to host and home state jurisdictions where there exist robust mechanisms for enforcement.

The aim of the rest of this chapter is to assess major international initiatives taken to date to address corporate responsibility. This will serve as a background to understanding the thrust of this book. First, we shall examine major international instruments and their applicability or otherwise to MNCs and second, we shall examine major attempts by various international organisations to control MNCs.

---

2 S. Stefans, "The Amorality of Profit: Transnational Corporations and Human Rights" (2002) 20 *Berkeley Journal of International Law* 45.
3 J.A. Zerk, *Multinationals and Corporate Social Responsibility: Limitations and Opportunities in International Law* (Cambridge: Cambridge University Press, 2006). Some of these points are raised in my review of Zerk's book. See O. Amao, "Book Review: Multinationals and Corporate Social Responsibility: Limitations and Opportunities in International Law by Jennifer A. Zerk" (2007) 10 (1) *Journal of International Economic Law* 161.

International human rights instruments

The Universal Declaration of Human Rights and Corporations[4]

A major development in the twentieth century is the introduction of the Universal Declaration of Human Rights (UDHR). The horrors of Nazi Germany, which rode on the back of legal positivism, led to the decline of that theory and the renaissance of natural rights. Natural rights greatly influenced conventional international human rights norms.[5] The natural rights theorists put forward a theory of foundational or core rights, which each individual is entitled to by virtue of his humanity. As noted by Shestack,[6] the UDHR clearly reflects the natural law theorists' approach when it provides in its opening statement that "recognition of the inherent dignity and of the equal and inalienable rights of all members of the human family is the foundation of freedom, justice and peace in the world". Similarly article 1 provides that "all human beings are born free and equal in dignity. They are endowed with reason and conscience and should act towards one another in a spirit of brotherhood".

The UDHR which has many of its principles codified in the International Covenant on Civil and Political Rights (ICCPR) and the International Covenant on Economic, Social and Cultural Rights (ICESR) and later treaties on racial discrimination, women's rights and torture came to alter the status quo as regards the relationship between the states and their citizens.[7] These norms curtailed the sovereignty of states by recognising the individual citizen and regulating the relationship between the state and its nationals. Whether as duty holders or beneficiaries there is no consensus on the position of the corporation within the UDHR. The explicit duty holders under the declaration are states while the explicit beneficiaries are human beings. It has been suggested that the UDHR

---

4 Universal Declaration of Human Rights, GA res. 217A (III), UN Doc A/810 at 71 (1948).
5 J.J. Shestack, "The Philosophic Foundation of Human Rights" (1998) 20 (2) *Human Rights Quarterly* 201; B.H. Weston, "Human Rights" (1984) 16 (3) *Human Rights Quarterly* 257.
6 Ibid.
7 International Covenant on Civil and Political Rights, GA res. 2200A (XXI), 21 UN GAOR Supp. (no. 16) at 52, UN Doc. A/6316 (1966), 999 UNTS 171, entered into force 23 March 1976. International Covenant on Economic, Social and Cultural Rights GA Res. 2200A (XXI), 21 UNGAOR Supp. (no. 16) at 49, UN Doc. A/6316 (1966), 993 UNTS 3, entered into force 3 January 1976. International Convention on the Elimination of All Forms of Racial Discrimination (ICERD) (GA res. 2106 (XX), Annex, 20 UN GAOR Supp. (no. 14) at 47, UN Doc. A/6014 (1966), 660 UNTS 195), entered into force 4 January 1969. Convention on the Elimination of All Forms of Discrimination Against Women, GA res. 34/180, 34 UN GAOR Supp. (no. 46) at 193, UN Doc. A/34/46, entered into force 3 September 1981. Convention against Torture and Other Cruel, Inhuman or Degrading Treatment (1984, 1465 UNTS 85).

could be read to incorporate the corporations as duty holder. This view is predicated on the preamble to the UDHR, which states that:

> Every individual and every organ of society, keeping this declaration constantly in mind, shall strive by teaching and education to promote respect for these rights and freedoms and by progressive measures, national and international, to secure their universal and effective recognition and observance.

This view thus seeks to interpret "organs of society" as used in the UDHR to include corporations.[8] However, this view is based on a rather tenuous argument, which fails to appreciate the context in which the UDHR arose. The apparent reality is that the UDHR at the time of its conception did not impose any duty on corporations to promote and protect human rights. According to Meyer, human rights obligations for MNCs as a function of legal rights based on the UDHR are a "null set".[9] The wording of the preamble may at best be interpreted in the manner suggested to encourage corporations to voluntarily observe human rights standards. It is arguably not feasible to construe any responsibility on corporations by this interpretation. Interestingly the twin covenants of the UN do not contain this phrase. According to the European Union:

> According to the Universal Declaration on Human Rights and the International Covenant on Civil and Political Rights, every individual and every organ of society is under a responsibility to strive for the promotion and observance of human rights. The EU stresses that such a provision does not constitute direct legal obligations for companies under human rights law, unless the company performs public functions, which may invoke state responsibility. Such a provision could allocate responsibility to corporations, but the legal obligations rest with states. The Covenants, Conventions and Declarations that lay at the basis of human rights responsibilities and duties have been negotiated, signed and ratified by states, which also bear prime responsibility for their implementation.[10]

8 R. Goel, *Guide to Instruments of Corporate Responsibility: An Overview of 16 Key Tools for Labour Fund Trustees* (Toronto: York University, 2005). See also P.T. Muchlinski, "Human Rights and Multinationals: Is there a Problem?" (2001) 77 (1) *International Affairs* 31, 40.

9 W.H. Meyer, "Human Rights and MNCs: Theory Versus Quantitative Analysis" (1996) 18 (2) *Human Rights Quarterly* 368, 369.

10 "EU Reply to the OHCHR Questionnaire on Responsibilities of Transnational Corporations and Related Business Enterprises with Regard to Human Rights", online, available at: www2.ohchr.org/english/issues/globalization/business/docs/replyfinland.pdf (accessed 20 September 2010). See also D. Kinley and J. Tadaki, "From Talk to Walk: The Emergence of Human Rights Responsibilities for Corporations at International Law" (2003–2004) 44 *Virginia Journal of International Law* 931, 948–949.

However, an interesting relationship has emerged between corporations and human rights. This relationship equates the corporate form to the individual and thus views the corporation as an entity that is capable of having its rights violated.[11] The reason for this generally could be found in the view that corporations operate in a private sphere governed by contracts as opposed to government. Most legal systems therefore extend human rights to corporations to the extent that they are capable of exercising them.[12] Therefore, while corporations could not directly be held responsible for violations of human rights as provided for under the UDHR they have the ability to exercise the rights provided in various human rights documents in domestic courts (the wider implications of this will be discussed in Chapter 3).

European Convention on Human Rights (ECHR)[13]

The Convention for the Protection of Human Rights and Fundamental Freedoms (also widely referred to as the "European Convention on Human Rights" and "ECHR") differs significantly from other regional and global human rights frameworks in that it offers wide-ranging protection for business entities, non-profit organisations and natural persons.[14] The term "everyone" which appears many times in the convention also applies to corporations. This is underscored by section 34 of the ECHR, which confers jurisdiction on the European Court of Human Rights (ECtHR) to receive applications from any person, non-governmental organisation or group of individuals claiming to be the victim of violations of rights by contracting states.[15] As Emberland notes, "the court has never doubted that a company is a 'non-governmental organisation' within the meaning of Art 34, and the convention's system of private litigation therefore is open for corporate persons".[16] Emberland observes that despite interpretative and practical challenges, which sometimes occur in the application

---

11 M. Addo, "Human Rights and Multinational Corporations" in M. Addo ed., *Human Rights Standards and the Responsibility of Transnational Corporations* (Netherlands: Kluwer, 2004), 3. See also M. Addo, "The Corporation as Victim of Human Rights Violation" in M. Addo, ed., *Human Rights Standards and the Responsibility of Transnational Corporations* (Netherlands: Netherlands, 2004), 187: Muchlinski (note 8), 32.

12 See Y. Ghai, "Human Rights and Social Development: Toward Democratization and Social Justice" (United Nations Research Institute for Social Development, Democracy, Governance and Human Rights Programme Paper Number 5, 2001).

13 Convention for the Protection of Human Rights and Fundamental Freedoms, 213 UNTS 222, entered into force 3 September 1953, as amended by protocols nos 3, 5, 8 and 11 which entered into force on 21 September 1970, 20 December 1971, 1 January 1990 and 1 November 1998 respectively.

14 M. Emberland, *The Human Rights of Companies: Exploring the Structure of ECHR Protection* (Oxford: Oxford University Press, 2006), 31.

15 Ibid., 4.

16 Ibid.

of convention rights to companies, the notion of companies enjoying rights is well settled under the ECHR.[17]

Between 1998 and 2003, of the 3,307 judgements delivered by the ECtHR, 126 or 3.8 per cent of the total number originated through processes filed by companies or individuals representing corporate interests.[18] Companies' cases are brought within a small range of ECHR provisions including article 6(1) on due process guarantees, alleged breaches of article 1 of the first protocol on property protection and illegitimate interference with freedom of expression guaranteed under article 10. It must be observed that local companies rather than MNCs have mostly availed themselves of protection under the ECHR. MNCs are also capable of invoking the provisions of the ECHR,[19] but these opportunities have been under-explored. The ECHR thus affords considerable protections to corporations which can be invoked by MNCs. However, corporations cannot be sued under the provisions of the convention. According to Wouters and Chanet, in today's Europe the ECHR "is seen more as an instrument that provides *rights* for corporations rather than one that lays down obligations for them unless they are vested with state powers and/or control by states".[20]

A relevant third international human rights instrument is the African Charter on Human and Peoples' Rights (African Charter) which is a more recent development. To avoid needless repetition, the instrument shall be discussed later in Chapter 5.

International institutions

With the exclusion of direct responsibility for MNCs under international law instruments, various international organisations especially under the auspices of the UN have attempted to find ways to control MNCs. Surveys of the major attempts are presented below.

The International Labour Organisation's Tripartite Declaration of Principles Concerning Multinational Enterprises and Social Policy (Tripartite Declaration)[21]

The Tripartite Declaration was the first effort by the international community to set corporate responsibility standards for MNCs.[22] In devising a

---

17   Ibid.
18   Ibid., 14.
19   *British American Tobacco Ltd* v. *Netherlands*, ser. no. A331 (1996) 21 EHRR 404.
20   J. Wouters and L. Chanet, "Corporate Human Rights Responsibility: A European Perspective" (2008) 6 (2) *Northwestern Journal of International Human Rights* 262, 263.
21   Tripartite Declaration of Principles Concerning Multinational Enterprises and Social Policy (1977) 17 ILM 422, para. 6 (1978).
22   See A. Al Faraque and M.D. Zakir Hossain, "Regulation vs Self Regulation in Extractive Industries: A Level Playing Field" (2006) 3 *Macquarie Journal of International and Environmental Law* 47, 57.

new world order following the First World War, the high contracting party under the Treaty of Versailles[23] realised that universal peace can only be achieved through the institutionalisation of social justice. According to the preamble to article 13 of the Treaty of Versailles the high contracting parties "moved by sentiments of justice and humanity as well as by the desire to secure the permanent peace of the world" agreed to the establishment of the International Labour Organisation (ILO). The parties also sought to initiate international action to improve labour conditions world-wide.[24] However, the establishment of the ILO was not done wholly for the purpose of world peace, justice and humanity. According to the ILO:

> The third motivation was economic. Because of its inevitable effect on the cost of production, any industry or country adopting social reform would find itself at a disadvantage vis-à-vis its competitors. The Preamble states the failure of any nation to adopt humane conditions of labour is an obstacle in the way of other nations which desire to improve the conditions in their own countries.[25]

Thus, there was the implicit factor of creating a level playing field for economic growth. Employers in the private sector were in support of the idea of an international labour body (which was an additional burden on business) for other reasons, the fear of revolution brought about by the advancement of socialist and communist ideas and the belief that the ILO as a vehicle for social compromise would be an effective check against uprisings made employers' supportive of the idea. Attempts to oppose the establishment of the ILO were also countered by the allegations made against corporations in the Second World War industrialist cases.[26] The ILO was established in 1919.

The ILO became involved in issues concerning the control of MNCs in the 1970s. Its strategy was to develop guidelines for MNCs' operations. The ILO embarked on the drawing up of a guideline for MNCs for several reasons. By the 1960s the involvement of MNCs in the violation of human rights sparked discussions in many international fora on the need to regulate their conduct and to properly define the terms of their relationship with host countries. Another factor that gave support to the argument for regulation was the growing gap between the established nations of the North and the nascent states of the South. The states perceived MNCs as part of the reason for the increasing gap and this generated hostilities toward MNCs. Trade Union activism at the international level on the abuse of corporate power by MNCs also bolstered the effort. According to

23 Treaty of Versailles (1920) ATS 1.
24 E. Lee, "Globalization and Labour Standards: A Review of Issues" (1997) 136 (2) *International Labour Review* 173–188.
25 See International Labour Organization "ILO History", online, available at: www.ilo.org/public/english/about/history.htm (accessed 20 September 2010).
26 See the Second World War industrialist cases discussed in Chapter 1.

the ILO, "since labour related and social policy issues were among the specific concerns to which MNE activities gave rise, the ILO was inevitably drawn into international guidelines in its sphere of competence".[27]

The Tripartite Declaration of Principles concerning Multinational Enterprises and Social Policy was passed on 16 November 1977 after deliberations between governments, labour organisations and employer groups and then revised in 2000 and in 2006. There are five major sections in the declaration. The first section urges MNCs to respect national sovereignty, laws and policies of host states and urges host governments to treat MNCs and local companies equally. The section further urges regular consultation between business, labour and government. The second section encourages MNCs to generate secured employments, use appropriate technologies and observe appropriate employment policies. The third section addresses the training, retraining and promotion of workers. The fourth focuses on wage rates, benefits, conditions of work including occupational safety and health. The last part is on freedom of association and the right to organise, collective bargaining, consultation, examination of grievances and settlement of industrial disputes.

The Tripartite Declaration turned out to be more of a defensive mechanism and a public relations exercise to appease growing hostility from the states of the South and trade unions. This is because unlike the procedure for the examination of complaints against infringement of trade union rights under other ILO conventions,[28] the declaration does not provide for a complaints procedure against companies or governments. It is a voluntary instrument and no reporting is required. Companies are not required to endorse or sign up to the declaration. However, periodic surveys are conducted to monitor the usage of the declaration by MNCs, governments, employers' organisations and workers' organisations. A summary and an analysis of the replies received from ILO member governments and employers' and workers' organisations are submitted to the ILO governing body for discussion.

A procedure approved by the governing body in 1980 (revised in 1986) allows for the submission of requests for interpretation in cases of dispute on the meaning/application of the provisions of the declaration.[29] This

27 International Labour Organization, "Multinational Enterprises and Social Policy", online, available at: www.oit.org/public/english/employment/multi/tripartite/history. htm (accessed 8 March 2009).

28 For example the Committee on Freedom of Association reviews complaints concerning violations of freedom of association, whether or not a member state has ratified the relevant conventions. The relevant conventions are Freedom of Association and Protection of the Right to Organise Convention, 1948 Convention no. 87 and the Right to Organise and Collective Bargaining Convention, 1949, Convention no. 98.

29 Procedure for the Examination of Disputes Concerning the Application of the Tripartite Declaration of Principles Concerning Multinational Enterprises and Social Policy by Means of Interpretation of Its Provisions (adopted by the Governing Body of the International Labour Office at its 232nd Session (Geneva, March 1986)).

procedure has, however, been employed in a way that renders it almost meaningless. In two cases where trade union bodies tried to use the provisions to review the actions of MNCs, the cases were unsuccessful. One of the requests was submitted by the International Union of Food, Agricultural, Hotel, Restaurant, Catering, Tobacco and Allied Workers' Associations (IUF) in 1992. The submission was based on paragraphs 1, 2, 8 and 45 of the Tripartite Declaration and it sought to establish whether or not Pepisco Company, an MNC operating in Burma, had, by choosing to operate in a country where human rights and labour rights were severely curtailed, put itself in a position where it could not possibly observe the principles of the declaration.[30] The request was declared not receivable by a committee of the ILO on multinational enterprises consisting of an employers' group and some government representatives on the ground that it was dangerous and ill-advised to link investments with human rights or trade union records of a country. According to the committee, the situation envisaged under the procedure were those concerning labour-management disputes and in that particular case there was no evidence of any actual dispute between workers and management or government leading to a disagreement in interpretation. Similarly, a request by the International Federation of Chemical, Energy, Mine and General Workers' Unions (ICEM) in 1993, which sought to establish whether a subsidiary of Exxon in Malaysia was entitled to prevent one of its employees from attending an ILO meeting and withholding certain information from him was inconclusive.[31] In that case, the secretary-general of the union involved was appointed to attend a sectoral tripartite meeting. The union official requested the employer (Exxon) to grant him union paid leave in order to attend the session. He also requested the company to provide him with company safety and health information for use at the meeting. The company granted him leave without pay, refused to provide company safety and health information and statistics on the ground that these were proprietary and only for the use of the company. Based on those facts, a request was subsequently submitted for the interpretation of paragraphs 37, 38 and 39 of the declaration. The committee gave two alternative interpretations but failed to approve either of them and left the matter unresolved. The relevance of the declaration has thus been undermined by its unenforceability. The Tripartite Declaration has therefore been of little consequence in practice.

The United Nations Centre on Transnational Corporations (UNCTC)

A more robust attempt was made to control MNCs under the auspices of the UN by the establishment of the UNCTC. In order to confront the

---

30 *IUF Case* (1992) (GB.254/MNE/4/6).
31 *ICEF Case* (1993–1995) (GB.264/13, Appendix).

challenges posed by MNCs and due to enormous pressure put on it by the countries of the South, the United Nations Economic and Social Council set up a group of eminent persons in 1973 to examine the nature and impact of MNCs on development process.[32] It is interesting to note that the immediate rationale of UN's action in this area was at the initiation of Chile which was at the time dealing with the revelation of the alleged role of US based corporation, ITT, in the political instability in the country.[33] One of the group's recommendations was the establishment of the United Nations Commission on Transnational Corporations, a permanent inter-governmental forum for deliberations on issues related to MNCs. The recommendation also led to the establishment of the UN permanent programme on MNCs carried out by the UNCTC. The UNCTC commenced its work in November 1974. The three main objectives of the centre were:

> To further the understanding of the political, economic, social and legal effects of MNCs activity, especially in developing countries;
>
> To secure international arrangements that promote the positive contributions of MNCs to national development goals and world economic growth while controlling and eliminating their negative effects; and
>
> To strengthen the negotiating capacity of host countries, in particular developing countries, in their dealings with MNCs.[34]

One of the major tasks to which the centre dedicated itself was the formulation of a code of conduct for MNCs.[35] This was in direct response to developing countries' agitations for international control of MNCs under a new international economic order to safeguard their natural resources, trading rights, as well as secure access to capital and technology.[36] A draft code was

32 See United Nations, *The Impact of Multinational Corporations on Development and on International Relations* (United Nations Publication, Sales no. E.74.II.A.5) and United Nations, *Multinational Corporations in the World Development* (United Nations Publications, Sales no. E.73.II.A.11).

33 See ECOSOC Resolution 1721 (LIII) adopted 28 July 1972, meeting 1836. See also L. Sergelund, "Thirty Years of Corporate Social Responsibility within the UN: From Codes of Conduct to Norms" (Sixth Pan-European Conference on International Relations, Turin, Italy 12–15 September 2007). See generally on UN's decision to intervene in the regulation of MNCs, S.J. Rubin, "Reflections Concerning the United Nations Commission on Transnational Corporations" (1976) 70 *American Journal of International Law* 73.

34 United Nations, *The United Nations Code of Conduct on Transnational Corporations, United Nations Centre on Transnational Corporations*, UNCTC Current Studies, ser. A, no. 4 (New York, 1986).

35 F.E. Nattier, "Regulation of Transnational Corporations: Latin American Actions in International Fora" (1984) 19 *Texas International Law Journal* 265, 280–282.

36 Ibid.

adopted by the UN in 1983 and revised in 1988 and 1990.[37] The code recognised some important rights for investors but also emphasised the need for foreign investors to obey host country laws, follow host country economic policies and avoid interference in the host country's domestic political affairs. There was no direct reference to human rights in the first draft of the code. However, the 1990 version contained a direct reference to fundamental freedoms and international standards of human rights. It provides in paragraph 14 that "transnational corporations shall respect human rights and fundamental freedoms in countries in which they operate ... and shall not discriminate on the basis of race, colour, sex, religion, language, social, national and ethnic origin or political or other opinion".

As earlier indicated in Chapter 1, economic instability and mounting debt crises forced the countries of the South that called for a code under a new international economic order to abandon the idea. The countries that had previously championed the UN code and struggled to make it into a treaty had to discard the idea in the early 1990s as a compromise to secure foreign investments, assistance for development and forgiveness of mounting foreign debt.[38] Also the change in the attitude of UNCTC and the commission contributed to the stalling of the Code. The Cold War climate of confrontation and mistrust changed attitudes and focussed attention on the positive impact of MNCs on development. The emergence of a new economic orthodoxy, neo liberalisation, which encouraged liberalisation, privatisation and deregulation, further undermined the UNCTC effort. The centre was closed in 1993, bringing to an end the effort by the centre to draft a code for the control of MNCs.[39]

The OECD Guidelines for Multinational Enterprises[40]

Another international initiative in this area is the guideline produced under the auspices of the Organisation for Economic Cooperation and Development (OECD). The guideline was originally negotiated in 1976 as part of the OECD Declaration on International Investment and Multinational Enterprises. It was revised in 1991 to take into account environmental con-

---

37   See Draft United Nations Code of Conduct on Transnational Corporations, UN Centre on Transnational Corporations, Special Session (7–18 March 1983 and 9–20 May 1983): UN Doc.E/C.10/1982/6(1986); Code of Conduct on Transnational Corporations, UN ESCOR, Organisational Session for 1988, Provisional Agenda Item 2, at 4, UN Doc. E/1988 (39(Add.1) (1988); Development and International Economic Cooperation: Transnational Corporations, UN Doc E/1990/94(1990).

38   S.R. Ratner, "Corporations and Human Rights: A Theory of Legal Responsibility" (2001) 111 *Yale Law Journal* 450–459.

39   D. Abrahams, "Regulations for Corporations: A Historical Account of TNC Regulation" (Geneva: UNRISD, 2005).

40   Organisation for Economic Cooperation and Development Guidelines for Multinational Enterprises, 15 ILM. 9 (1976).

siderations and was further updated in the year 2000.[41] The negotiators of the guidelines were the participating countries of the OECD, business associations, trade unions and some civil society organisations. The guidelines set out "the principles for acceptable behaviour for corporations in the social and environmental sphere globally".[42] The document has been described as the most comprehensive document on CSR.[43] According to Queinnec, one of the original features of the Norms set out in the OECD guidelines is that they apply "both to member states in charge of implementing them and to the multinational enterprises whose activities these guidelines are supposed to govern (whether they operate on the territory of a member country or are based there)".[44]

Murray in her analysis of the OECD guidelines opines that the guidelines were a product of four themes or strands in the debate about MNC in the 1970s.[45] The first strand comes from the question of power relations between MNCs and host countries especially in the countries of the South. This was the period when the South advocated the creation of a new international economic order, which would among other things, ensure that states were able to exercise control over foreign direct investment and the activities of MNCs within their territories. What the countries of the South sought, were binding rules to ensure that the MNCs did not interfere with the polity of the host community and did not serve the interest of foreign countries whilst doing business in host states. However, the final outcome of the OECD negotiations did not reflect these aspirations. One of the major compromises made in the negotiations was that the operation of the guidelines would be limited to the OECD area itself, thereby excluding to a large extent non-OECD states from its protection. Nonetheless, the guidelines made some minor concessions to host countries which are general and ambiguous. The guidelines commit OECD member states to working with non-OECD states to improve welfare and the living standards of all people. It also requires MNCs to obey the domestic law of the states in which they operate.

The second dominant strand identified by Murray was the desire of corporations and some OECD states to protect foreign direct investments and MNCs' operations from being interfered with by host governments.[46] This strand shaped the outcome of the negotiations so much that it has cor-

---

41 OECD Guidelines for Multinational Enterprises, OECD Doc. DAFFE/IME(2000)20 (2000). Text of the revised version of the OECD Guideline for Multinational Enterprises is online, available at: www.oecd.org/ (accessed 5 May 2008); French (note 1).

42 S. Macleod and D. Lewis, "Transnational Corporations: Power, Influence and Responsibility" (2004) 4 (1) *Global Social Policy* 77.

43 Goel (note 8), 65.

44 Y. Queinnec, *The OECD Guidelines for Multinational Enterprises: An Evolving Legal Status* (Paris: Sherpa, 2007), 6.

45 J. Murray, "A New Phase in the Regulation of Multinational Enterprises: The Role of the OECD" (2001) 30 (3) *Industrial Law Journal* 255.

46 Ibid., 256.

rectly being described as the overriding purpose of the declaration.[47] The motivation accounts for the "national treatment" requirement of the declaration which is to the effect that MNCs should be treated no less favourably than domestic companies. The declaration thus seeks to create greater freedom for MNCs.

The third strand reflected the intervention of the EU and others who were concerned with the problem of organised labour within the MNCs. The chapter on employment and industrial relations in the guidelines guarantees rights to collective bargaining within the MNC and if necessary in the multinational context. The fourth strand, which is crucial to the nature of the document eventually produced, is the debate concerning the nature and status of the declaration. Most home states and MNCs were opposed to any form of legally binding instrument. While there was a proposal to create binding obligations, the United States, Switzerland and Germany retaliated by proposing a binding code to protect foreign direct investment.[48] The compromise reached was to succumb to the demand of the MNCs and the states demanding for a non-binding treaty. The guidelines were therefore couched as recommendations from the OECD states to MNCs.

The guidelines were revised in 2000. The revised guidelines reduced the focus on MNCs' compliance with national law and practice to an emphasis on MNCs' obligations in relation to a range of international standards.[49] The revised guidelines make direct reference to some important international instruments such as the Universal Declaration of Human Rights and the ILO Declaration on Fundamental Principles and Rights at Work. MNCs are urged to comply with these instruments in line with host states' international obligations and commitments. Another significant point to note in the revised version is that it expanded the scope of its applicability to corporations operating "in or from" OECD territories.[50] Global production was also covered by the revised guidelines, which appeal to MNCs to encourage, where practicable, business partners including suppliers and contractors to follow the guidelines in their business dealings. In the field of labour standards, the revised guidelines in its chapter on industrial relations employ the language of regulation in specifying standards to be met by MNCs which was, with the exception of the standards on organising and collective bargaining, absent from the earlier version. The guidelines supplement the core ILO standards and create additional ones on occupational health and safety for requirements.

Despite these changes, which arguably can be considered as an attempt to strengthen the guidelines, one factor that remained unchanged and

---

47 Ibid.
48 Ibid., 260.
49 OECD Guidelines for Multinational Enterprises, OECD Doc. DAFFE/IME(2000)20 (2000).
50 Ibid.

which belies all the changes made to the document is that the guidelines were to remain not legally binding. According to Murray "the guidelines adopt the jargon of modern management theory to make explicit their principle of self regulation".[51] And as she correctly concludes:

> The fact that the new package of demands placed on MNCs continued to be non-legally binding suggests that, on a deeper level, the desire of states to encourage the unfettered flow of FDI and other Transnational economic activity is the fundamental motivation given expression in the guidelines.[52]

At the negotiations of the guidelines, the business community aimed for a voluntary guideline. The Business Industry Advisory Council (BIAC), which is one of the bodies required to be consulted by the OECD's Committee on International Investment and Multinational Enterprises (CIME) in its task of coordinating exchange of views, stated clearly that the guidelines "must remain voluntary – not legally binding. They are not designed to replace national or international legislation or individual or sectoral code".[53] For example, when the Dutch government proposed to require MNCs to comply with the guidelines as a prerequisite for obtaining export credit and subsidies, the BIAC opposed it, urging other countries not to follow such precedent.[54] It would appear that for business, the guidelines may represent no more than a corporate marketing opportunity rather than an authentic opportunity to moderate corporate behaviour.

The guidelines are implemented and promoted through National Contact Points (NCPs) which members are obliged to set up pursuant to the OECD Council Decision of June 2000.[55] States are given wide latitude in respect of the structural arrangement in this regard.[56] The NCPs promote the guidelines, entertain enquiries and resolve problems in specific process of implementation. The NCPs also handle complaints against companies for violations of its principles. They also gather information on experiences at the national level on the implementation of the guidelines. These experiences are shared at the general meetings and included in annual reports submitted by the NCPs to CIME.[57] However, most of the

---

51 Murray (note 45) 265.
52 Ibid., 266.
53 Macleod and Lewis (note 42).
54 Ibid.
55 Council decision of June 2000, online, available at: www.oecd.org/document/39/0,334 3,en_2649_34889_1933095_1_1_1_1,00.html (accessed 23 September 2010).
56 Macleod and Lewis (note 42).
57 See generally C.N. Francoise, "A Critical Assessment of the United States' Implementation of the OECD Guidelines for Multinational Enterprises" (2007) 30 *Boston College International and Comparative Law Review* 223.

NCPs have been criticised as being unresponsive and unaccountable.[58] This criticism has been levied against NCPs in major member states including Japan, Korea, United States, Ireland and Canada.[59] The NCPs were criticised by the Trade Union Advisory Committee in its 2001 report for underperforming.[60] For example, as of 2007, 16 communications were submitted to the US NCP which represents the greatest number to any member state. This underscores the low usage of the procedure. Most of these cases were not made public and where they are made available only brief details are provided making information on implementation scarce.[61] Recently, the special representative of the UN secretary general on the issue of human rights and transnational corporations and other business enterprises has called for a review of the guidelines to make them more specific and comprehensive.[62] In April 2010, the adhering governments agreed on the terms of reference for carrying out an update of the guidelines.[63] The terms include technical updates, clarification and further guidance on the application of the guidelines to supply chains, elaboration on the application of the human rights element under Chapter II and the consideration of making due diligence one of the operational principles of the chapter, update on disclosure standards, revision or expansion or elaboration of Chapter VI on combating bribery, application of the guidelines to environmental issues, possible expansion of Chapter VII on consumer issues, public disclosure of taxes, royalties and other payments and improvement of implementation procedure.

The United Nations' Global Compact (UNGC)

Following the failure of the UNCTC to come up with a code for the control of MNCs, the next significant development at the UN level was the introduction of the UNGC. The Global Compact programme was initiated by Kofi Anan, the former United Nations secretary general. The UNGC's operational phase was launched at UN headquarters in New York on 26 July 2000. The UNGC is a voluntary initiative designed to help fashion a more humane world by enjoining businesses to follow ten principles

58 Goel (note 8).
59 Ibid.
60 Macleod and Lewis (note 42).
61 Francoise (note 57), 230.
62 Promotion and Protection of all Human Rights, Civil, Political, Economic, Social and Cultural Rights, including the Right to Development; Protect, Respect and Remedy: A Framework for Business and Human Rights; Report of the Special Representative of the Secretary General on the Issue of Human Rights and Transnational Corporations and other Business Enterprises, John Ruggie, A/HRC/8/5, 7 April 2008 (the Ruggie Report). Online, available at: http://198.170.85.29/Ruggie-report-2010.pdf (accessed 20 September 2010).
63 OECD, "Terms of Reference for an Update of the OECD Guidelines for Multinational Enterprises" (May 2010).

concerning human rights, labour, the environment and corruption.[64] The ten principles enshrined in the Global Compact document were derived from the Universal Declaration of Human Rights,[65] the 1992 UNCED Rio Declaration,[66] the four fundamental principles and rights at work adopted at the 1995 World Summit for Social Development[67] and the UN Convention against Corruption.[68] The aim of the initiative was to get business to internalise these principles in their practices.[69] According to Ruggie, "companies are encouraged to move toward 'good practices' as defined through multi-stakeholder dialogue and partnership, rather than relying on their often superior bargaining position vis-à-vis national authorities".[70]

The UNGC has been in existence for more than a decade and its success as a tool for controlling corporations is doubtful. Many of the norms it promotes are ambiguous in content and are not reflective of international legal norms.[71] Two important factors militate against companies signing up to the UNGC: One is the fear of litigation based on the principles set forth in the UNGC. This is especially so in the case of US based corporations particularly in the wake of the *Kasky* v. *Nike Inc*[72] law suit. In that case, Nike was sued *inter alia* for false advertisement based on its voluntary claims. The suit was eventually settled at a substantial cost to the company. It is therefore possible that corporations may be sued based on their claim of compliance with the UNGC principles. The second factor is the transaction cost that may be involved in signing up to the

---

64 O.F. Williams, "The UN Global Compact: The Challenge and the Promise" (2004) 14 (4) *Business Ethics Quarterly* 755.

65 Universal Declaration of Human Rights, GA res. 217A (III), UN Doc A/810 at 71 (1948).

66 Rio Declaration on Environment and Development 31 ILM 874.

67 Report of the World Summit for Social Development, 1995, online, available at: www. un.org/documents/ga/conf166/aconf166-9.htm (accessed 22 September 2010).

68 United Nations Convention Against Corruption, online, available at: www.unodc.org/ unodc/en/treaties/CAC/index.html (accessed 22 September 2010).

69 It has also been argued that the Global Compact was an attempt by the UN to expand its reach from states to non-state actors in order revive and reinvent its relevance on the global stage. It is suggested that the move was recognition of the relevance of corporations in achieving sustainable globalisation. See S. Deva, "Global Compact: A Critique of the UN's 'Public–Private' Partnership for Promoting Corporate Citizenship" (2006–2007) 34 *Syracuse Journal of International Law and Commerce* 107–109. See J. Bendell, "Flagships of Inconvenience? The Global Compact and the Future of the United Nations" ICCSR Research Paper Series 2004, online, available at: www.notting-ham.ac.uk/nubs/ICCSR/research.php?action=single&id=58 (accessed 24 September 2010).

70 J.G. Ruggie, "Taking Embedded Liberalism Global: The Corporate Connection" in D. Held and M. Koenig-Archibugi, eds, *Taming Globalization: Frontiers of Governance* (Cambridge: Polity Press, 2003), 93.

71 French (note 1), 132; Deva (note 69), 129.

72 02 CDOS 3790.

compact. These factors perhaps explain the slow response of "big business", in the United States especially, to the compact.[73]

The UNGC is a completely voluntary initiative. Business may choose to sign or not to sign up to it. As many scholars on the subject have posited, the UNGC is neither a code nor regulation.[74] Thus it has no real enforcement mechanism. Corporations that sign up to it are required only to make an unambiguous statement of support and include some reference in their annual report or other public documents on the progress they are making on internalising the principles within their operations.[75] Companies are further required to submit a brief description of the report to the UNGC website. Failure to submit the brief description within two years of signing up and every two years thereafter will result in the defaulting company being removed from the list of participants. This is the most severe action the UNGC can take against an erring company.

The UNGC presently encourages participating companies to also participate in the Global Reporting Initiative (sometimes called the triple bottom line or sustainability reporting) but does not make it mandatory.[76] The lack of an objective and independent monitoring process makes the programme susceptible to being used merely as a public relation instrument by corporations knowing full well that they will not be called to account.[77] The strategy is all the more effective because such corporations may hide under the prestigious and plausible covering of the UN and need not necessarily follow the principles. The UNGC may also allow corporations to be selective as to what they comply with and flaunt their select compliance in their report while neglecting other areas. There is also the fear that the UNGC may have the effect of marginalising human rights in the long term by shifting focus away from it.[78] This is because more attention may be paid to such voluntary initiatives rather than on ways of improving human rights framework.

However, scholars in favour of the UNGC have argued that the UNGC has a different role from that for which a code is designed.[79] While emphasising that the compact is an attempt to retrieve the moral purpose of business, William concedes that "the Global Compact today is a far cry from a force that might shape significant changes in the moral values of the global community".[80] However, he emphasises that the UNGC is a beginning. According to William, the UNGC as envisioned by its authors, is an

---

73 Williams (note 64).
74 See for example Ruggie (note 70).
75 Williams (note 64), 756.
76 Ibid.
77 Ibid.
78 French (note 1), 133.
79 Williams (note 64); Ruggie (note 70).
80 Williams (note 64), 761.

incremental process of learning and improvement, rooted in local networks, sharing the same universal values, that is now only at the starting point.[81] According to Ruggie, the compact "operates on the premise that the socially legitimated good practices would help drive out the bad ones through the power of transparency and competition".[82] In Ruggie's view, the compact is a mechanism intended to engage companies in the promotion of UN goals, not to regulate them. Regulation, he reasons, is a perfectly valid objective, but it is not the only one that matters. However, he notes that experience learnt through the UNGC would inevitably lead to the desire for greater benchmarking and that some of the soft laws produced by voluntary initiatives may well develop subsequently into hard law.

In conclusion, the UNGC does not qualify as a legal standard. Its norms are fluid and uncertain. It has no viable enforcement mechanism. Its use as a standard setting mechanism is doubtful. However, its most important contribution may be its reinforcement of the idea that there is a moral purpose to business.

Norms on Responsibility of Transnational Corporations and other Business Enterprises with Regard to Human Rights[83]

In 2003, the United Nations Sub-Commission on the Promotion and Protection of Human Rights approved the "Norms on Responsibilities of Transnational Corporations and other Business Enterprises with Regard to Human Rights" (the Norms). The sub-commission consists of 26 experts elected by the UN Commission on Human Rights. The Norms were subsequently approved by the full commission in 2004, which thereafter disseminated the document for comment from businesses, governments and NGOs. However, the UN Commission on Human Rights failed to finally adopt the document.

The Norms consolidate a wide range of human rights norms specifically applicable to multinational corporations and other businesses. The Norms purportedly derive their legitimacy and binding character from the international conventions, standard, codes and other international instruments to which they refer.[84] The Norms refer to at least 56 instruments including

---

81 Ibid.

82 Ruggie (note 70).

83 Norms on the Responsibilities of Transnational Corporations and Other Business Enterprises with Regard to Human Rights, UN Doc. E/CN.4/Sub.2/2003/12/Rev.2 (2003). Approved 13 August 2003, by UN Sub-Commission on the Promotion and Protection of Human Rights Resolution 2003/16, UN Doc. E/CN.4/Sub.2/2003/L.11, 52 (2003).

84 D. Weissbrodt and M. Kruger, "Norms on the Responsibilities of Transnational Corporations and other Businesses Enterprises with Regard to Human Rights" (2003) 97 *American Journal of International Law* 901.

18 treaties, 11 multilateral instruments, three industry/commodity initiatives, six union/trade initiatives, 13 company codes and five NGO model guidelines.[85] The Norms are generally viewed as an attempt to establish an international framework for mandatory standards on CSR.[86]

According to Weissbrodt and Kruger "the Norms is an extension of human rights standards to the field of corporate social responsibility", they "represent(s) a landmark in holding businesses accountable for their human rights abuses and constitute a succinct, comprehensive, restatement of the international legal principles applicable to business".[87] In the authors' view, the Norms represent an important development as the document takes a different approach from other earlier international initiatives by being the first non-voluntary initiative adopted at the international level. While the Norms recognise the primary role of states in protecting and promoting human rights, they went further by putting direct obligations on companies to ensure that human rights are respected in their spheres of activity and influence. According to Baxi, the human rights responsibility of corporations under the Norms may be summed up as: "duties of non-benefit from human rights violations; duties of influence, and duties of implementation" which they are required to bear "within their respective spheres of activity and influence".[88]

The obligations placed on MNCs by the Norms are substantial. They include: obligations to treat workers equally and to provide equal opportunities;[89] obligations not to engage in or benefit from violations of human rights or humanitarian laws;[90] specific obligations to workers in the areas of compulsory labour, prohibition of child labour, provision of safe and healthy environment, provision of fair and progressive remuneration standards and right to collective bargaining;[91] respect of international and domestic law of host states including human rights obligations,[92] transparent obligations;[93] consumer protection[94] and environmental protection.[95]

---

85 U. Baxi, "Market Fundamentalisms: Business Ethics at the Altar of Human Rights" (2005) 5 *Human Rights Law Review* 1.

86 L.C. Backer, "Multinational Corporations, Transnational Law; The United Nations' Norms on the Responsibilities of Transnational Corporations as a Harbinger of Corporate Social Responsibility (2005–2006) 37 *Columbia Human Rights Law Review* 287; S.S. Thorsen and A. Meisling, "Perspectives on the UN Draft Norms" (Paper submitted to the IBA/AIJA Conference on Social Responsibility in Amsterdam, 25–26 June 2004).

87 Weissbrodt and Kruger (note 84).

88 Draft Norms at para. 1; Baxi (note 83), 9.

89 Para. 2 UN Draft Norms.

90 Ibid., para. 3.

91 Ibid., para. 5–9.

92 Ibid., para. 10.

93 Ibid., 11.

94 Ibid., 13.

95 Ibid., 14.

Backer has argued that the Norms attempt to shift corporate governance from a shareholder maximisation model to a public law model, imposing direct obligations on corporations to serve the community in which they operate in accordance with international standards.[96] According to him, the Norms suggest a stakeholder approach, substantially extending the concept of stakeholder to cover almost all elements of society.[97] The Norms are applicable worldwide regardless of corporate governance models in domestic laws.[98] Therefore, the extent to which the national corporate governance model permits or excludes other stakeholder issues will not matter.

Unlike earlier instruments, the Norms also attempt to introduce an effective implementation procedure in the framework. The Norms require businesses to adopt their substance as the minimum to be included in their company code of conduct or internal rules of operation and to further adopt mechanisms to ensure accountability within the company.[99] The Norms prescribe that in case of non-compliance a company will have to pay reparations. The United Nations is to play a monitoring and verification role, while states will use national law to ensure corporate accountability.

The Norms were largely welcomed by NGOs[100] and some academics[101] that perceived the document as a more effective way of holding MNCs accountable. According to Baxi "what makes the Norms, and the commentary, precious is the now proclaimed zero tolerance for egregious forms of business conduct and practices that transgress human rights and constantly reproduce human rights violations".[102] He posits that a single-minded pursuit of human rights-oriented future for globalisation and human development is perhaps the only pertinent way forward.[103]

---

96   Backer (note 86), 352.
97   Ibid., 358. Para. 22 of the Norms.
98   Para. 20 provides

> The term "transnational corporation" refers to an economic entity operating in more than one country or a cluster of economic entities operating in two or more countries – whatever their legal form, whether in their home country or country of activity, and whether taken individually or collectively.

99   Weissbrodt and Kruger (note 84).
100 In the face of stiff opposition to the Norms especially from the business community and some home country governments nearly 200 NGOs signed a letter of support for the Norms in 2004, online, available at: http://web.amnesty.org/library/Index/ENGIOR420052004?open&of=eng-398 (accessed 20 September 2010).
101 J. Oldenziel, "The Added Value of the UN Norms: A Comparative Analysis of the UN Norms for Business with Existing International Instruments" (SOMO Centre for Research on Multinational Corporations, 2005).
102 Baxi (note 85), 3.
103 Ibid.

However, not all shared this enthusiasm. MNCs, their umbrella organisations such as the International Organisation of Employers (IOE), the International Chamber of Commerce (ICC), the Confederation of British Industry (CBI), the United States Council for International Business and influential home states fiercely opposed the possibility of creating a binding obligation on corporations. The IOE and the ICC vigorously opposed the introduction of the Norms after their approval. They produced a 42-page legal document challenging the legality and relevance of the Norms.[104] The document accused the Norms of several infringements including: mistakenly placing human rights obligations on private business actors contrary to international law; shifting state responsibilities onto private business; misrepresenting international law by placing obligations on business which may ultimately undermine human rights and subject business to overarching and intrusive legislations such as mandatory reparation payment as a consequence of non compliance. They further alleged that the process of the adoption of the Norms was not transparent.[105] In a similar vein the Confederation of British Industry employed the services of Maurice Mendelson, QC to prepare its opposition on the Norms. Mendelson criticised the Norms on the following broad grounds:

i   It has little or no basis in existing international law.
ii It plays "fast and loose" with the established means of creating international law, and seeks to mix law, "soft law", guidelines, non-law and would-be law, not to mention assorted categories of rules, in a most unsatisfactory normative stew.
iii It runs counter to the general structure of international law which, for good reason, places the responsibility for ensuring good governance and respect for human rights on states and their instrumentalities.
iv It begs numerous questions, both of practice and principle.[106]

The United States Council for International Business (USCIB) criticised the Norms in similar terms, contending that the Norms were predicated on the erroneous "belief that human rights can best be advanced by circumventing national political and legal frameworks and establishing

---

104 Joint views of the IOE and ICC on the draft, "Norms on the Responsibilities of Transnational Corporations and Other Business Enterprises with Regard to Human Rights", online, available at: www.reports-and-materials.org/IOE-ICC-views-UN-norms-March-2004.doc (accessed 24 September 2010).
105 Ibid.
106 Opinion of Professor Emeritus Maurice Mendelson QC, "In the Matter of the Draft 'Norms on the Responsibilities of Transnational Corporations And Other Business Enterprises with Regard to Human Rights'", online, available at: www.reports-and-materials.org/CBI-Annex-A-Mendelson-opinion.doc (accessed 24 September 2010).

international legal obligations for multinational companies that do not exist at the national level or apply to domestic companies".[107]

Despite the controversy generated by the Norms, their introduction nonetheless focused the debate more directly on human rights responsibility of businesses. However, the conflicting positions have ensured the stalling of the Norms. As things stand today, it appears we are not getting nearer to a coherent regulation of MNCs, at least not under the framework provided by the Norms.

Following the stalemate over the adoption of the Norms, a special representative was appointed by the UN secretary general with a five-point mandate in order to find a way forward. In his first interim report, the special representative severely criticised the Norms, largely along the same lines as the views expressed by the business community. According to Ruggie:

> The Norms exercise became engulfed by its own doctrinal excesses. Even leaving aside the highly contentious though largely symbolic proposal to monitor firms and provide reparation payments to victims, its exaggerated legal claims and conceptual ambiguities created confusion and doubt even among mainstream international lawyers and other impartial observers. Two aspects are particularly problematic in the context of this mandate. One concerns the legal authority advanced for the Norms and the other the principle by which they propose to allocate human rights responsibilities between states and firms.[108]

The caustic criticism of the Norms by Ruggie, sounded the death knell for the Norms.[109]

The special representative of the secretary general on the issue of human rights and transnational corporations and other business enterprises

The special representative released his first report in April 2008.[110] The report was considered by the United Nations Human Rights Council in

---

107 See copy of document at United States Council for International Business (USCIB), "Talking Points on the Draft 'Norms on the Responsibilities of Transnational Corporations and Other Business Enterprises with Regard to Human Rights", online, available at: www.business-humanrights.org/Links/Repository/331222/jump (accessed 24 September 2010).

108 J. Ruggie, "Promotion and Protection of Human Rights: Interim Report of the Special Representative of the Secretary General on the Issue of Human Rights and Transnational Corporations and Other Businesses" (Commission on Human Rights, E/CN.4/2006/97).

109 Ibid.

110 Ruggie Report (note 62).

June 2008. In setting out the report, Ruggie succinctly stated the underlying challenge as follows:

> The root cause of the business and human rights predicament today
> lies in the governance gaps created by globalization – between the
> scope and impact of economic forces and actors, and the capacity of
> societies to manage their adverse consequences. These governance
> gaps provide the permissive environment for wrongful acts by com-
> panies of all kinds without adequate sanctioning or reparation. How
> to narrow and ultimately bridge the gaps in relation to human rights
> is our fundamental challenge.[111]

In the report, Ruggie proposes a three-pronged international framework
for corporate accountability for human rights which he referred to as the
"Protect, Respect and Remedy". The framework comprises of three core
principles (pillars) which "rest on differentiated but complementary
responsibilities".[112] The principles are state duty to protect against human
rights abuses by third parties, including private parties; corporate responsibility to respect human rights and the provision of more effective access
to remedies (judicial and non-judicial).

The first principle addressed the settled position in international law
that states have the primary duty to protect against human rights violations. The duty of host states in this regard is clear. However, what is not
clear is what is to be done in situations, such as those that abound in developing countries, where states lack the capacity or willingness to protect. A
thornier issue is the home state's responsibility to protect against violations of human rights by their corporations abroad on which issue, as
Ruggie correctly noted, experts disagreed.[113] These issues will be dealt with
extensively in Chapters 6 and 7 of this book.

Ruggie goes on to discuss corporate culture. His discussion here strad-
dles an area which, from the view of this book, is within the competence of
domestic jurisdictions (both host and home states). Corporate culture is
one of the pivotal areas in this context. According to Ruggie "governments
are uniquely placed to foster corporate cultures in which respecting rights
is an integral part of doing business".[114] Such approaches include sustainability reporting, widening fiduciary duties of directors, facilitating the use

---

111 Ibid., 3.
112 Ibid., 4.
113 R. McCorquodale and P. Simons, "Responsibility Beyond Borders: State Responsibility
     for Extraterritorial Violations by Corporations of International Human Rights Law"
     (2007) 70 (4) *Modern Law Review* 598; O. Amao, "Controlling Corporate Cowboys: Extra-
     territorial Application of Home Countries Jurisdiction to EU Corporations Abroad"
     (2007) *University College Dublin Law Review (Symposium Edition)* 67.
114 Ruggie Report (note 62) 10.

of shareholder proposals to curb human rights and the use of "corporate culture"[115] as opposed to individual liabilities in determining corporate criminal liability and punishment.

Ruggie's argument that home states need to do more resonates with one of the core arguments of this book.[116] He notes the important point that the framework of foreign investment constrains the capacity of host states especially in developing countries to control corporations. They are skewed more in favour of MNCs. Citing the example of export credit agencies (ECAs), by which home states support exports and investments in regions and sectors that may be too risky for the private sector alone, he suggests that such arrangements should require that beneficiaries perform adequate due diligence on the potential human rights impact of their operations. This would ensure that adequate oversight is applied where needed and the withdrawal of state support where necessary. He suggests that the international level could support the states to achieve better control of MNCs in this area. Noting, for example, that the OECD guidelines[117] is one of the major standard setting instruments in the field of corporate responsibility, he suggests that there is a need to revise the guidelines to make it more specific and comprehensive.

On the second principle which is on corporate responsibility to respect, Ruggie focuses on the role of corporations themselves. He disagrees with attempts in the discourse that have tried to identify a limited set of responsibilities for which corporations should be held accountable. He is of the opinion that since companies have the potential capacity to impact all recognised rights, companies should consider all these rights. The duty to respect human rights, according to him, is defined by social expectations. The pertinent question, however, is whether social expectations are sufficient in themselves to guide corporate actions. This book will argue that while social expectations indicate the duty generally, there is a need for more clarity as to what is owed, which the law may be best placed to provide. Ruggie correctly notes that corporations' responsibility to respect exists independently of states' duties and as such, the popular argument that states have primary responsibility and that companies have secondary responsibility is irrelevant. Corporations thus have a primary duty to respect human rights.

In a striking sentence he correctly observes that voluntary corporate philanthropy which is widely practised as CSR cannot compensate for human rights abuses. According to him, "because the responsibility to respect is a baseline expectation, a company cannot compensate for

---

115 Corporate culture refers to a company's policies, rules and practices.
116 See Chapters 6 and 7.
117 Organisation for Economic Cooperation and Development Guidelines for Multinational Enterprises, 15 ILM 9 (1976).

human rights harm by performing good deeds elsewhere".[118] This underscores a widely canvassed argument that the duty of corporate actors to respect human rights transcends merely doing good.

How can corporations discharge the responsibility to respect? The answer, according to Ruggie, lies in *due diligence*, a concept which "describes the steps a company must take to become aware of, prevent and address adverse human rights impacts".[119] According to Ruggie's report, determining the scope of due diligence involves an inductive and fact-based process guided by three sets of factors. These factors include the context of the country in which corporations operate and human rights challenges are envisaged. The second is actual human rights impacts their activities may have in the country. The third is the possibility of contributing to human rights abuses through relationships connected with their activities. Ruggie suggests that companies should look to international bills of human rights and core ILO conventions for the substantive content of due diligence. He further suggests that a basic human rights due diligence should include the following: adoption of company's human rights policies; conducting human rights impact assessments; integration of human rights policies throughout a company; tracking performance through monitoring and auditing. He suggests industry and multi-stakeholder initiatives can help to facilitate due diligence. He notes that the UN Global Compact[120] has the capability to support due diligence.

The report deals with two specific concepts, which the mandate of the special representative required him to clarify: "sphere of influence" and "complicity". The sphere of influence concept was introduced by the Global Compact and was intended as a template to determine the extent of corporate responsibility to other stakeholders apart from shareholders. It attempted to delimit the scope of the impact of companies' activities that would trigger corporate responsibility. The concept was also employed in the draft version of the Norms. Ruggie concludes that the concept is not helpful because it is imprecise and ambiguous. He opines that

> The scope of due diligence to meet the corporate responsibility to respect human rights is not a fixed sphere, nor is it based on influence. Rather, it depends on the potential and actual human rights impacts resulting from a company's business activities and the relationships connected to those activities.[121]

---

118 Ruggie Report (note 62) 17.
119 Ibid.
120 The United Nations Global Compact is a voluntary initiative designed to help fashion a more humane world by enjoining business to follow ten principles concerning human rights, labour, the environment and corruption. See further Chapter 2.
121 Ruggie Report (note 62) 20.

While it is conceded that the sphere of influence concept as presently construed is of little use, there may still be the need to clarify the extent of corporate responsibility. The solution may be to employ the law in bringing clarity to this area.

With regard to the "complicity" concept which refers to indirect corporate involvement of corporate actors in human rights abuses in collusion with governments or other non-state actors, Ruggie notes the difficulty in specifying what constitutes complicity particularly from a legal perspective. However, he suggests that the due diligence approach that he proffers can help companies avoid complicity in human rights abuses. However, his suggestion does not address the necessity to have a clarification of complicity as it relates to corporate activities. Avoiding complicity in human rights abuses is one thing; determining culpability in cases of complicity is a completely different issue that needs to be addressed separately.

The third limb of Ruggie's framework is access to remedies. He recommends that home states should strengthen judicial capacity to hear complaints and enforce remedies against corporations operating from or based in their territory. He recommends that states remove obstacles to justice in their territories by victims of human rights violations.

Ruggie suggests that non-judicial mechanisms could be helpful if they meet certain principles which include: legitimacy; predictability; equitability; human rights standards compatibility and transparency. He makes similar suggestions in respect of company-based grievance mechanisms, state-based non-judicial mechanisms and multi-stakeholders or industry-based initiatives. However, the major challenge here is enforceability. Without effective enforcement mechanisms, any non-judicial mechanism employed is likely to be of little help.

Ruggie further suggests that there is the need to provide adequate information so that victims of human rights abuses are aware of available mechanisms and how to access them. He also hinted, albeit in brief, at the possibility of creating a global ombudsman which could receive and handle complaints. He did not deal with this in detail and it is doubtful whether consensus could be reached to create an ombudsman at international level in the foreseeable future.

In his 2010 report, Ruggie put forward suggestions towards operationalising the ideas spelt out in the earlier report.[122] The report examines possibilities at domestic and international level in the areas of law and policy.

At the state level, the report identifies specific priority areas which include: the enhancement of state's ability to meet their human rights obligations, consideration of human rights issues when states engage in business, facilitation of corporate culture respectful of human rights at home and abroad, development of appropriate policy guidelines to assist companies in areas of

---

122 Ruggie Report (note 62).

conflict and extraterritorial jurisdiction to remedy human rights violations committed abroad. This will necessarily involve a rethink of states' approach to treaty making and contracting internationally, bilateral investment treaties negotiation and host government investment agreements.

A significant proposal in this area is in respect of developing the concept of corporate culture. The report suggested that this can be achieved through corporate social responsibility (CSR) focused policies, statutory reporting requirements to include reporting on human rights risks, provisions on directors' duties (to include duty to consider human rights impact) and criminal law and process to accommodate the concept of "corporate culture" as a possible tool for compliance.[123]

The report addresses the scope of corporate responsibility to respect human rights. Ruggie's position is that this should be determined with reference to the International Bill of Human Rights, the ILO's eight core conventions and domestic human rights provisions in domestic law. Companies can seek to achieve the required standard by engaging with the due diligence process which include having adequate human rights policies, periodic human rights impact assessment, effective reporting systems and effective corporate grievance mechanisms. Muchlinski correctly points out that this is more of a "responsibility" than a "duty" because there is no legal requirement under international human rights law framework for MNC to observe human rights.[124] However, the report acknowledges that positive actions need to be taken by MNCs in this area.

Another area that the report addresses is access to remedy including: company-led mechanisms, state based (judicial and non-judicial) mechanisms and complementary initiatives by other stakeholders. He reiterates the principles that should govern these mechanisms as adumbrated in the earlier report.

It is expected that specific recommendations will be made in the special representative's final report.

Developments in international environmental law: a brief discussion

As environmental law is not the focus of this book, this section comprises very brief discussion of developments in international environmental law. It is generally acknowledged that MNCs dominate pollution-intensive industries such as chemicals, petroleum and manufacturing.[125] In environmental

---

123 P. Muchlinski, "The SRSG Reports on Further Steps Taken towards Operationalising the 'Protect, Respect and Remedy' Framework" (Institute for Human Rights and Business, 12/05/10).

124 Ibid.

125 A.M. Rugman and A. Verbeke, "Corporate Strategies and Environmental Regulations: An Organizing Framework" (1998) 19 *Strategic Management Journal* 363.

law discourse, one of the major challenges facing the field is providing for multinational corporate environmental liability.[126] A major obstacle to the legal control of corporations within the environmental field is the previously mentioned classical exposition of public international law as law governing states, which essentially leaves the control of MNCs within the domestic jurisdiction of states.[127] The problem is complex in the context of MNCs because of the network of their operation and their multi-jurisdictional presence. However, there have been developments in international environmental law that may have huge implications for future directions in this field.

Major environmental disasters in the 1970s and 1980s drew the attention of the world to the need to protect the environment by finding ways to control MNCs, which are the major violators. The first attempt at addressing this problem at the global level was the convening in 1972 of the UN Conference on the Human Environment in Stockholm. The Stockholm conference led to several environmental initiatives at the global level. These included a declaration containing a series of normative principles, a 109-point environmental action plan and a resolution recommending institutional and financial implementation by the United Nations. Following the recommendations, the UN General Assembly created the United Nations Environmental Programme (UNEP) which has since played an active role in facilitating the negotiation of global environmental treaties.

Several international treaties were to follow these developments. For example, as a result of the fear of the depletion of the ozone layer by commercially produced chemicals especially chlorofluorocarbons (CFCs), the Vienna Convention for the Protection of the Ozone Layer was convened in 1985.[128] The convention laid down general principles and an institutional framework to be made more specific in treaties or sub-treaties between parties to the main convention. This led to the intergovernmental negotiation resulting in the Montreal protocol on substances that deplete the ozone layer in 1987.[129] The protocol was precipitated by the discovery of the ozone hole over Antarctica.

In 1982, a follow-up conference was held in Nairobi, Kenya, which led to the establishment of the World Commission on Environment and Development under the chairmanship of the then prime minister of Norway, Gro Harlem Brundtland. The commission introduced the concept of "sustainable development" into international environmental

---

126 D.M. Ong, "The Impact of Environmental Law on Corporate Governance: International and Comparative Perspectives" (2002) 12 (4) *European Journal of International Law* 685.

127 Ibid.

128 Vienna Convention for the Protection of the Ozone Layer, 26 ILM 1516.

129 Montreal Protocol on Substances that Deplete the Ozone Layer, 16 September 1987, 26 ILM 1541.

law discourse and facilitated the preparation for the Conference on Environment and Development, which was held in 1992.

The concept of sustainable development as a universal goal was first recognised at the Rio Summit in 1992.[130] The Rio Summit resulted in several initiatives including an action plan for ten years known as Agenda 21, as well as the Rio Declaration on the Environment and Development,[131] the United Nations Framework Convention on Climate Change,[132] the 1992 Convention on Biological Diversity and the non-legally binding authoritative statement on the forests.[133] The most enduring legacy of the Rio Summit lies in its contribution to the development of a framework of international law principles. Drawing on international environmental policies, some first enunciated in the Stockholm Declaration, domestic environmental law and international thought and action on the subject, the Rio Summit established several important principles of international environmental law. These included: the precautionary principle; polluter pays principle; sustainable development; common but differentiated responsibility and environmental impact assessment.

What is the implication of these developments for MNCs? As Ong points out

> Multilateral environmental conventions bind their state parties but, although their provisions may naturally be expected to impinge on the activities of businesses and companies throughout the world, these entities are not directly mentioned, or indeed provided for at this level.[134]

The general environmental principles, therefore, have no special and specific role for companies.[135] He posits that as things stand today in the

---

130 Oldenziel (note 101).

131 Rio Declaration on Environment and Development 31 ILM 874.

132 United Nations Framework Convention on Climate Change, 9 May 1992, 31 ILM (1992) 849.

133 The 1992 Convention on Biological Diversity and the Non-legally-Binding Authoritative Statement on the Forests 31 ILM 849; since 1992 other important treaties and conventions have been signed which have bearing on the operation of companies. These include: The Cartagena Protocol on Biosafety (2000); the Kyoto Protocol; the Stockholm Convention on Persistent Organic Pollutants (2001); the Rotterdam Convention on Prior Informed Consent (1998) and the Aarhus Convention (1998) which was the first to link human rights with environmental rights: see further Oldenziel (note 101).

134 Ong (note 126); see also I. Bantekas, "Corporate Social Responsibility in International Law" (2004) 22 *Boston University International Law Journal* 309, 334.

135 Anderson also argues that "regulatory response to environmental damage by MNCs has been largely ineffective because international environmental treaties bind state parties, but do not place obligations directly on companies". M. Anderson, "Transnational Corporations and Environmental Damage: Is Tort Law the Answer?" (2002) 41 *Washburn Law Journal* 399.

absence of implementation at the national level companies can only be indirectly or voluntarily enjoined to apply the relevant environmental principles to their activities.[136] He further argues that the lack of effective implementation of internationally agreed environmental principles on corporate behaviour is compounded by the fact that states have failed to come up with an agreement on the question of liability for environmental damage. The lack of individual corporate liability in this area is mitigated by specific international civil liability regimes in certain specific areas such as radioactive fall-out from nuclear accidents and marine oil pollution damage from super tanker spills.[137] However, beyond these rather narrow confines there is no general international civil liability scheme providing for the compensation of corporate environmental damage. It is Anderson's contention, with which this author agrees, that there has to date been a "failure to address corporate environmental behaviour in either international law or comparative company law, leaving the bulk of regulatory burden to be borne by national systems of civil and criminal liability".

The weakness in the international framework is reflected in the problems encountered in the various attempts to bring cases in the United States under the Alien Torts Act (ATCA) against MNCs for *inter alia* environmental damage.[138] The recourse to this strategy in the first place is as a result of what is generally perceived as a "governance deficit" in the regulation of MNCs. The attempt to make MNCs liable for the international consequence of their operation has proved largely unsuccessful due to political opposition, problems of jurisdiction and company law.[139]

However, this situation on the international scene is in sharp contrast to the developments within domestic fora in the developed states of the North. The imposition of both civil and criminal corporate environmental liability in the United States, for example, has led commentators to posit that environmental protection has been one of the regulatory successes of the past decade.[140] Ong reviewed developments in the United States, United Kingdom, Australia, Canada, Hong Kong, Germany and Spain and concluded that all these jurisdictions reflect a "general trend towards the imposition of strict, non-fault based, liability for corporate environmental damage".[141] The United States has the most stringent corporate environmental civil liability regime with the introduction of the 1980 US Comprehensive Environmental Response, Compensation and Liability Act

136   Ong (note 126).
137   Ibid.
138   Ibid.
139   The Alien Torts Act claims are discussed fully in Chapter 5.
140   M.A. Eisner, "Corporate Environmentalism, Regulatory Reform, and Industry Self Regulation: Toward Genuine Regulatory Reinvention in the United States" (2004) 17 (2) *Governance: An International Journal of Policy, Administration, and Institutions* 145.
141   Ong (note 126).

(CERCA) otherwise known as "Superfund Act" which imposes strict liability and may allow the corporate veil of corporations to be lifted for the purpose of imposing liability for environmental damage. It thus exposes company directors, corporate officers, creditors and shareholders to personal liability in such cases. Furthermore, there are provisions in US environmental law, which allow private citizens to institute action against corporations and partnerships that have violated statutory provisions, regulations, orders or permits.[142] Also, an aggressive stance has been taken in the United States in respect of environmental offences. The United States is moving towards imposition of strict liability in this area. The demonstration of criminal intent is not required before a company or its officers may be found criminally liable.[143] Similar trends generally abound within the domestic jurisdictions of other states in the developed world.

While the domestic forum in the developed states of the North, which incidentally are home states to most MNCs, ensures that environmental well-being within the domestic jurisdiction is not sacrificed to corporations' pursuit of profit, the same cannot be said in respect of the capital-starved countries of the South, which lower labour, environmental and other regulatory standards in order to attract investment from MNCs. Even where countries of the South have strict environmental laws they often fail to enforce them. According to Schmidt,

> When a TNC [MNC] exploits a host country's natural resources and harms its land, developing countries often fail to enforce these laws because they fear the company will leave and take its jobs and dollars with it. Today, developing countries are asked to trade health and safety for the progress and prosperity promised by economic venture of TNCs. Presently, without any binding international law to protect host countries, individual nations find themselves in a difficult situation.[144]

The inevitable conclusion to be drawn from the developments in international environmental law is that developed countries tend to impose strict regulation on corporations where their activities directly pose a threat to the home states themselves but would not appear to be too interested in imposing such standards when the threat is far from home.

---

142 Ibid.
143 Ibid.
144 Schmidt makes reference to Brazil, Mexico, Indonesia and the Philippines in this regard. See T.M. Schmidt, "Transnational Corporate Responsibility for International Environmental and Human Rights Violations: Will the United Nations' Norms Provide the Required Means?" (2005) 36 *California Western International Law Journal* 217, 218.

Summary

Significant steps have been taken at the international level to control MNCs and to ensure that their activities do not lead to human rights violations. However, to date these steps have failed. The reason for the failure is mainly because of the ambiguous relationship between international law and MNCs. The failure of the various initiatives makes it imperative to explore alternative avenues for the control of MNCs.

3 Corporate social responsibility and its relationship to law

Introduction

This chapter looks at how the CSR philosophy has developed as an alternative way to address externalities emanating from operations of corporations. First, it traces the evolution of CSR. Then it asks the pertinent question: What is CSR? In order to properly address this question the chapter examines how the concept has been presented by disciplines that played important roles in its development. Then it examines the theoretical underpinnings of CSR asking the following questions: Does CSR suggest a moral responsibility for business? Does business have a moral responsibility? If, as this chapter posits, it does, what implications does CSR have for law? In answering these questions the chapter evaluates some suggestions that have been made on how the law should respond to CSR. The chapter explores the question of the morality of corporations, the relationship of the discussion to the concept of corporate personhood and the implication of corporate morality and personality for human rights law.

Evolution of the CSR concept

The evolution of the modern concept of CSR can be traced to developments in corporate governance in the United States.[1] However, there are landmarks in other parts of the world especially the European Union that have important bearings on the practice of CSR. The starting point is therefore a discussion of the emergence of the concept in the United States.

---

1 It is generally accepted that the concept of modern CSR first emerged as an issue in the United States. See C.A.H. Wells, "The Cycles of Corporate Social Responsibility: An Historical Retrospective for the Twenty-First Century" (2002) 52 *Kansas Law Review* 77. This assertion is, however, contested by some European scholars who argue that CSR in Europe predates its origin in the United States even though it was not referred to in such terms. See for example N. Eberstadt, "What History tells us about Corporate Social Responsibilities" (1973) 7 *Business and Society Review* 76.

The emergence of CSR in the United States

Developments in the US economy and industrial sector after the First World War had a significant impact on the construction of the role of business in society. With the modernisation of the US economy including its industrial sector, emphasis was placed on the profitability of business for investors. It was assumed that as long as business was profitable it was creating wealth for society and at the same time improving society's standard of living by the production of goods and services. This disposition influenced the landmark decision of the Michigan Supreme Court in *Dodge* v. *Ford Motor Co*[2] where the court stated that:

> A business corporation is organized and carried on primarily for the profit of the stockholders. The powers of the directors are to be employed for that end. The discretion of directors is to be exercised in the choice of means to attain that end, and does not extend to a change in the end itself, to the reduction of profits, or to the non-distribution of profits among shareholders in order to devote them to other purposes.

The emergence of the "trusteeship management concept" in the 1920s and 1930s based on the apparent diffusion of ownership from control changed, to some extent, the perception of the role of business in society.[3] The concept regarded corporate managers as fiduciaries who had the duty to maintain an equitable balance between shareholders and various other potential claimants on the corporation. This development raised the question of whether corporations have social responsibility and if so, what are their responsibilities and what is the basis of imposing such obligations.

Central to the debate within legal circles that triggered the modern debate on CSR was the question

> Whether the directors and managers of large, publicly held corporations should have a legal duty, when making decisions for the corporation, to take into account not only the needs of the shareholders but also other groups affected by the corporation's actions, such as its employees, customers, or the communities in which they are based.[4]

The question posed above was the backdrop of four decades of debate between Berle and Dodd based on the trusteeship principle. Professor Berle in his study of the emerging separation of ownership and control in

---

2 *Dodge* v. *Ford Motor Co* 204 Mich. 459, 170 N.W. 668. (Mich. 1919).
3 S. Saleem, *Corporate Social Responsibility Law and Practice* (London: Cavendish Publishing Limited, 1996), 11.
4 Wells (note 1).

the corporate structure canvassed the principle of trusteeship to deal with the new relationship.[5] Berle started the debate with his thesis that the powers and duties given to directors are "necessarily and at all times exercisable only for the rateable benefit of all the shareholders as their interest appears".[6] He argued that because shareholders put their investment at risk by investing in the company, the directors should be answerable to them and the powers and duties invested in them should be exercised only for their benefit and to maximise their profit.[7] He advocated the trust model under which directors and managers would be construed as trustees of the stockholders and subject to oversight by the Court of Equity.[8] One should not lose sight of the main reason behind his thesis which was to "establish a legal control which will more effectually prevent corporate managers from diverting profit into their own pockets" in the guise of discharging wider responsibilities to persons other than shareholders.[9] According to Wells, the period preceding Berle's article witnessed the emergence of large corporations owned by stockholders, mostly holding small amounts of publicly traded stock and managed by professionals with little interest in the firms. Accompanying this was the erosion of legal safeguards that once put strict limits on managers and the ability of managers to transfer power and wealth to themselves. Berle's aim was thus to protect the shareholders from the managers. This aim clearly distinguishes Dodd's position from that of Berle. Dodd sought to protect society from corporations.[10]

In May of 1932, Dodd replied to Berle's thesis, arguing that directors of large corporations owe duties not only to shareholders but also to the larger community and as such, directors should have the competence to take into consideration non-shareholder stakeholder interests. He opposed the idea of strengthening directors' duties to shareholders but rather favoured supporting what he claimed to be recent trends where corporations were being run for the benefit and general good of society. According to him, "public opinion, which ultimately makes law, has made and is today making substantial strides in the direction of a view of the business corporation as an economic institution which has social service as well as profit making function".[11] He argued that historically, the common

---

5   J.L. Weiner, "The Berle–Dodd Dialogue on the Concept of the Corporation" (1964) 64 *Columbia Law Review* 1458.

6   A. Berle, "Corporate Powers as Powers in Trust" (1931) 44 *Harvard Law Review* 1049.

7   Corporations and Markets Advisory Committee (CAMAC) "Corporate Social Responsibility Discussion Paper" (November 2005).

8   Wells (note 1).

9   E.M. Dodd, Jr., "For Whom are Corporate Mangers Trustees?" (1932) 45 *Harvard Law Review* 1145.

10   Wells (note 1).

11   Dodd (note 9), 1148.

law had treated business as a public rather than a purely private matter.[12] He further argued that because the state has conferred the privileges including perpetual succession and limited liability on the corporation, the corporation is expected to act in the general public interest. For Dodd, the growth of corporate power creates new responsibilities for corporations, which include the spread of corporate wealth to maintain social stability. The separation of ownership from control thus allowed corporate managers to address a wider constituency. The corporation should therefore be treated as a distinct legal personality and directors as trustees for the corporation and not for shareholders.

While agreeing with the major premise of Dodd's argument, Berle in his response contended that the argument is not practical. According to Berle,

> The industrial "control" does not now think of himself as a prince; he does not now assume responsibilities to the community; his bankers do not now undertake to recognize social claims; his lawyers do not advise him in terms of social responsibility. Nor is there any mechanism now in sight enforcing accomplishment of his theoretical function.[13]

According to Berle, if the directors' fiduciary obligation to shareholders is weakened or eliminated, the directors' duty becomes for all practical purpose absolute. For Berle, the primacy of shareholders in the corporate decision-making process cannot be abandoned until such time that it is possible "to offer a clear and reasonably enforceable scheme of responsibilities" to some other group(s).[14]

As Weiner correctly observed after critically analysing the two viewpoints, the main difference between the two relates "to the absence of machinery for enforcing a legitimate community demand".[15] In 1954 Berle seemed to have changed his position when he wrote,

> Twenty years, ago, the writer had a controversy with the late Professor E. Merrick Dodd, of Harvard Law School, the writer holding that corporate powers were powers in trust for shareholders while Professor Dodd argued that these powers were held in trust for the entire community. The argument has been settled (at least for the time being) squarely in favour of Professor Dodd's contention.[16]

12 See the insightful article on the Berle and Dodds debate by Weiner (note 5).
13 A.A. Berle, Jr., "For Whom Corporate Managers Are Trustees: A Note" (1932) 45 *Harvard Law Review* 1365, 1367.
14 Ibid.
15 Weiner (note 5), 1458–1467.
16 A.A. Berle, Jr., *The 20th Century Capitalist Revolution* (New York: Harcourt, Brace and Co., 1954), 169.

Professor Berle later explicitly supported the viewpoint of Professor Dodd when he wrote that "modern directors are not limited to running business enterprise for maximum profit, but are in fact and recognized in law as administrators of a community system".[17] Berle then advocated changes that would free managers from their singular duties to shareholders and allow the use of corporate wealth for societal good. He suggested the creation of society based on the corporation which has been described as European style corporatism based on corporate and government planning.[18]

The debate begun by Dodd and Berle continued into the 1960s and 1970s focusing primarily on the role of large corporations in the community. The period also witnessed the emergence of the use of shareholder proposals by proponents of the notion that corporations should have broader social responsibilities to influence the corporate decision-making process.[19]

Early criticisms of the CSR concept in the United States

As the debate over CSR was evolving, so was criticism of the concept. Most of the major critics wrote from the economic perspective. The concept was criticised for being vague in the tasks it set for itself, providing no viable alternative for the governance of the socially responsible corporation and its advocates' lack of faith in the free market system.[20] Rostow, in his economic defence of corporate law, argued that the proposals put forward by the CSR advocates would make managers autonomous free agents instead of agents for shareholders which would go against the economic justification of business and place too much faith in ordinary men.[21] According to him, pushing along that line is to deviate from the profit maximisation goal of business and the consequent distortion of market mechanisms with the possibility of market failure.[22]

In the 1960s Milton Friedman, the period's most prominent free market economist, put forward an influential argument against the emerging concept of CSR. Friedman's argument was based on economics and morality. He argued that the CSR agenda is aimed at replacing market mechanisms with political mechanisms in the determination of the allocation of resources, which according to him, can only lead to inefficiency.

---

17 Foreword to E.S. Mason, ed., *The Corporation in Modern Society* (Cambridge, MA: Harvard University Press, 1959).
18 R. Romana, "Metapolitics and Corporate Law Reform" (1984) 36 *Stanford Law Review* 923.
19 Corporations and Markets Advisory Committee (CAMAC) (note 7).
20 Wells (note 1).
21 E.V. Rostow, "To Whom and for What Ends is Corporate Management Responsible?" In E.S. Mason, ed., *Corporation in Modern Society* (Cambridge: MA: Harvard University Press,1961), 46–47.
22 Ibid.

He argued that managers are the employees of the owners of the corporation – the shareholders – and therefore it would be immoral for these employees to divert assets belonging to their employers to causes which are not for the benefit of the shareholders. The view propounded by Friedman is that the purpose of the corporation is to make profit for shareholders.[23] He contended that since shareholders are the owners of the company, they own the profits of the corporation and managers, as the agents of the shareholders, are duty bound to maximise shareholders' profit and not to donate shareholder funds to charity in the name of CSR. He further argued that having invested in corporations, shareholders are entitled to their profits. To him, so long as business creates value for its shareholders, society benefits.

In the 1980s and 1990s in the United States, the debate focused on the social consequence of corporate takeovers. The laws in the United States required directors of target companies to take into consideration the interests of shareholders in deciding whether to accept or reject a bid. This meant that regardless of the impact on employees or the host community, once a bid is beneficial the directors were bound to support it.[24] As the debate grew and the courts vacillated between whether to allow the target companies to take into consideration other interests in a takeover bid or uphold shareholder supremacy,[25] many states in the United States adopted what are generally known as constituency statutes which permit directors to widen the constituencies they take into consideration in such circumstances.[26] Pennsylvania enacted the first constituency statute in 1983. Other states soon followed, with 28 such statutes enacted by 1991. By 1999, 41 states had enacted constituency statutes.[27] The constituency statutes typically allow the board of directors to take into consideration the interests of employees, suppliers, customers and host communities in considering the best interest of the corporation. The constituency statute was as far as legislation has gone in protecting other stakeholders' interests in the United States.

The emergence of the neo-liberal free market ideology pushed the CSR agenda to the back stage in the United States. The dominance of the

23   M. Friedman, *Capitalism and Freedom* (Chicago: University of Chicago Press, 1962).
24   CAMAC (note 7).
25   For example, *Unocal Corp.* v. *Mesa Petroleum Co.* 493 A. 2d 946 (Del. 1985) the Delaware Supreme Court held that the board of directors of a target company could take into consideration other constituency interest apart from shareholders in their decision. The decision was qualified in a later decision of the same court in *Revlon. Inc* v. *McAndrews and Forbes Holdings. Inc* 506 A.2d 173 (Del. 1986) where it was held that the other constituency interests that could be considered are limited to ones that could produce a "rationally related benefit" to shareholders.
26   CAMAC (note 7).
27   R.J. York, "Visages of Janus: The Heavy Burden of Other Constituency Anti-Takeover Statutes On Shareholders and The Efficient Market for Corporate Control" (2002) 38 *Willamette Law Review* 187.

contractarian theory of the firm in the 1980s and its popularity and promotion by the law and economics school of law had a negative impact on the advancement of the CSR agenda and in its extreme form threatened the underpinnings of the concept.[28] This theme will be addressed in full later in this chapter.

CSR in the United Kingdom

It is generally accepted in the literature that CSR in the modern form emerged in the United Kingdom in the 1970s.[29] The absence of CSR in its modern form in the United Kingdom before the 1970s has been attributed to the heavy reliance on publicly owned enterprise in the performance of essential economic tasks and the involvement of the government with business. Three major factors can be attributed to the emergence of the modern concept of CSR in the United Kingdom.[30] The first is the development of the concept in the United States. The second is the United Kingdom's membership of the European Union (then known as the European Economic Community), which it joined in 1973. Generally, the company was regarded as one of the main vehicles of achieving EU social objectives. The implementation of EU treaties thus had significant impact on the conception of the corporation in the EU framework. Third, many government reports and private publications promoted the idea of corporate social responsibility.[31] Further impetus was given to the promotion of CSR in the United Kingdom following the initial adverse social impact of the Thatcher government's economic reform policy in the 1980s. Rioting among unemployed youths led companies to take greater interest in social stability and the conditions of the local area.[32]

CSR in Europe

The EU summit in Lisbon in March 2000 (which conceived what is now generally referred to as the Lisbon Agenda) decided to concentrate on corporate social responsibility as a way of linking economic, employment

---

28 See F.H. Easterbrook and D.R. Fischel, *The Economic Structure of Corporate Law* (Cambridge: Harvard University Press, 1991); R.H. Coase, "The Problem of Social Cost" (1960) 3 *Journal of Law and Economics* 15.

29 See K. Campbell and D. Vick, "Disclosure Law and Market for Corporate Social Responsibility" in D. McBarnet, A. Voiculescu and T. Campbell, eds., *The New Corporate Accountability: Corporate Social Responsibility and the Law* (Cambridge: Cambridge University Press, 2007), 241, 249.

30 Saleem (note 3), 13.

31 Ibid.

32 See S. Braun and T. Loew, eds., *Corporate Social Responsibility: An Introduction from the Environmental Perspective* (Berlin: German Federal Ministry for the Environment, 2006).

and social goals which lie at the core of the agenda.[33] The Lisbon Agenda was designed to make the European Union "the most competitive and dynamic knowledge-based economy in the world, capable of sustainable economic growth with more and better jobs and greater social cohesion".[34] To this end, the EU Commission produced a Green Paper – on "Promoting a European Framework for Corporate Social Responsibility" – which was followed in the year 2002 by a White Paper.[35] The EU further declared the year 2004 as the European Year for Corporate Social Responsibility.

These developments in the EU are hardly surprising as some issues which the CSR concepts address such as societal well-being and employees' welfare, have been at the heart of EU social policy for decades,[36] culminating in the legal frameworks found in the Single European Act of 1986, the Maastricht Treaty of 1992 and the Treaty of Amsterdam in 1997.[37] According to Lynch Fannon "fundamental to the expressed connection between competitiveness, employment and social policies is the 'stakeholder model of corporate governance' or 'social model of corporate governance as distinct from shareholder model of corporate governance espoused in the United States".[38] Therefore the corporation is "seen as one of a number of social partners all of whom have a role to play in contributing to the planning of both macroeconomics and social outcomes".[39] Furthermore the EU has always made human rights a priority in its framework.[40]

According to Burchell and Cook, the Green Paper linked the EU's social agenda with the CSR concept in addressing concerns regarding "employment and social consequences of economic and market integration and in adapting working conditions to the new economy".[41] The Green Paper states that the concept of CSR is an opportunity to involve

---

33 O. De Schutter, "Corporate Social Responsibility European Style" (2008) 14 (2) *European Law Journal* 203; J. Wouters and L. Chanet, "Corporate Human Rights Responsibility: A European Perspective" (2008) 6 (2) *Northwestern Journal of International Human Rights* 262.

34 European Commission, "Promoting A European Framework for Corporate Social Responsibility: Green Paper" (COM) 2001 366 final.

35 Commission of the European Communities, "Communication from the Commission Concerning Corporate Social Responsibility: A Business Contribution to Sustainable Development" COM (2002) 347 final.

36 I. Lynch Fannon, *Working within Two Kinds of Capitalism: Corporate Governance and Employee Stakeholding: US and EU Perspectives* (Oxford and Portland, OR: Hart Publishing, 2003), 88.

37 Ibid., 28.

38 I. Lynch Fannon, "The European Social Model of Corporate Governance: Prospects for Success in an Enlarged Europe" in P.U. Ali and G.N. Gregoriou, eds, *International Corporate Governance After Sarbanes – Oxley* (New Jersey: John Wiley & Sons, Inc, 2006), 423.

39 Ibid.

40 P. Craig and G. De Burca, ed., *EU Law: Text, Cases and Materials* (fourth edition, Oxford: Oxford University Press, 2007), chapter 11.

41 J. Burchell and J. Cook, "The Challenges of Corporate Social Responsibility: Lessons from EU Green Paper" Brunel Research in Enterprise, Innovation, Sustainability, and Ethics Working Paper no. 10, 2004.

companies in a partnership with other social partners, local authorities and other bodies that manage social services in other to strengthen their social responsibility. The Green Paper thus set out to explore what opportunity, if any the CSR concept offers in the attainment of EU social policy. The Green Paper encouraged extensive debate along three key themes. The first was the role of the EU in promoting CSR with emphasis on a uniform EU framework; second, the role of CSR in corporate business strategies and third, how to improve dialogue between companies and other stakeholders and the role of these actors within the concept. According to the Green Paper, EU companies should pursue social responsibility internationally as well as in Europe, including through their supply chains. A significant point to note is that the Green Paper recognised the role of regulation or legislation in the process when it states,

> Corporate Social Responsibility should nevertheless not be seen as a substitute to regulation or legislation concerning social rights or environmental standards, including the development of new appropriate legislation. In countries where such regulations do not exist, efforts should focus on putting the proper regulatory or legislative framework in place in order to define a level playing field on the basis of which socially responsible practices can be developed.[42]

In 2002 the EU followed up with the creation of the EU Multistakeholder Forum on CSR.[43] The forum was aimed at involving all affected stakeholders as a key to ensuring acceptance and credibility of CSR and better compliance with its principles. Among its objectives were to encourage exchange of good practices in CSR, develop a common EU approach and the identification of areas where EU action may be necessary. The forum's membership included employers' organisations, business groups, trade unions, non-governmental organisations (NGOs) and business groups. The final forum report was released in June 2004.[44] Two of the key points emphasised by the forum were that CSR is complementary to other approaches of ensuring high environmental and social performance. It was, however, observed that there are limits to CSR and it alone cannot be expected to ensure environmental and social improvement. It should therefore not be used to shift public responsibilities onto companies. The report went on to say that "when operating in developing countries and/ or in situations of weak governance, companies need to take into account

---

42 European Commission Green Paper (note 34).
43 For a detailed discussion on EU-Multistakeholder Form see De Schutter (note 33) 210.
44 European Multistakeholder Forum on Corporate Social Responsibility, Results – June 2004, Final Forum Report, online, available at: http://ec.europa.eu/enterprise/csr/forum_2002_04_index.htm (accessed 24 September 2010).

the different context and challenges, including poverty, conflicts, environment and health issues".[45]

The forum identified the main international and European principles, standards and conventions guiding companies and stakeholders in developing their CSR approaches. These include reference texts and instruments developed with the involvement of business and directly addressed to them which are: the ILO Tripartite Declaration of Principles Concerning Multinational Enterprises (MNEs) and Social Policy (1977, revised 2000), the UN Global Compact (2000). Other instruments addressed more widely to states and governments but containing values that can inspire companies in developing their CSR practices include: the UN Declaration on Human Rights (1948), the International Convention on Civil and Political Rights (1966), the International Convention on Economic, Social and Cultural Rights (1966) – (International Bill of Rights); the Council of Europe Convention for Protection of Human Rights and Fundamental Freedoms (1950); the EU Charter of Fundamental Rights (2000); the (Council of Europe) Social Charter (1961, revised 1996); the ILO Declaration on Fundamental Principles and Rights at Work (1998); the Rio Declaration on Environment and Development (1992) and its Agenda 21 (1992); the Johannesburg Declaration and its Action Plan for Implementation (2002); the UN Guidelines on Consumer Protection (1999); the EU Sustainable Development Strategy, as adopted by the European Council in Gothenburg Summit (2001) and the Aarhus Convention on Access to Information, Public Participation in Decision Making and Access to Justice in Environmental Matters.

The forum made several recommendations including: raising awareness of core values and key principles embodied in reference texts; collecting, exchanging and disseminating information about CSR; researching and improving knowledge about and action on CSR; enhancing the capacity of business to understand and integrate CSR; building capacity; including CSR in education and curricula; developing stakeholder dialogue; enhancing the role of public authorities and creating the right conditions for CSR. In respect of creating the right conditions for CSR the forum recommended that,

- EU institutions and governments step up their efforts towards a more co-coordinated policy approach, and they implement the Lisbon goal and Gothenburg Strategy;
- public authorities ensure that there is both a legal framework and the right economic and social conditions in place to allow companies which wish to go further through CSR, to benefit from this in the market place, both in the EU and globally.

45 Ibid.

It must be noted that although the above recommendation acknowledges the need for a legal framework, it favours a framework that provides incentives rather than stringent conditions with consequences.

In 2005, in the face of global competition and an ageing population, the EU Commission called for a fresh start to the Lisbon Agenda. To achieve this end, the commission launched a Partnership for Growth and Jobs in February 2005 and also renewed its Sustainable Development Strategy in December 2005. An informal meeting of heads of state and government in October 2005 "called for innovative answers to address competitive challenge while defending European values".[46]

On 22 March 2006, the European Commission unveiled its new CSR approach which was a significant shift from its earlier approach.[47] The commission made it explicit that CSR in Europe would remain company-led and voluntary. The commission stated that "CSR is fundamentally about voluntary business behaviour, an approach involving additional obligations and administrative requirements for business risks being counter-productive and would be contrary to the principles of better regulation".[48] According to the commission's vice president and commissioner for enterprise and industry, Gunter Verheugen: "A controversial discussion has been finished, at its heart: does CSR require a legal framework or should it be purely voluntary? We're not going to create any new bureaucracy but we will rather pursue a partnership approach."[49] Verheugen stated further that: "There will be no monitoring, no benchmarking, no naming and shaming, no reporting requirements. It is completely voluntary. We will never have a regulatory framework for CSR because it is a philosophy, a concept." The communication establishes a new European alliance for CSR, which is explained to be a "political umbrella for new and existing CSR initiatives by large companies, SMEs and their stakeholders".[50] According to the communication, the alliance is a concept drawn up on the basis of contributions from business active in the promotion of CSR. The alliance cooperates, collaborates and meets with business to develop joint projects. The alliance is open-ended; it is not a legal instrument, it is not required to be endorsed by companies and there are no formal requirements for supporting it. The European Multi Stakeholder

46 Ibid.
47 Ethical Corporation, "Pushing Business-Driven Corporate Citizenship" (2006), online, available at: www.ethicalcorp.com/ (accessed 24 August 2007). See also CSR Forum Review Meeting, 7 December 2006, Closing remarks Vice-President Verheugen, online, available at: http://ec.europa.eu/enterprise/csr/documents/ms_forum_1206/verheugen_forum_final.pdf (accessed 5 May 2008); Wouters and Chanet (note 33), 280.
48 Communication of the Commission "Implementing the Partnership for Growth and Jobs: Making Europe a Pole of Excellence on CSR", 136 Final of 22 March 2006.
49 Ethical Corporation (note 47).
50 Communication of the Commission (note 48).

Forum was revived to support the discussions and initiatives through a series of review meetings.

The communication was said to have represented a true victory for business.[51] The new approach attempts to align the EU stance on CSR to the business-led voluntary initiative ideology prevalent in the United States. It must be observed that the EU Parliament criticised the position taken by the commission in a subsequent resolution. However, in the resolution the European parliament took a rather ambiguous position as to whether a voluntary or regulatory approach should be taken.[52]

CSR in the context of developing countries

Questions have been raised as to whether there is any difference between the practices of CSR in developed countries when compared with developing countries. It has been suggested that the concept differs "according to national social economic priorities – which are themselves influenced by historical and cultural factors – and according to the different types of social actors that are demanding action on these priorities".[53] In the case of South Africa, for example, it was noted that the earlier practice of CSR was rooted in philanthropy. During the apartheid era it was common for businesses to make charitable donations and to seek patronage from local chiefs.[54] However, after the 1994 elections the business community took a more holistic approach to CSR and the government also embarked on series of legislative drives to back up the CSR agenda. The CSR agenda in South Africa is presently influenced by the need to respond to the legacies of apartheid and address local priorities. Prominent CSR initiatives in South Africa include the Black Economic Empowerment programme and the current heavy corporate involvement in the struggle against HIV/AIDS. Research in many parts of Africa has suggested that CSR is largely associated with philanthropy.[55]

CSR has developed more in recent times because of pressure on MNCs arising out of their operation in developing countries and the impact of their operations on human rights, labour issues and community

---

51 De Schutter (note 33), 216.

52 European Parliament Resolution of 13 March 2007 on Corporate Social Responsibility: A New Partnership (2006/2133(INI)) P6_TA(2007)0062; Wouters and Chanet (note 33), 281–282.

53 International Institute for Sustainable Development, "Perceptions and Definitions of social Responsibility" (Canada: May 2004), 3.

54 Ibid.

55 See M. Kivuitu, K. Yambayamba and T. Fox, "How can Corporate Social Responsibility Deliver in Africa? Insights from Kenya and Zambia" Perspectives on Corporate Responsibility for Environment and Development Number 3, July 2005, International Institute for Environment and Development. See also K. Amaeshi, A. Adi, C. Ogbechie and O. Amao "Corporate Social Responsibility in Nigeria: Western Mimicry or Indigenous Influences?" (2006) 24 *Journal of Corporate Citizenship* 83.

relations.[56] For example, CSR became a prominent issue in Nigeria in the 1990s following a series of human rights and environmental law infringements involving Shell. Shell has been a focus point in Nigeria "not only because the company is the largest oil producer and polluter in Nigeria, but also because unlike other major oil producers, Shell's operations are predominantly onshore and as such involve greater interactions with human settlements".[57] Indeed Shell's CSR activities have been described as "a classic business school case study".[58] The concept has since taken root in the oil and gas industry in Nigeria.[59]

It is significant to note that because of weak institutions and insufficient social provision in the developing countries compared to developed countries, CSR may be more important in the context of the former.[60] According to Dobbers and Halme:

> CSR theories, concepts and ideas primarily originate from market economy countries with relatively strong institutional environments in which regulation is efficient and fairly enforced. Yet in a number of emerging economies and developing countries with weak institutional environments underlined by arbitrary enforcement of law, bureaucratic inconsistency, insecurity of property rights and corruption, CSR may get a different twist.[61]

Defining CSR

Finding a generally acceptable definition for CSR has been a major challenge across disciplines. The situation has led to a proliferation of definitions and difficulty in understanding the concept and its relationship to law. It has been observed that companies, consultants, lawyers, NGOs and other interest groups have separate definitions for the concept.[62] Those

---

56 U. Ite, "Multinationals and Corporate Social Responsibility in Developing Countries: A Case Study of Nigeria" (2004) 11 *Corporate Social Responsibility and Environmental Management* 1.

57 K. Omeje, *High Stakes and Stakeholders: Oil Conflict and Security in Nigeria* (England: Ashgate, 2006), 58.

58 D. McBarnet, "Corporate Social Responsibility Beyond Law, Through Law, for Law: The New Corporate Accountability" in D. McBarnet, A. Voiculescu and T. Campbell, eds, *The New Corporate Accountability: Corporate Social Responsibility and the Law* (Cambridge: Cambridge University Press, 2007), 14.

59 U. Idemudia and U.E. Ite, "Corporate–Community Relations in Nigeria's Oil Industry: Challenges and Imperatives" (2006) 13 *Corporate Social Responsibility and Environmental Management* 194, 195.

60 P. Dobbers and M. Halme, "Editorial: Corporate Social Responsibility and Developing Countries" (2009) 16 *Corporate Social Responsibility and Environmental Management* 237.

61 Ibid., 242.

62 "The Importance of Corporate Responsibility" A White Paper from the Economist Intelligence Unit sponsored by Oracle, 2005.

who are most interested in the environment pay less attention to other factors. Those who support philanthropy emphasise the charitable component of CSR, while those who uphold human rights see CSR as mainly involving labour and human rights issues.[63] Quite apart from different definitions, it has also been observed that institutions and individuals change their definition of the concept over time. Blowfield and Frynas cite the example of the World Business Council for Sustainable Development (WBCSD), which defined the concept in 1998 as "the continuing commitment by business to behave ethically and contribute to economic development while improving the quality of life of the workforce and their families as well as of the local community and society at large".[64] In 2002, the WBCSD changed its definition to "the commitment of business to contribute to sustainable economic development, working with employees, their families, the local community and society at large to improve their quality of life".[65] The change was effected to accommodate the growing popularity of the concept of sustainable development. While this may not be a significant change, it demonstrates the fluidity of the concept and its amenability to different viewpoints.

The fuzziness of the concept and the fluidity of the definitions that have been offered for it have led to the suggestion that the concept may not be accurately defined but may be described. In 1979, a management scholar, Archie B. Carroll, proffered the most prominent definition of CSR which has been the starting point of most academic research into the concept. According to him, CSR encompasses the economic, legal, ethical and discretionary (philanthropic) expectations that society has of organisations at a given point in time. Carroll thus tried to accommodate all the competing definitions within his broad definition. The definition has been expanded and modified over the years by Carroll himself and other writers.[66] However, we may just note at this juncture that the concept is generally about how companies should respond to externalities[67] of their operations which are sometimes though not always illegal but which may

---

63 Ibid.
64 M. Blowfield and J.G. Frynas, "Setting New Agendas: Critical Perspectives on Corporate Social Responsibility in the Developing World" (2005) 81 *International Affairs* 499.
65 Ibid.
66 M. Foster and A. Meinhard, "Corporate Social Responsibility in the Canadian Context: The New Role of Corporations in Community Involvement and Social Issues" Center for Voluntary Sector Studies, Ryerson University, Faculty of Business, Working Paper Series no. 20, November 2002. G.P. Lantos, "The Ethicality of Altruistic Corporate Social Responsibility" (June 2001, CBFA Version); W. Visser, "Revisiting Carrroll's CSR Pyramid: An African Perspective" in E.R. Pederson and M. Huniche, eds, *Corporate Citizenship in Developing Countries* (Copenhagen: The Copenhagen Centre, 2006).
67 Externality is the term used by economists to describe the side effects or spill over effects from business activities. C. Meyer and J. Kirby, "Leadership in the Age of Transparency" *Harvard Business Review* (April, 2010) 38.

not stand up to societal expectations. It will be instructive to briefly look at how business organisations generally view the concept.

The business case for CSR

The business approach sees other stakeholder issues as something to be managed, like managing a product or brand. The approach thus attempts to extrapolate techniques rooted in financial management to the management of social and environmental issues.[68] Simply put, the business case for CSR is that CSR must be linked to better performance. That is, a link must be developed between "doing good" and "doing well". In other words participating in CSR should lead to improved profits.[69] However, while most people would admit that CSR yields intangible benefits, quantifying these benefits' impact on profit has remained problematic. Most research that has been done on the link between performance and CSR has produced mixed results.

Henderson has argued that the business response has been bifurcated. The first school are those business organisations he described as defensive and business-focused because they view the changes that go with the CSR agenda not as desirable for their own sake "but rather as necessary or prudent adaptations to a new and more demanding situation".[70] In addition, they view the changes as necessary for the benefit of the business and not for the sake of a wider goal of making the world a better place.[71] The second school are those that positively accepted CSR and have a broad focus of what the concept is. It is positive because it views the change as "recognizing and grasping new opportunities" and broadly focused because of its acceptance of a larger role for business.[72]

De Schutter summarised the arguments of the business approach as follows.[73] A first series of arguments is based on the internal workings of the company. First, it is argued that socially responsible conduct contributes to improving the workforce in terms of loyalty, commitment and productivity.[74] Second, it is argued that environmentally responsible conduct ensures efficient use of resources. Third, it is argued that CSR encourages voluntary dialogue with a variety of stakeholders and consequently builds

---

68 Blowfield and Frynas (note 64).

69 D.L. Brown, A. Vetterlein and A. Roemer-Mahler, "Theorizing Transnational Corporation as Social Actors: An Analysis of Corporate Motivations" (2010) 12 (1) *Business and Politics* 1; De Schutter (note 33) 205.

70 D. Henderson, *Misguided Virtue: False Notions of Corporate Social Responsibility* (New Zealand: New Zealand Business Roundtable, 2001), 11.

71 Ibid.

72 Ibid.

73 De Schutter (note 33).

74 Ibid., 217.

trust, increase companies' "licence to operate" and ensures community support. A second series of arguments is based on the contention that the market will increasingly reward socially responsible corporate practice.[75] Consumers may be more willing to buy products of socially responsible companies; investors may be more disposed to invest in such companies and public authorities may choose to award public contracts to such companies.

De Schutter correctly criticises the business approach by highlighting the ambiguities it creates. According to him, it creates a dependency of CSR on economic returns which may lead to adverse consequences. CSR will thus be treated as an investment decision which will only be embarked upon where profitable. He further contends that the argument is fragile because it is difficult to demonstrate the benefits of CSR practices in economic terms. He also argues that the concept creates an inaccurate impression that CSR will evolve naturally.[76]

The questions that arise from the discussion so far are the following: Does the law have a role to play in the modern discourse of CSR and if so, how is that role defined? These issues will be the focus of the following sections of the chapter.

CSR and the law: how should the law respond to the CSR concept?

In order to effectively understand the interplay between CSR and law it is necessary to distinguish the legal dimension of CSR from the perception of CSR as being outside the ambit of the law. Examples of those who take the latter view are the law and economic theorists. As Ward correctly points, out the most fundamental dividing line in the CSR debate is

> Between people who argue that CSR should be limited to consideration of "voluntary" business activities "beyond compliance" with legal baselines, and those who argue for a broader starting point, based on an understanding of the total impacts of business in society.[77]

The former approach tends to discourage the introduction of legislation or regulation as a response to issues raised in the CSR debate thereby

---

75 Ibid., 218.

76 Ibid., De Schutter therefore argues for a regulatory framework for CSR in the European Union. He argues that regulation is needed to ensure greater transparency and improved reporting in CSR instruments such as codes of conduct. He also argues that because the cost of private monitoring may be too high for some companies, particularly SMEs, there may be a need for the intervention of public authorities at the European level.

77 H. Ward, "Legal Issues in Corporate Citizenship" (Swedish Partnership for Global Responsibility, 2003), 8.

disconnecting the debate from discussion of corporate accountability through law.[78]

Ward further argues that failure to take into account the legal dimensions of CSR substantially weakens the chances of making progress in defining the proper balance between government, business and civil society. Ward advances several reasons why legal analysis should be factored into public policy and business strategy on CSR. First, the CSR debate has given rise to a number of legislative developments in areas such as mandatory social and environmental reporting or social labelling.[79] Second, some CSR tools have the potential to take on the colour of law; for instance, where codes of conducts are incorporated into contracts with supplier or employee[80] or where (as in the United States) corporations are held accountable for misleading advertisements or representations.[81] Third, in many developing countries, compliance with minimum legal standards especially for environmental, labour, fair competition and corporate governance are seen as part of the CSR agenda. Fourth, some CSR initiatives have given rise to consideration of legal issues in the intergovernmental context. An example is the concern of developing world's governments in the World Trade Organization in relation to the potential negative market access impacts of labelling or certification schemes and their compatibility with WTO regulations. Fifth, civil litigation actions against parent companies of multinational corporations are targeted at many of the issues on the CSR agenda.[82] Finally, according to Ward "the rigorous legal approach to analysis that is demanded by CSR-related litigation is helpful in unpacking some of the most difficult 'boundary' issues about the respective roles and responsibilities of business, civil society, and governments".[83]

The legal dimension of CSR views the concept as a means of employing legal changes to attain CSR objectives. CSR is thus regarded as a step towards standards, which would be regulated eventually.[84] This view seeks

78 Ibid.
79 Ibid., 1–2. See also H. Ward, "Corporate Social Responsibility in Law and Policy" in N. Boeger, R. Murray and C. Villiers, eds., *Perspectives on Corporate Social Responsibility* (Cheltenham: Edward Elgar, 2008), 18.
80 See C. Glinski, "Corporate Code of Conduct: Moral or Legal obligation" in D. McBarnet, A. Voiculescu and T. Campbell, eds., *The New Corporate Accountability: Corporate Social Responsibility and the Law* (Cambridge: Cambridge University Press, 2007), 119–147.
81 See *Nike, Inc.* v. *Kasky*, 123 S. Ct. 2554 (2003); *Kasky* v. *Nike, Inc.*, 79 Cal. App. 4th 165 (1st Dist. 2000; *Kasky* v. *Nike*, 27 Cal. 4th 939 (2002).
82 Civil litigation and accountability of MNCs shall be discussed in Chapter 7.
83 Ward (note 77).
84 I. Lynch Fannon, "Issues and Studies related to Corporate Governance and the Development of Socially Responsible Actors" Paper Presented at the International Research Colloquium on Accountable Governance, Queens University Belfast Colloquim, 20–22 October 2005. I. Lynch Fannon, "The Corporate Social Responsibility Movement and Law's Empire: Is there a Conflict?" (2007) 58 (1) *Northern Ireland Legal Quarterly* 15, 19.

to protect other constituents through changes to corporate law, contract law, civil liability laws, labour and human rights laws. Corporate law, for example, can do this through expansion of director's fiduciary duties, provision for independent directors, mandatory disclosure and social accounting, etc. Alternatively CSR is viewed as a complement to law by promoting social norms. Here other constituents are expected to be protected through self-regulation such as framework agreements and codes of conducts.

A variant of the latter group are the norms scholars within corporate law scholarship. The norms scholars make a distinction between legally enforceable rules that bind companies and non-legally enforceable rules and standards (NLERS) where behaviour is adhered to "through a privately enforced system of rewards and penalties".[85] The scholars sought to place these private systems within the corporate law structure. According to Lynch Fannon, there are two variants of this school. One part, which would seem to accommodate the CSR voluntary concept, is of the view that "norms will yield behaviour which is desirable but which it is argued law cannot and perhaps ought not deliver".[86] The second school appears to be driven more by the business case for CSR. To this school of scholars, all norm driven behaviour must be guarded by the primary purpose of the corporation, which is to maximise shareholders' wealth. Thus for any CSR initiative to be justifiable, it must be financially beneficial to the company and consequently its shareholders.[87] A good example of the latter group and its most prominent advocates is the law and economics school of law.

Undoubtedly, the law and economics jurisprudence has been dominant in the US legal jurisprudence for decades. This dominance has far reaching effects on academia, judicial decisions and the law making process generally. The dominance has also had a far reaching effect on the aspirations of the advocates of CSR. The Chicago school or neo-classical school of law and economics is widely regarded as the most influential within the economic analysis of law. At the heart of the school's economic analysis of law are three important propositions. The first is the proposition based on Adam Smith's idea that a free market unfettered by anything more than minimal state intervention is the most effective. The second is the standard economic assumption that humans are rational maximisers of their own satisfaction not only in the market but also in non-market spheres. The rational person faced with competing alternatives would employ a paradigm which compares marginal cost with personal benefit and will choose the course which best maximises his satisfaction or utility. The rational actor would continue on the same course until the marginal benefit is perceived to be greater

---

85 Lynch Fannon (2005) Ibid.
86 Ibid.
87 Ibid.

than the marginal cost.[88] Third is the concept of "efficiency as justice", which states that the "analysis of legal rules and legal decision-making should be evaluated from the perspective of economic efficiency".[89] There are two major paradigms of this proposition: Pareto efficiency and Kaldor–Hicks efficiency. Pareto efficiency is deemed by major proponents of the Chicago school to be inapplicable to legal analysis.[90] Simply put, according to the Pareto efficiency paradigm an activity would be regarded as efficient if one person can be made better off by it without making anyone worse off. The Kaldor–Hicks efficiency is the favoured paradigm. This paradigm focuses on wealth maximisation and serves as the theoretical basis of cost–benefit analysis. According to the paradigm it would not matter that an allocation of resources make some persons worse off, as long as those made better off by the allocation would be in a position theoretically to compensate those who have been made worse off. In such a situation, the allocation is considered efficient or wealth maximising. As Haugh pointed out the criterion is only hypothetical, there is no suggestion that those made better off should compensate those made worse off.[91]

The effect of this analysis on this discourse is the view that corporate law requires managers to pursue the single aim of the maximisation of stockholder profits. According to Easterbrook and Fischel:

> The role of corporate law here, as elsewhere, is to adopt a background term that prevails unless varied by contract. And the background term should be the one that is either picked by contract expressly when people get around to it or is the operational assumption of successful business firms. For most firms the expectation is that residual risk bearers have contracted for a promise to maximize long-run profits of the firm, which in turn maximizes the value of their stock. Other participants contract for fixed payouts – monthly interest, salaries, pensions, severance payments, and the like.[92]

The effect of this approach is to effectively exclude corporate social responsibility from the ambit of corporate law.

---

88 See for example R.A. Posner, *Economic Analysis of Law* (fifth edition, New York: Aspen Publishers Inc, 1989), 4.
89 Ibid., 12–16.
90 Ibid.
91 A. Haugh, "Law and Economics" in T. Murphy, ed., *Western Jurisprudence* (Dublin: Thompson, Round Hall, 2004), 325–350. The paradigm originally developed by Nicholas Kaldor and extended by J.R. Hicks was employed by Kaldor to explain the rationale for the abolition of Britain's protectionist Corn Laws in the 1930s. According to him the abolition of the Corn Laws was efficient because the gain to the country as a whole from the consequent free trade were likely to sufficiently outweigh losses to some corn farmer as a result of the abolition.
92 F.H. Easterbrook and D.R. Fischel, *The Economic Structure of Corporate Law* (Cambridge, MA and London: Harvard University Press, 1991) 36.

CSR and the law: perspectives

There are two main approaches identifiable in the literature that suggest a theoretical reconceptualisation of what regulation is in order for the law to be able to work effectively with CSR. These are the meta-regulatory approach advanced by Christine Parker[93] and the reflexive law theory[94] approach. Some legal scholars posit that the movement towards greater social responsibility is entering a phase where the parameters of responsibility are being defined. They stress that the law, especially human rights and international law, will have important roles to play in defining the parameters.[95] This point will be discussed in the last part of this chapter.

Meta-regulation and CSR

The concept of meta-regulation is used to capture developments at the intersection of state regulation and self-regulation, where government monitors the self-monitoring of corporations.[96] Parker summarised the approach as follows,

> Meta-regulation should be about requiring organisations to implement processes ... that are aimed at making sure they reach right results in terms of actions that impact on the world.... It recognises, however, that lawmakers and regulators may not know exactly what the "right" processes, and even the right results, will look like in each situation. The people who are involved in the situation are best placed to work out the details in their own circumstances, if they can be motivated to do so responsibly.

Parker thus argues that legal accountability for CSR must be aimed at making business enterprises put themselves through a CSR process aimed

---

93 C. Parker, *The Open Corporation: Effective Self-Regulation and Democracy* (Cambridge: Cambridge University Press, 2002).

94 R. Rogowski and T. Wilthagen, eds., *Reflexive Labour Law* (The Netherlands; Kluwer Law and Taxation Publishers, 1994); C. Barnard, S. Deakin and R. Hobbs, "Reflexive Law, Corporate Social Responsibility and the Evolution of Labour Standards: The Case of Working Time" (2004) ESRC Centre for Business Research, University of Cambridge Working Paper no. 294; G. Calliess, "Reflexive Transnational Law" *Zeitschrift für Rechtssoziologie* 23 (2002), Heft 2, S. 185: G. Teubner, "Global Bukowina: Legal Pluralism in the World Society" in G. Teubner, ed., *Global Law Without a State* (Brookfield: Dartmouth, 1997); D.J. Winders., "Combining Reflexive Law and False Advertising Law to Standardize 'Cruelty-Free' Labelling of Cosmetics" (2006) 81 *New York University Law Review* 454–486.

95 A. Clapham and S. Jerbi, "Categories of Corporate Human Rights Abuses" (2000–2001) 24 *Hastings International and Comparative Law Review* 339.

96 B. Morgan, "The Economisation of Politics: Meta-Regulation as a Form of Nonjudicial Legality" (2003) 12 *Social and Legal Studies* 489, 523.

at CSR outcomes.[97] According to her, the form of regulatory technique needed here need not take the form of the traditional hierarchical, legal regulation promulgated by nation states, rather such law might include international networks of governance and laws that authorise, empower, co-opts or recognise the regulatory influence of industry, professional or civil society bodies to set and enforce standards for CSR processes and outcomes.[98] It is thus obvious that meta-regulation is seeking a middle ground between positive law and self-regulation.

However, the concept may be open to criticism because of its indeterminate nature. It would appear that the concept would give legal backing to self-regulation and it is arguable that such a development will not improve accountability. The law may thus seem to be promoting a concept that would undermine the law itself. Furthermore, meta-regulation would seem to be delegating power to make rules and the power to determine the implementation and enforcement of such rules to corporations, thus creating a non transparent governance scenario. Ultimately, it does very little to improve accountability or improve the achievement of CSR objectives.[99]

Reflexive law theory approach

The theory shares some similarities with the meta-regulatory concept. Legal theorists including Gunther Teubner, Jurgen Habermas and Phillip Selznick have put forward this theory which involves what is usually called "reflexive", "procedural" or "responsive" law as a way to resolve the dichotomy between traditional law and self-regulation.[100] According to Cohen, reflexive law applies procedures to procedures (hence the reflexivity) steering and fostering self-regulation within social institutions.[101]

Reflexive law theory seeks to transform the concerns of post-structuralist and modern sociological systems theory into important questions for sociology and theory of law.[102] The challenge it poses is the rethinking of the understanding of the legal and social order, emphasising a shift from individualism in the "academic analysis of law and other social phenomena" to a study of the communicative processes which constitute legal and social

---

97 C. Parker, "Meta-Regulation: Legal Accountability for Corporate Social Responsibility?" in D. McBarnet, A. Voiculescu and T. Campbell, eds., *The New Corporate Accountability: Corporate Social Responsibility and the Law* (Cambridge: Cambridge University Press, 2007) 207.

98 Ibid., 208–209.

99 Parker has attempted to address some of these criticisms. Ibid., 229–236.

100 See J.L. Cohen *Regulating Intimacy* (New Jersey: Princeton University Press, 2002), 17.

101 Ibid., 4.

102 R. Rogowski and T. Wilthagen, *Reflexive Labour Law* (Deventer and Boston:: Kluwer Law and Taxation Publishers, 1994), 1–19.

systems.[103] It shifts focus away from the over reliance on command and control methods. The theory focuses on procedural norms ("auxiliary legislation") as opposed to substantive formalised rules. The procedural norms concentrate on the development of regulatory mechanisms, which are aimed at achieving intended outcomes by aggregating individual self-regulatory decisions.[104] It thus mobilises the self-referential capacities of institutions to enable them to best shape their response to complex problems.[105] The law thus avoids the need to directly regulate complex social areas but focuses on controlling the structure and processes of self-regulation appropriately.[106] Regulation and compliance is thus delegated to the level of individual corporations. According to Cohen, provided that certain procedural norms and principles of justice are respected, the relevant parties are free to strike whatever substantive agreements they wish. Thus unlike material law, reflexive regulation does not dictate any particular outcome.[107] This is one way in which the reflexive law theory approach differs from the meta-regulation approach which is aimed at CSR outcomes.

The theory recognises that the social context of law consists of "independent function systems" (autopoietic systems), which are functionally closed.[108] In this approach, the law will seek to find ways of working with the other subsystems such as self-regulation which is "seeking for example the alignment of regulatory norms set by legislators, legal norms generated as a response by the legal subsystem, and activities over which control is sought".[109] Reflexive law thus allow regulation to take advantage of the benefits of soft law: lower contracting costs, lower sovereignty costs, better adaptation to conditions of uncertainty and those requiring compromise.[110] Examples include narrow procedural processes, like the requirement that firms have compliance officers, legal rules e.g. senior members being liable for the misconduct of junior members and setting minimum standards for contents of codes of conduct.[111]

An important aspect of reflexive law is the position that formal state law is not the only significant form of norm. State law, though much more

---

103   Ibid., 4.
104   M. Davies, "A Crisis of Professional Self-Regulation – the Example of the Solicitors' Profession" Cardiff Centre for Law and Ethics (2005), online, available at: www.ccels.cf.ac. uk/ (accessed 6 May 2008).
105   Ibid.
106   Ibid.
107   Cohen (note 100), 4.
108   Rogowski and Wilthagen (note 102), 6.
109   C. Scott, "Regulation in the Age of Governance: The Rise of the Post Regulatory State" (2003) National Europe Centre Paper no. 100, Australian National University, 9.
110   F. Snyder, "Economic Globalisation and the Law in the Twenty-First Century", in A. Sarat ed., *The Blackwell Companion to Law and Society* (New York: Blackwell Publishing, 2004), 624–640.
111   Davies (note 104), 6.

formalised, is conceived as one among many competing normative systems. Following from this is the ability of the concept to accommodate the concept of a "global law without a state",[112] which would accord legitimacy to transnational global norms.[113] Norms are developed by communicative processes between subsystems. In this regard MNCs, civil society and international institutions (as opposed to communities and geographical groups) are all subsystems, which facilitate discourses and communication. The result would be quasi-contractual norms to solve regulatory problems.

Reflexive law is open to similar criticism as the meta-regulatory approach and in fact has generated more criticism along those lines. Cohen identifies three of the main criticisms of the theory.[114] First it has been argued that the theory is a new form of privatisation or neo corporatism allowing the delegation of authority and decision making to ultimately irresponsible powers. Second, it has also been argued that the paradigm undermines the rule of law and democracy. Third it is argued that the theories of legal paradigms generally are unconvincing because they rest on untenable premises. The concept has also been criticised for neither establishing formal rules of interaction nor directing substantive outcomes.[115]

From the discussion so far, it is noted that CSR is a concept that is in flux and there is need for a firmer underpinning for the concept rooted in the law.

Theoretical justification for CSR

Here the chapter considers the theoretical justification for CSR with emphasis on the importance of legal theories to the understanding of the concept. This is (more so) because the modern debate about the social responsibility of business was started by legal scholars as noted earlier in this chapter. Moir has rightly identified three theories, which may help in the analysis and explanation of the theoretical underpinnings of CSR. These theories are the stakeholder theory, the social contract theory and the legitimacy theory. However, it is suggested that the social contract model (which the legitimacy theory has some resemblance with) is most

---

112 Calliess (note 94), 9; Teubner (note 94) 3–38.
113 Calliess (note 94), 4, defines transnational law as

> A third-level autonomous legal system beyond municipal and public international law, created and developed by the law-making forces of an emerging global civil society, founded on general principles of law as well as societal usages, administered by private dispute resolution service providers, and codified (if at all) by private norm formulating agencies.

114 Cohen (note 100), 17.
115 W.A. Braunig, "Reflexive Law Solutions for Factory Farm Pollution" (2005) 80 *New York University Law Review* 1505, 1525.

compelling because of its completeness and logic and because of its influence on political organisations and societies in which corporations operate.[116] The chapter therefore pays particular attention to the social contract theory. However, before proceeding to address the social contract theory, I will briefly discuss the other two theories mentioned by Moir.

Stakeholder theories

According to Freeman a stakeholder is "any group or individual who can affect or is affected by the achievement of the firm's objectives".[117] Across disciplines it is generally agreed that stakeholders in this sense include shareholders, creditors, employees, customers, suppliers, public interest groups and government. Stakeholder theories address the question of which group in society corporations should be responsible to.[118] Stakeholders are typically analysed into primary and secondary stakeholders.[119] Primary stakeholders are those whose participation directly ensures the continuity of the corporation as a going concern. This group includes shareholders, employees and customers, and also includes what Clarkson describes as the public stakeholder group – governments and communities that provide necessary infrastructure, market and the enabling legal framework. The secondary groups are described as those who influence or affect or are influenced or affected by the corporation but are not involved in transactions with the company, nor are they necessary for its survival.[120] Scholars on the theory are divided on whether to consider the theory as a normative theory based on largely ethical propositions or an empirical/instrumental/descriptive theory.[121] Inquiries that have shaped the debate on CSR theories in this area include: determining whether stakeholder

---

116 Muchlinski also alluded to the relevance of the social contract theory as a justification for CSR. According to him, CSR "may be justified philosophically by appeals to a 'social contract' and to the need of all actors, including non-state actors, to observe the preservation of human dignity through adherence to fundamental human rights" P.T. Muchlinski, *Multinational Enterprises and the Law* (second edition, Oxford: Oxford University Press, 2007), 101.

117 Quoted in R.W. Roberts, "Determinants of Corporate Social Responsibility Disclosure: An Application of Stakeholder Theory" (1992) 17 (6) *Accounting Organisations and Society* 595.

118 See D. Matten and A. Crane, "Corporate Citizenship: Toward an Extended Theoretical Conceptualization" (2005) 30 (1) *Academy of Management Review*, 166; See also J. Moon, A. Crane and D. Matten, "Can Corporations be Citizens? Corporate Citizenship as a Metaphor for Business Participation in Society" (2005) 15 (3) *Business Ethics Quarterly* 429.

119 M.B.E. Clarkson, "A Stakeholder Framework for Analysing and Evaluating Corporate Social Performance" (1995) 20 *Academy of Management Review* 92.

120 L. Moir, "What do We Mean by Corporate Social Responsibility?" (2001) 1 *Corporate Governance* 16.

121 Ibid.

theory is part of motivation for business to be responsible and identification of relevant stakeholders to be taken into consideration by business managers. A model of stakeholder identification and salience was put forward by Mitchell *et al.*[122] The model was based on stakeholders possessing one or more attributes of power, legitimacy and urgency. What the model suggests is that firms would pay more attention to any stakeholder that possesses one or more of these attributes. Other researchers in the field have favoured this idea.[123]

Legitimacy theory

Legitimacy theory has been defined as a generalised perception that the actions of the organisation are proper or appropriate within a given social system.[124] Suchman identifies three types of organisational legitimacy as pragmatic, moral and cognitive.[125] Furthermore, he identifies three key challenges to legitimacy management, which are gaining, maintaining and repairing legitimacy. He posits that legitimacy management is dependent on communication.[126] Moir therefore suggested that in the debate on CSR it would be necessary to examine corporate communications.[127] The primary argument of legitimacy theory is that external factors influence corporate management to seek to legitimise activities. It has been observed that legitimacy may not necessarily be a benign process through which organisations obtain legitimacy from society.[128] An organisation may employ four different strategies when faced with the legitimacy threat: it may choose to educate its stakeholders about its intention to improve the organisation's performance; it may seek to change the organisation's perception of the event without changing performance; it may divert attention from the event or it may choose to change external expectations of its performance.[129] It therefore stands to reason that while legitimacy might be an important reason for corporations to undertake CSR it may not be the only reason. It has also been argued as an alternative view that since society grants power to business, society expects that the power be used responsibly. According to Moir, this would amount to a restatement of the social contract between the firm and society.[130]

122 R.K. Mitchell, B.R. Agle and D.J. Wood, "Toward a Theory of Stakeholder Identification and Salience: Defining the Principle of Who and What Really Counts" (1997) 22 *Academy of Management Review* 853.
123 Moir (note 120).
124 M.C. Schuman, "Managing Legitimacy: Strategic and Institutional Approaches" (1995) 20 *Academy of Management Review* 571.
125 Ibid.
126 See a fuller discussion of Schuman's idea in this regard in Moir (note 120), 16–22.
127 Ibid.
128 Ibid.
129 Ibid.
130 Ibid.

The aim of the rest of the chapter is to examine the social contract theory to see if it can ground sufficient legitimacy for the CSR concept. I will also consider the implications of this for law. I start by considering the questions posed by CSR from a legal perspective. Thereafter I consider how the legal conception of the corporation has affected the understanding of the moral responsibility of the corporation. I later return to the social contract theory as justification for CSR.

Understanding the emerging responsibilities of modern corporations: a social contract approach

The argument that is put forward here is that the modern corporation has acquired a status that is akin to that of a person under the law and should be treated as such in determining its social responsibility and its responsibilities under human rights law especially international human rights law. In arriving at this conclusion, this part of the chapter analyses the implications of CSR from a legal perspective, examines the moral foundation of the concept and places this examination within the context of the theoretical understanding of the personhood of the corporation. It is posited that since the social contract has been very influential in the construction of state and individual responsibility, it will be necessary to examine the role of the corporation within the social contract and thus understand the position of the corporation under international human rights law. The social contract concept has been very influential in the political context and the attempt here is to extend the concept to corporations in a logical way.

The original understanding of the social contract postulates that society decides to move from a situation of undefined rights and incessant conflict over resources to a society under a social contract whereby individuals agree to honour the rights of others in return for guarantees that their own rights will be respected and protected. The state is the repository in which individuals vest authority to ensure that the terms of the contract are complied with. The state thus mediates between individuals and between individuals and society. It is suggested that the idea of corporate social contract underlies the CSR concept. The idea is that the corporate social contract concerns "a firm's indirect societal obligations and resembles the 'social contract' between citizens and government traditionally discussed by philosophers who identified the reciprocal obligations of citizen and state".[131] Thus business should act in a responsible manner because it is part of society and also enter into a social contract with society. From this perspective CSR is described as "the obligation stemming from the implicit 'social contract' between business and society for

---

131 G.P. Lantos, "The Boundaries of Strategic Corporate Social Responsibility" (2001) 18 *Journal of Consumer Marketing* 599.

firms to be responsive to society's long-run needs and wants, optimizing the positive effects and minimizing the negative effects of its actions on society".[132]

What questions does CSR raise for law?

CSR has emerged as the voluntary way in which companies respond to issues for which it is generally assumed they have no legal responsibility such as the promotion and protection of human rights and social welfare.[133] The argument is always that as private actors, corporations are not designed to take on such responsibilities.[134] The move by companies to adopt CSR as a philosophy is partly driven by the difficulty which has been experienced in imposing such a concept on corporations by legally binding rules.[135] Furthermore, corporations generally argue against the construction of moral duty to act otherwise than for the interests of shareholders. However, because of the relentless pressure from civil societies, activists, media and consumers, corporations have found it fashionable to adopt the concept of CSR. This approach gives the leaders of the corporate domain the ability to determine what CSR should be and the scope of such voluntary responsibility.[136] The widespread acceptance of moral obligation can be inferred from the widespread adoption of voluntary initiatives such as statements of principles, codes of ethics, codes of conduct and voluntary social reporting.[137] According to Dickerson:

> The practical reality today is that some multinational corporations' actual behaviour is more respectful of non shareholder rights than the classic corporate social responsibility norms require. As a matter of conduct, multinationals recognize the rights of persons other than shareholders and a growing appreciation of the power of groups influence this evolving behaviour.[138]

132 Ibid., Lantos has, however, criticised the social theory for being vague, as it is not in writing, varies from place to place and does not indicate to what extent the corporation should be conceived as a public as against private enterprise and the relevance of firms' size to the equation.

133 J.A. Zerk, *Multinationals and Corporate Social Responsibility: Limitations and Opportunities in International Law* (Cambridge: Cambridge University Press 2006), 42.

134 Ibid. See also F.M. Idoho, "Oil Transnational Corporations: Corporate Social Responsibility and Environmental Sustainability" (2008) 15 (4) *Corporate Social Responsibility and Environmental Management* 210.

135 J. Dine, *Companies, International Trade and Human Rights* (Cambridge: Cambridge University Press 2005), 222.

136 C.M. Dickerson, "How Do Norms and Empathy Affect Corporation Law and Corporate Behaviour? Human Rights: The Emerging Norm of Corporate Social Responsibility" (2001–2002) 76 *Tulane Law Review* 1431.

137 McBarnet (note 58), 10.

138 Ibid. See also Zerk (note 133).

Considering such trends Jackson opines that corporations clearly assume significant non economic i.e. political, legal and moral roles as well as economic ones.[139] It has been observed that globalisation has made corporate decisions in respect of CSR subject, to some extent, to pressures from other sources such as home market consumers and complex problems from developing countries.[140]

These developments indicate the acceptance of self-imposed and self-defined responsibility by corporations on themselves akin to morality in the case of natural persons. According to Muchlinski, this trend shows that MNCs appear to be rejecting a purely non-social role through the adoption of codes of conduct and the trends appear to indicate an increasing social dimension to the role of MNCs.[141] However, as we shall see presently, commentators have debated whether or not it is possible to construct a moral responsibility framework for corporations.

One way in which CSR is interacting with the law is that legal standards are major sources of the non binding rules that are shaping corporate "conscience".[142] Norms of legal character, especially in the areas of international law of human rights, labour and environmental protection, national and supranational legislation is widely used to inform or guide corporate actions and reporting within the sphere of CSR.[143] Business principles of most corporations draw from these instruments. According to Buhmann, the striking feature is that despite the fact that CSR is generally understood as being voluntary and acting beyond legal compliance, many CSR demands from stakeholders and much corporate compliance action appears to be based on assessments of compliance with international law especially human rights and labour law.[144] As noted earlier, a recent trend which is still embryonic is that some governments are legislating on aspects of CSR especially in the areas of social reporting and directors' duties.[145] Indonesia has gone further by moving towards a broader legislative framework for CSR.

These developments raise fundamental questions in law: if these developments are construed as the assumption of morality or conscience by corporations, then what role (if any) does the law have to play in this

---

139 K.T. Jackson, "Global Distributive Justice and the Corporate Duty to Aid" (1993) 12 *Journal of Business Ethics* 547.

140 Dickerson (note 136).

141 P.T. Muchlinski, "Human Rights and Multinationals: Is there a Problem?" (2001) 77 *International Affairs* 37–38.

142 Parker (note 97), 208.

143 K. Buhmann, "Corporate Social Responsibility: What Role for Law? Some Aspects of Law and CSR" (2006) 6 *Corporate Governance* 188.

144 Ibid. See also W.C. Frederick, "The Moral Authority of Transnational Corporate Codes" 1999 (10) *Journal of Business Ethics* 165–167.

145 United Kingdom, France, Germany, Belgium, Sweden; see Buhmann (note 143) 7. See also McBarnet (note 58), 32–35.

regard? Mitchell and Gabaldon succinctly summarised these questions when they stated:

> The issue of corporate social responsibility poses the important ques-
> tion of whether the corporate tin man can itself be expected to behave
> humanly, that is be morally responsible, or whether its moral compass
> can only come from those who motivate it – its directors, officers, and
> employees. This directly poses the question of whether the corpora-
> tion can have a heart of its own, its own moral and psychological con-
> struct, or whether its morality can never be more than that of the
> individuals who comprise it.[146]

In Parker's opinion, law should attempt to constitute corporate "conscience" by getting companies to want to do what they should and not just
comply with legal requirements.[147]

This book contends that CSR as presently construed is largely a construct of moral responsibilities for companies.[148] It further contends
that there is a relationship between morality and the law and in doing
so, it rejects the positivist argument that there is no issue of morality in
law because there is no link between law and morality. It argues that
morality, which is driven by societal expectation, forms the basis of the
corporation's entrance into the existing social contract. It further
argues that the modern corporation has acquired the capacity to enter
into the existing social contract by virtue of the status the law has
afforded to it.

The shortcomings in the understanding of the nature of the corporation by ethicists and philosophers and the problem of ascribing morality to the corporation

It is posited here that the ambiguity that has attended legal theories as to
the nature of the corporate person has befuddled attempts by ethicists and
philosophers to analyse the relationship between the corporation and
morality. The arguments of Wolgast, Ewin, French, Goodpaster and
Mathews, and Donaldson will be used to illustrate this point.[149]

In Wolgast's view the problem with ascribing morality to the corporation is directly linked with the conception of the corporation as an

---

146 L.E. Mitchell and T.A. Gabaldon, "If I Only Had a Heart: Or, How Can We Identify a
Corporate Morality" (2001–2002) 76 *Tulane Law Review* 1645.
147 Parker (note 97).
148 However, the difference here is that unlike societal moral construct that are determined
by the society as a collective, the moral constructs in CSR practices are largely determined by the corporations themselves.
149 The relevant works of the writers referred to are cited below.

artificial person under the law.[150] According to her the corporation is in the class of artificial persons who act on behalf of stockholders. The concept thus facilitates the use by the same individuals of others' labour and expertise to increase the power and scope of their activities. The dilution created by the fragmentation caused by this arrangement negates the ascription of moral responsibilities as the intention of the principal and agents do not necessarily coincide.[151] The basis of her analysis is the legal conception of the corporation as an artificial person which, as we shall presently see, may not necessarily be the case because the metaphor is just one of the many conflicting legal theories of the corporation.

The artificial person distinction also grounded Ewin's argument when he concluded that:

> Because they are *artificial and not "natural" people*, corporations lack the emotional make-up necessary to the possession of virtues and vices. Their moral responsibility is exhausted by their legal personality. Corporations can have rights and duties; they can exercise the rights through their agents, and they can in the same way fulfil their duties. If necessary, they can be forced to fulfil their duties. The moral personality of a corporation would be at best a Kantian sort of moral personality, one restricted to the issues of requirement, rights, and duties. It could not be the richer moral life of virtues and vices that is lived by the shareholders, the executives, the shop-floor workers, the unemployed and "natural" people in general[152] (emphasis added).

Ewin was unequivocal in emphasising that the moral personality of corporations is severely limited and is exhausted by its legal personality. The consequence of the artificial legal construct of the corporation according to Ewin is that corporations might be logically locked into selfishness, which would leave them with a very limited and unsatisfactory moral personality. According to him:

> Of course, it might be very imprudent for them to look as though they were entirely selfish and might, with such a poor corporate image, have deleterious effects on their trading performance, but that is not sufficient to defeat the point and solve the problem. All that shows is that an efficient firm would be subtle about its selfishness, considering what promoted its interests in the long run, and would employ a good advertising agency.[153]

---

150 See E. Wolgast, *Ethics of an Artificial Person: Lost Responsibility in Professions and Organisations* (Stanford: Stanford University Press, 1992).
151 Ibid.
152 R.E. Ewin, "The Moral Status of the Corporation" (1991) 10 *Journal of Business Ethics* 749.
153 Ibid.

On this basis, Ewin rejected French's differing argument that "corporations can be full-fledged moral persons and have whatever privileges, rights, duties as are in normal course of affairs, accorded to moral persons".[154] French's argument stemmed from his belief that if corporations are not full members of the moral society, they "will avoid the scrutiny and control of moral sanction" and his aim was to subject them to moral sanction.[155] He argued that for an entity to be the subject of moral obligation it needs to be an intentional actor and since corporations have internal decision-making structures then they are moral persons as a collective.

French is not alone in his contention; Goodpaster and Mathew in a widely respected article subsequently argued that conscience can reside in corporations since corporations evince both rationality and respect in their goal-setting and decision-making capacities.[156] Goodpaster developed this idea further in 1983 in his article "The Concept of Corporate Responsibility" where he based his principle of "moral projection" on an analogy between corporations and persons.[157] It is worth noting here that Goodpaster made a clear distinction between the company and the persons that run them. According to him:

> The actions and decisions of corporations are not usually a simple function of any single manager's values. Even the chief executive officer of a corporation often must, in his or leadership role, work indirectly in efforts to guide the large organisation toward its goals … The point is that having a conscience in the running of a large corporation does not translate automatically into running a conscientious corporation. The latter requires an "institutionalization" of certain values, not simply the possession of those values in one part of the organisation (even if that part is at the top of the hierarchy).[158]

He therefore concluded that managing the "joint force" or the "personhood" imputed to the corporation by law and generally accepted accounting principles as well as the "personality" imputed in recent discussions of corporate "culture" demands a large unit of analysis.[159] In his view, the law should give enough freedom for companies to exercise moral responsibility.

154 P. French, *Collective and Corporate Responsibility* (New York: Columbia University Press, 1984).
155 Ibid., ix.
156 K. Goodpaster and J. Matthews, "Can a Corporation have Conscience?" (1982) 60 (1) *Harvard Business Review* 132.
157 K.E. Goodpaster, "The Concept of Corporate Responsibility" (1983) 2 *Journal of Business Ethics* 1.
158 Ibid.
159 Ibid.

In contesting Goodpaster's idea, Ranken resorted to the artificiality of the personhood of the corporation to conclude that the analogy of personhood is irrelevant and may be counter-productive by shifting the focus away from individual responsibility.[160] Ranken's argument is basically to reduce the corporation to people that run them. It shall be argued later on that this is not true in law. The above postulations arose from what it is perceived the law says corporations are. This was also the premise to Donaldson's view that the law seems to imply that corporations are artificial legal persons or "juristic persons" who are merely creations of the law. In his opinion the juristic personhood failed to establish full fledged moral agency.[161] In consequence of the heavy reliance on the artificial personhood metaphor, Donaldson concluded that the combined weight of such argument suggests that corporations fail to qualify as moral persons. They may be juristic persons, granted legal rights by courts and legislatures, they may be moral agents of some other kinds but they do not appear to be "moral persons" in any literal sense of the term.[162]

This narrow presentation of the theory of the legal personality of the corporation leads Donaldson on an untenable path in his quest to establish the moral status of the corporation. According to him it would be better to ask whether some corporations are moral agents and some are not, and would be better to proceed by specifying the conditions that any corporation would need to satisfy in order to qualify as a moral agent.[163] Once we have done this, it is then possible to ask whether or not a given corporation satisfies the conditions. Donaldson sets out some criteria for a corporation to become a moral agent but not a moral person.[164] To qualify as a moral agent, a corporation must be able to use moral reason in decision making, i.e. it must be morally accountable and it must have control over the structure of the decision-making process itself. He further posited that acute bureaucratic problems may deny or interfere with a company's ability to become a moral agent.

It is submitted here that Donaldson's approach is unhelpful as it sets different standards for different corporations, which is not how societal moral standards are constructed. Furthermore, it is questionable whether a company would willingly make itself a moral agent where such a step would put it at a competitive disadvantage. In the opinion of this writer, because of the focus on the narrow artificial construct of the corporation, the moral philosophers' and ethicists' attempts to analyse the moral responsibility of the corporation may have been impaired. The next

---

160 N.L. Ranken, "Corporations as Persons: Objections to Goodpaster's Principle of Moral Projection" (1987) 6 *Journal of Business Ethics* 633.

161 T. Donaldson, *Corporations and Morality* (New Jersey: Prentice Hall, 1982), 21.

162 Ibid., 23.

163 Ibid., 29.

164 Ibid., 126–127.

section considers the conception of the corporation from the standpoint of legal theorists.

The modern corporation and legal theories

To understand the responsibility (including the moral responsibility) of the modern corporation, it is essential to fully understand the concept of the personhood of the corporation from the legal theory perspective.[165] This is important because legal theorisation in this regard influences many fields' understanding of the purpose of the corporation and it has also helped in shaping the law.[166] In Bainbridge's view, corporate law scholarship requires a normative theory of the corporation and its place in policy, in other words "corporate law scholarship requires a model of the corporation upon which one may make predictions about how corporate actors will behave under a given legal regime and how courts should rule in particular cases".[167] According to Blumberg in his examination of three traditional corporate personality theories in American law:

> The three traditional theories have much more than philosophical interest. They have helped shape our law. The view of the corporation as an "artificial person" underlies entity law, the view of corporation with rights and duties separate from those of its shareholders, for ages past the prevailing view of Western jurisprudence ... The view of the corporation as an association or aggregate of the individuals composing it played an important role in the late nineteenth century in facilitating the development of the law to broaden and extend constitutional protections to corporations in order to protect economic interests of shareholders ... the corporation as a "real entity", is the view that has dominated corporation law for decades. It is especially evident in the attribution to corporations of constitutional rights similar to those of natural persons in most cases.[168]

The importance of metaphor in this connection was emphasised by Greenfield when he posited that "scholars have used metaphors – corporation as

165 Wood and Scharffs followed this approach in their 2002 article but reached a different conclusion from this book. See S.G. Wood and B.G. Scharffs, "Applicability of Human Rights Standards to Private Corporations: An American Perspective" (2002) 50 *American Journal of International Law* 531.

166 P.I. Blumberg, "The Corporate Personality in American Law: A Summary Review" (1990) 38 *American Journal of Comparative Law, Supplement. US Law in an Era of Democratization* 49.

167 S.M. Bainbridge, "Competing Concepts of the Corporation (aka Criteria? Just Say No)" (2002) 2 *Berkeley Business Law Journal* 77.

168 Blumberg (note 166), 49, 51.

person, corporation as creature of state, corporation as property, corporation as contract, corporation as community, to name the most prominent – as justifications for the imposition of, or freedom from, legal and ethical requirements".[169] Commenting on the practical implication of such endeavour Mitchell and Gabaldon stated that:

> Judgments as to which of these propositions is most nearly correct can make a difference as far as the kinds of duties and roles that should be assigned to corporate actors and the kinds of external constraints (such as employment discrimination and pollution control law) that should be applied to corporate entities. It is entirely possible that we currently regulate corporations and their constituencies as though one model were correct, whereas another one might be more apt. It is also possible, however, that there may be merit to acting as though one model or another is correct even in the face of evidence that it is not.[170]

According to Smith, something important is going on in the persistent and widespread idea of a business entity or "person" that deserves more study and may ultimately be fully explained by academics.[171] At the heart of such inquiry is the debate about corporate law's objectives in the light of increasing attention to social costs of the operation of corporations.[172] As Wood and Scharffs correctly noted, the underlying theory of the corporate person affects the content and scope of the rights and duties that are attributed to corporations.[173]

There are two broad approaches to corporate personhood: entity theory versus the corporation as an aggregate of natural persons. The two broad approaches have related subdivisions. The entity theory is related to the artificial person's versus natural person's distinction while the corporation as aggregate theory is related to the contractarian versus communitarian distinction. The next section examines these different theories of the corporation.

Artificial entity theory

This is variously referred to as the artificial person, fiction, concession or grant doctrine of the corporation. The notion is the foundation of the classic definition of corporation given by Chief Justice Marshall in the *Dartmouth College* case:

---

169 K. Greenfield, "From Metaphor to Reality in Corporate Law" (2001) 2 *Stanford Agora* 59.
170 Mitchell and Gabaldon (note 146).
171 T.A. Smith, "The Use and Abuse of Corporate Personality" (2001) 2 *Stanford Agora* 69.
172 See D. Millon, "The Ambiguous Significance of Corporate Personhood" (2001) 2 *Stanford Agora* 39; D. Millon, "Theories of the Corporation" (1990) *Duke Law Journal* 201.
173 Wood and Scharffs (note 165), 531, 544.

A corporation is an artificial being, intangible, and existing only in the contemplation of law. Being the mere creation of law, it possesses only those properties which the charter of its creation confers upon it, either expressly, or as incidental to its very existence.[174]

This theory, which has been very popular with the courts, has considerably influenced other disciplines to conceive the corporation as an artificial "person". According to this early version of the entity theory, the corporation was a separate person in the eyes of the law. However, the emphasis was on the personhood's artificiality which was based on the fact that its existence depended on action by the state.[175] The rationale for this is not farfetched as, up to the nineteenth century, private initiative alone was not enough to create a corporation; entrepreneurs required special acts of the legislature granting a charter to operate.[176] The legislature imposed limits on the corporation through the charters and the *ultra vires* doctrine confined the company to those bounds. Some notable American cases decided from this stand-point in the nineteenth century include *Louisville, Cincinnati and Charleston Railroad* v. *Leston*,[177] *Marshall* v. *Baltimore and Ohio R.R.*[178] and *Bank of Augustat* v. *Earle*.[179] The arguments of Donaldson, Ewin and Wolgast (discussed earlier) proceeded from this particular viewpoint which, it is submitted, is an incomplete understanding of the legal conception of corporate personhood.

Corporation as an aggregate of natural persons

This is also known as the association, aggregate or contract theory. The advent of large-scale enterprises led to a shift in the legal conception of the corporation. The artificial entity theory because of its justification of state regulation was found to be incompatible with the emerging economic structuring of large corporations. Recourse was had to the aggregate theory, which appeals to the individual rights of shareholders and the freedom of association, to justify the position that legislative interference was not needed. As Millon correctly pointed out, the corporation is perceived as the aggregate of natural persons that make it up in the sense of a partnership. It is therefore not an entity independent or distinct from its members.[180] Such reasoning supports understanding the company from the perspective of the persons that constitute it. Thus, whatever is done to

---

174 *Trustees of Dartmouth College* v. *Woodward*, 17 US 518 (1819).
175 Millon (2001) (note 172), 201.
176 Ibid.
177 43 US (2 How.) 497 1844.
178 57 US (16 How.) 314, 327–329 (1853).
179 38 US (13 Pet.) 519 (1839).
180 Millon (2001) (note 172), 39.

the corporation is done to the individuals constituting it.[181] The point here is that corporations are not persons at all (artificial or otherwise) and should not be subject to any special duties. Any regulation of the corporation has to be justified with respect to the individuals that own the corporation and their property and not an indeterminable concept of corporation.[182] This notion was reflected in notable nineteenth-century US decisions such as *Bank of the United States* v. *Deveaux*[183] where Chief Justice Marshall writing the unanimous decision of the court, held that in determining the diversity of jurisdiction for the purpose of the jurisdictional competence of the federal High Court, the case was controlled by the citizenship of the shareholders of the company and not an abstract concept.

The dependence of the concept mainly on the analogy made between corporations and partnership presented a problem of its own.[184] According to Millon

> Partnership law's traditional insistence on each partner's right to participate in control of the business implied that unanimous shareholder approval was necessary for corporate mergers and consolidations. Furthermore, the partnership analogy also suggested the possibility of shareholder liability in cases of firm insolvency.[185]

Thus the analogy placed some difficulty in corporate decision making and also allowed the possibility of individual shareholder liability. These difficulties later influenced the emergence of the natural entity theory which would have ironic consequences for corporate law theory.

Natural entity theory

Natural entity theory is also referred to as the person, real entity or realism theory. This is one important development in the late nineteenth and twentieth century to which most of the commentators from other fields have failed to pay much attention. The natural entity theory conceives the corporation neither as a legal fiction nor a contract between individuals, but a natural person with a pre-legal existence.[186] The theory derives

---

181 For example the US Supreme Court held in *Santa Clara* v. *Southern Pacific Railway* 118, US 394 (1886) that attempts to tax corporations directly implicated individual constitutional rights.
182 Smith (note 171), 69.
183 9 US (5 Ranch) 61 (1809).
184 Millon (2001) (note 173) 5.
185 Ibid.
186 A. Grear, "Human Rights – Human Bodies? Some Reflections on Corporate Human Rights Distortion, The Legal Subject, Embodiment and Human Rights Theory" (2006) 17 *Law Critique* 171, 185.

substantially from Otto Gierke's idea of naturalness embedded in groups and later work in the same vein by Maitland and Freund.[187] It is also associated with the continental theorists of the twentieth century who wrote about "group" or "corporate" personality as a challenge to individualism and an effort to come to terms with institutions of modern society.[188] In so classifying a corporation, it illegitimatises any attempt to single out corporations for special regulatory control. It thus justified the banishment of the state's role in the creation of companies to a secondary level while emphasising the natural evolvement of corporation from the "impersonal market forces".[189] This theory fits well with the emergence of large corporations as it deemphasised the role of the shareholders in the control of the company's affairs, transferring effective power to the board who acts for the corporate entity.[190] The status of companies as distinguishable from shareholders was thus recognised by legal theorists.[191] According to Cerri, the legal status of *person* has contributed to making corporations autonomous from public control and to shield their accountability while retaining correlative privileges.[192] The significance of this development is the minimisation of the state's role in the incorporation process in favour of the view that the corporation is the product of private initiative and inevitable market forces discouraged legal regulations that especially applied to corporations and increased accommodation of the separation of ownership from control and the focus on managers' accountability to shareholders.[193] One result of this conception is the ability of corporations to claim rights provided primarily for natural persons.[194]

These developments, however, led to another possibility spearheaded by Dodd who, arguing from the entity perspective and emphasising the

---

187 O. Gierke, *Political Theories of the Middle Age* (Translated by Frederic W. Maitland) (Cambridge: Cambridge University Press, 1990); E. Freund, *The Legal Nature of Corporations* (Chicago: University of Chicago Press, 1897); F. Maitland "The Corporation Sole" (1900) 16 *Law Quarterly Review* 335; J.A. Mack, "Group Personality – A Footnote to Maitland" (1952) 2 *Philosophical Quarterly* 249.

188 C.J. Meyer, "Personalizing the Impersonal: Corporations and the Bill of Rights" (1989–1990) 41 *Hastings Law Journal* at 581; J. Dewey, "The Historical Background of Corporate Legal Personality" (1926) 35 *Yale Law Journal* 655; P. Vinogradoff, "Juridical Persons" (1924) 24 *Columbia Law Review* 594.

189 Millon (2001) (note 172) 39.

190 Ibid.

191 Ibid.

192 L. Cerri, "Corporate Personhood and Economic Democracy" Paper presented at a workshop on Economic Democracy and European Left in the Age of Globalization organised by Centre for Marxist Studies (CSM) and Transform (European Network for Alternative Thinking and Political Dialogue 14–15 June 2003, Stockholm).

193 Ibid.

194 Blumberg (note 166), 49; C.J. Meyer, "Personalizing the Impersonal: Corporations and the Bill of Rights" (1989–1990) 41 *Hastings Law Journal* 577.

separateness of the corporation from its shareholders, called for a wider social responsibility for business. According to Dodd:

> If we think of it as an institution which differs in the nature of things from the individuals who compose it, we may then readily *conceive of it as a person*, which, like other persons engaged in business, is affected not only by the laws which regulate business but also by the attitude of public and business opinion as to the social obligations of business[195] (emphasis added).

The idea is compelling because if corporations are viewed as natural persons in some sense and accorded the negative right to freedom from coercion, then corporations should also have obligations just like humans.

Berle and Means' response to Dodd's article did not directly take on the issue of the personhood of the corporation. Rather they rehashed the property rights argument (corporations as aggregate of natural persons) in a depersonalised manner.[196] They asserted that the corporation is simply a property owned by shareholders and run by management as trustees. This idea was the foundation for Friedman's positions that the corporation is the property of shareholders and the management are employees of shareholders.[197] The corporation is thus a mere legal fiction for the use of shareholders and from this perspective, the argument of the personhood of the corporate entity is irrelevant. According to Friedman, "What does it mean to say that 'business' has responsibilities? Only people can have responsibilities".[198] The corporate person was thus reduced to the shareholders and their agents. At this juncture, is pertinent to consider two modern theories that have developed from earlier ideas and have been prominent in the discourse in recent times: the contractarian and the communitarian theories.[199]

Contractarian versus communitarian debate

The contractarian "nexus of contract" idea proceeded from the stand-point of Berle and Means[200] deemphasising the personality of the corporation.

---

195 E.M. Dodd, Jr., "For Whom are Corporate Managers Trustees?" (1932) 45 *Harvard Law Review* 1145.

196 A.A. Berle and G.C. Means, *The Modern Corporation and Private Property* (New York: Commerce Clearing House, 1932).

197 M. Friedman, "The Social Responsibility of Business is to Increase its Profits" in M.W. Hoffman and R.E. Frederick (eds), *Business Ethics, Readings and Cases in Corporate Morality* (New York: McGraw Hill, 1995), 133.

198 Ibid.

199 I. Lynch Fannon, *Working Within Two Kinds of Capitalism: Corporate Governance and Employee Stakeholding: US and EU Perspectives* (Oxford and Portland, OR: Hart Publishing 2003), 77–78.

200 Berle and Means (note 196).

Any notion of "corporate responsibility" or "citizenship" is denied.[201] The contractarian school is based on the law and economics contract theory, which sees the corporation as a microcosm of the larger market place.[202] The school has its foundation in the liberal-utilitarian models of Hobbes, Locke, Smith, Bentham and Mill[203] which emphasise the primacy of the law protecting rights and enforcing contracts. The theory conceives the company as a vehicle for contracting in which each constituency is placed within a contractual paradigm that only recognises bargained rights.[204] According to the theory the sole purpose of the corporation is to maximise shareholders' profit. All other constituencies within the corporation are protected to the extent of the provisions of the term of their contracts. To the contractarian school, the role of the state in corporate governance is "primarily to provide efficient default rules from which shareholders can choose to depart, and the few mandatory legal rules that do exist to restrain corporate behaviour are subject to evasion by choice of form".[205] Markets thus, to a large extent, set the terms of corporate activity, not the law.[206] The role of the law is therefore nothing more than to provide a set of loose contractual based rules to assist a collection of individuals in pursuing their interests in a free market.[207] According to Fischel, a prominent proponent of this school of thought: "Since it is a legal fiction, a corporation is incapable of having social or moral obligations, much in the same way that inanimate objects are incapable of having these obligations. Only people can have moral obligations or social responsibility."[208] The response of the communitarian school which presents a contrasting position to the contractarian school also side-stepped the argument as to the personhood of the corporation. The corporation is viewed by the communitarian school as a community of participants in which such values as trust and respect for others determine the success of the "venture". Although, the communitarian theorists have not fully defined the purpose of the corporation compared to the contractarian school, they introduce a new conception of the corporation through the recognition of the claims of other stakeholders. The model seeks to "regulate and define the legal institution of property

---

201 Millon 2001 (note 172).
202 Lynch Fannon (note 199), 80.
203 Ibid., 79.
204 Ibid., 77.
205 A. Winkler, "Case Studies in Conservative and Progressive Legal Orders: Corporate Law or the Law of Business? Stakeholders and Corporate Governance at the End of History" (2004) 67 *Law and Contemporary Problems*, 109.
206 Ibid. See also L. Mitchell, *Corporate Irresponsibility: America's Newest Export* (New Haven and London: Yale University Press 2001), 13.
207 Mitchell (note 206).
208 D.R. Fischel, "The Corporate Governance Movement" (1982) 35 *Vanderbilt Law Review*, 1259.

and contract in service of social values".[209] According to Parkinson[210] the idea behind this model is that the company is a complex social institution, which cannot be adequately conceptualised through the contractarian view or the concept of ownership. The model seeks to apply values, which are usually applied to non-commercial, social and political organisations in evaluating the governance of firms and in reforming the conception of the firm.[211]

The contractarian versus communitarian debates have driven the legal discourse on the purpose and nature of the corporation in recent years. According to Millon today's version of the debate over the desirability of shareholder primacy is largely conducted without regard to entity-based arguments over corporate personhood. The contractarians and communitarians focus on the insiders and corporate law therefore looks inward, at the relationship between corporation's various participants.[212]

Millon has suggested that perhaps the real challenge is to discard both entity- and aggregate-based arguments for responsibility and turn attention instead to the individual actors and the question of their responsibility, without regard to anyone's status in relation to a corporation.[213] It is argued, however, that the suggestion simply tries to wish away the legal theorisation about the company without taking into account the far-reaching impact legal theory has had on the conception of the corporation both within and outside the law. In addition, as Bainbridge observed in another context, one must have a positive and normatively viable conception of the entity being considered in order to be able to give specific evaluative criteria among others in analysing the role of such an entity.[214]

How are corporations conceived of today?

Following a thorough examination of the major theoretical conceptions of the corporation, Mitchell and Gabaldon considered which of the metaphors more accurately reflects the way corporations are treated today. Regarding the corporation as an aggregate of the natural persons model, they argued that save with the exception of laws relating to basic corporate liability for torts and crimes and some regulatory regimes such as the antitrust and securities regulation (which allows for corporate actors to be

209 I. Lynch Fannon, "The European Model of Corporate Governance: Prospects for Success in an Enlarged Europe" in P. Ali and G. Gregoriou, eds., *International Corporate Governance after Sarbanes-Oxley* (New Jersey: John Wiley & Sons 2006), 423.
210 J. Parkinson, "Models of the Company and the Employment Relationship" (2003) 41 *British Journal of Industrial Relations* 481.
211 Ibid.
212 Millon 2001 (note 172).
213 Ibid.
214 Bainbridge (note 167).

individually punished for unlawful conduct undertaken on behalf of corporations), the corporate entity is usually held accountable in most cases, implicating torts, crimes and statutory violations.

On the concept of the corporation as a person they concluded that:

> We think that for much of the twentieth and the twenty-first century, corporations pretty much have been regulated primarily according to the "corporations as individual, presumably, if not hopefully, with its own morality" model ... For example, the laws pursuant to which corporations are animated bestow upon them the same legal powers as individuals, and corporations are included, in the definition of the "persons" that can violate criminal laws. Whatever contemplation of morality inheres in criminal law, then, evidently does not discriminate between real people and corporations. Special accommodation of the corporation's fictional nature, as well as its sometimes extraordinary resources, sometimes is forced.[215]

This writer supports the conclusion of Mitchell and Gabaldon and would proceed to argue that based on this view the corporation has become an entrant into the social contract and should stand in the same position as individuals vis-à-vis international human rights norms.

The autonomy of the corporation

The position arrived at above recognises the autonomy of the corporation as a distinct "person" but contradicts Dan-Cohen's "personless corporation" which he described as an "intelligent machine".[216] It would be unrealistic to think of a corporation without human instrumentality. However, the very fact that the corporation acts through humans does not affect its separate identity. In the human world, children, the physically ill and people in persistent vegetative state are still humans with distinct personality despite the

---

215 Mitchell and Gabaldon (note 146), 1661. The conclusion of Mitchell and Gabaldon, in the view of this writer, is more representative of actual developments in this area of the law than the conclusions of Wood and Scharffs (note 165). Wallace also argued that corporate entities have gradually become endowed by civil and common law systems with capacity initially and normally attributable to natural persons. See C.D. Wallace, *The Multinational Enterprise and Legal Control: Host State Sovereignty in an Era of Economic Globalization* (The Hague: Martinus Nijhoff Publishers, 2002), 10.

216 M. Dan-Cohen, *Rights, Persons, and Organisations* (Berkeley: University of California Press, 1986), 49. Dan-Cohen constructed a hypothetical corporation which repurchased its own shares, sacked all its human personnel and replaced them with computers. He concluded that this possibility demonstrates that corporations are merely mechanical and not human and so they have no capacity to bear rights. However, as shown in this chapter this flies in the face of reality. Corporations have the capacity to bear rights and they have rights ascribed to them independent of their human participants.

fact they need to act through others. The point that is being made, and will be elucidated upon later in this chapter, is that the rights that are ascribable to the corporate entity as distinct from its shareholders and management have increased because of its acquisition of an autonomous identity.

Each human person that participates in the corporation, whether as shareholders or management or employees, cedes a certain amount of their autonomy as humans to the corporation. The shareholders give up the right to control their properties, employees their labour and management their services and how it is used. They are thus only participants in the larger autonomy of the corporation. The autonomy is different from that of individual participants because its exercise is distinct from that of the participants and is exercisable only in the name of the company. For example, under the company law of most jurisdictions, the directors who exercise the autonomy of the corporation have fiduciary duties to the company.

Analysing the company from this perspective is not new. However, this perspective has been neglected in the discourse.[217] The concept of the "enterprise-in-itself" which expresses the enterprise's autonomy as a social system and an economic power distinct from either managers or employees has been canvassed by German scholars in the past.[218] In more recent times, Teubner has engaged with this illuminating concept in his consideration of the expression "company's interest" in company law. Teubner posited that to speak of the company's interest is not the same thing as the interest of shareholders or employees but the interest of the enterprise "in itself". According to him:

> People and things are transferred into the enterprise's environment and the enterprise is constructed in radical fashion exclusively as an ensemble of communications. That is why the term "enterprise-in-itself" seems appropriate, underlining the self-reference and autonomy of the organisation.[219]

He argued that the ensemble is "effectively separated from acting individuals, whether shareholders, workers or management".[220] He further argued that because the modern corporation has gained a far-reaching autonomy from shareholders and management it has a wider role in the larger society.[221] He wrote:

---

217 G. Teubner, "Company Interest: The Public Interest of the Enterprise 'in Itself'" in R. Rogowski and T. Wilthagen, eds., *Reflexive Labour Law: Studies in Industrial Relations and Employment Regulation* (Deventer and Boston: Kluwer Law and Taxation Publishers, 1994), 22.
218 Ibid., 20.
219 Ibid., 25.
220 Ibid., 26.
221 Ibid., 26.

The company interest cannot be identified with the interest of the shareholders. Moreover, it is different from the interests of the interest-groups involved. None of the resource-holders, whether share-holders, workers, or management, are the "subject" of the company interest. It is the "corporate actor" itself, that is to say the autonomous ensemble of communications in its orientation towards broader social expectations. At the same time this rules out the overall economic system and the political system as subjects of this interest.[222]

Teubner's analysis goes against the long established definition of "company's interest" which equates the expression with the interest of share-holders.[223] However, by emphasising the autonomous nature of the modern corporation, Teubner's analysis is closer to reality than the traditional view. For example, when Dine considered the question who owns the assets of the company, she argued that the company should be seen as the true owner. According to her: "We should understand the company as truly owner of its assets with the managers exercising its ownership rights, at present uncontrolled since the claim to control by shareholders is seen to be an unfounded use of property rhetoric."[224] Thus, Dine underscores the distinct autonomy of the corporation. In the same vein Teubner observed elsewhere that "the historical liberation of the legal person and the emergence of the joint stock company as the typical large-scale organisation ... was concerned with the autonomy of the corporation vis-à-vis its environment and shareholders".[225]

Thus, it is argued that the modern corporation has gradually assumed a life of its own with distinct interests, different from that of shareholders and management. The implication of this autonomy is discussed in the following sections of this chapter.

The social contract as justification for CSR

The dominance of the social contract in political theorisation has led to interest in analysing the role of business in society from the perspective of a social contract. The social contract concept was developed by philosophers of the seventeenth and eighteenth century including Thomas Hobbes, John Locke and Jean-Jacques Rousseau. It is important to note as a starting point that the idea predates the nineteenth century modern

---

222 Ibid., 27.
223 For a discussion of the traditional view see D.J. Bakibinga, "Directors' Duty to Act Bona Fide in the Interest of the Company" (1990) 39 (2) *International and Comparative Law Quarterly* 451.
224 Dine (note 135) 263–264.
225 G. Teubner, "Unitas Multiplex: Corporate Governance as an Example" in Gunther Teubner, *Law as an Autopoietic System* (Oxford: Blackwell, 1993), 146.

joint stock and limited liability corporations by about 200 years. The social contract is an implied agreement by which people agreed to create government and maintain social order. It provides the rationale behind western democracies' ideology that the legitimate state authority must be derived from the consent of the governed. The view, in the context of this book, is that an implicit social agreement also exists between business and society. It is to this implicit agreement that we can look to identify the duties and rights of business vis-à-vis society. The contract is considered to be an evolving document. Perhaps one important contribution of Donaldson in this connection is his attempt to analyse the social contract between the corporation and society.[226] According to him the political social contract provides a clue for understanding the contract for business: if the political contract serves as a justification for the existence of the state, then the business contract by parity of reasoning should serve as justification for the existence of the corporation.

The social contract: Donaldson's approach

In his *Theory of Justice* John Rawls included corporations (as well as states and churches) along with individuals when he listed the parties in the "original position".[227] However, he accorded priority to individuals in the social contract and he did not explore in detail the corporation's status within the scheme. Donaldson resorted to the social contract theory in order to interpret the nature of the corporation's indirect obligations which according to him are notoriously slippery.[228] What he considered indirect obligations straddle the areas covered by CSR. However, in addressing the issue he relied on his idea of what the law says a corporation is, which as this chapter has shown earlier, is not the case.

Donaldson drew a parallel analogy to traditional devices in social contract theory and suggested looking at the state of nature which he called for his purpose "state of individual production", that is the state of affairs existing before the introduction of productive organisations. In the state of individual production, there would exist "economically interested persons who have not yet organised themselves or been organized into productive organisations".[229] The strategy according to him involves:

1   Characterising conditions in a state of individual production (without productive organisation).

---

226   Donaldson (note 161).
227   J. Rawls, *A Theory of Justice* (revised edition, Cambridge, MA: Harvard University Press, 1999), 126.
228   Donaldson (note 161) 36.
229   Ibid., 44–45.

2 Indicating how certain problems are remedied by the introduction of productive organisations.
3 Using the reasons generated in the second step as a basis for specifying a social contract between society and its productive organisations.

According to Donaldson, two principal classes of people stand to benefit or be harmed by the introduction of productive organisations: the consumers and the employees (i.e. society as consumers and employees).[230] It is, however, argued that narrowing down society to consumer and employees in analysing the social contract would impair Donaldson's attempt as it would be difficult to account for all the ramifications of the externalities of corporation from that perspective. Host communities, for example, are as much affected by companies' operations as consumers and employees.

What are the terms of the contracts? Donaldson broadly enumerated three.[231] According to him people as consumers would hope that the introduction of productive organisations would better satisfy their interests for shelter, food, entertainment, transportation, health care and clothing. There is therefore a promise from the standpoint of the corporation to "enhance the satisfaction of economic interests".[232] Second, people as workers would also expect to increase income potentials, diffuse personal liability and the adjustment of personal income allocation in a way that avoids the vicissitudes of life. However, the contract recognises that there are major drawbacks to the introduction of productive organisations just as there were drawbacks in the political social contract (governments' tendencies to abuse their power). He noted that potential harms to customers include pollution, depletion of natural resources, destruction of personal accountability and misuse of power. In the case of employees the harms include the alienation of workers, restriction of workers' control over working, conditions and the dehumanisation of the worker. Thus he posited that the social contract will specify that these negative consequences be minimised while the positive benefits are maximised. According to him, as part of such a social contract from the standpoint of consumers, productive organisations should minimise:

1 Pollution and depletion of natural resources,
2 Destruction of personal accountability,
3 The misuse of political power.

---

230 Note that in Donaldson's reply to Hodapp's criticisms of his attempt he argued that these two classes are broadly defined and before the hypothetical contract they are "prospective classes". See T. Donaldson, "Social Contracts and the Corporations: A Reply to Hodapp" 1989 (8) *Journal of Business Ethics* 133.
231 Donaldson (note 161) 45.
232 Ibid.

And from the perspective of the worker, corporations should minimise:

1   Workers alienation,
2   Lack of workers' control over working conditions,
3   Monotony and the dehumanisation of the worker.

Hence, the social contract according to Donaldson requires that productive organisations maximise evils relative to consumers' and workers' welfare. The question would then be how corporations make the necessary trade-offs. According to Donaldson, society might believe that on balance, people as workers stand to lose from the introduction of productive organisations, and that potential alienation, loss of control and other drawbacks make the overall condition of the worker worse than before. But if the benefit to people as consumers fully overshadows these drawbacks, the contract would still be expected to be enacted.

However, he placed an important caveat: people make trade-offs only on the condition that it does not violate a minimum standard of justice, for example by reducing a given class of people to inhuman existence, subsistence poverty or enslavement.[233] He thus posited that an inference could be drawn that a tenet of the social contract will be that productive organisations are to remain within the bounds of the general canons of justice. Recognising the limitation in deciding what justice requires, he opined that the application of the concept of justice to productive organisations appears to imply that productive organisations avoid deception or fraud, that they show respect for their workers as human beings and that they avoid any practice that systematically worsens the situation of a given group in society.

Criticisms of Donaldson's analysis

There have been many criticisms of Donaldson's analysis.[234] Hodapp's criticisms are particularly apposite because of his direct attack on the social contract theory. Donaldson has responded to Hodapp's criticisms[235] but I will consider the issues he raised from a legal point of view. Hodapp criticised Donaldson's social contract theory as a methodology which is circular, presupposing the information which it is supposed to generate. He argued that Donaldson had already assumed the purpose of the corporation before engaging in the imaginative process. He contended that unlike the threat (which Hobbes described) which may constrain those who might not wish to enter the social contract (remaining in a state of nature

---

233   Ibid., 53.
234   See for examples P.F. Hodapp, "Can There be a Social Contract with Business?" (1996) 9 *Journal of Business Ethics* 127 and G.C. Sollars, "The Corporation as Actual Agreements" (2002) 12 *Business Quarterly* 351.
235   Donaldson (note 230), 133.

with no protection under the social contract) no such threat can be found in respect of productive organisations because of the rights of individuals who set them up. Individuals who create productive organisations have natural rights which are attributable to the productive organisations and other people in the society may not brazenly override these rights based on their consumptive and employment rights. According to him,

> The conflict is not between an abstract entity without any natural rights and the rest of us who possesses consumptive and employment rights; rather the conflict is between individuals with productive rights who have created productive organisations and the rest of us who have consumptive and employment rights.[236]

He concluded that the business of business should be business. Hodapp then reached an unsupportable conclusion in respect of the political contract and the corporation when he said: "The Corporation is only an agent for the state and has no authority to make such contracts on its own behalf. It can only make such contracts on behalf of its principal, the state".[237]

Hodapp's assertion here can only be valid if the corporation can be completely equated with the individuals who set them up. This is not true as the corporation is not equated with its shareholders.[238] It has "its own interest" and a threat exists as to whether society will continue to allow it to exist in the form which it presently takes. Furthermore, his conclusion that the business of business is business will not stand up in the light of recent developments and business approaches to other stakeholder issues.[239] As to his conclusion that the corporation is an agent of the state, it is hard to imagine the modern corporation as an agent of the state. While the interests of the modern corporation and government sometimes coincide, they do not always coincide. His criticisms are based on one of the possible interpretations of the nature of the corporation, that is the "corporation as individual private property right".

The social contract, morality and corporations: a different approach

In a widely cited work, Wilson posited that:

> Corporations operate under the terms of two charters: a former written, legal charter; and an unwritten, but critically important, social

---

236 Ibid.
237 Ibid.
238 Dine (note 135) 45.
239 The contention that the corporation has only one goal, which is to maximise shareholders' profit is fading fast in the face of widespread practice of CSR.

charter … It is the unwritten charter of societal expectations that determines the values to which the corporation must adhere and sets the terms under which the public grants legitimacy to the corporation.[240]

Wilson contended that as business organisations become the principal form of economic organisation, the number of interested parties multiply, the relationships become more complex and the interests of more and more constituencies are involved. According to him,

> This expansion of constituencies and interests has progressively enlarged the social role and importance of the corporation, broadened its responsibilities, and underscored the fact that it must reflect the society's shared values – social, moral, political, and legal as well as economic. Building the corporation on a foundation of economic values alone has never been a satisfying solution, either for its members or society. Now it is not even a viable option.[241]

He thus posited that new rules are emerging from societal expectations (as demonstrated by the changing practices of companies to CSR) which corporations would have to contend with later.[242] According to Dine the expectation referred to by Wilson can only be found by developing jurisprudence which refines and makes precise the vague aspirational goals currently presented in CSR debates.[243]

This book argues that drawing from legal theorists' discourse on the nature of the corporation and emerging jurisprudence (discussed below) the corporation has moved from being just an artificial person to something similar to a natural person. This change should inform the understanding of the role of the corporation under the social contract. It is contended by this writer that the existence of the political social contract before the introduction of productive organisations or corporations has a bearing on any analysis of the social responsibility of business. The corporations entered the scene at a later stage and would thus negotiate a contract based on the existing political social contract. A distinction must be made between the earlier chartered corporation and the modern incorporated companies. This is important because persons or entities who are parties to the contract are expected to be independent, rational and equal participants.[244]

---

240   I. Wilson, *The New Rules of Corporate Conduct: Rewriting the Social Charter* (Westport, CT: Quorum Books, 2000), 3.

241   Ibid., 4.

242   Ibid., 33–137.

243   Dine (note 135) 234.

244   M.C. Nussbaum, "Beyond the Social Contract: Toward Global Justice" The Tanner Lectures on Human Values delivered at Australian National University, Canberra, 12 and 13 November 2002 and at Clare Hall, University of Cambridge, 5 and 6 March 2003.

The requirement of independence, rationality and equality would imply that the earlier chartered corporations, which were completely subject to state control, cannot reasonably be argued to have been a party to the social contract. This is mainly because of their lack of independence and the unequal status attached to them by virtue of the manner of their creation and the constraints placed on their operation by the state. The chartered corporations were simply instruments in the hand of the society. It is this kind of corporation that could probably come within Hodapp's analysis. One of the shortcomings of Donaldson's attempt is his failure to recognise this distinction.

However, the transition from chartered corporation to the incorporated modern company changed the complexion of the corporate form and its relationship with society. As argued earlier, the corporation gradually assumed a life of its own in law and in fact. It became distinct from shareholders and has an interest different from shareholders and management. It has autonomous status with important consequences in law. According to Cerri, the most striking consequence of corporate personhood is the use of constitutional amendment by American business corporations.[245] This has led to the courts treating the corporate form as an individual, a kind of person that can enjoy rights attributable to humans.[246]

For example, a significant development in the United States was in *Santa Clara County* v. *Southern Pacific Railroad Company*[247] where a private company was held to be a natural person under the US Constitution and to have the right to be protected under the Fourteenth Amendment.[248] Several judgements have followed this trend in the United States. The US Supreme Court in the *Santa Clara County* case refused to take argument on the personhood of the corporation:

> The court does not wish to hear [oral] argument on the question whether the provision of the Fourteenth Amendment to the Constitution, which forbids a state to deny to any person within its jurisdiction the equal protection of the law, applies to corporations. We are all of the opinion it does.[249]

---

245 Cerri (note 192).
246 P. Blumberg, "The Multinational Challenge to Corporate Law" (Oxford: Oxford University Press 1993), 30–45; C.J. Mayer, "Personalizing the Impersonal: Corporations and the Bill of Rights" (1989–1990) 41 *Hastings Law Journal* 577: See also J.D. Ohlins, "Is the Concept of the Person Necessary for Human Rights?" (2005) 105 *Columbia Law Review* 226–227.
247 118 US 394 (1886).
248 According to Mayer 1886 marked the year when the corporation was personified in the United States. See Mayer (note 246).
249 118 US 394 (1886), 396.

The decision in *Pembina Consolidated Silver Mining and Milling Co.* v. *Pennsylvania*[250] without saying explicitly that corporations are persons took the same approach. According to the US Supreme Court "under the designation of person [in the Fourteenth Amendment] there is no doubt that a private corporation is included".

The US Supreme Court finally equated the corporation with a person in *Covington and Lexington Turnpike Road Co.* v. *Sandford.*[251] The court relied on *Santa Clara* and *Pembina* among other cases. According to the court "corporations are persons within the meaning of the constitutional provisions forbidding the deprivation of property without due process of laws, as well as denial of the equal protection of the laws".

Furthermore, the Fifth Amendment of the US Constitution which provides that "nor shall any person be subject for the same offence to be twice put in jeopardy of life or limb" which directly refers to natural person with the use of "life or limb" has been applied to corporations by the court.[252] The US courts have also held that the First Amendment on freedom of speech is applicable to corporations.[253] In other cases the courts have ruled that the corporations are entitled to Fourth Amendment "search and seizure" protection,[254] freedom of speech,[255] the right to influence political elections or referenda through money spending,[256] the right to protection of commercial speech,[257] and the right to privacy.[258]

Commenting on these developments Mayer wrote:

> Too frequently the extension of corporate constitutional rights is a zero-sum game that diminishes the rights and powers of real individuals.... The legal system thus is creating unaccountable Frankensteins that have superhuman powers but are nonetheless constitutionally shielded from much actual and potential law enforcement as well as accountability to real persons such as workers, consumers, and taxpayers.[259]

As noted in Chapter 1, the jurisprudence of the European Court of Human Rights (ECtHR) in this regard is also interesting to note. While

---

250   125 US 181 (1888).
251   164 US 578, 592 (1896).
252   Blumberg (note 246) 59; See also *United States* v. *Martin Linen Supply Co.*, 430 US 564 (1977); *American Tobacco Co.* v. *United States*, 328 US 781 (1946); *United States* v. *Security National Bank*, 546 F. 2d 492 (2d Cir. 1970).
253   *First National Bank* v. *Bellotti* 435 US 765 (1978).
254   *Hale* v. *Henkel* 201 US 43 (1906).
255   *Buckley* v. *Valeo* 424 US 1 (1976); *First National Bank* v. *Bellotti* 435 US 765 (1978); *Austin* v. *Michigan Chamber of Commerce* 494 US 652 (1990).
256   *Central Hudson Gas and Electric Company* v. *Public Utilities Commission* 447 US 557 (1980).
257   *Pacific Gas and Electric Corporation* v. *Public Utilities Commission* 475 US 1 (1986); *International Dairy Foods Association* v. *Amestoy* 92 F.3d 67 (1996).
258   *See* v. *City of Seattle* 387 US 541 (1967); *Marshall* v. *Barlow's Inc* 436 US 307 (1978).
259   Mayer (note 246), 658–659; William Greider, in the same vein noted:

the ECtHR has not concerned itself much with the question of the person-hood of the corporation, it has made important pronouncements which implicate the status of the corporation in the interpretation of the provisions of the European Convention on Human Rights (ECHR).[260]

The ECHR offers wide ranging "human rights" protection for business entities despite the fact that these entities are not human.[261] According to Emberland, the term "everyone", which appears frequently in the convention, can also be applied to corporate entities.[262] The ECtHR has held that corporations possess the right to property in article 1 of the first protocol, the right to freedom of expression in article 10, the right to fair trial in article 6 and the right to respect for private life in article 8.[263] For example, the ECtHR has recognised that corporations enjoy the right provided under article 8(1) which provides that "everyone has the right to respect for his private and family life, his home and his correspondence". The court held in *Colas Est SA* v. *France*[264] that the right to protection of one's home extends to business premises.[265] The court has also allowed corporations to benefit from article 10(1) which provides that

> Everyone has the right to freedom of expression. This shall include freedom to hold opinions and to receive and impart information and ideas without interference by public authority and regardless of frontiers.

> In the modern era of regulation [corporate lawyers] are invoking the Bill of Rights to protect their organisations from federal laws ... Corporations in other words, claim to be "citizens" of the Republic, not simply for propaganda or good public relations, but in the actual legal sense of claiming constitutional rights and protections ... Whatever legal theories may eventually develop around this question, the political implication are profound. If corporations are citizens, then other citizens-the living, breathing kind-necessarily become less important to the process of self-government.
>
> (Quoted in R.A.G. Monks and N. Minnow, *Corporate Governance* (second edition, Malden: Blackwell Publishing, 2001), 13)

260 Convention for the Protection of Human Rights and Fundamental Freedoms, 213 UNTS 222, entered into force 3 September 1953, as amended by protocols 3, 5, 8 and 11 which entered into force 21 September 1970, 20 December 1971, 1 January 1990 and 1 November 1998 respectively.

261 M.K. Addo, "The Corporation as a Victim of Human Rights Violations" in Michael Addo, ed., *Human Rights Standards and the Responsibility of Transnational Corporations* (The Hague: Kluwer Law International, 1999), 187, 194.

262 M. Emberland, "Protection against Unwarranted Searches and Seizures of Corporate Premises under Art. 8 of the European Convention on Human Rights: The *Colas Est SA* v. *France* Approach" (2003) 25 *Michigan Journal of International Law* 77.

263 P.T. Muchlinski, "Human Rights and Multinationals: Is there a Problem?"(2001) 77 *International Affairs* 31.

264 App. no. 3797/97, ECtHR (16 April 2002).

265 Emberland (note 262).

This Article shall not prevent states from requiring the licensing of broadcasting, television or cinema enterprises.[266]

In *Autronic AG* v. *Switzerland*[267] the court held that:

> In the court's view, neither Autronic AG'S legal status as a limited company nor the fact that its activities were commercial nor the intrinsic nature of freedom of expression can deprive Autronic AG of the protection of Article 10 … The Article … applies to "everyone", whether natural or legal persons.

Thus the corporation is treated under the law as a person with the ability to enjoy human rights.

It thus stands to reason that having acquired such a personhood, the modern corporation should come within the existing social contract as a later entrant to join the state and the individual. If, as it is argued, the modern corporation is a later entrant to the existing social contract, what then is its relationship to the existing contract? It is posited that its entrance is conditioned by the terms of the existing contract as it has evolved over time. Second it is argued that since the corporation becomes a beneficiary under the contract it should have corresponding obligations the same way the social contract regulates the relationship between individuals, society and government.

The social contract, the law and international human rights law

The social contract theory has influenced much of our contemporary law so that it is not possible to ignore it in the discussion of the social responsibility of corporations. As Palmer noted, the constitutions of many states have been explicitly or implicitly founded upon the principles of the social contract.[268] However, the most important implication in this connection is its relationship with international human rights law. The human rights concept as we have it today and the concept of inalienable rights have their origin in the social contract tradition. The UN Human Rights Charter implicitly assumed as its foundation the concept of a social contract. The human rights discourse is overpowering as a standard setting paradigm at all levels of human relations and it is based on the idea that

---

266   See for examples *Sunday Times* v. *UK* A no. 30 (1980) 2 EHHR 245; *Markt intern Verlag GmbH and Klaus Beermann* v. *Germany* ser. A no. 165 (1990) 12 EHRR 161; *Groppera Radio AG and Ors* v. *Switzerland* A no. 173 (1990) 12 EHRR 321.

267   Ser. A no. 178 (1990) 12 EHRR 485.

268   E. Palmer, "Multinational Corporations and the Social Contract" (2001) 31 (3) *Journal of Business Ethics* 245.

there are rights inherent in every individual which are greater than the power of government and cannot be taken away by the government.

The idea of human rights can be traced to the concept of natural rights which is commonly used as a synonym for human rights.[269] There are two important ways in which human rights remains an offshoot of natural rights. First, like natural rights it ascribes rights to people in their natural capacity as human beings, i.e. merely being human justifies having certain entitlements. Second human rights provide standards by which we assess legitimacy of governments. Human rights are deemed to be beyond the prerogative of any authority. While aspects of human rights norms have been codified as binding legal instruments others are accepted as aspirational. An important point to note here is that human rights come with a duty imposed on others – if A has a right to life then B has an obligation not to take his life.

Human rights are described as the flip side of the duties under the social contract. It is a benefit derived from the social contract. The rights derived impose duties on all other members of the society and the government. If, as it is argued, the corporation is some kind of person and has all the attributes that allow the natural person to enter into the social contract and if it has been accorded rights attributable to the natural person, then it follows that it should be constrained in the same manner that the natural person is constrained under the law, including international human rights law. The argument is thus that the corporation as a person stands in the same position as the natural person vis-à-vis international human rights law and as such should have similar duties and responsibilities under international human rights law.

It is conceded that traditionally states were, and to a considerable extent continue to be, the main subject of international law, including international human rights law.[270] However, as many commentators have pointed out, developments in the last century have accommodated intergovernmental organisations into the category and individuals are increasingly being recognised as subjects of international law.[271] (Indeed Ochoa has even radically suggested that individuals should be recognised as participants in international law formation.[272])

---

269 Grear (note 186); P. Jones, "Human Rights" in E. Craig, ed., *Routledge Encyclopedia of Philosophy* (London: Routledge 2006), online, available at: www.rep.routledge.com (accessed 2 February 2010); see also B.H. Weston "Human Rights" (1984) 6 (3) *Human Rights Quarterly*, 258–259.

270 M. Shan Alam, "Enforcement of International Human Rights Law by Domestic Courts: A Theoretical and Practical Study" (2006) 53 *Netherlands International Law Review* 401; See also R.A. Mullerson, "Human Rights and the Individual as Subject of International Law: A Soviet View" 1 (1990) *European Journal of International Law* 33, 40.

271 Ibid.

272 C. Ochoa, "The Individual and Customary International Law Formation" (2007) 48 *Virginia Journal of International Law* 119.

The jurisprudence that has emerged from the International War Crimes Tribunal at Nuremberg and Tokyo, the International Criminal Tribunals for Rwanda and Yugoslavia have confirmed these developments.[273] One of the main principles that emerged from the Nuremberg trials and is a cornerstone of international criminal law, is that anyone who commits an act which constitutes a crime under international law is responsible for it and therefore liable to be punished for it. In the trial of the German Major War Criminals (HMSO)[274] the Tribunal stated:

> It was submitted that international law is concerned with the actions of sovereign states, and provides no punishment for individuals; and further, that where the act in question is an act of state, those who carry it out are not personally responsible, but are protected by the doctrine of sovereignty of the state. In the opinion of the tribunal, both these submissions must be rejected.
>
> Many other authorities could be cited, but enough has been said to show that individuals can be punished for violations of international law. Crimes against international law are committed by men, not by abstract entities, and only by punishing individuals who commit such crimes can the provisions of international law be enforced.

This principle of individual responsibility was also affirmed by article 7(1) and article 33 of the statutes of the International Criminal Tribunals for the former federal republic of Yugoslavia and article 6(1) and article 22 of the statutes of the International Criminal Tribunal for Rwanda.

Therefore, if the corporation has acquired a personhood status that enables it to enjoy rights accorded to the natural persons under both domestic and international law it should be amenable to human rights norms like the natural person. In light of these developments Kinley and Chambers have argued that: "Considering the imposition of fundamental, international legal obligations on such non state-actors as individuals and armed oppression groups, it would be anomalous for companies to remain almost wholly outside the ambit of international law."[275] It is instructive to note that while in the United States, the corporation have acquired significant natural person's status with the ability to enjoy constitutional rights protection; developments in the United States appear to be introducing the flip side of that personhood status. Significantly, the Alien Torts Claim Act litigation, which made corporations, to a limited extent, amenable to

---

273 Alam (note 270).
274 *The Trial of German Major War Criminals (HMSO)* Judgement (Lawrence LJ): 30 September 1946–1 October 1946, 41–42.
275 D. Kinley and R. Chambers, "The UN Human Rights Norms for Corporations: The Private Implication of Public International Law" (2006) 6 *Human Rights Law Review* 493.

account for egregious human rights violations, is indicative of the possibility of the flip side of the personhood of the corporation under the social contract taking root.[276]

Summary

This chapter has examined the rise of the CSR philosophy as an alternative offered by MNCs to address externalities of their operations instead of the traditional form of regulation. The chapter explored how the law is interacting with CSR. The chapter noted that CSR lacks coherence because of its lack of foundational basis and the indeterminate nature of its ambit. The chapter argued that the concept needs to be grounded in law in order to be meaningful. The chapter contended that the arguments from other fields in the analysis of the social responsibility of corporations have been influenced by an understanding of what the law says the corporation is which they have confined to the artificial personhood perspective. The chapter showed how this is a limited understanding of legal theorisation of corporations. It was further argued that the CSR concept as presently construed by corporations and as demonstrated by emerging corporate practice is an acceptance of moral and social responsibility by corporations which the law should respond to appropriately. The chapter used insights from the influential social contract theories in defining the moral responsibility of business. It was argued that having been accorded the status of the natural person under the law, the corporation is a later entrant into the social contract on the same footing with the natural person. This position is buttressed by the continuing extension of rights of the natural person to corporations in different jurisdictions. It is argued that the modern corporation is treated as a natural person by its ability to enjoy human rights and this recognition should have reciprocal obligations by placing the corporation on the same footing as an individual under international human rights law. It is therefore posited that to the extent that international human rights law recognises individual responsibility, such responsibility should also be applicable to corporations. This conceptual development will also have significant implications for domestic regimes.

---

276 See Dickerson (note 136).

4 Legal and institutional framework and the control of multinationals in developing countries with a focus on Nigeria

It is generally assumed that home jurisdictions, especially in the countries of the South, are impotent when it comes to the control of multinational corporations (MNCs).[1] While this assertion is largely correct, this book contends that there cannot be an effective control of MNCs whether at international or regional level without a corresponding development of a minimum institutional framework at the domestic level.[2] This chapter uses the Nigerian legal framework for the regulation of MNCs as an example with a view to determining the weaknesses in the domestic forum, asking what minimum standards should be in place and how such standards can be achieved. References shall also be made to other relevant jurisdictions. The issues raised in this chapter relate to understanding the gap within the domestic context that has made corporate social responsibility (CSR) important in the circumstances. It further analyses the issues that have emerged from the operation of MNCs within the local context and the recourse by corporations to the concept of CSR. The chapter's position is that while CSR practices by MNCs are becoming more widespread, the development cannot replace the need for effective home state regulation. It also examines the weaknesses in the domestic legal framework and suggests viable possibilities within the local context that may enhance the control of MNCs. The areas of law that are relevant in the control of MNCs which are examined in the chapter include company law, tort law, human rights law, criminal law, labour law and anti-corruption regulation.

---

1 See J. Woodroffe, "Regulating Multinational Corporations in a World of Nation States" in Michael Addo, ed., *Human Rights Standards and the Responsibility of Transnational Corporations* (The Hague: Kluwer Law International, 1999), 131–142, 139; D. Kinley and J. Tadaki, "From Talk to Walk: The Emergence of Human Rights Responsibilities for Corporations at International Law" (2003–2004) 44 *Virginia Journal of International Law* 931, 933; T. McInerney, "Putting Regulation before Responsibility: Towards Binding Norms of Corporate Social Responsibility" (2007) 40 *Cornell International Law Journal* 171; D. Brown and N. Woods, *Making Global Self-Regulation Effective in Developing Countries* (Oxford University Press, Oxford, 2007) 1.
2 See McInerney (note 1) 171 at 189–190, 191–192.

MNCs and CSR in Nigeria

CSR practices are most prominent in the oil and gas sector in Nigeria and among MNCs which have been operating in Nigeria for a long time. The major tools of CSR employed by MNCs in Nigeria include corporate codes of conduct, voluntary social reporting and community development projects. The areas covered by these CSR initiatives include human rights, labour issues, transparency, bribery and corruption, employees' welfare, environmental issues, disclosure of information and consumer protection.[3] Most, if not all, of these areas are traditionally governed by hard law. It thus seems inappropriate that CSR is conveniently described as going beyond the requirements of the law.[4] The question then is why has CSR become so important for the operation of MNCs in Nigeria and why is the law taking a back seat? According to a report on Statoil, a Norwegian MNC in Nigeria,

> Because of past and present experiences with petroleum activity in the Niger Delta, with widespread environmental destruction and little or no economic development, the population is deeply suspicious towards oil companies. Because of this, Statoil has to prove itself when it comes to corporate social responsibility in Nigeria.[5]

A closer look at the domestic forum (in this case Nigeria) reveals that the gaps within the domestic law, complemented by the absence of an enforceable international framework for controlling MNCs has amplified the importance of CSR. However, commentators have noted that the adoption of CSR as a strategy in Nigeria has failed to remove the suspicion and conflicts that exist between MNCs and other stakeholders.[6]

Brief history of MNCs in Nigeria

The first MNCs entered the Nigerian jurisdiction during the colonial period under the British. It may thus be instructive to note the trend of

---

3 See for examples Shell Nigeria Annual Report, *People and the Environment* (2006); Shell's General Business Principles, online, available at: www.shell.com.ng/home/content/ nga/aboutshell/who_we_are/our_values_and_principles/ (accessed 26 September 2010); S. Amadi, M. Germiso and A. Henriksen, *Statoil in Nigeria: Transparency and Local Content*, Report Number 1/2006 (Oslo: Framtiden, I vare hender, 2006) 19.

4 C. Parker, *The Open Corporation: Effective Self-Regulation and Democracy* (Cambridge: Cambridge University Press, 2002); D. McBarnet, A. Voiculescu and T. Campbell, eds., *The New Corporate Accountability: Corporate Social Responsibility and the Law* (Cambridge: Cambridge University Press, 2007).

5 Amadi *et al.* (note 3).

6 U. Idemudia and U.E. Ite "Corporate-Community Relations in Nigeria's Oil Industry: Challenges and Imperatives" (2006) 13 *Corporate Social Responsibility and Environmental Management*, 194.

domestic law from this period in order to appreciate the dynamics of domestic regulation as regards MNCs. The British colonial administration established the basis of the modern Nigerian legal and institutional framework. One of the major aims of the British colonial administration was to make the colonies self sufficient and profitable.[7] This aim influenced major decisions that were taken in the country that impacted on the operations of corporations in those early days. A significant early development was that in 1900 all mineral rights were nationalised and vested in the British crown and in 1907, contrary to widespread traditional practices of communal landholding, all lands were also nationalised and vested in the British crown.[8]

The policies of the colonial administration gave the pioneering British companies a free space in which to operate. The companies operated under a favourable legal regime because of their links to the colonial power.[9] During the colonial era and before the discovery of oil, the most important mineral resource produced in Nigeria was tin.[10] To exploit this resource, the British company, the Niger Company, set up the Naraguta Tin Mining Company under the charge of an engineer, H.W. Laws. In 1904, Laws led a military campaign on the location of the resource, the Jos Plateau, and took over control of the area from indigenous people who were actively engaged in mining activities in the area. Though there was no official policy statement by the colonial government as to the displacement of indigenous people by the company, Lord Lugard, the head of the British administration in Nigeria stated that:

> Minerals can only be discovered and exploited by the science and capital of Europeans, and to them the government can provide at once more security and more control than native chiefs and can allocate the royalties for the good of the country as a whole.[11]

Colonial administration and the oil industry

Oil prospecting started in Nigeria in 1906.[12] However, legislation was not introduced to govern the oil industry until the end of 1914 with the

---

7 M.S. Steyn, *Oil Politics in Ecuador and Nigeria: A Perspective from Environmental History on the Struggles between Ethnics Minority and National Governments* PhD Thesis submitted to the Faculty of Humanities (Department of History) University of the Free State, Bloemfontein, South Africa (2003), 74, 147.

8 Ibid., 148.

9 B.O. Nwabueze, *A Constitutional History of Nigeria* (London: C. Hurst & Co Publishers, 1982), 35–37.

10 J.H. Morrison "Early Tin Production and Nigerian Labour on the Jos, Plateau 1960–1921" (1977) 11/2 *Canada Journal of African Studies* 205, 205.

11 Ibid., 208.

12 Steyn (note 7), 180.

introduction of the Oil Ordinance no. 17. Under the law, oil exploration and exploitation was limited to British citizens and British companies.[13] In 1937, an exploration licence covering the entire mainland of Nigeria was granted to Shell-BP by the British colonial government.[14] The area covered was 357,000 square miles. The company was able to explore and select 15,000 square miles of the original concession without competition, thus securing a first mover advantage over later entrants to the market.[15] In 1958, the company discovered oil in commercial quantities in Oloibiri in the present Rivers State.[16] By 1959, on the brink of Nigeria's independence, the sole-concessionary right granted to Shell-BP had been reviewed and companies of other nationalities from Europe and the United States were brought into the field. These companies include Mobil, Gulf, Agip, Safrap (now Elf), Tenneco and Amoseas (now Texaco and Chevron).[17] In 1959, the Petroleum Profits Tax Ordinance legislated for the equal division of the profits accruing from oil exploration between the companies and the country for the first time.

Legal developments after Nigeria's independence and the indigenisation policy: a synopsis

Nigeria became independent in 1960 and legislative changes were introduced that altered the status quo. As noted above, for example, Shell-BP had to surrender some of its oil concessions and other MNCs were allowed into the field.[18] Independence brought many more changes. Legislation was brought in to control some aspects of the operations of foreign companies, including the following major initiatives. The Exchange Control

---

13 It has, however, been noted that this provision resulted in a paradox because the first company ever to undertake oil exploration in Nigeria albeit unsuccessfully due to the First World War was the German Bitumen Company. See P.D. Okonmah, "Right to Clean Environment: The Case for the People of Oil-Producing Communities in Nigerian Delta" (1997) 41/1 *Journal of African Law* 43, 44; B. Manby, *The Price of Oil: Corporate Responsibility and Human Rights Violations in Nigeria's Oil Producing Communities* (New York: Human Rights Watch, 1999), 27; Y. Omoregbe, "The Legal Framework for the Production of Petroleum in Nigeria" (1987) 15 *Journal of Energy and Natural Resources Law* 273, 274.

14 The exploration rights were granted through exploration concessions based on the powers vested in the British government under Order no. 19 of 1909, Laws of Southern Nigeria, Mineral Oil Acts of 1914, Cap 120 Laws of Nigeria, 1958, Mineral Oil Ordinance no. 17, 1937. See also Manby (note 13), 27.

15 J.G. Frynas, M.P. Beck and K. Mellahi, "Maintaining Corporate Dominance after Decolonization: The 'First Mover Advantage' of Shell-BP in Nigeria" (2000) 27/85 *Review of African Political Economy* 407, 407–409.

16 Ibid.

17 Ibid.

18 B. Onimode, "Imperialism and Multinational Corporations: A Case Study of Nigeria" (1978) 19 *Journal of Black Studies* 207.

Act, 1962,[19] set out the rules governing the investment of non-resident capital in Nigerian businesses and defined methods of transfer of foreign interests to non-residents and residents. Section 10(1)(a) of the Act significantly restricted foreign exchange transactions in Nigeria by providing: "No person shall, except with the permission of the Minister – (a) Transfer any security or create or transfer any interest in a security, to or in favour of a person resident outside Nigeria." The Act thus restricted the ability of foreigners, including corporations to enter the Nigerian market. The Act further restricted the repatriation of foreign investment unless approved by the authorities. Similarly, the Nigerian Immigration Act, 1963, required a foreigner to obtain permission before he/she could set up or operate a limited liability company.[20] A major development was the introduction by a military government in 1968 of the first local company law after independence (which was renamed by the following civilian regime as the Companies Act, 1968).[21] The Companies Act introduced the requirement for the reincorporation of a foreign corporation as a Nigerian company before it could operate in Nigeria. This requirement is still part of Nigerian law to date.[22] The implications of this requirement will be examined in more detail later in this chapter. The rationale for this move must be viewed in the context of the importance attached to sovereignty by nascent states of the South at independence.[23]

The Nigerian indigenisation policy

Like most other nascent nations at independence Nigeria had a distrust of foreign domination of the economic sphere. The general belief was that MNCs, because of their close links to the former colonialists, might impede economic development.[24] The country's leaders in the 1970s thus perceived the process of indigenisation as a way of asserting the nation's right under international law to exercise sovereignty over natural resources in her territory and to regulate foreign participation and exercise the right to naturalise such investments.[25] After independence, successive governments were initially interested in nationalising certain sectors of the economy (i.e. airlines, shipping and external communications).[26]

---

19 Cap 113, Laws of the Federation of Nigeria (LFN) 1990.
20 Nigerian Immigration Act 1963, Cap 171, LFN, 1990.
21 Nigeria's Company Act, 1968.
22 See section 54 Companies and Allied Matters Act, Cap 59, LFN, 1990.
23 T.I. Ogowewo, "The Shift to the Classical Theory of Foreign Investment: Opening up the Nigerian Market" (1995) 44 *International and Comparative Law Quarterly* 915.
24 Ibid. See Also V. Akpotaire, "The Nigerian Indigenization Laws as Disincentives to Foreign Investments: The End of an Era" (2005) 3 *Business Law Review* 62.
25 F.C. Beveridge, "Taking Control of Foreign Investment: A Case Study of Indigenization in Nigeria" 1991 (40) *International and Comparative Law Quarterly* 302–333.
26 Ibid., 307.

The limited nationalisation arrangement still left a vast space of Nigerian economy under the control of foreign MNCs.

The Nigerian government decided to adopt a more rigorous strategy in its Second National Development Plan (1970–1974) which was to embark on partial and sometimes total nationalisation of foreign controlled enterprises.[27] However, when the enabling legislation was passed two years later (the Nigerian Enterprises Promotion Decree, 1972), the legislation proposed a gradual indigenisation of the economy through the transfer of foreign holdings to indigenous people.[28] It thus aimed at increasing local participation but not at actually eliminating foreign investments. The approach was not effective and the law was generally viewed as not achieving its aims.[29] A second decree was enacted, the Nigerian Enterprises Promotion Decree, 1977 (now renamed the Nigerian Enterprises Promotion Act, 1977), which was largely similar to the earlier legislation but which increased government participation in some businesses such as the banking sector.[30]

A paradigm shift came about in the 1980s with the emergence of economic liberalisation, deregulation and the privatisation of state owned corporations and interests. The shift came as a result of the International Monetary Fund and the World Bank neoliberal agenda which conditioned loans and other assistance to countries on market liberalisation.[31] In 1989, the Nigerian Enterprises Promotion Act was introduced, which repealed the Act of 1977. The new Act was Nigeria's first step towards the deregulation and liberalisation of its economy. The Act opened the field once again for 100 per cent foreign participation in most sectors of the Nigerian economy subject to necessary approvals by the government.[32] Since then Nigeria has wholeheartedly embraced neo-liberal free market economics and has embarked on massive privatisation and commercialisation of the economy.[33]

---

27   Ibid.
28   Ogowewo (note 23), 925.
29   Ibid., 314.
30   This was followed by the Nigerian Enterprises (Issue of Non-voting Equity Shares) Act, 1987.
31   World Bank, *Annual Report* (Washington, DC: World Bank, 1997); World Bank, *World Bank Development Indicators* (Washington, DC: World Bank, 1997); World Bank, *The East Asian Miracle: Economic Growth and Public Policy* (New York: Oxford University Press, 1993); World Bank, *Adjustment in Africa: Reform, Results and the Road Ahead* (Oxford: Oxford University Press, 1994); E.A. Calamitsis, "Adjustment and Growth in Sub-Sahara Africa: The Unfinished Agenda" (1997) 1 *Finance and Development* (IMF) 1; Independent Evaluation Office of the IMF, "Issue Paper for an Evaluation of Structural Conditionality in IMF-Supported Programs" (Washington, DC: International Monetary Fund, 2005).
32   See sections 4, 5 and 6 of the Nigerian Enterprises Promotion Act, 1989, See also A. Jimoh, *Nigerian Investment Law and Business Regulations* (Lagos: Learned Publishments Limited, 2002), 64; Akpotaire (note 24).
33   Public Enterprises (Privatization and Commercialization) Act 1999.

The Nigerian context in modern times

The impact of MNCs operations is most obvious in the oil production and extraction industry. Nigeria is currently the largest producer of crude petroleum in Africa, the fifth largest producer within OPEC and the eighth largest exporter of crude oil in the world. Crude oil accounts for around one-third of GDP, 75 per cent of public revenue and 95 per cent of exports[34] The major MNCs in today's Nigeria include the Anglo-Dutch Royal Shell (Shell),[35] which is the biggest oil producer in Nigeria producing more than 40 per cent of Nigeria's total output. There are also the US domiciled corporations, Exxon-Mobil and Chevron/Texaco, which produce about 38 per cent of Nigeria's output. Other US based corporations in Nigeria are Ashland, Sun Oil and Conoco. In addition there are Total (France), Agip International (Italy), Statoil (Norway) and Sasol (South Africa). There are recent entrants into the Nigerian oil industry from Asia especially China.

It is significant to note that home governments have had and in some cases still have substantial interests in these companies. This is particularly true of Europe based MNCs (with the exception of Shell) and Sasol from South Africa. The shares of the US based MNCs are largely held by institutional investors thereby obscuring the extent (if any) of the state governments' shareholding interests in these companies. In the case of Statoil, the Norwegian state, through the Ministry of Petroleum and Energy, holds 67 per cent of the company's shares.[36] Total was founded after the Second World War at the behest of the French government which held shares in the company. The French government held shares in the company reaching up to 34 per cent. However, the French government's shareholding was reduced to 5 per cent in 1992 and in its 2000 annual report Total stated that the French government had divested itself of its shares.[37] In 1999, Total had merged with Elf Aquitane, a company in which the French government had a golden share.[38] However, the European Commission forced the government to relinquish its golden share. In *Commission of the European Communities* v. *French Republic*[39] it was held that the golden share held by the French government was inconsistent with the country's obligations under

---

34 Manby (note 13), 6–10.

35 Primarily listed on the London Stock Exchange and the Amsterdam Stock Exchange.

36 See the official website of Statoil, online, available at: www.statoil.com/en/InvestorCentre/Share/Shareholders/Pages/StateOwnership.aspx (accessed 26 September 2010).

37 *Total Fact Book* (Total Publications,1995), 21 (no longer available online).

38 Note that Elf Aquitane was created in 1941 by the French government. In 1986 14 per cent of the company's share was sold to the public. By 1995, the French government share was reduced to 10 per cent. In 1996 the French government sold the rest of its stake but retained a golden share.

39 Case C-483/99 – European Court Reports 2002 p.i–04781. See also L.C. Backer, "The Private Law of Public Law: Public Authorities as Shareholders, Golden Shares, Sovereign Wealth Funds, and the Public Element in Private Choice of Law" (2008) 82 (5) *Tulane Law Review* 1801, 1816.

article 73b of the Treaty Establishing the European Community (EC Treaty) (article 56 EC).[40] Agip International (more popularly known by its original Italian name Eni) was founded in 1959 by the Italian government. The company was privatised in 1992. However, under article 6 of the company's by-laws, no shareholder, except the Italian government can directly or indirectly own more than 3 per cent of the company's share capital. The Italian government, through the Ministry of Economy and Finance, own 20.31 per cent of Agip International's share capital.[41] Sasol was established by the South African government in the late 1920s. Currently, two South African government-owned companies hold the majority of the shares in the company. The Public Investment Corporation Limited[42] holds 15 per cent of the shares and the Industrial Development Corporation of South Africa Limited[43] holds 7.8 per cent of the shares.[44]

All the foreign MNCs in the oil and gas sector operate in partnership with the Nigerian National Petroleum Corporation (NNPC), a state owned corporation. The NNPC was set up originally as the Nigerian National Oil Corporation (NNOC) in 1971 to engage in the prospecting, producing and marketing of oil and to acquire an equity stake in foreign MNCs operating in Nigeria.[45]

A closer look at the typical structure of MNCs in the oil industry in Nigeria reveals the following: a parent company mostly in Europe or the United States; subsidiaries incorporated as Nigerian corporations which engage in joint venture partnership with the federal government of Nigeria through NNPC, typically in a ratio of 55–60 per cent to the government and 40–45 per cent to the corporation. The shareholders of the parent company are predominantly in the home countries.[46] The MNCs

40 The French government repealed article (1) and (3) of Decree no. 93-1298 of 13 December 1998 which legally vested the state with the golden share by Decree no. 2002–1231.

41 See *Eni Annual Report*, 2006, 104–106, online, available at: http://www.eni.com/en_IT/attachments/publications/reports/reports-2006/annual_2006.pdf.

42 Established by the Public Investment Corporation Act no. 23 of 2004.

43 Established by the Industrial Development Act, no. 22 of 1940.

44 See Sasol, *Annual Review and Summarised Financial Information*, 2006, 125, online, available at: http://www.sasol.com/sasol_internet/frontend/navigation.jsp?navid=17200010&rootid=4.

45 The company was set up in response to OPEC Resolution no. XVI. 90 of 1968 which urged member countries to "acquire 51 percent of foreign equity interests and to participate more actively in all aspects of production".

46 For example, Exxon Mobil is owned by NNPC (60 per cent) and Mobil Oil (40 per cent). Shell Petroleum Development Corporation shareholding structure comprises NNPC (55 per cent), Shell International (30 per cent), Elf Petroleum (10 per cent), Agip Oil (5 per cent). Chevron Nigeria Limited is owned by NNPC (60 per cent) and Chevron Texaco (40 per cent). Nigeria Agip Oil Company is owned by NNPC (60 per cent), Agip Oil (20 per cent) and Phillips Petroleum (20 per cent). Elf Nigeria Ltd is owned by NNPC (60 per cent) and TotalElfFina (40 per cent) and Texaco Overseas (Nigeria) Petroleum Company is owned by the NNPC (60 per cent), Chevron (20 per cent) and Texaco (20 per cent).

maintain managerial control of the enterprise. The government contributes proportionately to the cost of carrying out the oil operations and receives a share of the production in the same proportion. The fact that by agreement the MNCs maintain managerial control implies that the MNCs not only dictate the pace and pattern of the industry according to their objective of ensuring maximum production for profit[47] but also makes the government heavily dependent on their operations.[48]

At this juncture, it is pertinent to examine the institutional framework for the control of MNCs in Nigeria and their limitations.

Nigerian company law and the control of MNCs

A major way through which a state controls corporations, both local and foreign, is through its domestic company law.[49] A consideration of the provisions of Nigerian company law is therefore important to understanding the regulatory framework in which MNCs operate in Nigeria.

A brief history of Nigerian company law

The abolition of the slave trade and the formal establishment of British authority over its Nigerian colony saw a rapid growth both in internal and external trade in nineteenth-century Nigeria.[50] The early companies in Nigeria were based in Britain. By virtue of colonial statutes enacted between 1876 and 1922, the law applicable to companies in Nigeria at this time consisted of the common law, the doctrines of equity and the statutes of general application in England on the first day of January, 1900 subject to any later relevant statute.[51] The implication of this approach was that common law concepts such as the concept of the separate and independent legal personality of companies as enunciated in *Salomon* v. *Salomon*[52] was received into the Nigeria company law and has since remained part of the law.[53] However, with continued growth of trade, the colonialists felt it

---

47   C. Hassan, J. Olawoye and K. Nnadozie, "Impact of International Trade and Multinational Corporations on the Environment and Sustainable Livelihoods of Rural Women in Akwa-Ibom State, Niger Delta Region Nigeria" (2002), online, available at: www.gdnet.org/ (accessed 1 February 2009).

48   M.J. Watts, "Righteous Oil? Human Rights the Oil Complex, and Corporate Social Responsibility" (2005) 30 *Annual Review of Environment and Resources* 373.

49   N.H.D. Foster and J. Ball "Imperialism and Accountability in Corporate Law: The Limitations of Incorporation as a Regulatory Mechanism" in S. Macleod, ed., *Global Governance and the Quest for Justice: Corporate Governance* (Oxford: Hart Publishing, 2006), 93.

50   J.O. Orojo, *Company Law in Nigeria* (third edition, Lagos: Mbeyi & Associates, 1992).

51   Ibid., 17–18.

52   *Salomon* v. *Salomon and Co* (1897) AC 22.

53   Orojo (note 50), 17.

was necessary to promulgate laws to facilitate business activities locally. The first company law in Nigeria was the Companies Ordinance of 1912, which was a local enactment of the Companies (Consolidation) Act, 1908 of England. The current company law of Nigeria – the Companies and Allied Matters Act, 1990 (CAMA) – is largely modelled on the UK Company Act, 1948.[54]

Local incorporation as a strategy for control

As stated earlier, the first measure aimed at controlling MNCs directly was introduced under the Nigerian Companies Act, 1968. The Act introduced the requirement of local incorporation with the aim of bringing MNCs under the ambit of Nigerian company law and to make them comply with requirements under the Act such as disclosure of accounts and regulation of directors and shareholders. This provision has remained part of Nigerian company law till now. Section 54 of the CAMA, 1990 provides that:

> Subject to sections 56 to 59 of this Decree every foreign company which before or after the commencement of this Decree was incorporated outside Nigeria, and having the intention of carrying on business in Nigeria shall take all steps necessary to obtain incorporation as a separate entity in Nigeria for that purpose, but until so incorporated, the foreign company shall not carry on business in Nigeria or exercise any of the powers of a registered company and shall not have a place of business or an address for service of documents or processes in Nigeria for any purpose other than the receipt of notices and other documents, as matters preliminary to incorporation under this Decree.

It must be observed that this provision is unique to Nigerian company law – the UK company law which was the basis of the CAMA contained no such provision. In the United Kingdom a foreign company is not required to reincorporate but required to file its names and addresses of the persons authorised to accept services on its behalf with the Registrar of Companies.[55] Ogowewo has challenged the usefulness of this requirement which according to him only has symbolic value and constitutes an unnecessary restriction on foreign investment.[56] A worrisome aspect of the provision in

---

54 A. Guobadia, "Protecting Minority and Public Interests in Nigeria Company Law: The Corporate Affairs Commission as a Corporations Ombudsman" in F. MacMillan, *International Corporate Law Annual Vol. 1* (Oxford and Portland, OR: Hart Publishing, 2000), 79.

55 See section 691 of Companies Act, 1985.

56 Ogowewo (note 24), 925.

the context of this book is that it makes it easier for the parent companies of subsidiaries of MNCs in Nigeria to deny liabilities for any adverse consequence of the operation of their subsidiaries since they are incorporated and legally recognised as Nigerian companies. This argument was rigorously canvassed in a suit brought by a community in the oil producing area against Mobil and its parent company in the United States.[57] Another implication of this legislation is that it may impede the ability of Nigerians seeking redress from MNCs to approach the home jurisdiction of the parent companies.

However, an alternative understanding of the implications of this provision may be gained if approached from the "the incorporation" and "real seat" theory which divides the European company law system.[58] The incorporation theory connects the company to the jurisdiction where it was incorporated and the company may develop activities in other states without losing its original status.[59] The incorporation theory thus recognises all foreign legal entities according to the rules applicable in the state of origin.[60] One of the main advantages of the incorporation technique is that whatever happens, the company can act according to the rules of its domestic jurisdiction even if operating in a foreign company.[61] On the other hand, the real seat doctrine does not recognise companies that claim to belong to a jurisdiction which is not the one in which their real seat is established. According to Wymeersch:

> Real seat systems … are more oriented towards exercising close control over the entities that operate within their jurisdiction. These jurisdictions will refuse such companies, whether by disqualifying them, or by submitting them to their own legal order in cases when in fact the company is being managed within their own territory.[62]

Germany had a strict application of the real seat theory before the ruling of the European Court of Justice (ECJ) in the *Überseering* case.[63] Under German case law, a foreign company establishing its seat in Germany would not be regarded as a German company but as an unincorporated

---

57   *Mobil Producing (Nig.) United* v. *Monokpo* (2003) 18 NWLR (Pt 852) 346. This distinction was also employed by the Court of Appeal in granting a stay of execution of a judgement in favour of an oil community which judgement was against Shell for gas flaring in *Shell Petroleum Development Company (SPDC) of Nigeria* v. *Dr Pere Ajuwa and Honourable Ingo Mac-Etteli* Court of Appeal, Abuja Division, no. CA/A/209/06, 27 May 2007.

58   Eddy Wymeersch, "The Transfer of the Company's Seat in European Company Law" (2003) 40 *Common Market Law Review* 661.

59   Ibid., 661.

60   Ibid., 661–662.

61   Ibid., 667.

62   Ibid., 662.

63   *Überseering*, C-208/00 (2002) ECR I-9919.

association or as a private firm without the benefit of shareholders' limited liability.[64] It also lacks the capacity to sue and be sued. The company was required to be formed all over again in order to operate in Germany. In the *Überseering* case, the European Court of Justice ruled that this requirement was incompatible with the freedom of establishment guaranteed in articles 43 and 48 EC for a member state to deny legal capacity to a company formed in a member state which moves its central place of administration to another member state. The rationale underlying the real seat theory has been said to be the protection of creditors, minority shareholders and employees which is consistent with the stakeholder orientation of German corporate law.[65]

To a certain extent, Nigerian company law reflects the real seat theory as it was applied in Germany. However, there are areas of difference. First, foreign companies are subject to the Nigerian jurisdiction by the fact that they are doing business in Nigeria and not just because they are incorporated there. This is in line with practices in other common law jurisdictions.[66] Second, section 60 of CAMA allows foreign companies to sue and be sued in Nigeria in its name or the name of its agents. The courts in Nigeria have held that a company incorporated other than in Nigeria can bring an action in the Nigerian courts.[67]

The point to note is that if the legal framework in Nigeria is effective, the Nigerian government will have a better legal basis for regulating subsidiaries of MNCs through the provisions of section 54 of CAMA. However, as the legal framework in Nigeria is not effective, the benefit of the provision is limited and indeed could even have the opposite effect as argued earlier.

Groups of companies under Nigerian law

Another issue to examine is the approach of Nigerian company law to groups of companies and to see whether this impacts in any way on the

---

64 Wymeersch (note 58), 670.

65 K. Baelz and T. Baldwin, "The End of Real Seat Theory (Sitztheorie): The European Court of Justice Decision in *Ueberseering*" (2002) 3 (12) *German Law Journal,* 2–3.

66 *Okura and Co. Ltd* v. *Forsbacka Jernverks Aktiebolag* (1914) 1 KB 715. See also *Offshore International SA* v. *Federal Board of Inland Revenue* (1976) 1 NTC 385 where a Nigerian court held that a company incorporated in Panama, having its principal office in Texas and no place of business in Nigeria was liable to pay tax for the operation of its business carried out through a subsidiary in Nigeria under the Nigerian Companies Income Tax Act.

67 See *Kitchen Equip (W.A.) Ltd* v. *Staines Catering Equip International Ltd* Suit no. FCA/L/17182 OF 28/2/83; *Nigerian Bank for Commerce and Industry* v. *Europa Traders (UK) Ltd* (1990) 6 NWLR 36, 41 CA; *Ishola* v. *Societe Generale Bank (Nig.) Ltd* (1997) 2 NWLR (Pt. 488) 406 SC; *UBN Plc* v. *Jase Motors (Nig.) Ltd* (1997) 7 NWLR (Pt. 513) 387 CA; *Watanmal (Singapore)* v. *Liz Olofin andCo* (1998) 1 NWLR (Pt. 533) 311 CA; *Ritz and Co KG* v. *Techno Ltd* (1999) 4 NWLR (Pt.598) 298 CA; *Saeby* v. *Olaogun* (2001) 11 WRN 179 SC.

operations of MNCs. The main question here is whether an MNC can be held liable for the acts of its subsidiary under Nigerian law. The default rule in Nigeria, like in other common law jurisdictions is that a holding company and its subsidiaries are each distinct and separate legal persons.[68] It is also the position of Nigerian law that a subsidiary is not an agent of the parent company but a different entity.[69] Theoretically, however, it may be possible to proceed against the parent company of an MNC under Nigerian law in very limited circumstances but the problem would be the ability to enforce any judgement obtained. As stated earlier, a foreign company, regardless of whether or not it is incorporated in Nigeria can sue and be sued in the Nigerian courts if it does business in Nigeria. Second, Nigerian company law recognises the relationship between holding, subsidiary and wholly-owned subsidiary companies. According to section 338 of the CAMA, a company is deemed to be a holding company of another if the company is its subsidiary[70] and a company is deemed to be a subsidiary of another if that other company is a member of it and controls the composition of its board of directors or holds more than half of its nominal equity share capital or if the other company is a subsidiary of any company which is that other's subsidiary.[71] The Act further provides that a body corporate is deemed to be the wholly owned subsidiary of another if it has no member except that other's wholly owned subsidiaries and its or their nominees.[72]

Under the CAMA, the veil of incorporation of the subsidiary may be lifted to reach the holding company in certain circumstances. This includes the requirement to prepare financial statements, where a group of companies is virtually a partnership and where one company is a trustee of another,[73] or where the Corporate Affairs Commission is investigating the affairs of a company under section 316, or where a company is acting as an agent of shareholders or created as a sham.[74] The court is also empowered to disregard the legal personality of a subsidiary in appropriate cases in the interest of justice. The last ground is wide and could accommodate a variety of issues.

However, the limitation in lifting the veil of the subsidiary of MNCs to reach the holding company has been pointed out by the leading authorities on Nigerian company law. Orojo asserts that the fact that a company has a wholly owned subsidiary in a foreign country would not make the

68 *M.O. Kanu and Sons* v. *FBN Plc* (1998) 11 NWLR (Pt. 572) 116, 121.
69 *Musa* v. *Ehidiamhen* (1994) 3 NWLR (Pt. 334) 554 CA.
70 Section 338 (5) CAMA, 1990.
71 Sections 338(1)(a) and (b) CAMA, 1990.
72 Section 338(5)(b) CAMA, 1990.
73 See section 345; see also *DHN Food Distributors Ltd* v. *London Borough of Tower Hamlets* (1976) 3 All ER 462.
74 See *Public Finance Securities Ltd* v. *Jefia* (1998) 3 NWLR (Pt. 543) 602, 604 CA.

parent company subject to the jurisdiction of that foreign country and if the foreign country gives judgement against the parent company, the courts would refuse to enforce it.[75] The consequence is that assuming that a Nigerian court gives judgement against the US or EU based parent company of the subsidiary of an MNC, it is most likely that the US or EU court would treat the parent and subsidiary as different entities and would refuse to enforce the judgement. A subsidiary is more than likely to be viewed as a separate entity in the unlikely event that the veil is lifted and the parent company found liable. Therefore, it would be difficult to enforce any judgement obtained in the host state in a foreign country.[76]

Disclosure requirements and CSR: mandatory disclosure requirements under company law and MNCs in Nigeria

Corporate social reporting has been subject of debate in the past decades.[77] Companies have generally argued that this aspect of reporting should be left for companies to engage in voluntarily. Over the years, companies by themselves or in conjunction with other private institutions developed various concepts to implement voluntary social reporting. Such attempts include the so called "triple-bottom line reporting",[78] global reporting initiative, and the Institute of Social and Ethical Accountability Standard AA 1000. Villiers notes that despite the attention paid to the concept by corporations, this aspect of corporate disclosure remains underdeveloped. According to her, the barriers to its development include the voluntary nature of the reporting, lack of clear definition of social and environmental reporting and lack of clarity as to the scope and contents of such reporting.[79] It is posited that as long as the practice remains voluntary, these barriers would remain. Some legal commentators and mandatory CSR advocates have argued that there is a need to regulate this area of reporting. According to Greenfield:

---

75 Orojo (note 50), 85.

76 J. Dine, *Companies, International Trade and Human Rights* (Cambridge: Cambridge University Press, 2005), 49.

77 C. Villiers, *Corporate Reporting and Company Law* (Cambridge: Cambridge University Press, 2006), 229; P.T. Muchlinski, *Multinational Enterprises and the Law* (second edition, Oxford: Oxford University Press, 2007), 375.

78 The phrase "triple bottom line" was coined by the social scientist John Elkington in 1994. See J. Elkington, "Towards the Sustainable Corporation: Win–Win–Win Business Strategies for Sustainable Development". (1994) 36 (2) *California Management Review* 90; J. Elkington, *Cannibals with Forks: The Triple Bottom Line of the 21st Century Business* (Gabriola Island, Canada: New Society, 1998). The concept demands that a company's responsibility should be to stakeholders (anyone who is influenced, either directly or indirectly, by the actions of the firm) rather than shareholders.

79 Villiers (note 77), 229.

The traditional fixation on financial reporting is under-inclusive. Even though a company's narrow-gauged financial reports are popularly cited as a measure of the company's worth, they do not come close to reporting a business's true value. Companies should be measured on more than their finances – if externalities count, we must try to count them. These reports do not disclose the value of the company to its workers or to the communities in which it does business. They do not report on the environmental costs of the company's products or services except in so far as such costs are relevant to shareholders (such as the costs arising from lawsuits). They do not report whether the company has been complicit in human rights violations.... When public policy requires corporations to report only on finances, corporate decision-makers will, accordingly, make decisions as if that is their only concern. If public policy required corporations to make a more robust accounting of their activities, corporate decision makers would take a broader view of their responsibilities. Corporate decision makers urged to focus only on shareholder return inevitably will make decisions differently than those who are urged to take account of broader social goals.[80]

Mandatory disclosure requirements thus present an important strategy by which the law is being employed to promote CSR.[81] Disclosure regimes are gradually, if slowly, changing to reflect new developments in business activities. Villiers argues in her book, which is an exploration of the disclosure requirements of companies in their reporting that problems exist in the disclosure regime, partly because it fails to keep pace with the speed of changes in business activities and partly because its character is shaped by the traditional shareholder-centred legal model of the company.[82] She argues that:

The corporate reporting and disclosure system is closely tied to the profit maximization goal of shareholders and therefore focuses

---

80 K. Greenfield, "New Principles for Corporate Law" (2005) 1 *Hastings Business Law Journal* 87, 91–92.

81 A World Bank publication explained the development as follows:

Company reporting on non financial policies and impact has become a tool within the CSR agenda. Social and environmental reporting by companies or so-called "triple bottom line" reporting on environmental, social, and economic impact has attracted government attention in many high-income countries, although it is difficult to find examples of developing country public sector action in this area. Public sector initiatives related to reporting include requirements for mandatory disclosure against social or environmental indicators or development of guidelines for voluntary reporting.

(See T. Fox, H. Ward and B. Howard, "Public Sector Roles in Strengthening Corporate Social Responsibility: A Baseline Study" (World Bank, October 2002), 15)

82 Villiers (note 77), xi.

primarily on financial accounting and reporting. This narrow focus influences developments relating to social and environmental reporting so that stakeholder advocates are likely to be disappointed if they rely on the disclosure system in its present form to take their objectives forward.[83]

While explaining that corporations as presently regulated only have a duty to report on financial matters, Villiers concludes that "a clear rationale for mandatory social and environmental reporting is required".[84] She explicitly agrees with Monaghan that reporting should be considered as one of the many tools that can potentially enhance corporate accountability.[85]

UK company law has moved slightly away from the sole focus on financial reporting.[86] The British government is looking to reintroduce the Operating and Financial Review legislation[87] which was repealed in 2006 and replaced with the business review requirement in the director's report. The law requires quoted companies to publish annual operating and financial review covering social and environmental issues. It among other things requires companies to identify material social and environmental risks and to disclose information in respect of these risks. This requirement to report on non financial matters may facilitate a more transparent approach to CSR in the United Kingdom.

A significant development in this respect took place in France in 2001. According to Dhooge, "in response to the indivisibility of business activities and human rights and the relevancy of information relating to their interaction to investors and other stakeholders, France's *Assemblee Nationale* mandated social disclosure as part of its Nouvelles Regulations Economiques (NRE)".[88] France amended its laws in 2001 to require extensive disclosure of social and environmental issues by corporations. Notably, article 116 of the New Economic Regulation of France made it mandatory

---

83 Ibid., xii.
84 Ibid.,261.
85 P. Monaghan, "Does Reporting Work? The Effect of Regulation" (2003) *Accountability Quarterly*, 4–5. Also quoted with approval by Villiers (note 77), 261.
86 D. McBarnet, "Corporate Social Responsibility Beyond Law, Through Law, for Law: The New Corporate Accountability" in D. McBarnet, A. Voiculescu and T. Campbell, eds, *The New Corporate Accountability: Corporate Social Responsibility and the Law* (Cambridge: Cambridge University Press 2007), 33.
87 SI 2005/1011 The Companies Act (Operating and Financial review and Directors' Report etc.) Regulation, 2005.
88 See L.J. Dhooge, "Beyond Voluntarism: Social Disclosure and France's Nouvelles Regulations Economiques" (2001) 21 *Arizona Journal of International and Comparative Law*, 441, 443; see also A. Voiculescu, "The Other European Framework for Corporate Social Responsibility: from the Green Paper to New uses of Human Rights Instruments" in D. McBarnet, A. Voiculescu and T. Campbell, eds., *The New Corporate Accountability: Corporate Social Responsibility and the Law* (Cambridge: Cambridge University Press 2007), 365 at 376–377.

for all companies traded on the French stock exchange to report annually on the social and environmental impact of their activities commencing from 2003.[89] Article 116 was implemented by Decree Number 2002-221 of 20 February 2002 which established nine separate categories of social information that must appear in the annual report.[90] These include matters relating to human resources, community issues and engagement, labour standards, health and safety and environmental issues. The requirement of the French law has been said to be a legal expression of the triple bottom line.[91] Commenting on the relevance of the French example to the CSR debate in other countries, Antal says:

> The French example highlights the role of the state in these fields. In contrast to other national contexts, where CSR activities are considered as exclusively private initiatives clearly separate from any intervention of public actors, the French State has played a central role in the traditional practices, and in the process of changing these practices, be it by legislation or by more informal forms of influence, such as the case of the Global Compact.[92]

The most radical legislative intervention so far was introduced in Indonesia in July 2007. The Indonesian parliament passed a new company law: the Limited Liability Company Law, 2007 to replace its former company law, the Limited Liability Company Law no. 5 of 1995. At the same period, a new investment law was introduced: Investment Law no. 25 of 2007. These laws were passed after a debate on CSR policies involving corporations (mainly MNCs and large Indonesian companies), NGOs, trade unions and affected communities and politicians. Corporations and some politicians opposed a mandatory CSR policy because, according to them, such a move is an additional tax on companies, it also opens companies to

89 Article 116 provides as follow:

> The report [of the board or executive board] contains information, the list of which is determined by a decree of the Council of State, about the way the company takes into account the social and environmental consequences of its activity.
>
> (Law no. 2001-420 of 15 May 2001, JO, 16 May 2001, 7776)

90 See Decree no. 2002-221 of 20 February 2002, JO, 21 February 2002, p. 3360, Articles 148–142.

91 A. Berthoin Antal, "Corporate Social Responsibility in France: A Mix of National Traditions and International Influences" (2007) 46 (1) *Business and Society* 9, 16. According to Antal

> The mere fact of imposing a common framework on reporting by defining a precise list of social and environmental criteria to report on is still a mark of the role the French State intends to play in the field, whereas the governments of most other countries remain quite reluctant to intervene.

92 Ibid., 26.

predatory and corrupt practices from politicians and may ultimately encourage capital flight.[93] The argument put forward by those in favour of mandatory CSR policy, according to Rosser and Edwin, are that "the role of companies in society was increasingly being seen in terms of stakeholders' interests, not just shareholders' interests", voluntary CSR practices are "often sporadic" and narrowly focused and also that the practices are generally carried out only by large companies while small firms pay little attention to them.[94] Despite the opposition, the laws were passed in 2007. In these laws, the Indonesian government moved to make CSR a mandatory concept for companies. The objective of this move is to employ CSR as a means of engaging the private sector in building a welfare society and the reduction of the gap between companies and local communities. The relevant provisions of the laws are quoted below.

Article 74 of the Limited Liability Company Law, 2007 on Social and Environmental Responsibility provides as follows,

1　Companies conducting business activities in the field of and/or related to natural resources have the obligation to carry out Social and Environmental Responsibility.

2　Social and Environmental Responsibility as referred to in paragraph (1) is the company's obligation, which is budgeted for and calculated as a cost of the company, and which is implemented with attention to appropriateness.

3　Companies which do not carry out their obligation as referred to in paragraph (1) shall be subject to sanctions according to the provisions of laws and regulations.

4　Further provisions on Social and Environmental Responsibility shall be regulated by Government Regulation.

Article 74 clearly makes social and environmental responsibility compulsory for companies "conducting business activities in the field of and/or related to natural resources". Article 66 further requires companies to report on how they have implemented corporate social and environmental responsibility in their annual reports.

Article 1 of the law defines social and environmental responsibility as, "the company's commitment to participate in sustainable economic development in order to improve the quality of life and beneficial environment, both for the company itself, the local community, and society in general". Investment Law no. 25, 2007 provides in article 15b that "each investor is obliged to ... carry out corporate social responsibility".

93　A Rosser and D Edwin, "The Politics of Corporate Social Responsibility in Indonesia" (2010) 23 (1) The Pacific Review 1, 8.

94　Ibid., p11.

The government is yet to issue the regulation referred to in article 74(4) setting out specifically matters such as social and environmental responsibilities, sanctions for non compliance and mechanisms for monitoring and control. The law is in its infancy and it is still too early to evaluate its effectiveness.

Disclosure requirements under Nigerian law

Despite the overarching importance of promoting corporate responsibility in the Nigerian environment, little attention has been paid to utilising social reporting as a means of promoting corporate responsibility. Prior to 1968, there was no provision for mandatory reporting of any form under Nigerian company law. The Companies Act, 1968 introduced the concept of mandatory reporting which was modelled on disclosure provisions in the UK Company Act, 1948. The scope of the disclosure requirements under the Act has been expanded under the CAMA. Section 331 of the Act requires every company to keep accounting records sufficient to show and explain its transactions. In addition it must disclose its financial position with reasonable accuracy. The record must contain entries from day to day of all monies received and expended by the company and matters in which such transactions were made. It must also contain a record of the assets and the liabilities of the company. The records are required to be kept in the registered office of the company or other places in Nigeria as the director may think fit and should at all times be open to inspection by the officers of the company.[95]

Section 334 of the Act mandates the director of the company to prepare a financial statement in respect of each financial year. The information required to be disclosed includes:

1   statement of the accounting policies;
2   the balance sheet as at the last day of the financial year;
3   a profit and loss account or, in the case of a company not trading for profit, an income and expenditure account for the financial year;
4   notes on the accounts;
5   the auditor's report;
6   the director's report;
7   a statement of the source and application of funds;
8   a value added statement for the financial year;
9   a five-year financial summary;
10 in the case of a holding company, the group financial statement.[96]

---

95   Section 332 (1) CAMA.
96   See section 344 (2) CAMA.

An interesting aspect of the requirements is the provision in (8) that the statement should include "a value added statement for the financial year" which the leading authority on Nigerian company law has described as "a requirement to report the wealth created by the company during the financial year and its distribution among various interest groups such as the employees, governments, creditors, proprietors and the company".[97] In practice, however, this provision has been limited to shareholders, government and creditors. The only exception under the Act are three heads of information relating to the employment of disabled persons; health, safety and welfare at work of the company's employees and employees' involvement and training which are required to be included in the annual report.[98] Reporting requirements under the current law in Nigeria are thus largely fixated on financial reporting and do not accommodate issues raised within the CSR debate.

The discussion so far has shown that despite the potential of domestic company law as a tool for controlling MNCs, Nigerian company law has not risen to the challenge. Considering the importance of CSR and control of MNCs within the Nigerian context, it is rather surprising that there is no significant attempt to utilise the potential of company law in this respect. This may be due to the fact that policy makers and the legislature in Nigeria are not aware of the viable possibilities available under company law. The situation is similar in most developing countries.

Domestic tort law and MNCs

Most of the cases that have been brought so far on issues concerning corporate responsibility have been brought under tort law. There are exceptions to this trend which shall be discussed in later chapters of this book. Nigerian tort law, like most other areas of laws, has its root in the common law. Complainants claiming under tort law have two possible remedies: monetary compensation for damages or an injunction. However, injunctions are granted at the discretion of the court based on equitable principles developed by the courts. Injunctions are rarely granted against MNC operations in the oil industry.[99] For example, in *Irou* v. *Shell-BP*[100] the plaintiff whose land, fish pond and creek had been polluted by Shell-BP operations sought an injunction to restrain the company from further pollution. The High Court refused to grant the injunction sought because "the interest of third persons must be in some cases considered, for

97 Orojo (note 50), 378.
98 See section 342 CAMA.
99 J.G. Frynas, "Legal Change in Africa: Evidence from Oil-Related Litigation in Nigeria" (1999) 43 *Journal of African Law* 121.
100 Unreported Suit no. W/89/71, Warri High Court.

example, where injunction would cause stoppage of trade or throwing out a large number of work people". The court ruled further that to grant an injunction would disturb the oil industry which is the main source of the country's revenue. A similar request for an injunction against Shell-BP for illegally flaring gas was rejected in *Chinda* v. *Shell-BP*.[101] A major exception to this trend is *Gbemre* v. *Shell*[102] which is discussed later in this chapter.

Many of the claims that have been brought in Nigerian courts have been brought under the head of negligence. The burden of proof is placed on the plaintiff to show that the defendant owed him a duty of care and that that duty was breached, leading to the damages alleged. In proving a breach of duty, the plaintiff must prove that the MNC committed a tort against the plaintiff and also that the company acted negligently. Discharging this burden has proved to be an obstacle in the majority of the cases brought under this head. In *Seismograph Services* v. *Mark*[103] despite the fact that the trial judge found as a matter of fact that the defendant's (Seismograph) boat tore through the plaintiff's (Mark) net, carrying away floaters and other fishing items belonging to the plaintiff, the trial judge held that the plaintiff had failed to show the duty of care owed to him by the plaintiffs.[104] The judge was of the opinion that the defendant must be shown to have operated its boat negligently and the mere fact that the boat damaged the plaintiff's property is not enough.[105]

The application of the tort principle of *res ipsa loquitur* has made the difference in a few cases. In a claim for oil spill damage in *Mons* v. *Shell-BP*,[106] the plaintiffs were awarded compensation on proving damages without providing evidence based on the pleading of *res ipsa loquitur*. According to the court in that case,

Negligence on the part of the defendants has been pleaded, and there is no evidence of it. None in fact is needed, for they must naturally be held responsible for the results arising from escape oil which they should have held under control.[107]

Cases have been brought under the head of nuisance with less success. A claim based on private nuisance was brought in *Seismograph Service* v.

---

101 (1974) 2 RSLR 1.
102 *Jonah Gbemre* v. *Shell Petroleum Development Company Nigeria Ltd, Nigerian National Petroleum Corporation and Attorney General of the Federation,* Decision of the Federal High Court of Nigeria in the Benin Judicial Division Holden at Court Benin City (Suit No FHC/B/CS/53/05, 14 November 2005).
103 (1993) 7 NWLR 203.
104 Similar conclusions were reached in *Seismograph Services (Nigeria) Ltd* v. *R.K. Ogbeni* (1976) 4 SC 85 and *Chinda and Ors* v. *Shell-BP* (1974) 2 RSLR1.
105 *Seismograph Services* v. *Mark* (1993) 7 NWLR 203.
106 *Mons* v. *Shell-BP* (1970–1972) 1 RSLR 71.
107 Page 73 of the judgement.

Akporuovo[108] on the ground that the defendant's (Seismograph) seismic operation had caused vibrations which destroyed three buildings belonging to the plaintiff (Akporuovo), two out-houses and other household goods. The trial court awarded damages in favour of the plaintiff but on appeal to the Supreme Court the award was set aside on the ground that the evidence adduced at the trial was insufficient to ground the plaintiff's liability. Similarly in *Amos* v. *Shell-BP*[109] which was a case based on public nuisance, a community brought an action against Shell-BP and its subcontractor (Niger Construction Company) for constructing a dam across a creek which led to the flooding and eventual drying up of the creek downstream. The consequence of this was that the plaintiffs' farms were flooded, transportation by river was disrupted and consequently goods could not be transported. The court dismissed the claim on the ground that the creek was a public water-way and the plaintiff had not sufficiently proved any special damage to them. The suit was also found to be procedurally flawed for misjoinder of plaintiffs who should have sued separately since they had separate claims.

Cases have also been brought under the strict liability rule in *Ryland* v. *Fletcher*[110] which is still operative under Nigerian law and in many commonwealth countries. However, the rule has been applied with mixed results. The Nigerian courts have held that oil in the ground which is in its natural state does not come under the rule but if it is channelled through pipes or gathered into pipes the rule applies.[111] The Court of Appeal applied the principle in *Shell Petroleum Development Corporation (Nig) Ltd* v. *Amaro*[112] In that case, the plaintiffs sued Shell for damages caused by spillage of oil from Shell's pipeline. As a result of the spill, the plaintiffs suffered loss of income from fishing, destruction of fishing grounds and fishing materials, destruction of economic trees and domestic materials. The court held that;

> A person who is in possession or in control of land (such as appellant herein) and keeps on such land petroleum products "exists under the rule in *Rylands* v. *Fletcher*". It must be said also that the establishment of crude oil pipeline on land with the potential of escape or spill of its contents is clearly non natural use of land.[113]

---

108 *Seismograph Service* v. *Akporuovo* (1974) All NLR 95.
109 *Amos* v. *Shell-BP* 4 ECSLR 486.
110 *Ryland* v. *Fletcher* (1868) (1) LR HL 330, The rule is to the effect that anyone bringing onto land, in the course of non-natural use of land, something likely to do mischief if it escapes is, prima facie answerable for all damages which are the natural consequence of its escape.
111 *SPDC* v. *Chief Graham Otoko and five others* (1990) 6 NWLR (Part 159) p. 693 at p. 724.
112 (2000) 10 NWLR 248.
113 Page 273 of the judgement.

The rule was partly applied successfully in *Umudje* v. *Shell-BP*.[114] In that case the part of the plaintiff's claim which was that materials escaped from Shell-BP's waste pit onto the plaintiffs' farms, ponds and lakes, damaging the farms and killing the fish in the ponds and lakes was held to come within the rules. The Supreme Court held that the rule applied in this scenario and Shell-BP was liable for damages. The court, however, refused to apply the rule to a part of the claim which was that the defendant's action also led to the blockage of stream which led to the starvation of fish in the ponds. The reason for the court's refusal was that nothing had escaped in this instance. The later part of the decision demonstrates the limitation in the application of the rule. Furthermore, there are various exceptions to the rule.[115] The defendant will not be liable if he can show that the damage was done by an "act of God", or with the consent of the plaintiff, or by a statutory authority or the independent act of a third party.[116] MNCs have thus been able to hide under these exceptions, particularly the independent third party exception, to avoid liability.[117] In *Shell* v. *Otoko*[118] communities in an oil producing area brought an action against Shell for damages caused by an oil spill. Shell claimed that the oil spill was caused by the act of an unknown third party who removed a screw from a damaged Shell facility. The court agreed with Shell and the company was held not liable.

The tort principles give room for wide discretion which allow the judges to rule either way. In most of the cases the decisions have gone against litigants claiming against MNCs. This scenario underscores why the tort approach is not sufficient. The tort approach also takes an ex post approach by the emphasis on compensation and damages, whereas an ex ante approach which will prevent the undesirable event happening at all will be preferable.

MNCs and human rights in Nigeria

The question of the extent of the violation of human rights by MNCs in Nigeria has been the subject of considerable debate. The paucity of legal mechanisms for ventilating human rights abuse complaints against MNCs mean that many of the issues remain allegations by citizens and local and international civil society organisations. There is, however, a general consensus among writers on the subject that there are important issues implicating human rights violations emanating from the operations of MNCs in

---

114 *Umudje* v. *Shell-BP* (1975) 9–11 SC 155.
115 Okonmah (note 13), 49–50.
116 G. Kodlinye, *The Nigerian Law of Torts* (Ibadan: Sweet & Maxwell, 1982), 116–117.
117 See for example *Shell* v. *Otoko* (1990) 6 NWLR (Pt.159) 693.
118 *Shell* v. *Otoko* (1990) 6 NWLR (Pt.159) 693.

Nigeria.[119] It is pertinent to commence this discussion of MNCs and human rights in Nigeria with a synopsis of human rights under Nigerian law.

Nigerian constitutional law and human rights (the human rights sphere under Nigerian law)

Since achieving independence, Nigeria has enshrined provisions on human rights in its Constitution. The first set of fundamental rights and basic freedom provisions were introduced into the Nigerian Constitution on the advice of the Willink Commission set up by the British Colonial Administration to consider the position of minority groups in relation to majority groups after independence.[120] The original agitation of the minorities was for the creation of separate states for them. However, the Willink Commission recommended the inclusion of fundamental rights provisions in the Nigerian Constitution as an effective way of dealing with minority issues.[121] The Nigerian Independence Constitution of 1960 contained provisions on human rights which have featured in all subsequent Constitutions that came afterwards. It must be observed that under the various military governments that have ruled at various times in the past, the provisions were suspended and this has had far reaching negative effects on the promotion and protection of human rights in the country. Between 1960, when Nigeria became an independent nation and 1999, there were six successful military coups lasting for a cumulative period of 30 years.

The pre-1979 Constitutions concentrated on natural rights (i.e. inalienable rights including rights to life and pursuit of happiness, freedom of speech, freedom of association and equality before the law). Little attention was paid to civil and political rights while economic, political and social rights were ignored.[122] The 1979 Constitution of Nigeria widened the scope of rights. Substantive rights were widened to include: the rights to life, to the dignity of the human person, to personal liberty, to private and family life, to freedom of expression, press, peaceful assembly, association, freedom from discrimination and right to ownership of property.[123]

---

119 See for example F.M. Edoho, "Oil Transnational Corporations: Corporate Responsibility and Environmental Sustainability" (2007) *Corporate Social Responsibility and Environmental Management* 1; R. Boele, H. Fabig, D. Wheeler, "Shell, Nigeria and the Ogoni: A Study in Unsustainable Development: 1. The Story of Shell, Nigeria and the Ogoni People – Environment, Economy, Relationships: Conflict and Prospects for Resolution" (2001) 9 *Sustainable Development* 74–86.

120 Manby (note 13), 4.

121 M. Akpan, "The 1979 'Nigerian Constitution and Human Rights" (1980) 2 *Universal Human Rights* 23.

122 Ibid.

123 Chapter IV of the Nigerian Constitution, 1999.

The Constitution also contained procedural rights including: the right to habeas corpus; the right to a public hearing; right to counsel of choice; the presumption of innocence in criminal trials; the right of information in an arrest or detention; protection from *ex post facto* laws; double jeopardy and self incrimination. Last, the Constitution prevented the government from acquiring any private property without prompt payment of compensation. Furthermore it placed a duty on the government to provide opportunity to any person claiming such compensation a right of access for the determination of his interest in the property and the amount of compensation in a court of law or tribunal or body having jurisdiction in respect of the matter.[124]

The 1979 Constitution also introduced political, social, educational and economic rights into the Nigerian Constitution. These rights were contained in chapter II of the Constitution under the heading "Fundamental Objectives and Directives of Principles of State Policy". However, by virtue of section 6(6)(c) these rights were non justiciable and the courts held this to be the case for over three decades after the introduction of the rights.[125] Section 15 of the Constitution placed an obligation on the government to provide adequate facilities to encourage free mobility of people, goods and services, secure residence rights for every citizen, encourage intermarriage among various groups and promote or encourage the formation of associations that cut across ethnic, linguistic or other social barriers. Section 17 covered social rights which include the right of equality, obligations and opportunities before the law; the duty of government to act humanely; the independence, impartiality, integrity and accessibility of the courts of law; opportunity to secure adequate means of livelihood and to secure suitable employment; just and humane conditions of work and adequate facilities for leisure and for social, religious and cultural life; safeguards as to the health and safety in the workplace, adequate medical and health facilities for all persons; right to equal pay for equal work, protection of children, young persons and the aged and provision of public assistance in case of need. Section 18 conferred educational rights and sets down the responsibility of government to eradicate illiteracy.

It must be observed on a general note that section 41 of the Constitution allowed the government to derogate from the rights provided in the interest of defence, public safety, public order, public morality, public health or for the purpose of protecting the rights and freedoms of other persons. The High Courts in Nigeria are vested with the responsibilities of adjudicating on the enforcement of the human rights provisions in the Constitution.

---

124   Section 40(1) of the Nigerian Constitution, 1999.
125   See for example *Okojie* v. *AG Lagos State* (1981) 2 NCLR 337.

Though the 1979 Constitution was replaced with the 1999 Constitution the provisions in respect of human rights have remained the same.

An interesting development occurred in 2002 when the Supreme Court of Nigeria ruled for the first time that the rights contained in Chapter II of the Constitution (Fundamental Objectives and Directives of Principles of State Policy) may be enforceable in certain circumstances. In *Attorney-General of Ondo State* v. *Attorney-General of the Federation and 35 Others*[126] one of the issues that the Supreme Court had to determine was whether a law made pursuant to sections 13 and 15 (5)[127] (which are under the non justiciable provisions) by the National Assembly is *ultra vires* the powers of the parliament and therefore unenforceable. The court also considered whether the law could be enforced against a private person (including a company) as the law purported to do. The National Assembly had enacted the Anti Corruption Bill pursuant to the stated sections in order to deal with the prevalent issues of corruption in Nigeria. The Supreme Court observed:

> It has been argued that the Fundamental Objectives and the Directive Principles of State Policy are meant for authorities that exercise legislative, executive and judicial powers only and therefore any enactment to enforce their observance can apply only to such persons in authority and should not be extended to private persons, companies or private organisations. This may well be so, if narrow interpretation is to be given to the provisions, but it must be remembered that we are here concerned not with the interpretation of a statute but the Constitution which is our organic law or grundnorm. Any narrow interpretation of its provisions will do violence to it and will fail to achieve the goal set by the Constitution. Corruption is not a disease which afflicts public officers alone but society as a whole. If it is therefore to be eradicated effectively, the solution to it must be pervasive to cover every segment of the society.

The court went on to hold that even though the provisions of the chapter are unenforceable, the National Assembly has the power to legislate on the provisions and make them enforceable against government bodies and also private persons including companies. According to the court, item 60(a) of the Exclusive Legislative List of Part I of the Second Schedule to the Nigerian Constitution empowers the National Assembly to legislate for the federation or any part thereof for the purpose of promoting and enforcing the observance of the Fundamental Objective and Directive

---

126 *Attorney-General of Ondo State* v. *Attorney-General of the Federation and 35 Others* (2002) 6 SC (Part. 1), 1.

127 The sections provides as follows 13: "It shall be the duty and responsibility of all organs of government, and of all authorities and persons, exercising legislative, executive or judicial powers, to conform to, observe and apply the provisions of this Constitution"; 15 (5): "The State shall abolish all corrupt practices and abuse of power."

Principles contained in chapter II. Therefore any step taken by the National Assembly in the furtherance of these goals is valid and enforceable in the Nigerian courts. Thus these provisions may be more potent than previously thought.

It is significant to note that a similar approach was taken by the South African courts in respect of section 7(2) of the Constitution of South Africa which requires the state to respect, promote and fulfil the rights in the Bill of Rights. The court held that the section applied also to provisions that are considered non justiciable. According to the court "given that socio-economic rights are expressly included in the Bill, the question is not whether they are justiciable, but how to enforce them in a given case".[128]

Nigeria and international human rights law

Apart from human rights provisions under the Constitution, Nigeria has ratified nine out of the 13 core international human rights treaties in force today. These include: the International Convention on the Elimination of All Forms of Racial Discrimination (1969), the International Covenant on Civil and Political Rights (1993); the International Covenant on Economic, Social and Cultural Rights (1993); the Convention on the Elimination of all Forms of Discrimination against Women (1985); the Convention against Torture and Other Cruel, Inhuman and Degrading Treatment or Punishment (2001); the Convention on the Rights of the Child (1991); the optional protocol to the Convention on the Rights of the Child on the Involvement of Children in Armed Conflict (2000) and the optional protocol to the Convention on the Rights of the Child on the Sale of Children, Child Prostitution and Child Pornography (2000). However, the impact of these instruments on Nigeria is less than one would have expected. This is because Nigeria has failed to ratify necessary instruments that will enhance their application. For example, Nigeria has not acceded to the first optional protocol to the International Covenant on Civil and Political Rights (1976) and thus does not recognise the competence of the Human Rights Committee to entertain individual complaints regarding the violation of the covenant. Similarly, Nigeria has not signed the optional protocol on the Convention against Torture (2002) and does not recognise the competence of the Committee against Torture to receive communications from individuals under article 22 of the convention. Also, Nigeria has not taken its reporting obligations under the treaties seriously. Its reports have been few and far between.[129]

---

128 *Government of the Republic of South Africa and Ors* v. *Grootboom and Ors; Grootboom* v. *Osstenberg Municipality and Ors* CCT38/00 (2000). See also *Port Elizabeth Municipality* v. *Various Occupiers* CCT53/03 (2004), *Minister of Health* v. *Treatment Action Campaign* CCT8/02 (2002), *Khosa and others* v. *Minister of Social Development* CCT13/03 (2003).

129 Human Rights Committee, "Concluding Observations of the Human Rights Committee: Nigeria 16/09/95" UN DOC. A/51/40, para. 42.

However, on a more positive note, Nigeria has ratified the African Charter on Human and Peoples' Rights[130] and incorporated it into domestic law through the African Charter on Human and Peoples' Rights (Ratification and Enforcement) Decree.[131] It has thus been held to be part of Nigerian domestic law[132] which can be enforced through the procedure provided under the Nigerian Constitution.[133]

In *Abacha* v. *Fawehinmi*[134] the Nigerian Supreme Court had the opportunity to clarify the status of the African Charter under Nigerian law. In that case, Gani Fawehinmi, a human rights activist and lawyer in the country had been arrested and detained for a week without being presented with an arrest warrant or given reasons for his arrest. He was held in total isolation before being transferred to another prison. Fawehinmi challenged the detention on the ground that it violated his fundamental rights under articles 4, 5, 6 and 12 (3) of the African Charter. The Supreme Court held that since the African Charter had been incorporated into the Nigerian domestic legal system, it was a statute with international flavour. Therefore if there is a conflict between it and another domestic statute, its provisions will prevail over those other statutes because it is presumed that the legislature does not intend to breach an international obligation. It was thus held that the African Charter possesses a "greater vigour and strength than any other domestic statute". The implication of this decision for MNCs is discussed in the following section in the context of an important later decision of the federal High Court in *Gbemre* v. *Shell and Two Others*.

Controlling MNCs through human rights provisions: the case of Gbemre *v.* Shell and two others[135]

Background to the case

More gas is flared in Nigeria than anywhere else in the world.[136] Oil companies flare gas because they find it profitable to do so where oil deposit is mixed with gas.[137] Gas flaring causes pollution of the local environment

---

130 (1981) 21 ILM 58.

131 Cap 10 vol. 1 LFN 1990.

132 *Garba* v. *Lagos State Attorney General* Suit ID/599m/91 and *Agbakoba* v. *Director State Security Services* (1994) 6 NWLR 475.

133 *Nemi* v. *The State* (1994) 1 LRC 376 (Nigeria, SC) See also F. Viljoen, "Application of the African Charter on Human and Peoples' Rights by Domestic Courts in Africa" (1999) 43 *Journal of African Law* 1.

134 *Abacha* v. *Fawehinmi* (2000) 6 NWLR Pt. 660.

135 *Jonah Gbemre* v. *Shell Petroleum Development Corporation of Nigeria Ltd and Others* (Suit No: FHC/B/CS/53/05, Federal High Court, Benin Judicial Division, 14/11/05.

136 Friends of the Earth, "Press Release: Shell Fails to Obey Gas Flaring Order" (2007), online, available at: www.foe.co.uk/resource/press_releases/shell_fails_to_obey_gas_fl_02052007.html (accessed 26 September 2010); Okonmah (note 13).

137 Omoregbe (note 13), 284.

affecting human, animals and vegetation and has also been said to contribute to climate change.[138] According to a report:

> The air pollution stems firstly from the sheer quantities of hydrocar-
> bons being burnt off, but also because the gas being burnt is not only
> natural gas (mostly methane), but also heavier gas types and pollut-
> ants like hydrogen sulphide (H_2S), which give off more air pollution.
> In addition to nitrogen and sulphur oxides (which cause respiratory
> problems and acid rain) and unburnt methane 26, the flaring also
> gives off cancer inducing benzene and other toxic gases. In addition
> you have CO_2, which is not a big local problem, but should worry the
> global community, and indeed Africa and Nigeria, which can be hit
> pretty hard by global warming. The CO_2 emissions from flaring in
> Nigeria were estimated at 34 million tons for the year 2002.[139]

It has been reported that local people in the oil producing area complain
of respiratory problems such as asthma and bronchitis and other ailments
such as cancer, leading to premature death.[140] Pollution also contributes
to acid rain corroding villagers' buildings. Local people complain of
intense heat and roaring noise emanating from gas flaring. This practice
is in stark contrast to practices in the developed world where associated
gas is used or re-injected into the ground. In Western Europe, for
example, 99 per cent of associated gas is used or re-injected.[141] The Nigerian government's efforts to contain the problem have been suspect and
this may be due to institutional capture because of the heavy reliance of
government on revenue from the industry. Under the Associated Gas Re-
Injection Act of 1979, which was the first legislation to deal with gas flaring
in Nigeria, oil companies were requested to submit schemes for the viable
utilisation of all associated gas and re-injection programmes. All companies were to stop flaring gas by 1 January 1984. A drastic penalty of for-
feiture of all concessions was imposed for flaring after that date. However,
the government relaxed the provisions in 1984 before they were to take
full effect. The government enacted the Associated Gas Re-injection Act[142]
which generally prohibited gas flaring but the law (and the regulation[143]
made under it) gave way to companies by allowing a continuation of gas
flaring where a ministerial certificate is issued to that effect. It is unclear
whether such certificates are issued in Nigeria because the issuance or non

138 Ibid.
139 Amadi (note 4), 19.
140 See the sworn affidavit of the plaintiff in *Gbemre* v. *Shell* (note 135).
141 Omoregbe (note13), 284.
142 Cap 26 LFN, 1990.
143 Associated Re-Injection (Continued Flaring of Gas) Regulation, 1985.

issuance of such certificates is not made public and cannot be challenged by a private individual. Furthermore, the discharge in harmful quantities of any hazardous substance into the air or upon land and water without permission is also criminalised under sections 21(1) and (2) of the Federal Environmental Protection Act. However, the use of the phrase "lawful permission" gives the government the discretion to permit the flaring of gas by companies.

Gbemre v. *Shell*

This case was brought by Jonah Gbemre on behalf of himself and the Iwhereken Community in Delta State in the Niger Delta area of Nigeria against Shell Petroleum Development Company Nigeria Ltd, The Nigerian National Petroleum Corporation and the attorney general of the federation. The case was brought under the fundamental rights enforcement procedure in the Nigerian Constitution alleging violations of both constitutional provisions and the African Charter. The plaintiffs claimed that the oil exploration and production activities of Shell which led to incessant gas flaring had violated their right to life and the dignity of the human person under sections 33 (1) and 34 (1) of the Constitution and articles 4, 16 and 24 of the African Charter. The plaintiffs alleged that the continuous gas flaring by the company had led to poisoning and pollution of the environment which exposed the community to the risk of premature death, respiratory illnesses, asthma and cancer. They also alleged that the pollution had affected their crop production thereby adversely affecting their food security. They claimed that many of the natives had died and many more were suffering from various illnesses. The community was therefore left in a state of gross underdevelopment. The defendants opposed the case on several grounds including that the articles of the African Charter referred to did not create enforceable rights under the Nigerian Fundamental Rights Enforcement procedure. However, they failed to follow up their arguments during the proceedings due to procedural issues. The judge therefore proceeded to judgement without any findings of fact which left the judgement bereft of any in-depth legal analysis. In its judgement, the federal High Court held that the constitutionally protected rights include rights to clean, poison-free, pollution-free environment and that the actions of Shell in continuing to flare gas in the course of their oil exploration and production activities in the applicant's community violated their right to life and/or the dignity of the human person under the Constitution and the African Charter. Even though there is no apparent justiciable right to a "clean poison-free, pollution-free and healthy environment" under the Nigerian Constitution, the court relied on a cumulative use of constitutional provisions with the provisions of the African Charter (especially article 24) to recognise and apply a fundamental right to a "clean poison-free, pollution-free and healthy environment".[144] This is in line with the decision of the African commission in the *SERAC* case, though the court did not refer to the case in its judgement.[145] The implication of this decision is that there is a possibility of resorting to the African Charter for rights that are not available under national law.

The plaintiffs' counsel had further argued that the provisions of the Associated Gas Re-injection Act (Continued Flaring of Gas Regulations) 1984 and the Associated Gas Re-Injection (Amendment) Decree no. 7 of 1985, which allow for continuation of gas flaring, were inconsistent with the right to life (which includes the right to a healthy environment) guaranteed under the Constitution. The court agreed with this argument and held that statutes permitting flaring of gas in Nigeria, with or without permission, are inconsistent with the Nigerian Constitution and, therefore, unconstitutional. The court therefore directed the attorney general of the federation and the Minister of Justice to take steps to amend the statutes governing gas flaring to bring them in line with provisions on fundamental rights under the Constitution. The significance of this is that fundamental rights protection is held as an objective which other regulations must meet in order to be valid under the law. This clearly invalidated the discretion given by existing statutes to the government to permit gas flaring where it deemed fit. The court consequently restrained the company from further flaring gas in the plaintiffs' community.

Employing human rights provisions for the first time, this case signalled a significant shift in the control of MNCs under Nigerian law. It is also important to note that the provisions employed were not only constitutional provisions but also the wider provisions under the African Charter. The human rights approach enabled the court to grant an injunction to protect rights considered to be fundamental and which cannot be ignored on a balance of convenience test as in the case of injunctions under tort law. Another critical point to note here is that the fundamental right enforcement procedure is much faster than other litigation procedures in Nigeria. This case took less than a year to conclude, while cases brought using other procedures take an average of three years in the Court of First Instance.[146] Furthermore, the decision's explicit recognition of non-state actors' (i.e.

---

144 G. Fortman, "'Adventurous' Judgments: A Comparative Exploration into Human Rights as a Moral-Political Force in Judicial Law Development" (2006) 2 *Utrecht Law Review* 22.

145 The African Commission on Human and Peoples' Rights held in *SERAC* v. *Nigeria* (2001), Communication no. 155/96 (African Commission on Human and Peoples' Rights) that the failure of the Nigerian government to prevent the escape of toxic waste from oil reserves violated the right to health (article 16) and the right to a clean environment (article 24) of the African Charter. The Nigerian government had argued that the rights are vague and incapable of legal enforcement. The SERAC case is discussed fully in Chapter 5.

146 J.G. Frynas, "Problems of Access to Courts in Nigeria: Results of a Survey of Legal Practitioners" (2001) 10 *Social Legal Studies* 397, 410.

corporations') duties vis-à-vis human rights signals the possibility of horizontal application of human rights provision to corporations in Nigeria.

The criminal liability of corporations under Nigerian law

Even though the concept of corporate criminal liability is recognised under the current law,[147] its practical application to corporations has been at best lukewarm. Before the enactment of the CAMA, the concept was rooted in the common law, under which the acts of certain agencies of a corporation may be regarded as that of the corporation itself and the criminal acts of the agencies thus become attributable to the corporation.[148] Under the criminal code (similar provisions are contained in the penal code applicable in the North) persons subject to criminal liability are defined to include corporations. To buttress this position, section 18(1) of the Interpretation Act[149] defines "person" to include "any body of persons corporate or incorporate".

With the coming into force of CAMA in 1990, a specific statutory basis was added to corporate criminal liability.[150] Section 65(1) provides that:

> Any act of the members in general meeting, the board of directors, or of a managing director while carrying on in the usual way the business of the company shall be treated as the act of the company itself and the company shall be criminally and civilly liable therefore to the same extent as if it were a natural person.

Furthermore section 66 provides that subject to the provisions of section 65, the acts of any officer or agent of a company will be deemed to be the act of the company and the company will be liable in such circumstances provided the company is acting through its members in a general meeting, board of directors or managing director, expressly or impliedly authorised the act. As Okoli correctly observes, the involvement and guilt of the "directing mind and will" must be present in order to impute criminal liability to a corporation. This view was judicially expressed in *Adeniji* v. *State*[151] where it was held:

---

147   See chapter 1 and section 515 of the Nigerian Criminal Code.
148   See C. Okoli, "Criminal Liability of Corporations in Nigeria: A Current Perspective" (1994) 38 *Journal of African Law* 35, 35. See also the English cases of *Lennard's Carrying Company* v. *Asiatic Petroleum* (1915) AC 705, 713–714, *Bolton* v. *Graham* (1956) 3 All ER 624, 630 and the Nigerian case of *AG (Eastern Region) Amalgamated Press* (1956–1957) IERLR 12. On corporations and criminal responsibility generally, see C. Wells, *Corporations and Criminal Responsibility* (second edition, Oxford: Oxford University Press, 2001) 84.
149   Cap 192, LFN, 1990.
150   Okoli (note 148), 104.
151   (1992) 4 NWLR (Pt.234) 248, 261.

There is no doubt therefore that the company could be made liable criminally for the actions of natural persons in control or with necessary authority and who are regarded as the alter ego of the company and such natural persons could be treated as the company itself. Corporations being a legal fiction can only act and think through their officials and servants. For the purpose of imposing criminal liability upon corporations other than vicarious responsibility, the conduct and accompanying mental state of senior officers, acting in the course of their employment, can be imputed to a corporation.

It is also important to note that under Nigerian law a company may be liable under the criminal law for acts done which are *ultra vires* its activities as contained in its memorandum and articles of association.[152]

It is thus clear that under Nigerian criminal law, in order to establish the criminal responsibility of corporations, the liability of the agent must be established. This area of law has not been tested against MNCs and the likelihood of using criminal law in this respect is remote as the states' Department of Criminal Justice and the Nigerian Police Force, who are vested with powers to institute criminal proceedings and prosecute, have not utilised these powers in cases of complaints against MNCs.

Workers' protection and MNCs

It is difficult to get an accurate figure for the number of people employed by MNCs in Nigeria because most MNCs do not publish adequate data.[153] However, corporations like Shell provide limited information on their workforce on their website. Shell is the largest multinational corporation in Nigeria. Shell has interests in four main companies in Nigeria which are Shell Petroleum Development Corporation Ltd, Shell Nigeria Exploration and Production Company, Nigeria LNG Ltd and National Oil and Chemicals Marketing Company. The corporation currently employs about 5,000 workers directly including 4,950 Nigerians. However, substantial parts of its workforce are employed indirectly through contractors. About 20,000 people are employed this way.[154] The same pattern of employment is followed by other oil corporations in Nigeria, although the numbers differ. A 2003 survey produce the following figures for some companies in the oil sector in Nigeria.

---

152 See section 65(b) CAMA and the decision in *James* v. *Mid-West Motors Ltd* (1978) NSCC 536.
153 Amadi *et al.* (note 4).
154 Online, available at: www.shell.com/home/Framework?siteId=nigeria (accessed 26 September 2010).

Table 4.1

Company	Number of permanent workers	Number of casual/contract workers	Percentage of workers on casual/contract	Total
Nigerian Agip Oil Co.	211	1,500	87.7	1,711
Elf Petroleum	199	550	73.4	749
Elf Oil	42	132	75.9	174
Shell Petroleum	520	8,000	93.9	8,520
Mobil Producing	492	2,200	81.7	2,692
Mobil Oil	0	492	100.0	492
Nidogas	15	150	90.9	165
National Oil	51	178	77.7	229
Smithnigeria	25	80	76.2	105
Schlumberger Group	250	1,000	80.0	1,250
African Petroleum Plc	300	376	55.6	676
NNPC	9,000	3,000	25.0	12,000
Total Nigeria Ltd	136	534	79.7	670
Lighthouse Petroleum	58	105	64.4	163
Comex Nig. Ltd	52	150	74.3	202
Remm Oil Service	120	350	74.5	470
Devtag Drilling Co. Ltd	96	300	75.8	396
Tidex Nig. Ltd	65	120	64.9	185
Consolidation Oil	300	600	66.7	900
Chevron	450	3,000	87.0	3,450
Trans Pecan Sedco Forex	50	150	75.0	200

Source: NUPENG, 2003.[1]

Note

1 National Union of Petroleum and Natural Gas Workers (NUPENG), "The Evil Menace of Contract/Casual Labour, Victimisation of Union Officials and Anti-Union Posture of Nigerian Employers" (Lagos: NUPENG Publications, 2003).

The recourse by corporations to the use of casual and contract employment, which involves replacing full time jobs with part time workers, employed on week-to-week basis is a major concern in the sector.[155] A second type of contract employment in the sector is the hiring of workers on short term individual contracts or simply as contractors. These innovations are brought about by corporations in order to circumvent traditional labour law.[156] These schemes allow corporations to take advantage of the workforce and mean that these categories of workers have severely limited rights against the corporations. They are not entitled to packages like pensions, sick pay and holiday rights. In addition, since they are not direct employees, corporations can easily use their position to force these workers to accept low wages for their services. Furthermore, because of the ambiguous nature of the status of these workers, their ability to unionise and engage in collective bargaining is severely limited. Indeed, casual workers and contract staff are left out of most, if not all collective agreements signed with MNCs in Nigeria.[157] The corporations thus avoid responsibility for these workers, which account for the majority of their work force.[158]

The situation in the Oil and Gas Free Zone[159] further exemplify the lax environment in which MNCs operate. More than 30 oil and gas companies operate in this area employing thousands of people. The zone was created under the Export Processing Zone Programme which was introduced in Nigeria through the Nigerian Export Processing Zones Decree.[160] The special zone was created for the oil industry in 1996 by the Oil and Gas Export Free Zone Decree no. 8 1996. Labour incentives to companies operating in this area and other free trade zones come in the form of erosion of labour standards. There is a ten-year amnesty on trade unions, strikes or lockouts following the commencement of operations in the zone.[161] The provision effectively denies workers fundamental rights recognised under

155 O. Ezigbo, "FG To Tackle Oil Majors, Banks over Unfair Practices" *Thisday Newspapers* 11 August 2007, online, available at: www.thisdayonline.com (accessed 11 December 2007).

156 It must be observed that this development is not limited to developing countries as benign variants of it are practiced in some developed countries.

157 See E.E. Okafor, "Globalisation, Casualisation and Capitalist Business Ethics: A Critical Overview of Situation in the Oil and Gas Sector in Nigeria" (2007) 15 (2) *Journal of Social Science* 169, 173 detailing the consequences of casualisation and contract employment practices in the oil industry in Nigeria.

158 O.S. Luwoye, "Casualization and Contract Employment in the Nigeria Oil and Gas Industry" (2002), online, available at: www.pengassan.org/Publications.1.htm (accessed 2 June 2007).

159 Established by Decree no. 8, 1996.

160 Decree no. 34 of 1991. The decree was replaced in 1992 by the Nigerian Export Processing Zones Decree no. 63 of 1992.

161 Section 18(5) Nigerian Export Processing Zones Decree no. 63 of 1992, section 18(5) Oil and Gas Export Free Zone Decree no. 8 1996.

the Nigerian Constitution and the ILO conventions which guarantee the rights of free assembly and association and protects workers' rights to form or belong to trade unions[162] The law provides that the Free Zone Authority instead of workers' organisation or workers' union shall handle the resolution of disputes between employers and employees in the zone.[163] The law has also been criticised for not allowing any unauthorised person to enter, remain or reside in the zone.[164] According to Ikeyi, a literal interpretation of the section means that persons including Nigerian citizens do not have an unimpeded right to enter the zones. This is in breach of constitutional right to free movement and the economic need for free mobility of labour[165] and external monitoring of the labour situation is seriously impeded.

Employees of MNCs have always been in disagreement with management over arbitrary mass termination of employment contracts of workers without adequate compensation or pension scheme to take care of their future. In 2004 for example, there was a disagreement between Shell workers and management over its "Securing our Future" programme. Under the programme Shell laid off almost half of its Nigerian workforce. Despite several representations from the two workers' unions in the oil and gas sector – Petroleum and Natural Gas Senior Association of Nigeria (PENGASSAN) and National Union of Petroleum and Natural Gas Workers (NUPENG) – the corporation failed to enter into negotiations with the unions. Trade union attempts to have the government intervene in the row failed, as the government was unwilling to interfere with the MNC's operation.

The three primary laws controlling the activities of MNCs in relation to their employees in Nigeria are the Nigerian Constitution, 1999; the Companies and Allied Matters Act, 1990; and the Nigerian Labour Act, 1971. Most of the constitutional provisions which could have served as benchmarks for determining the standards required of employers in respect of their employees are unenforceable by virtue of section 6(6)(c) of the Constitution. The only provision in the Constitution that appears to directly benefit workers is the right to peaceful assembly and association provided for under section 40 of the Constitution. The section apparently gives constitutional backing to trade union activities. This provision has proved inadequate to cater for employees' interests, as the law is observed more in the breach than in its observance.

---

162 ILO Convention no. 87 on Freedom of Association and Protection of the Right to Organize; Convention no. 98 on the Right to Organize and Collective Bargaining. See also N. Ikeyi "The Export Processing Zones and Foreign Investment Promotion in Nigeria: A Note on Recent Legislation" (1998) 42 *Journal of African Law* 223, 227.

163 Section 18(5) Nigerian Export Processing Zones Decree no. 62 of 1992.

164 Ibid., section 13; section 13, Oil and Gas Export Free Zone Decree no. 8 1996.

165 Ikeyi (note 163), 229–230; US Department of State, Country Report on Human Rights Practices, 2003 (Released by Bureau of Democracy, Human Rights and Labour, 25 February 2004.)

More directly dealing with corporations is the Companies and Allied Matters Act, 1990. However, the Act does not recognise the wide variety of stakeholders embraced by the CSR concept and thus pays insignificant attention to employees' interests. Section 342, the only section to address employees' interests, creates a duty to include in the annual reports some issues relating to employees but the provision is of no real value to workers.

The Labour Act, 1971 is the principal legislation on labour law. There are four major parts in the act. The first part deals with protection of workers' wages and their contracts of employment. The second part regulates the recruitment of workers within and outside Nigeria. The third part governs the employment of special classes of workers: apprentices, women and young persons. It also covers issues relating to forced labour and other miscellaneous matters. The fourth part covers supplemental matters and the administration of the act. However, despite the fact that the act, which came into force in 1971, covers these areas, its provisions appear too weak and outdated to be capable of addressing issues that have emerged from modern day industrial relations. For example, the Act makes no provision in respect of the regulation of casualisation and contract employment thereby leaving these all-important areas unregulated. Also the law was drafted before the concepts of export processing zones and free trade zones emerged in Nigeria where MNCs have significant operation. It is therefore not surprising that the law did not take cognisance of labour-related issues in these zones. Also despite the fact that the Act makes it illegal for an employee to make the membership or non-membership of a trade union a condition in a contract of employment, the law does not guarantee the right of workers to trade union activities. However, this is now guaranteed under the Constitution.[166] Furthermore, job security, a major concern of workers is not addressed. Apart from making provisions in respect of the length of notice required before an employee's employment can be terminated, the Act does not put in place any safety net to cushion the effect of such termination on the employee. Another major drawback of the Act is its weak enforcement process. The Act provides for criminal sanctions in case of non compliance and it also provides for the use of inspectors to prevent the breach of its provisions.[167] However, the criminal sanctions have never been enforced in the country and inspections are rarely carried out.

The implications of the developments discussed so far are multifaceted. First, there has been a dramatic increase in the use of temporary workers by MNCs.[168] This has led to incessant complaints about the marginalisation

---

166   Section 9(10) Labour Act, 1971; see section 40 of the 1999 Constitution.
167   See sections 77 and 78 Labour Act, 1971.
168   PENGASSAN (2004). "Memorandum to the House of Representatives Committee on Petroleum and Natural Resources", online, available at: www.pengassan.org/ (accessed 21 February 2007).

of Nigerian workers in MNCs.[169] Second, bargaining power is tilted more in favour of MNCs, which have the capacity to hire and fire at will.[170] It is therefore not surprising that there is constant friction between Nigerian employees and management of MNCs.[171] For example in 2004 the French company, Total, was shut down for one week by employees demanding better conditions of employment. Exxon Mobil had to contend with a similar dispute at the same period. Oil workers unions constantly issue warnings of industrial action to correct the perceived unjust treatment of workers.[172] The situation belies the commitment expressed by corporations in codes of conduct to their workers.

MNCs and anti-corruption laws

An area of corporate activity which involves CSR issues is the area of corporate involvement in corruption. Corruption has been described as the "most debilitating of the social and economic ills plaguing Nigeria".[173] In the Transparency International Corruption Perception Index 2009, Nigeria was ranked 130 out of 180 countries, the 180th country being the country perceived to be most corrupt.[174] In a 2002 decision the Supreme Court of Nigeria noted,

> It is a notorious fact that one of the ills which have plagued and are still plaguing the Nigerian nation is corruption in all facets of our national life. It is an incontrovertible fact that the present economic morass and or quagmire in which the country finds itself is largely attributable to the notorious virus, which is known as corruption.[175]

In several reports in the past few years MNCs have been implicated in corrupt practices of significant magnitude. A few examples illustrate this point. In 2003 Halliburton, a US-based MNC admitted to the Security Exchange Commission in the United States that "low-level employees"

169 Ezigbo (note 155).
170 E. Chianu, "Towards Fair Hearing for all Nigerian Employees" 2007 (1) *CALS Review of Nigerian Law and Practice* 29.
171 Okafor (note 157).
172 NUPENG–PENGASSAN (2004) Communiqué Issued at the End of the Joint National Executive Council Meeting of NUPENG–PENGASSAN held at Metropolitan Hotels Calabar 26 February 2005.
173 N.S. Okogbule, "An Appraisal of the Legal and Institutional Framework for Combating Corruption in Nigeria" (2006) 13 *Journal of Financial Crime* 92, 93; See also O. Oko, "Subverting the Scourge of Corruption in Nigeria: a Reform Prospectus" (2002) 34 *International Law and Politics* 397, 404.
174 Online, available at: www.transparency.org/policy_research/surveys_indices/cpi/2009/cpi_2009_table (accessed 26 September 2010).
175 *AG Ondo State* v. *AG Federation and Ors* (2002) 27 WRN 1.

paid bribes to officials of Nigeria's Federal Inland Revenue Service in 2001 and 2002 to obtain favourable tax treatments.[176] Similarly an international consortium comprising Brown and Root (KBR) (the British subsidiary of Halliburton), Technips of France, Snamprogetti Netherlands BV and JGC corporation of Japan were investigated for allegedly offering a bribe of USD 180 million to Nigerian officials to secure the contract to build the Bonny Island Liquefied Natural Gas (LNG) plant.[177] Technips, KBR and Snamprogetti recently admitted their role in the scandal.[178] Also in 2007 Vetco Gray Controls Inc, Vetco Gray Controls Limited and Vetco Gray UK Limited, a wholly-owned subsidiary of Vetco International Limited, all pleaded guilty to offering USD 2.1 million bribe to employees of the Nigeria Customs Service.[179] A curious case involving corruption in Nigeria was settled out of court in 2003.[180] In that case Alan Ferguson, a British oil executive sued his employer Baker Hughes Corporation, a company engaged in oil and gas drilling operations in Nigeria, in a court in Houston Texas in which he alleged that his employment was terminated because he refused to pay a bribe to secure a contract in Nigeria in 1999. Despite the fact that the case was settled out of court, it forced the company to admit improper dealings by its employees in another country (Kazakhstan).[181] Most recently, a former manager of a US-based multinational, Wilbros Group Inc was indicted for giving US$6 million bribe to secure a US$387 million contract to build gas pipelines in Nigeria.[182]

Corruption and human rights

The question whether there is a link between human rights and corruption has been the subject of academic consideration in the recent past. This is particularly so because there are no human rights conventions that provide for a right to be free from corruption.[183] The Seoul International

---

176   "The Cheney Factor" *Houston Chronicle*, February 22, 2004.

177   See IRIN (the humanitarian news and analysis service of the UN Office for Coordination of Humanitarian Affairs) "Nigeria: Why Obasanjo's War on Corruption is Faltering", online, available at: www.irinnews.org (accessed 14 August 2008).

178   Ejiofor Alike, "Halliburton: Technip to Pay $338m to Settle US Bribery Charges" *Thisday*, 29 June 2010; Tokunbo Adedoja, "Dutch Firm to Pay $240m Fine for NLNG Bribery Scam" *Thisday*, 8 July 2010.

179   C. Ogbu, "Corruption: US Firms Probes Operations in Nigeria" *Punch Newspapers*, 28 June 2007.

180   *Ferguson* v. *Baker Hughes Inc* no. 2002-14960 (Tex.Dist.Ct. filed 25 March 2002).

181   *US* v. *Baker Hughes Services International Inc*, Case no. H-07-129, United States District Court, Southern District of Texas).

182   See *United States of America* v. *Jason Edward Steph*, United States Courts for the Southern District of Texas, Houston Division, Criminal no. H 07–307.

183   A.M. Truelove, "Oil, Diamonds, and Sunlight: Fostering Human Rights through Transparency in Revenues from Natural Resources" (2003–2004) 35 *George Town Journal of International Law* 207, 209.

Anti Corruption Conference of 2003 declared that large scale corruption should be designated as a crime against humanity and should fall in the same category as torture, genocide and other crimes against humanity. The conference posited that all human beings have a basic right to live in a corruption-free society.[184] According to a United Nations Development Programme (UNDP) paper:

> A corrupt state creates a vicious circle in which the state quickly loses its authority and ability to govern for the common good. Corruption makes it possible for critics to be silenced, for justice to be subverted and for human rights abused to go unpunished. When corruption reigns, basic human rights and liberties come under threat and social and economic contracts become unpredictable. Therefore corruption affects both civil and political rights as well as economic rights.[185]

Many legal commentators argue that corruption should be characterised as a violation of human rights.[186] As Truelove correctly notes the main idea behind characterising corruption as a violation of human rights is that corruption perpetuates discrimination, prevents the full realisation of human development by negatively affecting economic, social and cultural rights and leads to authoritarian and repressive behaviour that impedes civil and political rights, distorts provisions of social services and hampers economic development.[187]

Corruption and the law in Nigeria

Under the criminal and the penal codes[188] there are provisions dealing with the issue of corruption.[189] A major shortcoming of these provisions,

---

184 The Seoul International Anti Corruption Conference of 2003, "The Seoul Findings", online, available at: www.11iacc.org/ (accessed 24 June 2010); see also the 2006 Guatemala Conference which further reiterated the links between corruption and abuse of human rights, *Declaration of the 12th International Anti-Corruption Conference* (Guatemala City, Guatemala, 18 November 2006).

185 See T. Pilapitiya, "The Impact of Corruption on the Human Rights Based Approach to Development" (United Nations Development Programme, Oslo Governance Centre: The Democratic Governance Fellowship Programmes, September 2004), 9–10. See also C. Raj Kumar, "Corruption and Human Rights: Promoting Transparency in Governance and the Fundamental Right to Corruption-Free Society in India" (2003–2004) 17 *Columbia Journal of Asian Law*, 31, 38–40.

186 Truelove (note 183); C. Grossman, "Introduction" in *The Experts Roundtable: A Hemisphere Approach to Combating Corruption* (2002) 15 American University International Law Review 759, 763; N. Kofele-Kale, "Partimonicide: The International Economic Crime of Indigenous Spoliation" (1995) 23 (1) *Vanderbilt Journal of Transnational Law* 45.

187 Truelove (note 183), 210.

188 The criminal code operates in the Southern part of Nigeria and is largely derived from English law while the penal code operates in the Northern part of Nigeria and accommodates the Sharia system.

189 Sections 98–99 of the Criminal Code, S. 115–122 of the Penal Code, Nigeria.

however, is that they are narrowly focused on the public service without paying adequate attention to the private sector. This has prevented a holistic approach to the problem of corruption through the criminal law system.[190] Apart from criminal law provisions, several other measures have been passed to tackle the problem. These include the Public Officers (Investigation of Assets) Decree (no. 5 of 1996), Public Complaints Bureau, the Corrupt Practices Decree (no. 38 of 1975), Code of Conduct Bureau and Tribunal, Recovery of Public Property (Special Military Tribunal) Decree (21 of 1986). However, these measures were largely ineffective because they were introduced under repressive and corrupt military regimes and were also largely focused on the public service.

Some important steps that have implications for the control of MNCs have been taken in recent times. The first is the enactment of the Independent Corrupt Practices and Related Offences Act, 2000 which established the Independent Corrupt Practices Commission (ICPC). It must be observed that even though section 6 of the act, which confers duties on the ICPC, seems to focus on public bodies, other sections of the Act consistently extend the scope of the Act to private companies. A major power invested in the ICPC is the power to examine the practices, systems and procedures of public/corporate bodies and where in its opinion such practices, systems or procedures aid or facilitate fraud or corruption, it can direct a review of such fraud-aiding practices or systems. This has been said to be the most potent of the ICPC's powers.[191]

It is instructive to note that section 2 of the Act defines a "person" to whom the Act applies to include a natural person, a juristic person or any body of persons corporate or incorporate while "an official" to whom the Act applies is defined as a director, functionary, officer, agent, servant, privy or employee serving in any capacity whatsoever in the public service or other public body, or in any private organisation, corporate body, political party, institution or other employment whether under a contract of services or contract for services or otherwise and whether in an executive capacity or not.

The above provisions show that the Act covers the activities of MNCs. It is therefore curious that the ICPC since its inception has not deemed it fit to extend its operations to MNCs. A case in point is the *SAGEM* case. In 2003–2004, the ICPC investigated allegations of bribe given by a France based MNC, SAGEM to some government officials. The commission eventually brought charges against the government officials but not the MNC as an entity.[192]

---

190 Okogbule (note 173).
191 O.F. Arowolo, "In the Shadows of EFCC: Is the ICPC Still Relevant?" (2006) 9 *Journal of Money Laundering Control* 203, 206.
192 IRIN (note 177).

Another major institution that was established to tackle the problem of corruption was the Economic and Financial Crime Commission (EFCC) established under the Economic and Financial Crimes Commission (Establishment) Act 2004. Section 46 of the Act defines economic and financial crime as the non-violent criminal and illicit activity committed with the objectives of earning wealth illegally either individually or in a group or organised manner thereby violating existing legislation governing the economic activities of government and its administration and includes any form of fraud, narcotic drug trafficking, money laundering, embezzlement, bribery, looting and any form of corrupt malpractices, illegal arms deal, smuggling, human trafficking and child labour, illegal oil bunkering and illegal mining, tax evasion, foreign exchange malpractices including counterfeiting of currency, theft of intellectual property and piracy, open market abuse and the dumping of toxic wastes and prohibited goods.

The scope of the commission's duties is very wide and includes:

1   Investigation of all financial crimes such as advance fee fraud (otherwise known as 419), money laundering, counterfeiting, illegal charge transfer, futures market fraud, fraudulent encashment of negotiable instruments of fraudulent diversion of funds, computer credit card fraud, contract scam, forgery of financial instruments and the issuance of dud cheques.
2   Adoption of measures to identify, trace, freeze, confiscate, or seize proceeds derived from terrorist activities, economic and financial crimes related offences, or the properties, the value of which correspond to such proceeds.
3   Adoption of measures to eradicate and prevent the commission of economic and financial crimes with a view to identifying individuals, corporate bodies or groups involved.
4   Determination of the extent of financial loss and such other losses by government, private individuals or organisation.
5   The collection of all reports relating to suspicious financial transactions and analysis and dissemination to all relevant government agencies.
6   Maintaining liaisons with office of the attorney general of the federation, Nigeria Customs Service, Immigration and Prison Service Board, Central Bank of Nigeria, Nigeria Deposit Insurance Corporation, National Drug Law Enforcement Agency (NDLEA), all government security and law enforcement agencies and such other financial supervisory institutions, in the eradication of economic and financial crimes.
7   Any other such activities as are necessary to give effects to the functions conferred on the commission under the act.[193]

---

193   See section 5 of the Economic and Financial Crimes Commission (Establishment Act) 2002.

The commission is also charged with the enforcement of key legislation governing economic and financial crime. These include the Money Laundering Act, 2004; the Advance Fee Fraud and Other Fraud Related Offences Act, 1995; the Failed Banks (Recovery of Debts) and Financial Malpractices in Banks Act, 1994, as amended; the Banks and other Financial Institutions Act, 1991, as amended; Miscellaneous Offences Act, 1990; and any other law or regulations relating to economic and financial crimes, including the criminal code and the penal code. Economic and financial crimes under the criminal code and the penal code were brought within the remit of the EFCC because of the failure of the state's criminal justice departments and the police to administer criminal law effectively.

Thanks to its broad powers and the wide definition of what constitutes economic and financial crime, the EFCC has power to monitor and investigate corrupt practices of MNCs. In its three years of existence the commission has investigated a number of high profile cases mainly involving allegations against public officers. However, its activities have not yet made any real impact in the private sector,[194] with the operations of MNCs completely escaping the commission's scrutiny.

Controlling MNCs under host state law: possibilities in Nigeria

It is the position of this book that despite obvious gaps within the domestic context, there are opportunities for the control of MNCs in Nigeria. These opportunities are also considered as ways by which the law can robustly work with CSR to make the concept more meaningful. However, in order for these opportunities to come to fruition the institutional and the legal framework in Nigeria must be reformed. Some suggestions are offered below.

Reconstructing the role of the corporation

As noted in Chapter 2, the theoretical framework is important in the design of the regulatory framework for corporations. It is opined that it is necessary to reconceptualise the corporation under Nigerian law in order to make it more amenable to regulation to achieve social goals.[195] Most countries of

---

194   E.M.N. Okike, "Corporate Governance in Nigeria: The Status Quo" (2007) 15 *Corporate Governance* 173, 187.

195   This writer agrees with the argument by Professor Greenfield that "corporate law can be part of the wider task of regulating corporations in particular and business in general". According to Greenfield

> The rules that govern corporations should more expressly take into account the fact that corporations are collective enterprises that demand investment from a number of different sources. These investments come in various forms: inflows of

the South have adopted the US model of corporate governance. This has led to the assumption that in corporate governance modelling "in Asia or Africa, in South America or the former Russian republics, as well as in Europe, and everywhere else on the globe, there is only one way – the American way".[196] Thus the conception of the company under the current framework in Nigeria follows the Anglo-American Contractarian Model. Companies are thus viewed as private actors to be run exclusively for the interests of shareholders. Under the Companies and Allied Matters Act 1990[197] the principal legislation on companies in Nigeria, the shareholders are recognised solely as the members of the company.[198] To further underscore the recognised interest within a registered corporation, the Act makes the Constitution of a company i.e. the memorandum and article of association of the company a contract between the company and its members (shareholders) and officers (management) on the one hand and between members and officers on the other.[199] (One contract governs the relationship between the company and others (shareholders and management) while the other governs the relationship between the shareholders and management among themselves). Under the act, the directors of the company owe duties to the company and its shareholders only and have no responsibility or legal capacity to embark on any public duty.[200] The Companies Act thus lends support to the shareholder supremacy and shareholder wealth

---

> capital from shareholders and creditors; cash inflows from customers; infrastructural support from governments and communities; and effort, intelligence, and direction from employees. Whereas corporate law presently focuses on the financial investments of shareholders only, it could, and should, be adjusted to take into account the contributions of "non-equity investors". Adjusted in this way, corporate law will make it more possible for corporations to serve their purpose of facilitating the creation of wealth, broadly defined and distributed. Instead of shareholder primacy being the lodestar for corporate decision making, corporations should be governed by the maxim of "abundance for all".
>
> (Kent Greenfield, "Reclaiming Corporate Law in a Gilded Age" (2008) 2 (1) *Harvard Law and Policy Review* 1)

196 D.M. Branson, "The Very Uncertain Prospect of 'Global' Convergence in Corporate Governance" (2001) 34 *Cornell International Law Journal* 321.

197 This was originally modelled on the UK Company Act, 1948. Guobadia (note 54).

198 See section 79 Companies and Allied Matters Act, 1990. See also Orojo(note 50), 250.

199 Section 41(1) of the Act provides as follows:

> Subject to the provisions of this Decree, the memorandum and articles when registered shall have the effect of a contract under seal between the company and its members and officers themselves whereby they agree to observe and perform the provisions of the memorandum and articles, as altered from time to time in so far as they relate to the company, members or officers as such.

200 See section 279 of the Companies and Allied Matters Act, 1999. See also Orojo (note 50), 321.

maximisation goal of the neo-liberal school. This position has been slavishly followed by the Nigerian courts, who have consistently ruled in favour of the supremacy of shareholders.[201]

The Nigerian situation can be contrasted with recent developments in the United Kingdom, which has moved towards a slightly different conception of the corporation. Under section 309 of the Companies Act, 1985, directors are required to have regard to the interests of employees. On 8 November 2006 the Company Act (UK) 2006 received royal assent.[202] The new Act *inter alia* extended directors' duties by introducing a new general statutory duty to "promote the success of the company" by considering *inter alia* not only the long-term business consequences of decisions but also the wider social responsibility factors such as the impact of the company's operations on the community and the environment and the interest of the employees.[203] In promoting the success of the company, directors are enjoined to consider the principle of enlightened shareholder value, which allows for the consideration of other stakeholder issues. The new legislation thus imports wider corporate social responsibility factors into the issues that directors must take into consideration when making decisions. Nevertheless, it must be observed that the effectiveness of these duties is undermined by the provision that they are owed to the company and consequently are only enforceable by the company.[204]

This model is not reflective of the practical situation in Nigeria and it has only succeeded in creating a yawning gap between theory and reality. According to Branson, the US forms of corporate governance are simply not responsive to the problems that the growth of large MNCs portends.[205]

Can corporations be treated as public actors?

This part of the chapter addresses some arguments underlying the need to construe MNCs as public actors. To make this point the chapter examines the shareholding structure of MNCs in Nigeria, the nature of the resources the corporations are exploiting and the effects of the conceptualisation of the corporate form on other stakeholders such as the host communities and employees. In considering the shareholding structure of MNCs in Nigeria the chapter uses Shell Petroleum Development Corporation (SPDC) as an example. SPDC has the biggest operation in Nigeria. A 2004 assessment[206] of its operation shows that it owns 87 flow stations, eight gas

201 See for example *Kotoye* v. *Saraki* (1994) 7 NWLR (Pt. 357) 414,467.
202 Company Act (UK) 2006.
203 This replaces section 309 of the 1985 act. See section 172 Companies Act (UK) 2006.
204 See section 171 (1) Companies Act (UK) 2006.
205 Branson (note 196).
206 Amnesty International, "Nigeria: Are Human Rights in the Pipeline?" (2004), online, available at: http://web.amnesty.org/library/Index/engafr440202004 (accessed 26 September 2010).

plants, about 100 producing oil fields with over 1,000 oil wells and runs a network of pipelines through the Niger Delta stretching over 6,000 km. It produces about half of the country's daily production estimated to be 900,000 barrels per day.[207]

A look at the SPDC's shareholding structure reveals that its majority shareholder with 55 per cent is the wholly owned and statutorily established federal government of Nigeria public organisation, Nigerian National Petroleum Corporation (NNPC).[208] Its other shareholders are three European Companies, Shell International (30 per cent), Elf Petroleum (10 per cent) and Agip Oil (5 per cent). The three European companies are publicly quoted with their shareholders mainly in Europe. However, the management and control of the company is vested in Shell International, which runs the company created by the joint venture.

An important question that arises out of the shareholding structure of Shell in Nigeria is whether the MNC by subsuming itself in a structure that made it a minority shareholder to a government corporation has not implicitly assumed a public function. If examined from the perspective of the worker, for example, under section 318 (1) of the Nigerian Constitution, employees of a company where any level of government holds controlling share or interest are considered to be working in the capacity of a public officer and thus protected under the Public Officers Protection Act.[209] This has been held to be the case in respect of domestic companies in which the government holds majority shareholding.[210] However, the courts have not applied the same approach to workers of MNCs.[211]

Another important factor that places MNCs in Nigeria in a peculiar situation is the nature of the resources they are exploiting. Section 44(3) of the Nigerian Constitution vests the entire property and control of oil and natural gas in the government of Nigeria, to be managed for the benefits of Nigerians. Furthermore, under chapter II of the Constitution on fundamental objectives and directive principles of state policy, duties and responsibilities are placed on the government under section 16(b) and 16(c) to "control the national economy in such manner as to secure the maximum welfare, freedom and happiness of every citizen on the basis of social justice and equality of status and opportunity" and to "manage and operate the major sectors of the economy". It would thus seem that having passed the management of these resources (through exploration and production) to MNCs, the government has passed a function of a public

---

207 Online, available at: www.nigeria-oil-gas.com/ (accessed 2 May 2008).
208 The corporation is established under the Nigerian National Petroleum Act, Cap 320, Laws of the Federation of Nigeria, 1990.
209 Cap 379, Laws of the Federation of Nigeria, 1990.
210 *Olatubosun* v. *NISER* (1988) 3 NWLR (Pt. 80) 25.
211 See for example the Nigerian Supreme Court decision in *Chukwumah* v. *Shell Petroleum* (1993) 4 NWLR (Pt.289) 512 SC.

nature to the MNCs. This book posits that by vesting managerial powers over oil and gas in the MNCs, the government has also transferred responsibility to the companies and therefore the MNCs should be accountable for the exercise of this public function.[212] If it is accepted that a function of a public nature has been invested in MNCs, it is argued that the corporations in this context are more than private interests. It is further suggested that the corporate governance structure in Nigeria should be reflective of the role of corporations within Nigerian society. The point therefore is that the conception of the corporation in Nigeria may be undermining the spirit of the Nigerian Constitution.[213]

The impact of MNCs on communities in their areas of operation has also called into question the role of corporations in such communities. Hassan *et al.* carried out research on the impact of MNCs in the oil and gas sector on women in one of the oil-producing states in Nigeria.[214] Their findings encapsulate the far-reaching impact of the corporations on local communities. The writers found that prior to the discovery of oil in the Niger Delta of Nigeria, the people of the area made their living from the exploitation of the resources of the land, water and forestry as farmers, fishermen and hunters. However, the effects of the operation of MNCs have changed the situation in the area. According to Hassan *et al.*,

> The people cannot farm or fish because of oil spillage and pollution, they can hardly obtain potable water and their health is in severe jeopardy. The ecological problem in the Niger Delta is that multi-national companies and the government are exploiting the ecosystems for resources beyond the level of sustainability. The environment has been exploited and damaged to such an extent as to be unable to continue providing the resources that people of the oil communities depended upon prior to the commencement of oil exploration and production activities.
>
> The activities of the oil companies have seriously affected local livelihoods due to water pollution, take-over of fishing grounds by equipment and installation and damage to fishing nets. Men are now forced to go farther out to sea for fishing which is more time-consuming and dangerous.... The danger of fishing on the high seas is high as some fishermen simply do not return.

212 D. Donald and A. Hutton, "Public Purpose and Private Ownership: Some Implications of the 'Great Capitalist Restoration' for the Politicization of Private Sector Firms in Britain" (1998) 32 *Journal of Economic Issues* 457.
213 This is not only true of the Nigerian case but as Mitchell noted, the exportation of the US model to Germany through investment has led to a distortion of the corporate form as envisaged under the German Constitution. See L. Mitchell, *Corporate Irresponsibility: America's Newest Export* (New Haven and London: Yale University Press, 2001), 257, 261.
214 Hassan *et al.* (note 47).

Health problems were generally reported due to the heat and air pollution resulting from gas flaring as well as water pollution due to oil spoilage. Sexually transmitted diseases have become more prevalent as well due to greater demand for commercial sex workers by oil workers and associated social problems related to large-scale in-migration of strangers.

These findings were corroborated by a 2004 Amnesty International report, which concluded that, "in 40 years of operation, oil companies have left large areas of the Niger Delta unusable for farming, due to frequent oil spills, leakages, and the effect of gas flaring or other accidents".[215]

Hassan *et al.* further highlighted the conflict situation that has become one of the prominent consequences of the activities of MNCs. They classified the conflict into three types – conflict between corporations and youths in the community; between leaders of the community and the youths; and between oil companies and women of the community. According to the researchers, the sources of the conflict include expectations of employment and contracts by young people whose means of livelihood have been wiped out by the corporations and the sharing of largesse that MNCs or their contractors usually give to community leaders to seek support for their activities. Another source of conflict is the failure of corporations to fulfil the promises they made to communities. Hassan *et al.* cite the example of Mobil, which failed to fulfil a promise to install a gas turbine to give uninterrupted electricity supply to one community. The above empirical research, though centred on a particular part of the country, can be used as a guide to understanding the many ways MNCs have affected the day-to-day life of a large number of people.

These negative externalities of MNC operations have raised the question of whether corporations ought to be responsible for people affected by their operations and if so how. The position of corporations has always been that as non-state actors they have no legal obligations either in international law or domestic law regarding the protection of human rights or the provision of public infrastructural facilities.[216] They may choose to protect human rights voluntarily and provide infrastructural facilities on a philanthropic basis but have no legal obligation to do so.

One interesting development is that the failure or inability of the Nigerian government to provide basic infrastructural facilities[217] in areas of

215 Amnesty International (note 210).

216 Ibid.; Edoho (note 119).

217 According to Amnesty International (note 210),

> Nigerian Federal Government has invested little of these resources in the Niger Delta, where the oil producing communities reside. Poverty in this area is widespread. Roads are in a constant state of disrepair; power outages are frequent; the water available is of poor quality and is often contaminated; schools are almost non-existent; and state-run hospitals and clinics are under-equipped or short-staffed, or both.

operation of MNCs has led to a situation where the people within these societies look to MNCs to fulfil this role. The rationale for this expectation is that since the corporations are directly responsible for causing many of these negative externalities they should provide the solutions to them. Okafor opined that communities in the sector are able to hold corporations responsible for their poor development because government has long abdicated its role and since become "invisible" in these communities.[218] The only entities therefore visible to the community are the corporations. As noted earlier, corporations generally deny any responsibility in this regard on the ground that as private actors they are not designed to bear such responsibility. However, despite their position, MNCs have funded several dozen projects of roads, clinics, schools, transport and other infrastructure, in the communities surrounding their operations. According to Amnesty International the reasons why corporations undertake these activities vary. Some companies undertake the activities out of a sense of philanthropy, some in order to secure their license to operate, some in their enlightened self-interest and some to "buy" peace from communities that are suspicious or resentful of their presence.[219]

The question is how to construct the proper function of MNCs in an economy like Nigeria in view of the roles they have implicitly assumed in the society due to their enormous power. In other words, is it tenable to simply argue that MNCs, as described above, with their enormous influence on society are private actors? The answer should be in the negative.

The conception of the MNC as a private actor has had adverse effects on employees of corporations in Nigeria as earlier discussed. Viewed from the communitarian perspective the situation of the employee in Nigeria would not accord with the social role of the corporation, which recognises the stake of the employee in the governance structure of the corporation. In the first place unlike the shareholder, the employee has firm-specific investment in the enterprise and should therefore have prior claim to certain incidents of ownership[220] including elements of voice and control over the disposal of corporate property and property rights in their employment.[221] The effort and sacrifice an employee invests in a corporation is another important factor. Also a broader understanding of the role

---

218 L. Okafor, Enhancing Business-Community Relations: The Role of Volunteers in Promoting Global Corporate Citizenship (Lagos, Nigeria: UNDP/UNV, 2003).

219 Amnesty International (note 210) noted that some projects have worked well and delivered services where none were previously provided, others did not and some are even non-existent. However, the aim of this chapter is not to evaluate the performance of these initiatives but to note the fact of the existence of such initiatives.

220 I. Lynch Fannon, *Working within Two Kind of Capitalism: Corporate Governance and Employee Stakeholding: US and EU Perspectives* (Oxford and Portland, OR: Hart Publishing, 2003), 82.

221 Ibid., 91.

of the corporation based on distributive justice would further support the enhancement of the position of the employee as stakeholder. The steps towards realising this goal will not be feasible as long as the contractarian ideology holds sway in Nigeria.

Considering the impact of corporations on society Lipton and Rosenblum described the corporation (in the United States and United Kingdom) as:

> The central productive element of the economies of the United States and United Kingdom. The health and stability of these economies depends on the ability of corporations to maintain healthy and stable business operations over the long term and to compete in world markets. The corporation affects the destinies of employees, communities, suppliers and customers.[222]

Given the corporations' importance in the "super power" economies of the United Kingdom and United States one can easily imagine the gargantuan implications their operations have for an economy like Nigeria's where the annual GDP largely depends on their functioning. If one imagines a hypothetical situation where the MNCs refused to operate for a sustained period, the socio-political institutions of Nigeria would be brought to their knees.[223] Viewed from this perspective, taking into consideration also the nature of the resources involved and the participation of the federal government in the operations of the MNCs it is unrealistic to sustain the conception of the corporation as a private actor in such circumstances. The merits of the EU model for Nigeria are discussed in the next section.

The social model of the corporation and the Nigerian situation

The discussions so far have shown the level of socio-economic and political involvement of MNCs in Nigeria and their relevance in corporate governance modelling. The NNPC in Nigeria acknowledged this fact when it stated that:

> It is well known that oil and gas are the driving forces of the Nigerian economy. Whilst it is true that the industry provides employment for large numbers of local people, its sheer magnitude means that it also has an impact on the lives of many who are not directly connected to it. This impact may be economic, with the state of health of the industry

---

222 M. Lipton and S. Rosenblum, "A New System of Corporate Governance: the Quinquennial Election of Directors" (1991) 58 *University of Chicago Law Review*, 187, 192.
223 Watts (note 48).

being closely linked to the overall economic welfare of the nation, or environment, since much structural development in Nigeria is linked to this crucial sector.[224]

It is therefore not completely accurate to describe the purpose of corporations working within such circumstances as creating wealth just for shareholders. As Testy observes:

> Because society is plagued by systemic subordination that prevents equality of opportunities, a market system, including a system of corporate governance, that awards rights only to those who can bargain and pay for them themselves deepens the divisions between the haves and the have-nots in society.[225]

Therefore shareholders should be seen as one of the constituents of the community for which the corporation is to create wealth.[226] According to Winkler "because of its broad social impact, only a distorted view of the firm would see shareholders as the sole constituency group".[227] In construing the purpose of the corporation Patricia Hewitt, former Secretary of State for the Department of Trade and Industry in the United Kingdom (introducing Operation and Financial Review and Directors Report Legislation) said as follows:

> What are companies for? The primary goal is to make a profit for their shareholders, certainly. But the days when that was the whole answer are long gone. We all have higher expectations of companies not simply to perform well in the short term, but to have an effective strategy for delivering long-term profitability.... We save for the years ahead, not the months ahead, and we need the companies in which we invest to share our own horizons.
>
> We expect companies to generate the wealth that provides good public services and a decent standard of living for everyone. We need continuing recognition that wealth creation demands honest and fair dealings with employees, customers, suppliers and creditors. Good working conditions, good products and services and successful relationships with a wide range of other stakeholders are important assets, crucial to stable, long-term performance and shareholder value.

---

224 Online, available at: www.abuja.net/biz3.htm (accessed 2 May 2007).
225 K.Y. Testy, "What Is the 'New' Corporate Social Responsibility? Linking Progressive Corporate Law with Progressive Social Movements" (2002) 76 *Tulane Law Review* 1227, 1251.
226 Lynch Fannon (note 220), 85.
227 A. Winkler, "Case Studies in Conservative and Progressive Legal Orders: Corporate Law or the Law of Business? Stakeholders and Corporate Governance at the End of History" (2004) 67 *Law and Contemporary Problems* 109.

We expect companies to create wealth while respecting the environment and exercising responsibility towards the society and the local communities in which they operate.... For this reason, I believe that increased, high quality shareholder engagements is vital to creating the modern economy that we all want.[228]

The above quoted statement is a fair description of the EU. A social model of the corporation has existed in Europe for more than 30 years and is a pragmatic expression of the communitarian model of corporate law and its foundation.[229] The ideas behind this model are reflected in many EU policy documents.[230] While the EU is like the United States in having many regulations protecting shareholders, the major difference between the United States and the EU approach is that the EU went further by facilitating regulations to protect non-shareholding stakeholders in significant ways. It is noted that corporate governance in EU member states differ in some respects from each other. The UK (and the Irish) systems have more in common with the United States when compared with other European models hence the common nomenclature "Anglo-American Model". However, in other European countries, the dominant corporate governance models are the communitarian model and the stakeholder models of the corporation. The link between the two models is the extension of the responsibilities of the corporation to other constituent groups.[231] It is pertinent to observe that the corporation at inception in the United Kingdom started out with a public dimension. According to Dodd the common law had historically treated business as public rather than private.[232] According to Kirkbride and others "governance in the public interest was the accepted doctrine" and "whilst individuals could own shares in the corporations and sell them, serving shareholder interest was not the primary purpose of corporations".[233]

228 Quoted in C.A. Williams and J.M. Conley, "An Emerging Third Way? The Erosion of the Anglo-American Shareholder Value Construct" (2005) 38 *Cornell International Law Journal.* 493.
229 The communitarian versus contractarian debate on corporate governance was discussed in Chapter 3. See also Lynch Fannon (note 220), 88.
230 For examples the "EU Green Paper Promoting a European Framework for Corporate Social Responsibility" (2001); The EU Working Time Directive (93/104/EC) as amended by Directive 2000/34/EC and Council Directive 96/34/EC (1996) OJ L145/4 on the Framework Agreement on Parental Leave.
231 M.P. Broberg "Corporate Social Responsibility in the European Communities: The Scandinavian Viewpoint" (1996) 15 *Journal of Business Ethics* 615; S. Donnelly, A. Gamble, G. Jackson and J. Parkinson, *The Public Interest and the Company in Britain and Germany* (Anglo-German Foundation, London, 2000); A. Gamble and G. Kelly "The Politics of the Company" in John Parkinson, Andrew Gamble and Gavin Kelly, *The Political Economy of the Company* (Oxford and Portland: Hart Publishing, 2000), 21–50.
232 E. Merrick Dodd, Jr. "For Whom Corporate Managers are Trustees: A Note" (1932) *Harvard Law Review* 1145.
233 J. Kirkbride, S. Letza, X. Sun and C. Smallman, "The Boundaries of Governance in the Post-Modern World" (2008) 59 (2) *Northern Ireland Legal Quarterly* 161, 162.

The EU social model based on the communitarian school of thought is reflective of the situation in Nigeria, unlike the present US contractarian model. The model sees the corporation as an appropriate subject of state legislation "where the object of this regulation is to achieve broadly sketched social, employment or economic policies".[234] Furthermore, the model allows for the regulation of external corporate relationships with other stakeholders and also for the governance structure within the corporation to recognise the claim of other stakeholders.[235] The acceptance of the corporation as a public actor gives legitimacy to the efforts of the legislatures both at the national and supranational level to regulate corporate activities as it affects many areas of life.[236]

The MNCs in Nigeria should be viewed not in the abstract but in the context in which they operate. The corporate governance structure in Nigeria would be more relevant to the regulation of corporations to achieve wider social goals if it were founded on a social model.

Advantages of a social model for Nigeria

The advantages of a move towards a social model would not only be beneficial to stakeholders but also to corporations. MNCs presently face diverse stakeholder claims, to which they have found it difficult to effectively respond. Their attempted responses mostly end in dispute with stakeholders as to the adequacy and appropriateness of the response offered. First, if adopted, such a model of corporate governance would make corporations receptive to legislation geared towards social goals. This would spell out the framework for responding to social issues. Many directives of the EU address social issues such as working conditions, regulation of atypical employment and environmental compliance. Second, the suspicion that has attended the social responsibility agenda of corporations operating in the South would be lessened. There has not been much trust in the voluntary approach of corporations to social responsibility.[237] An important point here is that a change in the governance structure would alter the perception in Nigerian society of oil corporations as exploiters whose only

234 I. Lynch Fannon, "From Workers to Global Politics; How the Way we Work Provides Answers to Corporate Governance Questions" in J. O'Brien, ed., *Governing the Corporation, Regulation and Corporate Governance in an Age of Scandal and Global Market* (London: Wiley Publications, 2005).

235 Lynch Fannon (note 220), 85.

236 Ibid., 132.

237 J. Frynas. "The False Developmental Promise of Corporate Social Responsibility: Evidence from Multinational Oil Companies" (2005) 81 *International Affairs* 581–598. See also Christian Aid's report, *Behind the Mask: The Real Face of Corporate Social Responsibility* (2004), online, available at: www.globalpolicy.org/socecon/tncs/2004/0121mask.pdf (accessed 2 May 2008).

interest is profit. Nigerians, especially in the area of operation of MNCs, view the relationship with MNCs as "them" against "us". This perception has led to incessant conflicts between the corporations and stakeholders. The shift would also enhance the partnership between the government and the corporations for developmental purposes.

A shift towards a social model would necessarily influence government policy decisions and regulation of corporations generally and MNCs in particular. Stakeholder issues such as employee representation on boards of corporations, which have not featured in the Nigerian company governance discourse to date, could be brought to the fore. It is significant that in European countries such as Germany, employees are represented on supervisory boards and have an equal say on some issues such as responding to takeover bids.[238]

In a report on the public interest and companies in the United Kingdom and Germany it was concluded *inter alia* that one of the strongest pressures and rationales for changes in these two European countries comes from the EU through its directives. According to the authors, the EU has emerged as a crucial arena for the definition and implementation of the public interest in relation to the company.[239] This influence, has for example strengthened the constitutionalisation of the company in Germany, where employees enjoy a right to consultation and, in some cases, participation in setting company policy on working conditions.[240]

As discussed earlier in this chapter, the governance model adopted has had dramatic effects on mandatory corporate reporting in the United Kingdom and France. It is suggested that the UK and French experiences could contain useful lessons for Nigeria in any future consideration of company law reform.

Some suggestions for reform in Nigeria

It is acknowledged that the social model in the EU has developed over time through many different legislative paths, including employment legislation, social security and central planning in the construction of the corporation as a social actor, but this book suggests that some key elements of Nigerian company law could be modified in an attempt to reconstruct the purpose of the corporation in Nigeria. Suggestions are also made in other areas of the law.

The US contractarian conservative, private, shareholder-wealth-maximisation model which is dominant in most of the countries of the South including Nigeria has proved irrelevant in addressing the issues raised by the operations of MNCs. The model is not only problematic from

---

238 Williams and Conley (note 228).
239 Donnelly *et al.* (note 231), 56.
240 Ibid.

the other stakeholders' perspective but also constrains the ability of MNCs to address conflicting demands made on them in consequence to their operations. Furthermore the model ignores the local context in which MNCs operate and distances the corporation from society. In the Nigerian context, the model can also be seen as being in conflict with the spirit of the Nigerian Constitution. While this chapter does not suggest doing away with the private structure of corporation, it advocates harnessing the potential of the private structure for the public interest. Addressing other stakeholders' issues will not be possible without making reforms to corporate law in a way that opens up the corporation to other stakeholder issues. It is in the light of this that this chapter is urging a shift in Nigerian corporate governance to a progressive, public, stakeholder-protection/ social-responsibility model. It is suggested that such a shift would effectively reposition the corporations within the context of their operations.

For example, directors' duties under the Companies and Allied Matters Act should be widened to accommodate duties to other stakeholders. At present under the Companies and Allied Matters Act, the directors of the company owe duties only to the company, interpreted as its shareholders, and thus have no legal responsibility or capacity to embark on any other duty apart from their duty to the company and its shareholders.[241] The proposed change would allow the directors to take appropriate account of the interests of non-shareholding stakeholders. As a start non-shareholding stakeholders could be defined to include employees and people within the area of operation of companies who are directly affected by their activities. The provision on directors' duties in the United Kingdom is instructive in this regard.[242] Section 172(1)(c) of the Companies Act 2006 on the general duty of directors to act in ways that "promote the success of the company" also obliged directors to have regard to the "impact of the company's operations on the community and the environment".

In the United States, the idea of widening directors' duties beyond the traditional scope is slowly emerging. Two famous decisions from the state of Delaware point in this direction. In the *re Caremark International Inc.*[243] case the Delaware Court of Chancery put forward an expanded view of directors' duty in relation to directors' supervisory duty over employees. According to the court,

> A director's obligation includes a duty to attempt in good faith to assure that corporate information and reporting system, which the

---

241 See section 279 of the Companies and Allied Matters Act, 1990. See also Orojo (note 55), 295–321. However, section 38 of CAMA, which is on powers of the company, allows the company to make donations except to a political party or political association.
242 See Companies Act, 2006 (UK).
243 Derivative litigation 698 A 2d 959 (Del.Ch.1996).

board concludes is adequate, exists, and that failure to do so under some circumstances may, in theory at least, render a director liable for losses.[244]

This is a duty to monitor corporate operations which goes beyond the traditional duty of care/good faith. The opinion was confirmed by the Supreme Court of Delaware in *Stone* v. *Ritter*[245] although the decision was confined to situations where there is sustained or systematic failure of the board of directors to exercise oversight.

Furthermore directors' reports under the Act should include reporting on companies' social responsibility performance. At present, the directors' report requirement under section 342 of the Act relates solely to the company's financial performance with the exception of the requirement that three heads of information relating to employment and employees be included which are: employment of disabled persons; health, safety and welfare at work of company employees and employees' involvement and training. The developments in Indonesia and France discussed earlier could be helpful in this regard.

It is furthered suggested that section 5 of CAMA which mandates foreign companies to be locally incorporated before they can carry on business in Nigeria be expunged from the law as it is counterproductive. It only provides a stronger shield for parent companies of MNCs without being of any special advantage to the country.

The implementation of the above modest suggestions would enable the courts to interpret the relationship between the corporation and other stakeholders on the basis of the social model.

MNCs in Nigeria operate in a complex and often chaotic situation. They are faced with conflicting demands from various stakeholders including the government, local communities and employees. The MNCs have thus been constrained to use the CSR concept as a means of balancing these conflicting interests.[246] However, because of the ill-defined nature of what is required and the means of addressing them, these initiatives have had little effect in resolving conflicting interests. The result is the constant friction between stakeholders and sometimes violent interruption of the operations of MNCs in the country. It is posited that the suggestions above would bring clarity to the situation and give MNCs more precise tools in addressing stakeholder issues. By expanding directors' duties some measure of legal backing would be given to company CSR practices.

---

244 Ibid.
245 911 A 2d 362 (Del. 2006).
246 K Amaeshi, A. Adi, C. Ogbechie and O. Amao, "Corporate Social Responsibility in Nigeria: Western Mimicry or Indigenous Influence" (2006) 24 *Journal of Corporate Citizenship* 83.

Second, expanding directors' reports to include social responsibility issues would make the CSR initiatives of MNCs more transparent. Finally, introducing minimum standards required in this regard would obviate recurrent dispute among stakeholders as to what is required.

Maximising the benefits of Gbemre *v.* Shell: *the human rights dimension*

The decision in *Gbemre* v. *Shell*[247] has shed light on a possibility which has not received much attention in the Nigerian context. The decision has not only shown that the human rights approach is practical and realistic but that it also has some significant advantages over other approaches. As shown earlier, the approach would check government complicity and complacency in respect of MNCs' abuse. Second, it avoids the procedural drawbacks associated with other approaches. It is much faster thereby making it more cost effective and it also accommodates the application of supranational norms i.e. the African Charter. The success of this approach would largely depend on lawyers in Nigeria taking up the benefits it offers and judges' ability to appreciate the approach as demonstrated in *Gbemre* v. *Shell*. Furthermore, considering that many of the provisions implicating issues raised in CSR are contained in chapter II of the Constitution on Fundamental Objective and Directive Principles of State Policy and in view of the Supreme Court decision in *AG Ondo and Ors* v. *AG Federation and Ors*[248] (discussed earlier) there is a duty on the legislature to adopt a more proactive attitude to activate the constitutional provisions under Chapter II.

Other areas

It is further suggested that there are provisions under the criminal and penal codes, the Independent Corrupt Practices and Related Offences Act, 2000 and the Economic and Financial Crimes Commission (Establishment) Act, 2004 to deal with the issue of corporate involvement in corruption as it affects all facets of life including human rights. Section 65(1) of CAMA has made it easier to ascertain the *mens rea* of a corporation. Furthermore the wide powers conferred on the EFCC should be exercised not only to monitor and investigate public bodies but also private organisations. Furthermore, Nigerian law has proved outdated and completely

---

247 *Jonah Gbemre* v. *Shell Petroleum Development Company Nigeria Ltd, Nigerian National Petroleum Corporation and Attorney General of the Federation,* Decision of the Federal High Court of Nigeria in the Benin Judicial Division Holden at Court Benin City (Suit No FHC/B/CS/53/05, 14 November 2005).

248 *AG Ondo and Ors* v. *AG Federation and Ors* (2002) 6 SC (Part. 1), 1.

inadequate to deal with the labour relations issues arising out of MNCs' operations. The need for reform of Nigerian labour/employment laws is more urgent than ever as the impact of MNCs continues to grow. The arrival of MNCs from Asia especially from China has exacerbated this problem.

Recent development: the Nigerian Corporate Social Responsibility Bill 2008

In March 2008, a Private Members Bill was introduced in the Nigerian Parliament for the establishment of a corporate social responsibility commission.[249] Though the Bill is in its early stages and its drafting is apparently poor and substantially ambiguous, it is pertinent to examine the Bill and the potential implications of its provisions for MNCs.

The objectives of the Bill are expressed in the explanatory memorandum:

> This Bill seeks to provide for comprehensive adequate relief to communities which suffer the negative consequences of the industrial and commercial activities of companies operating in their areas.
>
> The Bill seeks to create a specific body for the execution of this highly important social responsibility.
>
> It also provides for penalty for any breaches of corporate social responsibility.

The Bill takes a territorial approach which will not answer many of the challenges posed by the multi-jurisdictional structure of MNCs. However, it does contain provisions which are designed to change companies' (including MNCs' subsidiaries) approach to CSR in Nigeria.

There is an attempt under the Bill to widen the group of stakeholders to which corporations are responsible. Under section 5(1)(k), the CSR Commission is required to "ensure that companies are accountable not only to employees and their trade unions, but to investors, consumers, host communities and the wider environment". This obviously runs contrary to sections 41 and 279 of the principal statute on companies in Nigeria, the Companies and Allied Matters Act (CAMA) of 1990, which only recognises the traditional stakeholders: shareholders.

Section 5(1)(i) of the Bill makes corporate philanthropy mandatory. It specifies a minimum amount of money that should be invested in CSR by companies. The section requires companies to spend not less than 3.5 per

---

249 Bill for an Act to Provide for the Establishment of the Corporate Social Responsibility Commission (Nigerian CSR Bill), online, available at: www.femiamao.com/files/CSR_BILL.pdf (accessed 26 September 2010).

cent of their gross annual profit for a given year on CSR projects. Again, this provision attempts to allocate companies' resources in a way which is contrary to directors' statutory duties under section 279 of CAMA.

The Bill mandates annual social and environment impact reporting but places the responsibility for ensuring this on the commission.[250] Therefore, it does not alter the reporting scheme under CAMA, which requires only financial reporting.

The commission has the responsibility to create a standard for CSR consistent with international standards. This takes standard setting away from the voluntary initiatives of companies.[251] Furthermore, the commission is to develop guidelines on environmental standards expected of companies. It is not clear how this will work out given the existing regulatory framework for the environment in the country.[252] The commission also has the task of pegging and monitoring the implementation of local contents in terms of employment and sourcing of raw materials by companies.[253] CSR is to be integrated into Nigerian trade policies but taking into consideration WTO rules. The Bill also seeks to introduce social responsibility compliance labels in Nigeria to be awarded to companies that comply with CSR standards.[254]

The extent of each company's responsibilities will be determined by organisational size and the magnitude of investments.[255] This is a curious and ambiguous yardstick for determining responsibility as the social and environmental impact of corporations' operations may not necessarily be an issue of size and magnitude of investment.

For companies that default or fail to adhere to CSR standards, the Bill imposes sanctions through fines, temporary closure and suspension of operations. The fines stipulated are not less than 2 per cent of gross annual profit of a company on first conviction and on subsequent conviction not less than 3.5 per cent of its annual gross profit.[256] A company's officers may be liable in cases where a company fails to comply with the Bill and the company's officers wilfully obstruct the operations of the commission or its authorised staff. Such officers may be liable to imprisonment for a period of not less than six months.[257]

The apparent conflict of this Bill with the existing company law statute, the Companies and Allied Matters Act, 1990, is a major flaw in its drafting. Perhaps the drafters should have taken a cue from the approach taken by

250 Nigerian CSR Bill, section 5(1)(h).
251 Ibid., section 5(1)(a).
252 Ibid., section 5(1)(m).
253 Ibid., section 5(1)(b)(m).
254 Ibid., section 5(1)(0).
255 Ibid., section 5(1)(g).
256 Ibid., section 7(3).
257 Ibid., section 7(4)(1).

the Indonesian Parliament which has introduced the most radical legislative change in this area to date by amending its company laws as discussed earlier. While it is too early to assess the impact of the Indonesian approach, amending conflicting legal norms in company law will remove the conflict that has arisen in the case of the Nigerian CSR Bill.

Summary

This chapter explored the legal and institutional framework for the control of MNCs using Nigeria as a case study. The chapter noted that because of the colonial origins of Nigerian law and the close links between MNCs and the British authorities, pre-independence legislation in Nigeria was skewed in favour of MNCs. The colonial past has also influenced the post-independence attempt to put some measure of control over MNCs. The gaps within the local legal framework have left many issues within the CSR domain. Nevertheless, there are opportunities under the law in Nigeria for effective control of MNCs. In this regard, the chapter examined the areas of company law, tort law, human rights law, criminal law, labour law and anti-corruption law that could be employed to control MNCs. The chapter went further to identify areas of Nigerian law which need reform in order to deal effectively with issues raised by CSR. The chapter drew insights from different jurisdictions including Indonesia, France, the United Kingdom and the United States. This chapter underscores the relevance of domestic law in the control of MNCs. It is not suggested that the domestic level, or any level for that matter, is sufficient, but that there is a need to engage with all levels of governance in the control of MNCs. The regulatory frameworks at the domestic level in developing countries have largely been ignored to date and it is submitted that there is a need to engage with possibilities at this level.

5 Regional human rights system and multinational corporations

The case of the African regional human rights system

Introduction

This chapter continues with the overall goal of this book: exploring solutions to the control of multinational corporations (MNCs) at the domestic level with complementary mechanisms at regional and international levels. The aim of this chapter is to examine the African human rights system as a case study at the regional level, to evaluate how it has impacted on the control of MNCs and to examine its potential for the future. The theme of the chapter is important because it focuses on a heretofore under-explored avenue for the control of MNCs. The chapter concedes that the African human rights system is relatively young and cannot provide all the solutions to the numerous issues surrounding the control of MNCs in the continent. However, it is strongly suggested that the regional human rights system's emerging approach to state responsibility could galvanise the weak host states to be more effective because of its emerging approach to state responsibility.

The position of this writer is that, since host states have the primary obligation to control MNCs, it would be productive to explore frameworks that could strengthen and complement home states' capacity to control MNCs. The chapter provides a brief description of the African human rights system. It discusses the relevance of the African Charter to private and other legal persons including MNCs. It examines recent jurisprudence of the African Commission on Human and Peoples' Rights (the African Commission). The chapter explores the potential of the African Union (AU) court system in the control of MNCs. The chapter also examines The African Convention on Preventing and Combating Corruption and the implication of the convention for MNCs. The chapter concludes that the African system, though nascent, is a necessary complement to the ability to hold MNCs accountable at the host state level and other regional arrangements at the international level.

State responsibility in context: state responsibility for human rights violations by private actors under international law

The African system, to a large extent, follows the "state responsibility" approach as developed in international law.[1] It is therefore pertinent to begin this chapter with a discussion of state responsibility for violation of human rights by non-state actors under international law. It is argued in this chapter *inter alia* that in order to be more effective in the control of MNCs, the African system needs to advance beyond the current position of the principle of state responsibility under international law.

Under the classic doctrine of international law, states are responsible for upholding human rights.[2] United Nations treaties firmly establish that states are the primary duty bearers for the protection of human rights.[3] However, some of the UN treaty provisions either directly or indirectly impose obligations on states to regulate businesses in a way that ensures that they do not violate human rights. The earlier treaties such as the International Covenant on Civil and Political Rights (ICCPR),[4] International Covenant on Economic, Social and Cultural Rights (ICESCR)[5] and International Convention on the Elimination of All Forms of Racial Discrimination (ICERD) impose general obligations on states to ensure the enjoyment of rights and prevent non-state actor abuse.[6] Later treaties took

---

1 According to R. Murray,

> Because the African system has not rejected so called Western notions and concepts of international law and indeed has embraced some of them wholeheartedly, it would be illegitimate to reject the underlying concepts of international law as being wholly invalid.
> (R. Murray, *The African Commission on Human and Peoples' Rights and International Law* (UK: Hart Publishing, 2000) 50)

See also J. Udombana, "Between Promise and Performance: Revisiting States' Obligations under the African Human Rights Charter" (2004) 40 *Stanford Journal of International Law* 105, 121.

2 N. Jagers, *Corporate Human Rights Obligations: in Search of Accountability* (Antwerp: Intersentia, 2002), 137.

3 J.G. Ruggie, "Business and Human Rights: The Evolving International Agenda" (2007) 101 *American Journal of International Law* 819; see also Chapter 1.

4 International Covenant on Civil and Political Rights, GA res. 2200A (XXI), 21 UN GAOR Supp. (no. 16) at 52, UN Doc. A/6316 (1966), 999 UNTS 171, entered into force 23 March 1976.

5 International Covenant on Economic, Social and Cultural Rights GA res. 2200A (XXI), 21 UN GAOR Supp. (no. 16) at 49, UN Doc. A/6316 (1966), 993 UNTS 3, entered into force 3 January 1976.

6 See for example article 2(1)(d) of the International Convention on the Elimination of All Forms of Racial Discrimination (ICERD) (GA res. 2106 (XX), Annex, 20 UN GAOR Supp. (no. 14) at 47, UN Doc. A/6014 (1966), 660 UNTS 195), entered into force 4 January 1969 which requires each state party to prohibit racial discrimination by "persons, group or organizations". Article 2 of the ICCPR imposes a duty on states to ensure to all individuals the recognised rights. See also H.J. Steiner, P. Alston and R. Goodman *International Human Rights in Context* (third edition, Oxford: Oxford University Press, 2008) 188.

a more direct approach. The Convention on the Elimination of All Forms of Discrimination Against Women (CEDAW),[7] the Convention on the Rights of the Child (CRC)[8] and the Convention on the Rights of Persons with Disabilities[9] address business directly and in more detail.[10] The reason why the principle is relevant in the context of this chapter is that, since MNCs are not recognisable entities under international law, the principle provides an indirect way by which MNCs could be held accountable under international law. International human rights bodies have in their practices applied the general principles of state responsibility to human rights matters.[11] Commentators have also expressed the view that principles of state responsibility are applicable to human rights.[12]

State responsibility is an old principle of international law and it arose originally where one state committed an international wrong against another.[13] The rule has not only been elevated to the status of a general principle of international law, but has also been described by the Permanent International Court of Justice as a "greater conception of law" which would lead to payment of reparation where the principle is breached.[14]

---

7 Convention on the Elimination of All Forms of Discrimination Against Women, GA res. 34/180, 34 UN GAOR Supp. (no. 46) at 193, UN Doc. A/34/46, entered into force 3 September 1981.

8 Convention on the Rights of the Child, 20 November 1989, 1577 UNTS 3.

9 The Convention on the Rights of Persons with Disabilities and its optional protocol were adopted by the United Nations General Assembly on 13 December 2006 and opened for signature on 30 March 2007.

10 The Convention on the Elimination of All Forms of Discrimination Against Women (CEDAW) under article 2(e) imposes obligation on the states to take all appropriate measures to eliminate discrimination against women by any person, organisation or enterprise. Article 4(c) of the UN Declaration on the Elimination of Violence Against Women (A/RES/48/104, eighty-fifth plenary meeting, 20 December 1993) obliges states to "exercise due diligence to prevent, investigate and in accordance with national legislation, punish acts of violence against women whether those acts are perpetrated by states or private persons". See further article 2: Convention Against Torture and Other Cruel, Inhuman or Degrading Treatment (1984, 1465 UNTS 85), article 4: Convention on the Prevention and Punishment of Crimes Against Internationally Protected Persons Including Diplomatic Agents (1973, 1035 UNTS 167), article 11: Convention on the Safety of UN and Associated Personnel (1994, 2051 UNTS 303), article 15: International Convention on the Suppression of Terrorist Bombings (1997, 2149 UNTS 256).

11 Jagers (note 2),146.

12 See for example C. Warbrick "The European Convention on Human Rights and the Prevention of Terrorism" (1983) 32 (1) *International and Comparative Law Quarterly* 82; Jagers (note 2), 146; R. McCorquodale and P. Simons, "Responsibility Beyond Borders: State Responsibility for Extraterritorial Violations by Corporations of International Human Rights Law" (2007) 70 (4) *Modern Law Review* 598, 601–602.

13 R. Rosenstock, "The ILC and State Responsibility" (2002) 96 *American Journal of International Law* 792; D.M. Chirwa, "The Doctrine of State Responsibility as a Potential means of Holding Private Actors Accountable for Human Rights" (2004) 5 *Melbourne Journal of International Law* 1, 4.

14 *Chorzow Factory (Germany v. Poland) (Merits)* (1928) PCIJ (ser. A) no. 13.

According to Chirwa, the principle emanates "from the nature of the international legal system, which relies on states as a means of formulating and implementing its rules, and arises out of the twin doctrines of state sovereignty and equality of states".[15]

The rationale for the concept, especially in the context of human rights law, is that because international human rights law imposes a duty on states to protect people from violations of human rights, states have the duty to ensure that private actors do not violate human rights. Consequently if private actors violate human rights, states will be held responsible for failing to prevent such violations within their territories. States are not directly liable for the violations by private actors but for the failure to prevent the violations. International legal responsibility of non-state actors, such as MNCs, thus remains indirect: in order to be held responsible, an MNC's conduct must breach positive international law in a manner that is attributable to the state or a state must have violated one of its own obligations in relation to the regulation or supervision of an MNC's conduct.[16] The concept was largely developed through international judicial decisions. However, the United Nations decided to codify the rules on state responsibility and in 1949 it set up the International Law Commission (ILC) for that purpose. The revision and negotiations of the articles on responsibility of states for internationally wrongful acts (ILC articles) by the ILC took five decades. It should be noted that the ILC focused on secondary rules (consequences for breaching of primary rules) of state responsibility that would apply to a variety of situations as opposed to primary rules of substantive international law.[17] The articles were finally adopted by the ILC in 2001.[18] The ILC articles have not yet been adopted as a treaty and so technically are not binding. However, since the ILC articles codified existing case law and international law, they are regarded as providing evidence of established and developing international law.[19]

---

15 Chirwa (note 13), 5.

16 J. Brunnee, "International Legal Accountability through the Lens of the Law of State Responsibility" (2005) 36 *Netherlands Yearbook of International Law* 21–56, 42.

17 See M. Milanovic, "State Responsibility for Genocide" (2006) 17 (3) *European Journal of International Law* 553, 559–561; Rosenstock (note 13), 793.

18 International Law Commission, *Articles on Responsibility of States for Internationally Wrongful Acts*, as contained in the *Report of the International Law Commission on the Work of its 53rd Session*, August 2001, UN GAOR, 56th Sess. Supp. no. 10, UN Doc A/56/10 (SUPP) 2001.

19 The ICJ cited an earlier draft text of the ILC articles in *Gab íkovo-Nagyamaros Project (Hungary/Slovakia)* ICJ Reports 1997, 7, 38–41. The ICJ referred to the same draft in *Legal Consequences of the Construction of a Wall in the Occupied Palestinian Territory*, International Court of Justice, 9 July 2004, Advisory Opinion, ICJ Reports 2004, 136. The ILC articles were also cited by the International Tribunal on Law of the Sea in *M/V "Saiga" (no. 2) (St. Vincent and the Grenadines v. Guinea)* (Int'l Trib. Law of Sea 1 July 1999) 38 ILM 1323 (1999); cf. Milanovic (note 17) 560, who said that "The ILC's work is certainly not gospel and its authority, as well as that of the ICJ for that matter, does not place it or the ICJ beyond criticism".

Others have argued that since they also represent the views of highly regarded international law scholars they could be considered as having authoritative force.[20]

Under article 2, state responsibility would arise where two elements are established: (*a*) the existence of conduct consisting of an act or omission which is attributable to the state under international law; and (*b*) that the conduct constitutes a breach of international obligations of the state. These two elements are well established by international judicial decisions as principles of international law.[21]

The most relevant articles in the context of this chapter are articles 5 and 8. Article 5 provides as follows,

> The conduct of a person or entity which is not an organ of the state under Article 4 but which is empowered by the law of that state to exercise elements of the governmental authority shall be considered an act of the state under international law, provided the person or entity is acting in that capacity in the particular instance.

According to the commentary published by the ILC on the articles,[22] the term "entity" in the provision may include public corporations, semi-public entities, public agencies of various kinds and private companies provided that they are empowered by state law to exercise elements of governmental authority.

Article 8 provides as follows,

> The conduct of a person or group of persons shall be considered an act of a state under international law if the person or group of persons is in fact acting on the instructions of, or under the direction or control of, that state in carrying out the conduct.

Under the article, the conduct of private persons would be imputed to a state where private persons are acting on the instructions of the state in carrying out a wrongful act and where private persons act under the state's directions and control.

Under articles 5 and 8, the complainant has the burden of establishing state control of the non-state actor. The threshold for discharging the

---

20 Chirwa (note 13), 5; D. Caron, "The ILC Articles on State Responsibility: The Paradoxical Relationship between Form and Authority" (2002) 96 *American Journal of International Law* 857, 867.

21 See *Treatment of Polish Nationals and other Persons of Polish Origin or Speech in Danzig Territory*, 1932, PCIJ, ser. A/B, no. 44, 4; *SS "Wimbledon"* 1923, PCIJ, ser. A, no. 1; *Greco-Bulgarian "Communities"*, 1830, PCIJ, ser. B, no. 17, 32; *Reparation for Injuries Suffered in the Service of the United Nations*, ICJ Reports 1949, 174, 180.

22 United Nations, *Draft Articles on Responsibility of States for Internationally Wrongful Acts with Commentaries 2001* (United Nations: 2005), 92.

burden is high, ranging from a demonstration of "effective control" to establishing a relationship of "complete dependence".[23] Consequently, before a state can be held liable under the principle of state responsibility there must be sufficient nexus between the state and the act of the non-state actor.[24]

The requirement that for state responsibility to arise a connection has to be established between the state and the wrongful act is a major limiting factor on the application of the principle. This may make it difficult to attribute the conduct of private actors to states. Furthermore, the enforcement of the principle is dependent on action by another state or states. This is because as a general rule under classic international law only states have the right to bring a complaint against another state for violation of international law. There are exceptions to this rule, such as, the individual's ability to seek redress against the state under international human rights law.[25]

A relevant question in the context of this book is whether the conduct of a state owned corporation can be imputed to the state by the simple fact that it is state owned. Crawford summarises the ILC's position as follows:

In discussing this issue it is necessary to recall that international law acknowledges the general separateness of corporate entities at the national level, except in those cases where the "corporate veil" is a mere device or vehicle for fraud or evasion. The fact that the state initially establishes a corporate entity, whether by special law or otherwise, is not a sufficient basis for the attribution to the state of the subsequent conduct of that entity. Since corporate entities, although

---

23 See *Military and Paramilitary Activities in and Against Nicaragua (Nicaragua v. United States of America (Merits)* (1986) ICJ Reports 14, 58–63 where the court held that for conduct to give rise to state responsibility, the state must have "effective control" of the non-state actor. In *Prosecutor v. Tadic* (Appeals Chamber Judgement) Case IT-94-1-A (15 July 1999), the International Tribunal for Former Yugoslavia stated that a lesser standard could be applied depending on the facts of each case. However, the ICJ employed similar standards to the one employed in *Nicaragua* in *Bosnia and Herzegovina v. Serbia and Montenegro* (2007) ICJ Reports 2007 requiring a relationship of "complete dependence" between the state and the non-state actor and "effective control" over the latter. The ICJ rejected the opinion in *Tadic* reasoning that the case was not about state responsibility as such and that the tribunal was not in any case a judicial tribunal that deals with the issue of state responsibility. See further M. Gibney, "Genocide and State Responsibility" 2007 (4) *Human Rights Law Review* 760, 763.

24 Chirwa (note 13), 9.

25 See for example article 34 of the European Convention on Human Rights (213 UNTS 222) and protocol 11 to the Convention for the Protection of Human Rights and Fundamental Freedoms (ETS 155, entered into force, 1 November 1998) which allow for individual complaints. See also Steiner *et al.* (note 6), 891 on individual communications under UN human rights treaties.

owned by and in that sense subject to the control of the state, are considered to be separate, prima facie their conduct in carrying out their activities is not attributable to the state unless they are exercising elements of governmental authority within the meaning of Article 5.... On the other hand, where there was evidence that the corporation was exercising public powers, or that the state was using its ownership interest in or control of a corporation specifically in order to achieve a particular result, the conduct in question has been attributed to the state.[26]

Therefore under international law on state responsibility, the ownership of a corporation by the government is not crucial to determining state responsibility of state owned corporation. What is important is how the corporation is used by the state. However, as will be shown in this chapter, this is not necessarily the case in respect of the African regional human rights systems' approach.

The European Court of Human Rights and the Inter-American Court of Human Rights have handled many cases involving state responsibility. However, the ECtHR has handled more cases than the Inter-American Court.[27] The cases that have been decided by the ECtHR show how the principle of state responsibility is being employed to hold states accountable for failure to prevent violations of human rights under regional conventions. The approach of the ECtHR exemplifies the relevance of the state responsibility to the control of private parties including corporations. The first two cases examined below are particularly relevant because they involved private companies.

In *Lopez Ostra* v. *Spain*,[28] in the town of Lorca in Spain, a limited company called SACURSA had a plant for the treatment of liquid and solid waste. The plant was built with state subsidy on municipal land 12 metres away from the applicant's home. The plant started operating in July 1988 without licence from the municipal authorities required by Spanish regulation. The complainant alleged that the plant emitted fumes, repetitive noise and strong smells which adversely affected the living conditions of her family and caused her and her family serious health problems. The Spanish authorities were not directly responsible for the acts in question. The court, however, found that the municipal authority permitted its land

26 J. Crawford, *The International Law Commission's Articles on State Responsibility: Introduction Text and Commentary* (Cambridge: Cambridge University Press, 2002) 112; see also Chirwa (note 13), 7–8.

27 Chirwa (note 13), 24; B. Conforti, "Exploring the Strasbourg Case-Law: Reflections on State Responsibility for Breach of Positive Obligations" in M. Fitzmaurice and D. Sarooshi, eds, *Issues of State Responsibility before International Judicial Institutions* (Oxford and Portland: Hart Publishing, 2004), 129.

28 *Lopez Ostra* v. *Spain* (1994) 20 EHRR 277.

to be used and the state also provided subsidy for the building of the plant. The court held the state responsible because it failed to secure the right to private and family life provided for under article 8 of the ECHR.

In *Guerra and Others* v. *Italy*,[29] the applicants' lived in a town which was about 1 km from a company's chemical factory. During the course of its production process the company released large quantities of inflammable gas and other toxic substances such as arsenic trioxide. There was an explosion at the factory in 1976 leading to the release of tonnes of chemicals containing arsenic trioxide. The incident led to the hospitalisation of 150 people for arsenic poisoning. The applicants alleged that the Italian authorities had failed to ensure that the public were informed of the risks posed by the factory's operations and what was to be done in the event of an accident. The applicants were not complaining about an act of state but rather the failure of the state to act. The ECHR held that the Italian authorities were in breach of article 8 of the ECHR (the right to private and family life) because it failed to act to protect the people from the emissions and explosions.

These cases show that a state may be liable for the violations of human rights by a third party not because the state is directly liable but because of the failure to prevent the third party from violating others' rights within the state's territory. It is pertinent to note that the African Commission on Human and Peoples' Rights has made reference to judgements of the ECtHR in its decisions.

The African regional human rights system

The African Union (AU), which was influenced to a large extent by the European Union model, was conceived as a supranational body. The AU was established in 2001 as a successor to the Organisation of African Unity (OAU).[30] The main aims of the AU include the integration of the African economy, defence mechanism and political governance.[31] The purposes the AU is designed to serve include the securing of the continent's democracy, human rights and sustainable economy.[32]

The predecessor organisation to the AU, the OAU was established on a different basis. The OAU was established in 1963 with the aim of fighting colonialism and apartheid in South Africa.[33] The OAU did not engage

---

29 *Guerra and Others* v. *Italy* 26 EHRR 357.
30 See the Constitutive Act of the African Union adopted in Lomé, Togo, 11 July 2000, vol. 40 United Nations Treaty Series, UN Certification Number 1–37733 (hereafter called "Constitutive Act of the AU").
31 Article 3, Constitutive Act of the AU.
32 Article 4(m) and (n), Constitutive Act of the AU.
33 See the Charter of the Organization of African Unity, adopted 25 May 1963 entered into force 13 September 1963, 479 UNTS 39.

much with human rights issues except in the context of self determination and apartheid in South Africa.[34] The lack of emphasis placed on human rights under the OAU was due to the strong bias in favour of non-interference in other states' internal affairs. A major development under the auspices of the OAU, however, was the introduction of the African Charter in 1981. The African Charter, which to date is the continent's principal human rights instrument, entered into force in 1986.[35] The charter has its independent commission in Banjul, Gambia. As Lloyd and Murray correctly observe, during its existence, human rights matters were often detached from other OAU bodies and left within the remit of the African Commission on Human and Peoples' Rights.[36] Another major development occurred in 1988 when the Assembly of Heads of State and Government of the OAU adopted an additional protocol to the African Charter to establish an African Court of Human and Peoples' Rights.[37] The implications of these developments shall be discussed fully later in this chapter.

The AU appears to provide a vibrant and more transparent approach to human rights when compared to the OAU.[38] The Constitutive Act of the AU incorporated all of the objectives and principles of the OAU in its provisions. However, it went further by providing for the promotion of democratic principles and institutions, popular participation and good governance, and most importantly in the context of this chapter, the promotion and protection of human rights.[39] The principles of the Constitutive Act also expressly include respect for democratic principles, human rights, the rule of law and the promotion of social justice to ensure balanced economic development.[40]

To improve the efficacy of its human rights system, the AU departed from earlier emphasis placed on non-interference with the internal affairs of member states under the OAU by making provision for the imposition of sanctions on member states that fail to comply with the decisions and policies of the AU.[41] The AU Constitutive Act provides for the following institutions: an Assembly and Executive Council; a Pan-African Parliament;

---

34 A. Lloyd and R. Murray "Institutions with Responsibility for Human Rights Protection under the African Union" (2004) 48 (2) *Journal of African Law* 165, 166.

35 The African Charter was adopted 27 June 1981 and entered into force on 21 October, 1986 OAU Doc. CAB/LEG/67/3 Rev. 5.

36 Lloyd and Murray (note 34), 171.

37 The Protocol to the African Charter on Human and Peoples' Rights on the Establishment of an African Court on Human and Peoples' Rights – adopted in Ouagadougou, Burkina Faso, 10 June 1998, entered into force 25 January 2004.

38 Lloyd and Murray (note 34), 171.

39 Article 3, Constitutive Act of the AU.

40 Article 4, Constitutive Act of the AU.

41 Lloyd and Murray (note 34), 172.

an African Court of Justice; a Permanent Representatives Committee; an Economic, Social and Cultural Council; a Peace and Security Council; Specialised Technical Committees and Financial Institutions. Many of these institutions have the potential to deal with human rights issues.[42] Thus, as will presently be shown, some of these institutions are important in the state responsibility approach to the prevention of violation of human rights by private actors under the African human rights system.

The African Charter on Human and Peoples' Rights and Private Parties/MNCs

The scope of the African Charter

The African Charter combines elements of international law with African concepts of rights. According to Udombana, the African Charter is

> More than just a matter of public international law or international customary law; it is a synthesis of universal and African elements. Its organizing principle is the balance between tradition and modernity, not only between African tradition and the modernity of international law, but also between African modernity and the tradition of international law.[43]

The African Charter recognises a wide range of internationally accepted human rights norms. However, the charter recognises not only civil and political rights but economic, social and cultural rights. Furthermore, it recognises individual rights as well as collective rights. The charter imposes correlative duties on individuals contained in many human rights instruments and goes further to impose autonomous duties not connected with rights.[44] The civil and political rights that are recognised under the charter include: prohibition of discrimination (article 2); equality (article 4); bodily integrity and the right to life (article 4); dignity and prohibition of torture and inhuman treatment (article 5); liberty and security (article 6); fair trial (article 7); freedom of conscience (article 8); information and freedom of expression (article 9); freedom of association (article 10); assembly (article 11); freedom of movement (article 12); political participation (article 13);

---

42 Ibid., 173.
43 J. Udombana "Between Promise and Performance: Revisiting States' Obligations under the African Human Rights Charter" (2004) 40 *Stanford Journal of International Law* 105, 110.
44 The preamble and articles 27 through 29 of the African Charter recognise private duties. See also J. Udombana, "Between Promise and Performance: Revisiting States' Obligations under the African Human Rights Charter" (2004) 40 *Stanford Journal of International Law* 105, 111.

property (article 14); and independence of the courts (article 26). Some important civil and political rights are not explicitly mentioned in the charter. Such rights include the right to privacy and the right against forced labour. Other rights such as the right of political participation and fair trial rights are not well protected when compared with other international standards.[45] However, as will be elaborated upon later on in this chapter, the African Commission on Human and Peoples' Rights has interpreted the provisions in the charter to include unenumerated rights.

Perhaps more significant for the purposes of the current discussion is the inclusion of socio-economic rights in the charter alongside civil and political rights. According to Heynes and Killander, this approach emphasises the indivisibility of human rights and the importance of developmental issues within the African context.[46] The socio-economic rights that are expressly mentioned in the charter include: the right to work under equitable and satisfactory conditions (article 15); the right to health (article 16) and the right to education (article 17).

In a development reminiscent of the jurisprudence on unenumerated rights under the Irish constitution,[47] the African Commission on Human and Peoples' Rights in *SERAC* v. *Nigeria*[48] held that there are rights which are not explicitly mentioned in the charter but which should be regarded as being implicitly included. Such rights identified in the *SERAC* case include:

The right to housing or shelter deduced from the provisions on health, property and family in the Charter.[49]

The right to food deduced from the right to life, right to dignity, right to health and right to economic, social and cultural development.[50]

The commission went on to hold that all rights under the African Charter are enforceable. It would thus not matter whether the rights are civil and

---

45   C. Heynes and M. Killander, "The African Regional Human Rights System" in F. Gomez Isa and K. De Feyter (eds.) *International Protection of Human Rights: Achievements and Challenges* (Bilbao: University of Deusto, 2006) 507, 514–515.

46   Ibid., 507, 516.

47   See for examples G. Casey "Are there Unenumerated Rights in the Irish Constitution" (2005) 23 (8) *Irish Law Times* 123–127; G. Hogan, "Unenumerated Personal Rights: Ryan's Case Re-evaluated" (1990/92) 23/27 *Irish Jurist* 95.

48   *Social and Economic Rights Action Centre (SERAC) and The Centre for Economic and Social Rights (CESR)* v. *Nigeria* (2001), Communication no. 155/96 (African Commission on Human and Peoples' Rights), online, available at: www1.umn.edu/humanrts/africa/comcases/155-96b.html (accessed 26 September 2010). This decision is discussed fully later on in this chapter.

49   Articles 14, 16 and 18 of the African Charter. See paragraph 60 of *Serac* v. *Nigeria* (note 48).

50   Articles 4, 5, 16 and 22 of the African Charter.

political rights or economic rights or unenumerated rights. Any right specified under the charter would be enforceable through the communication procedure of the commission. Shelton observed in this regard:

> The Commission decision that all rights in the African Charter are enforceable and may be subject to the system's communication procedure advances the African system well ahead of other regional systems – which have moved tentatively toward allowing petitions for economic, social and cultural rights, and which only partially recognize a right to environment.[51]

The commission's approach to the enforcement of the charter against non-state actors is examined in the next section of this chapter.

The African Commission on Human and Peoples' Rights, the African Charter and multinational corporations

The African Commission on Human and Peoples' Rights was established under the African Charter.[52] The commission was modelled on the European Human Rights Commission (since abolished) and the Inter-American Commission on Human Rights.[53] The commission's functions are stated in article 45 of the charter and they include the promotion of human rights, the protection of human rights under the African Charter, the interpretation of the African Charter and any other functions assigned to the commission by the Assembly of Heads of State. The commission also has the task of preparing cases for submission to the African Court on Human and Peoples' Rights.[54] The commission thus has both protective and promotional responsibility. Its protective responsibility involves receiving communications on violations of rights protected under the charter, communicating them to states and investigating them with the view of reconciling parties. The decisions are also included in the commission's

---

51 D. Shelton, "Decision Regarding Communication 155/96 (*Social and Economic Rights Action/Center for Economic and Social Rights* v. *Nigeria*). Case no. ACHPR/Comm. A044/1" (2002) 96 (4) *American Journal of International Law* 937, 942.

52 Article 30 of the African Charter. The African Commission on Human and Peoples' Rights is not formally an organ of the AU, since it was created by a separate statute.

53 The European Commission on Human Rights was abolished by protocol 11 (note 25). The Inter American Commission on Human Rights is an autonomous organ of the Organization of American States (OAS). It was created in 1959 to promote and protect human rights in the Americas pursuant to the OAS Charter (119 UNTS 3 as amended) and the American Convention on Human Rights (OAS Treaty Series no. 36, 1144 UNTS 123, entered into force 18 July 1978).

54 Article 5 of the protocol to the African Charter On Human and Peoples' Rights on the Establishment of an African Court on Human and Peoples' Rights (note 35).

activity report. The commission does not by itself enforce its decisions but occasionally grants interim/provisional measures to avoid irredeemable harm.[55] In *International PEN and others* v. *Nigeria*, the commission held that such provisional measures are binding.[56] The African Commission on Human and Peoples' Rights has existed for about 20 years. Some doubts have been expressed about the retention of the commission as it was not mentioned in the Constitutive Act of the AU as one of its organs.[57] However, the commission has played a significant role in the development of the African human rights system to date as discussed in the following sections.

The African Commission's jurisprudence

Although the African Charter directly refers only to communications from states, the commission also accepts communications from non-state actors under the provision for "other communications".[58] This makes it possible for individuals and NGOs to bring complaints before the commission. However, a communication can only be brought against a state party to the charter and not against private persons or individuals.[59] Hence, a private person or individual can only be implicated when a state is held liable for the violation of human rights. This is in line with the principle of state responsibility as enunciated under international law as discussed earlier.

The commission had an opportunity to examine the scope of state responsibility for violations of human rights by non-state actors under the African Charter in *Zimbabwe Human Rights NGO Forum* v. *Zimbabwe*.[60] The complaint arose from acts which took place after a constitutional referendum held in Zimbabwe in February 2000 in which the majority of citizens voted against a government proposal. The complaint alleged that groups

---

55 Rules 111 of the Rules of Procedures of the African Commission on Human and Peoples' Rights adopted 6 October 1995 allows the commission to grant interim provisional orders. See U.O. Umozorike, "The African Charter on Human and Peoples' Rights: Suggestions for more Effectiveness" (2007) 13 *Annual Survey of International and Comparative Law* 179, 186.

56 See *International PEN and Others* v. *Nigeria*, African Commission on Human and Peoples' Rights, Comm. no. 137/94, 139/94, 154/96 and 161/97 (1998). See also R. Wright, "Finding an Impetus for Institutional Change at the African Court on Human and Peoples' Rights" 24 *Berkeley Journal of International Law* 463, 471.

57 Umozorike (note 54) 179, 181.

58 Articles 55–59 African Charter; see also C.H. Heynes and M. Kilander (note 45), 509, 525.

59 See article 47 of the African Charter.

60 *Zimbabwe Human Rights NGO Forum* v. *Zimbabwe* Communication 245/02, Annexure 3 to the African Commission on Human and Peoples' Rights Twenty-first Activity Report (July–December 2006).

of militias made up of youths and supporters of the Zimbabwe African National Union Patriotic Front (ZANU (PF)) and other militias intimidated and harassed people opposed to the government's reforms including members of the opposition. In the violent climate of that period several people were alleged to have lost their lives. The complaint alleged that these acts began during the country's election in June 2000 and lasted until November 2001. The government in Zimbabwe subsequently issued a general amnesty for politically motivated crimes[61] which absolved most of the persons and groups involved in the violence from prosecution.[62] The Clemency order defines "politically motivated crime" as:

a   Any offence motivated by the object of supporting or opposing any political purpose and committed in connection with:

   i The Constitutional referendum held on 12 and 13 February 2000; or
   ii The general Parliamentary elections held on 24 and 25 June 2000; whether committed before, during or after the said referendum or elections.

In its handling of this complaint, the commission considered *inter alia* three questions relevant to this chapter: 1. Who is a non-state actor? 2. What is the extent of state's responsibility for non-state actors? 3. What is the implication of Clemency Order no. 1 of 2000? The commission defined a non-state actor in similar terms as the ILC and international law. According to the commission,

The term "non-state actors" has ... been adopted by the international community to refer to individuals, organisations, institutions and other bodies acting outside the state and its organs. *They are not limited to individuals since some perpetrators of human rights abuses are organisations, corporations or other structures of business and finance, as the research on the human rights impacts of oil production or the development of power facilities demonstrates*[63] (emphasis added).

---

61 Clemency Order no. 1 of 2000 (Zimbabwe).
62 The commission held in that case that the clemency offered to perpetrators of "any politically motivated crimes" effectively forecloses the complainant or any other person from seeking redress in Zimbabwean courts or accessing any other local remedy. The commission therefore held that this act of state prevented victims from seeking redress and also encouraged impunity. Zimbabwe was held to have violated its obligation under articles 1 and 7 of the African Charter.
63 *Zimbabwe Human Rights NGO Forum* v. *Zimbabwe* Communication 245/02, Annexure 3 to the African Commission on Human and Peoples' Rights Twenty-first Activity Report (July–December 2006), para. 136.

In answering the second question, the commission drew a thin line between the ruling party, ZANU (PF) as a private entity and the Zimbabwean government. The commission held that ZANU (PF) was a political party in the country, different and distinct from the government. In reaching this conclusion, the commission considered it immaterial that some of the members of the government also held high ranking positions within the party. According to the commission:

> In the opinion of this Commission, the ZANU (PF) is a political party (the ruling party) in Zimbabwe and just like any other party in the country, distinct from the government. It has an independent identity from the government with its own structures and administrative machinery, even though some of the members of the Zimbabwe Government – cabinet ministers, also hold top ranking positions in the party. For example, President Robert Mugabe is the President and First Secretary General of the Party. This Commission also holds that the War Veterans Association is a group of ex-combatants of the Zimbabwe liberation struggle. President Mugabe was the Patron during the period under consideration.[64]

The commission continued:[65]

> It is not the view of the African Commission that the ZANU (PF) and the Zimbabwe Liberation War Veterans Association are structures of the Government or organs of the State. The complainant did not supply the African Commission with documentary evidence to prove this relationship. *Even if President Mugabe is Patron of the War Veterans and exercises control over the group*, this does not make the war veteran association part of government or State machinery (emphasis added).

The position of the commission on this point is open to several criticisms. Even though ZANU (PF) is distinct from the government, the fact that the party was the ruling party and members of the government held high ranking positions within the party should point towards a close connection between the government and the non-state actor. In relation to the war veterans, the commission seems to be saying that "control" is not important in determining state responsibility. This would appear to run contrary to the ICJ decision in *Nicaragua* v. *United States of America* and *Bosnia* v. *Serbia* which suggests that "control" is essential to a finding of state responsibility.[66] It is also hard to imagine how the commission expected the

---

64 Ibid., para. 138.
65 Ibid., para. 139.
66 *Nicaragua* v. *USA* (1986) ICJ Reports 14 and *Bosnia and Herzegovina* v. *Serbia and Montenegro* (2007) ICJ Reports.

complainant NGO to come by documentary evidence to prove "control" if it could not infer "control" from the facts before it. Human rights violators using non-state actors as proxies hardly leave paper trails.

The commission thereafter proceeded to consider the extent of state responsibility for non-state actors under the African Charter. The commission affirmed that states have responsibility under article 1 of the African Charter to "recognize the rights … and undertake to adopt legislative or other measures to give effects to them".[67] According to the commission,

> Any impairment of those rights which can be attributed under the rules of international law to the action or omission of any public authority constitutes an act imputable to the state, which assumes responsibility in the terms provided by the African Charter.[68]

The commission went further to say that

> An act by a private individual and therefore not directly imputable to a state can generate responsibility of the state, not because of the act itself, but because of the lack of *due diligence* to prevent the violation or for not taking the necessary steps to provide the victims with reparation.[69]

However, in this case the commission said that the complainant not only failed to demonstrate collusion by the state to either aid or abet the non-state actor in committing the violence but equally failed to show that the state remained indifferent to the violence that took place.[70] The commission purported to apply the decision of the Inter-American Court in *Velásquez* v. *Honduras* where the *due diligence* principle was established.[71] In *Velásquez* v. *Honduras* it was held that a state is in violation of its duty to protect human rights where it allows private persons or groups to act in a way that is detrimental to the enjoyment of human rights. However, as Beyani rightly pointed out, the commission adopted an elastic view of the

---

67 *Zimbabwe Human Rights NGO Forum* v. *Zimbabwe* Communication 245/02, Annexure 3 to the African Commission on Human and Peoples' Rights 21st Activity Report (July–December 2006), para. 142.
68 Ibid., para. 142.
69 Ibid., para. 143.
70 Ibid., para. 163. The commission noted in paragraph 161 p. 86 that the state indicated the measures it took to deal with the alleged violations which include amendment of legislation, arrest and prosecution of some perpetrators, payment of compensation and ensuring investigation of other complaints. The commission stated that the complainant did not dispute this claim but contended that the measures did not come early enough and were in any case inadequate. The commission therefore held that the measures put in place by the state were sufficient to defeat the claim of state responsibility under article 1 of the African Charter.
71 *Velásquez Rodriguez* v. *Honduras* IACtHR ser. C 4 (1988).

effect of that decision.[72] The commission was of the opinion that a state would only be liable if there was a lack of due diligence to prevent the violation or respond to the violation as required under the African Charter and if there was collusion by the state to aid or abet the non-state actor in committing the violation. The commission therefore held that the complainant had to show that there was collusion by the state to aid or abet the non-state actors in committing the violations, which it held they failed to do. A closer look at *Velásquez v. Honduras* shows that the interpretation given to it by the commission was too narrow. The *Velásquez* case involved a student, Manfredo Velásquez, who was alleged to have been detained without warrant, tortured by police and consequently disappeared without trace. The Honduran government contended that the allegations against the police were not true and that there was no credible evidence to prove otherwise. In its decision in that case, the Inter-American Court of Human Rights articulated what is widely considered the first truly comprehensive statement of a state's human rights obligation.[73] The court stated as follows:

172. [...] An illegal act which violates human rights and which is initially not directly imputable to a State (for example, because it is the act of private person or because the person responsible has not been identified) can lead to international responsibility of the State, not because of the act itself, *but because of the lack of due diligence to prevent the violation or to respond to it as required by the Convention.*

176. The State is obligated to investigate every situation involving a violation of the rights protected by the Convention. If the State apparatus acts in such a way that the violation goes unpunished and the victim's full enjoyment of such rights is not restored as soon as possible, the State has failed to comply with its duty to ensure the free and full exercise of those rights to the persons within its jurisdiction. *The same is true when the State allows private persons or groups to act freely and with impunity to the detriment of the rights recognized by the Convention.*

182. The Court is convinced, and has so found, that the disappearance of Manfredo Velásquez was carried out by agents who acted under cover of public authority. *However, even had that fact not been proven, the failure of the State apparatus to act, which is clearly proven, is a failure on the part of Honduras to fulfill the duties it assumed under Article 1(1) of the*

---

72 C. Beyani, "Recent Developments in the African Human Rights System 2004–2006" (2007) *Human Rights Law Review* 582, 607.

73 M. Freeman, *Truth Commission and Procedural Fairness* (Cambridge: Cambridge University Press, 2006), 6.

Convention, which obligated it to ensure Manfredo Velásquez the free and full exercise of his human rights (emphasis added).

Therefore, a correct interpretation of *Velásquez* v. *Honduras* is that where there is a failure to prevent violations by non-state actors and if the possibility of violation is reasonably foreseeable,[74] this will amount to failure of due diligence and the state will be liable. There is therefore no onus on the complainant to establish collusion. A similar approach was taken by the Inter American Court in the case of the *"Street Children" (Villagran-Morales et al.)* v. *Guatemala.*[75] In that case it was alleged that members of the security force of Guatemala kidnapped, tortured and murdered five children. The court considered *inter-alia* what is required to hold a state responsible for the actions of others. The court unequivocally affirmed its position in the *Paniagua Morales et al.* case[76] and said:

> Lastly, the Court has maintained that [un]like domestic criminal law, it is not necessary to determine the perpetrators' culpability or intentionality in order to establish that the rights enshrined in the Convention have been violated, nor is it essential to identify individually the agents to whom the acts of violation are attributed. *The sole requirement is to demonstrate that the state authorities supported or tolerated infringement of the rights recognized in the Convention.* Moreover, the state's international responsibility is also at issue when it does not take the necessary steps under its domestic law to identify and, where appropriate, punish the author of such violations[77] (emphasis added).

The implication of the African Commission's decision is that a state may be liable for the violation of human rights by non state actors such as MNCs only where there is an established collusion between the state and such private actors.

Furthermore, it is difficult to understand how the commission could hold that the state had taken adequate measures which would absolve it of responsibility for the activities of the non-state actors in the face of the clemency order which effectively absolve the non-state actors. In respect of the order, the commission held:

> That by passing the Clemency Order no. 1 of 2000, prohibiting prosecution and setting free perpetrators of "politically motivated crimes",

---

74 Beyani (note 72), 607.
75 *Case of the "Street Children" (Villagran-Morales* et al.*)* v. *Guatemala* Judgement of 19 November 1999.
76 *Paniagual Morales* et al. *Case,* Judgement of 30 May 1999, ser. C no. 37.
77 Case of the *"Street Children" (Villagran-Morales* et al.*)* v. *Guatemala* Judgement of 19 November 1999, para. 75.

including alleged offences such as abductions, forced imprisonment, arson, destruction of property, kidnappings and other human rights violatins (*sic*) the State did not only encourage impunity but effectively foreclosed any available avenue for the alleged abuses to be investigated, and prevented victims of crimes and alleged human rights violations from seeking effective remedy and compensation.[78]

It is argued that the singular act of enacting the clemency order shows clearly that the state deliberately frustrated any measure it claimed it put in place, therefore negating the claim of due diligence. It further shows that the state took proactive steps to condone human rights violations by non-state actors. If *Velásquez* v. *Honduras* had been correctly interpreted by the commission, state responsibility for the actions of the non-state actors would have been found.

The commission directly dealt with the issue of state responsibility for human rights violations by MNCs in *SERAC* v. *Nigeria*.[79] The next section of the chapter discusses this important case in the jurisprudence of the commission.

SERAC *v.* Nigeria: *implications for MNCS*

The case of *SERAC* v. *Nigeria* has been the subject of much academic commentary since the decision was handed down in 2002.[80] However, not much analysis has been done on the implication of the decision for MNCs.[81] The communication leading up to the decision was filed by two NGOs: the Social and Economic Rights Action Centre and the Centre for Economic and Social Rights. The communication was against the Nigerian

---

78   *Zimbabwe Human Rights NGO Forum* v. *Zimbabwe* Communication 245/02, Annexure 3 to the African Commission on Human and Peoples' Rights Twenty-first Activity Report (July–December 2006), para. 211.

79   *Social and Economic Rights Action Centre (SERAC) and The Centre for Economic and Social Rights (CESR)* v. *Nigeria* (2001), Communication no. 155/96 (African Commission on Human and Peoples' Rights), online, available at: www1.umn.edu/humanrts/africa/comcases/155-96b.html (accessed 26 September 2010).

80   D. Shelton, "Decision Regarding Communication 155/96 (*Social and Economic Rights Action/Center for Economic and Social Rights* v. *Nigeria*). Case no. ACHPR/Comm. A044/1" (2002) 96 (4) *American Journal of International Law* 937; F. Coomans, "Case Comment: The Ogoni Case before the African Commission on Human and Peoples' Rights" (2003) 52 (3) *International and Comparative Law Quarterly* 749; J.C. Nwobike, "The African Commission on Human and Peoples' Rights and Demystification of Second and Third Generation Rights under the African Charter: *Social and Economic Rights Action Center (SERAC) and the Centre for Economic and Social Rights (CESR)* v. *Nigeria* (2004–2005)" 1 *African Journal of Legal Studies* 129.

81   An exception is J. Oloka-Onyango, "Reinforcing Marginalized Rights in an Age of Globalization: International Mechanisms, Non-State Actors, and the Struggle for Peoples' Rights in Africa" (2002–2003) 19 *American University Law Review* 851.

government. However, most of the complaints which formed the basis of the communication emanated from actions taken by or involving the operations of Shell Petroleum Development Corporation (SPDC), a subsidiary of Shell International, which was in a consortium with the Nigerian National Petroleum Corporation (NNPC).[82] The communication stated that the government of Nigeria was involved in oil production through the NNPC. The communication alleged that the operations of SPDC caused environmental degradation and health problems among the Ogoni people. The communication further alleged that the oil consortium exploited oil reserves with no regard for the health or environment of the local communities, disposing toxic wastes into the environment and local waterways in violation of international standards. The activities of SPDC, according to the communication, led to the contamination of water, soil and air which had serious short- and long-term impacts. The communication alleged that that the Nigerian government condoned and facilitated the violations by placing legal and military powers at the disposal of the oil companies. It alleged that the government further participated in the violations by executing some Ogoni leaders and through the use of security forces killing many innocent civilians and destroying villages, homes, crops and farm animals. The communication accused the government of failing to monitor the activities of the oil companies, failing to conduct environmental impact studies, preventing independent scientists carrying out the environmental impact studies and keeping information on oil production from local communities.

When the communication was brought in 1996, Nigeria was under a military government. Despite the fact that the government was notified of the communication, it failed to respond to it. Nigeria returned to civilian rule in 1999 and the new civilian government responded to the communication through a *note verbale* delivered during the commission's November 2000 session. The Nigerian government did not contest the claim. The government stated that "there is no denying the fact that a lot of atrocities were and are still being committed by the oil companies in Ogoni Land and indeed in the Niger Delta area".[83] The government asserted however, that it was taking remedial measures to correct the situation.

This communication is important in the context of this chapter because it implicates the operations of an MNC. Most of the violations complained of emanated from the direct activities of the MNC. It thus raises the question of what the commission should do about the responsibility of the

---

82 The NNPC is a Nigerian state-owned corporation created under the Nigerian National Petroleum Decree no. 33 of 1977.

83 *Social and Economic Rights Action Centre (SERAC) and The Centre for Economic and Social Rights (CESR)* v. *Nigeria* (2001), Communication no. 155/96 (African Commission on Human and Peoples' Rights), para. 42.

non-state actor itself. It has been argued that even though many human rights violations committed by MNCs can be approached through the prism of state responsibility, there are gaps when issues of relative power of MNCs and economic necessity of the concerned states are taken into account.[84] The problem becomes more apparent when the issues concerning the control of MNCs are taken within the broader context of the challenges presented by globalisation.[85] Hence, it may be argued that it is necessary for the African Commission to go beyond the concept of state responsibility in these types of cases and to pronounce on the responsibility of the MNCs under the African Charter.

Even though the *SERAC* case communication was taken against the Nigerian government, the main target was SPDC. The majority of the allegations put forward in the communication emanated from the operations of the oil company. These included:

1   Environmental degradation and health problems resulting from the contamination of the environment
2   Exploitation of oil reserves with no regard for the health or environment of the local community
3   Disposing toxic wastes into the environment and local waterways in violation of applicable international law
4   Neglect and/or failure to maintain company's facilities thereby causing numerous avoidable spills in the proximity of villages
5   Contamination of water, soil and air causing serious short and long-term health impacts, including skin infections, gastro intestinal and respiratory ailments and increase in the risk of cancers and neurological and reproductive problems
6   Employing legal and military powers of the state to violate rights.

In contrast, the allegations against the Nigerian government mainly related to condoning and facilitating violations by oil companies:

1   Condoning and facilitating the violations of rights by the SPDC by placing legal and military powers of the state in its hands
2   Failure to monitor operations of the oil companies and also to require safety measures that are standard procedures within the industry
3   Withholding of information from the communities on the danger posed by oil companies operations
4   Use of the Nigerian security forces in the aid of the companies' operations.

84   Oloka-Onyango (note 81), 897.
85   Ibid.

The commission underscored the first line responsibility of states in the protection of human rights by holding that African governments have a duty to monitor and control the activities of MNCs.[86] The commission held further that African states should also ensure respect for economic, social and cultural rights. Relying on its earlier decision in the *Union des Jeunes Avocats/Chad*[87] case and the decision of the Inter-American Court of Human Rights in *Velásquez Rodriguez* v. *Honduras*[88] as well as that of the European Court of Human Rights in *X and Y* v. Netherlands,[89] the commission held that governments have the duty to protect their citizens through appropriate legislation and effective enforcement and also to protect them from damaging acts that may be perpetrated by private parties.[90] The commission restricted itself to the responsibility of the Nigerian government and said nothing about the MNC. It criticised the way in which the Nigerian government related to the MNC, finding that the government had failed to exercise the necessary degree of care required in the circumstances.[91] The Nigerian government was found to have facilitated the destruction of communities and also to have given the "green light" to private actors, especially the oil companies, to devastatingly affect the well-being of the Ogonis.[92] According to the commission:

> The Government of Nigeria facilitated the destruction of the Ogoniland. Contrary to its obligations and despite such internationally established principles, the Nigerian Government has given green light to private actors, and the oil companies in particular, to devastatingly affect the well-being of the Ogonis. By any measure of standards, its practice falls short of the minimum conduct expected of governments, and therefore, is in violation of the African Charter.[93]

The commission thus laid the responsibility for all the violations that had been committed by the non-state actor on the Nigerian state.[94] The state was found liable for violations of rights protected under the African Charter by SPDC.

---

86 See also Shelton (note 51), 941.
87 *Union des Jeunes Avocats/Chad* Communication 74/92, Ninth Annual Activity Report of The African Commission on Human And Peoples' Rights – 1995/96 AHG/207 (XXXII).
88 *Velásquez Rodriguez* v. *Honduras* Judgement of July 19, 1988, ser. C, no. 4 FACT.
89 *X and Y* v. *Netherlands* 91 ECHR (1985) (ser. A) at 32.
90 *Social and Economic Rights Action Centre (SERAC) and The Centre for Economic and Social Rights (CESR)* v. *Nigeria* (2001), Communication no. 155/96, African Commission on Human and Peoples' Rights, para. 57.
91 Ibid., para. 59.
92 Ibid., para. 58.
93 Ibid., para. 58.
94 Oloka-Onyango (note 81), 901.

It is important to note that in this particular case, the commission did not require proof of complicity between the Nigerian state and the non-state actor. Furthermore, the commission did not delve into the issue of the degree of control exercised by the Nigerian government over the SPDC before reaching its conclusions. One would be tempted to conclude that the commission was setting a much lower standard for finding state responsibility for the wrongful acts of non-state actors. However, such suggestion would not be compelling in the face of the later decision in *Zimbabwe Human Rights NGO Forum* v. *Zimbabwe.*[95]

Viewed from the perspective that most of the allegations emanated from the direct activities of SPDC, it would appear that there is a gap in the focus on state responsibility, while the primary violator's responsibility is not addressed. However, as Oloka-Onyango correctly points out, the position of the commission appears consistent with the long accepted position under international human rights law that the state is the primary actor responsible for the promotion and protection of human rights, irrespective of the size or relative economic clout of the private actor vis-à-vis the state.[96] While the position in international law may be valid as a general proposition, there are additional dimensions in the relationship between MNCs and governments in developing countries which may warrant a different approach. On this point Duruigbo observes as follows:

> The situation is even worse in the case of developing countries which in their quest and scramble for economic investments of multinational companies, are too enfeebled to regulate or control the multinationals. Indeed, the companies are more likely to show a preference for those countries with lax regulations over multinational business activity. The absence in developing countries of technical expertise and legal development necessary to monitor or regulate complex activities such as environmental pollution also militates against any efforts by these countries to control the activities of multinational corporations.[97]

The decision in the *SERAC* case may therefore be criticised because it was directed solely to the Nigerian state and omitted consideration of the accountability of the non-state actor. According to Oloka-Onyango, this omission becomes more glaring because the criminal law or regulatory mechanisms of the host state were inadequate to deal with the problem.[98]

95 *Zimbabwe Human Rights NGO Forum* v. *Zimbabwe* Communication 245/02, Annexure 3 to the African Commission on Human and Peoples' Rights 21st Activity Report (July–December 2006).
96 Oloka-Onyango (note 81), 901.
97 E. Duruigbo "Multinational Corporations and Compliance with International Regulations Relating to the Petroleum Industry" (2001) *Annual Survey of International and Comparative Law* 101, 139; quoted also by Oloka-Onyango (note 81), 903.
98 Ibid., 903.

He posits that because of the difficulty in using domestic institutions to deal with issues emanating from the operations of MNCs, there is a need for mechanisms such as the commission to delve deeper when confronted with cases like *SERAC*.[99] This is particularly true in view of the fact that the African Charter articulates issues of duties and responsibilities of other actors apart from states.[100] He contends that the African Commission could have gone further because the conditions for a finding of liability on the part of SPDC were all present in the case. According to Oloka-Onyango, where an MNC is directly involved with the host country in human rights violations, direct liability should be found.[101] There was evidence before the commission that the oil companies knew that their businesses were involved in state sponsored violations and that the company committed several violations itself. Oloka-Onyango concludes that notwithstanding the first line responsibility obligation placed on states, the commission could have examined the issue of the direct liability of the oil company more extensively. If this approach were to be taken, it would be a departure from the position in international law principle on state responsibility discussed earlier. The African regional system is a treaty-based arrangement which can go further than international law principles. It is up to the AU institutions to determine the direction the regional system takes. In view of the challenges posed by MNCs in Africa, it is suggested that a more proactive approach in the manner suggested by Oloka-Onyango would be a welcome development. The decision of the commission is in the form of recommendations for the erring state to comply with. One of the criticisms levelled against the commission's procedure is the lack of clarity in the enunciation of required remedies.[102] If the commission were to pronounce on the liability of the non-state actor, this would go a long way to provide clarity and assist state parties in knowing what to do to remedy the situation. Deterrent direct effect on individual and private MNCs therefore diminished significantly because of the issues raised above.

The main reason why the commission's ability is severely constrained here is because of the fact that it is not a court and depends on states for the implementation of its recommendations. It has been suggested that the establishment of a court will address the problem by depoliticising the process and providing for binding judgement.[103] This does not, however,

---

99 Ibid., 904.

100 Ibid., 910.

101 Ibid., 904.

102 F. Viljoen and L. Louw, "State Compliance with the Recommendations of the African Commission on Human and Peoples' Rights (1994–2004)" (2007) 101 *American Journal of International Law* 1, 32.

103 R. Murray, *The African Commission on Human and Peoples' Rights and International Law* (Oxford and Portland, OR: Hart Publishing, 2000), 22.

diminish the significance of the African system in respect of strengthening the state responsibility approach.

The limitations of the commission's procedure

Despite its potential as an institution to protect and promote human rights, the commission has its limitations. State parties generally refuse to cooperate with the commission during investigation, hearing of cases and implementation of decisions. In respect of the implementation, it has been suggested that the commission, in most of its decisions, has failed to enunciate clear and specific remedies which may affect compliance.[104] This places a question mark on the commission's overall relevance.[105] The commission has also been criticised for its lack of independence. This is because of its close links with African heads of state and government.[106] Under article 33 of the African Charter, the 11 members of the commission are elected by secret ballot by the Assembly of Heads of States and Government, from a list of persons nominated by the state party to the charter. This ensures that states have significant control over the commission. A major limitation on the commission's authority is the provision in article 59 of the charter which directs that measures taken within the provisions of the charter are to remain confidential until the Assembly of Heads of State and Government decide otherwise. Considering that one of the major weapons in the enforcement of human rights is the attendant publicity, this provision whittles down the power of the commission. Another major drawback is the restriction on access by non-state actors such as NGOs and individuals. Under article 58 of the charter, communications received from non-state parties must "relate to special cases which reveal the existence of a series of serious or massive violations of human and peoples' rights".[107] The charter does not define what is "special cases" or "serious or massive violations of human and peoples' rights". This provision could potentially be used to deny access to an otherwise relevant application. Furthermore, such communication must not be "written in disparaging or insulting language".[108] The determination of what is

---

104 Ibid., 32.
105 R. Wright, "Finding an Impetus for Institutional Change at the African Court on Human and Peoples' Rights" (2006) 24 *Berkeley Journal of International Law* 463, 471–472.
106 Ibid., 472.
107 Article 58, African Charter.
108 Article 56, African Charter. The commission sometimes apply this rule strictly to deny the admissibility of a petition. In *Ligue Camerounaise des droits de l'homme* v. *Cameroon*, Communication no. 65/92 (1997) the commission ruled that phrases such as "regime of torturers" and "government barbarisms" are insulting languages under article 56 which rendered the communication inadmissible.

considered a disparaging or insulting language is left to the commission. The commission has, however, interpreted these provisions liberally.[109]

The African Court on Human and Peoples' Rights (ACrtHPR)

The African Charter does not itself provide for the creation of a court. The ACrtHPR was established by an additional protocol to the African Charter adopted by the Assembly of Heads of State and Government of the OAU in 1998.[110] The protocol came into force in 2004. The court consists of an independent 11-member panel. Under the protocol, the court is empowered to exercise jurisdiction over all human rights instruments "ratified by the states concerned".[111] It has been suggested that this may include regional, sub-regional, bilateral and multilateral international treaties.[112] This may be important because a person whose rights are not adequately protected under the African Charter can invoke other treaties which state parties have signed up to.[113] This is in stark contrast to the jurisdiction of the commission which is limited to the interpretation and application of the African Charter.

The court has both advisory and contentious jurisdiction in respect of the rights contained in the African Charter. The court is generally empowered to receive complaints alleging violations of the African Charter submitted by states, the African Commission on Human and Peoples' Rights, African intergovernmental organisations and (subject to certain restrictions which are discussed in the following section), NGOs and individuals.[114] It has jurisdiction to entertain requests for advisory opinions from member states, the AU and its organs or any other organisation recognised by the regional body.[115]

109 See for example *Social and Economic Rights Action Centre (SERAC) and The Centre for Economic and Social Rights (CESR)* v. *Nigeria* (2001), Communication no. 155/96 (African Commission on Human and Peoples' Rights, *Zimbabwe Human Rights NGO Forum* v. *Zimbabwe* Communication 245/02, Annexure 3 to the African Commission on Human and Peoples' Rights Twenty-first Activity Report (July–December 2006).

110 The protocol to the African Charter on Human and Peoples' Rights on the Establishment of an African Court on Human and Peoples' Rights – adopted in Ouagadougou, Burkina Faso, 10 June 1998, entered into force 25 January 2004. Hereinafter Protocol Establishing an African Court on Human and Peoples' Rights.

111 Ibid., article 3(1).

112 R.W. Eno "The Jurisdiction of the African Court on Human and Peoples' Rights" (2002)2 *African Human Rights Law* Journal 223, 226: N.J. Udombana, "Towards the African Court on Human and Peoples' Rights: Better Late Than Never" (2000) *Yale Human Rights and Development Law Journal* 45.

113 Ibid.

114 Article 5, Protocol Establishing an African Court on Human and Peoples' Rights.

115 Article 4, Protocol Establishing an African Court on Human and Peoples' Rights, Lloyd and Murray (note 34), p166.

For the purpose of exercising its contentious jurisdiction, the court can exercise compulsory (automatic) or optional jurisdiction. Under its compulsory jurisdiction, article 5(1) provides that the following are entitled to submit cases to the court:

1 the African Commission;
2 the state which has lodged a complaint to the African Commission;
3 the state party against which the complaint has been lodged at the commission;
4 the state party whose citizen is a victim of a human rights violation;
5 African intergovernmental organisations.

Furthermore under article 5(2) matters may be referred to the court by a state party that has an interest in a case in which it was not originally involved.

The court's optional jurisdiction is for other claimants such as individuals and NGOs. The access of such non-state actors is severely restricted. The court can only allow cases brought by other claimants, first, where a state party has made an express declaration accepting the court's jurisdiction to hear such a case.[116] Second, the court reserves a discretionary power to grant or deny access as it deems fit in particular cases.[117]

The statute of the African Court on Human and Peoples' Rights has taken effect with the requisite ratification. To date only one state, Burkina Faso, allows applications from non-state entities.[118]

Access to the court

A major area of concern is the restriction on individual access to the court. Under article 5(1) of the African protocol, the commission, state parties and African intergovernmental organisations have direct access to the court. However, individuals and relevant NGOs with observer status with the commission can only be given access if the state concerned makes a declaration accepting the competence of the court to receive such cases.[119] Even if a state makes such a declaration, the court still has discretion on whether to admit the case or not. Juma has described these hurdles placed on the access to the court as an "assault on the African human rights system".[120]

---

116 Ibid., article 34(6).
117 Ibid., article 5(3).
118 U.O. Umozorike, "The African Charter on Human and Peoples' Rights: Suggestions for more Effectiveness" (2007) 13 *Annual Survey of International and Comparative Law* 179, 190.
119 Article 34(6) Protocol Establishing an African Court on Human and Peoples' Rights (note 110).
120 D. Juma, "Access to the African Court on Human and Peoples' Rights: A Case of the Poacher turned Gamekeeper" (2007) 4 (2) *Essex Human Rights Review* 1, 3.

It is observed that the approach of the African system in requiring state declaration is in line with the procedural law of other human rights systems.[121] It has been posited however, that the lack of direct access under the Inter-American Court system has been one of its greatest weaknesses because it limits the role of the victim and requires the intervention of the Inter-American Commission to refer individual cases to the court.[122] The position is different under the European system. Under protocol 11 of the ECHR

> The Court may receive applications from any person, non-governmental organisation or group of individuals claiming to be the victim of a violation by one of the high contracting parties of the rights set forth in the Convention or the protocols thereto.[123]

The provision in the African Court on Human and Peoples' Rights' protocol may have been included to encourage countries to sign up to it without fear that the platform would be used against them by non-state entities. According to Eno:

> While the limitation under Article 5(3) of the Protocol on the African Court may be necessary to bring states on board to ratify the Protocol, it is nevertheless disappointing and a terrible blow to the standing and reputation of the African Court. After all, it is individuals and NGOs, and not the African Commission, regional intergovernmental organizations or state parties who would be the primary beneficiaries and users of the African Court. The Court is not an institution for the protection of rights of states. A human rights court exists primarily for protecting citizens against the state and other government agencies.[124]

Another area where access to the court is unduly restrictive is the provision that only "relevant NGOs having observer status before the African Commission" have access to the court.[125] As Eno correctly notes, this is a unique and potentially dangerous restriction.[126] There is no guide to

---

121 See article 41 ICCPR (no. 6); article 21(1) Convention against Torture (GA res. 39/46 (annex, 39 UN GAOR Supp. (no. 51) at 197, UN Doc. A/39/51 (1984)); articles 25(1) and 46(1) European Convention for the Protection of Human Rights and Fundamental Freedoms (213 UNTS 222 as amended); article 44(1) of the American Convention on Human Rights. See also Eno (note 112), 230.
122 Wright (note 56), 478.
123 Protocol 11 to the Convention for the Protection of Human Rights and Fundamental Freedoms (note 26), article 34 which replaced article 44 of the European Convention.
124 Eno (note 112), 231.
125 Article 5(3), Protocol Establishing an African Court on Human and Peoples' Rights (note 114).
126 Eno (note 112), 231.

determine what is meant by a relevant NGO. Eno therefore argues that the determination may be left within the competence of the commission which may consider those NGOs that have been submitting their periodic reports to it. The implication of this is that NGOs which do not have observer status with the commission would be excluded completely.[127] This is significantly different from the position under the inter-American system. The inter-American system permits any NGO legally recognised in one or more member states to lodge a petition with the American Commission which may transmit the case to the Inter-American Court for judgement where necessary.[128]

It is thus apparent that there are gaps under article 5(3) which have potential implications for using the African Court on Human and Peoples' Rights to check human rights violations by non-state actors such as MNCs. It is most unlikely that the African Commission, regional intergovernmental organisations or state parties who have unqualified access to the court would bring proceedings implicating the operations of MNCs. Most of the cases that have been brought in such circumstances have been spearheaded by NGOs and individuals. With the restrictions placed on NGOs and individual access, the possibility of using the ACrtHPR to check MNCs does not look very promising. However, if the court adopts a liberal attitude to the interpretation of these provisions as the commission did, the provisions may not necessarily constitute impediments in this regard.

Exhaustion of local remedies under article 56

Under article 6 of the protocol establishing the court, the court is required to take into consideration the provisions of article 56 of the African Charter when ruling on the admissibility of cases. Article 56 requires that domestic remedies must be exhausted before communications (in relation to the procedure of the commission) are accepted. If this provision is applied restrictively by the court, it may discourage access to the court by individuals and NGOs. For example, where domestic remedies are not effective and adequate it may be unjust to require the exhaustion of such remedies. It has therefore been suggested that the rules of procedure for the court should contain explicit reference to the fact that domestic remedies must be both effective and adequate or exhaustion will not be required.[129] Such provision could follow the example of the Inter-American Commission's rules of procedure which provide as follows:

> 1   In order to decide on the admissibility of a matter, the Commission shall verify whether the remedies of the domestic legal system

---

127   Ibid.
128   Article 44 American Convention on Human Rights; Eno (note 112), 231.
129   Wright (note 56), 479.

have been pursued and exhausted in accordance with the generally recognized principles of international law.

2   The provisions of the preceding paragraph shall not apply when:

    a   the domestic legislation of the state concerned does not
afford due process of law for protection of the right or rights
that have allegedly been violated;

    b   the party alleging violation of his or her rights has been
denied access to the remedies under domestic law or has been
prevented from exhausting them; or,

    c   there has been unwarranted delay in rendering a final judge-
ment under the aforementioned remedies.

3   When the petitioner contends that he or she is unable to prove
compliance with the requirement indicated in this article, it shall
be up to the state concerned to demonstrate to the Commission
that the remedies under domestic law have not been previously
exhausted, unless that is clearly evident from the record.[130]

The African Commission has been inconsistent in its decisions on the
application of article 56 to its processes. It has insisted on effective
domestic remedies in some cases.[131] In others it has not, interpreting the
provision strictly.[132] If the court adopts a restrictive approach, further
access to the court will be hampered.

Confidentiality requirement

As noted earlier, there is an emphasis on confidentiality under the African
Charter. Article 59 of the charter provides that all measures taken within

---

130 Rules of Procedure of the Inter-American Court of Human Rights, Annual Report of
the Inter-American Court of Human Rights, 1991, OAS Doc. OEA/ser.L/V/III.25 doc.7
at 18 (1992), reprinted in Basic Documents Pertaining to Human Rights in the Inter-
American System, OEA/ser.L.V/II.82 doc.6 Rev.1 at 145 (1992).

131 *Constitutional Rights Project* v. *Nigeria (in respect of Wahab Akamu, G. Adega, and others,*
African Commission on Human and Peoples' Rights, Comm. no. 60/91 (1995); *Interna-
tional PEN and Others* v. *Nigeria,* African Commission on Human and Peoples' Rights,
Comm. no. 137/94, 139/94, 154/96 and 161/97 (1998), *Media Rights Agenda, Constitu-
tional Rights Project* v. *Nigeria,* African Commission on Human and Peoples' Rights,
Comm. no. 105/93, 128/94, 130/94, 152/96 (1998).

132 In *Legal Defence Centre* v. *The Gambia,* African Commission on Human and Peoples'
Rights, Comm. no. 219/98 (2000) the commission held that there was a failure to
exhaust local remedies even though the petitioner was barred from re-entering the state
and therefore could not access the local court. Similar approach was followed in *Kenya
Human Rights Commission* v. *Kenya,* African Commission on Human and Peoples' Rights,
Comm. no. 135/94 (1985), *Mohammed Lamine Diakite* v. *Gabon,* African Commission on
Human and Peoples' Rights, Comm. no. 73/92 (2000).

the provisions of the charter in respect of matters, including communications, shall remain confidential until the Assembly of Heads of State and Government shall otherwise decide. This provision gives leverage to heads of state and government to exert improper influence over proceedings. In respect of the court, article 10(1) of the protocol establishing the court provides that the court shall conduct its proceedings in public; however, it shall conduct proceedings in camera as may be provided for in the rules of procedure. Considering that publicity is a major way by which states can be compelled to comply with decisions of human rights bodies, these provisions reduce the threat of adverse publicity from the court's decisions for states. It has been suggested that the rule should stipulate that confidentiality would apply only in certain cases such as the necessity to protect the privacy of individuals to avoid abuse.[133]

The African Court of Justice and Human Rights: potential implications

The Court of Justice of the African Union is one of the organs of the AU specified under article 5(1) of the Constitutive Act of the AU. At its third ordinary session in July 2004, the Assembly of Heads of State and Government of the African Union adopted a resolution to the effect "that the African Court of Human and Peoples' Rights and the Court of Justice should be integrated into one court".[134] At the African Union Summit in July 2008 the Court of Justice was merged with the ACrtHPR and renamed "African Court of Justice and Human Rights".[135] The court takes over the adjudicatory duties of the African Commission on Human and Peoples' Rights. The merger of the Court of Justice and the ACrtHPR and its incorporation of the adjudicatory functions of the commission are significant because these changes would affect some of the issues discussed earlier in this chapter. These include access to the court, scope of jurisdiction and enforcement of decisions.

Under the statute establishing the African Court of Justice and Human Rights individuals and NGOs are eligible to submit cases to the court in respect of rights guaranteed by the Charter on the Rights and Welfare of the Child, the protocol to the African Charter on Human and Peoples' Rights on the Rights of Women in Africa, or any other legal instrument relevant to human rights ratified by the states parties concerned.[136]

---

133 Wright (note 56), 482.
134 See Decision on the Seats of the Organs of the African Union, Assembly/AU/Dec. 45 (III) Rev.1; Decision on the Merger of the African Court on Human and Peoples' Rights and the Court of Justice of the African Union. Doc. Assembly/AU/Dec. 83(v). Adopted in Sirte, Libya 4–5 July 2005.
135 Protocol on the Statute of the African Court of Justice and Human Rights. Adopted by the Eleventh Ordinary Session of the Assembly of the African Union, held in Sharm El-Sheikh, Egypt, 1 July 2008.
136 Article 30 of the Statute of the African Court of Justice and Human Rights.

However, there is no direct access for NGOs and individuals to the court unless the state party against which a complaint is made has made special declaration to accept the court's competence to hear cases brought by NGOs and individuals.[137] This provision is similar to the requirement under article 34(6) of the protocol establishing the ACrtHPR. The provision is more restrictive when compared with the restriction placed by article 58 of the African Charter in respect of access of non-state parties to the commission discussed earlier in this chapter. It is unlikely that states will be eager to make such voluntary declaration that will potentially expose them to more litigation. The similar provision in the ACrtHPR has received very little patronage. In fact only two states (Burkina Faso and Mali) have made the necessary declaration to allow access. Furthermore, NGOs are required to be accredited to the AU or its organs before they can be allowed access to the court.

Direct access to the court is available to the state parties, the Pan-African Parliament and other organs of the AU, the African Commission, the African Committee of Experts on the Rights and Welfare of the Child, African intergovernmental organisations accredited to the AU or its organs and African national human rights institutions.[138]

There are provisions in the protocol establishing the court which may potentially make it more effective than the ACrtHPR and the African Commission. The court has competence to exercise jurisdiction over the following: the Constitutive Act of the AU; African Union treaties and other subsidiary legislation; international law; all acts, decisions, regulations and directives of the AU and agreements concluded between parties among themselves or with the AU.[139] The jurisdiction of the court is thus very wide when compared to the European Court of Human Rights and the Inter-American Court of Human Rights which each enforce one treaty. The court is further empowered either on its own motion or on an application by the parties to grant provisional measures (such as injunctions) to preserve the respective rights of the parties.[140]

The enforcement of the judgement of the African Court of Justice is more robust than that of the ACrtHPR and the African Commission. State parties are obliged to comply with the decisions of the court.[141] However, where a party fails to comply, the court may upon application by either party to a dispute refer the matter to the AU Assembly, which may decide

---

137 Article 8(3) of the protocol on the Statute of the African Court of Justice and Human Rights and article 30(f) of the Statute of the African Court of Justice and Human Rights.
138 Ibid., article 29.
139 Ibid., article 31.
140 Ibid., article 35.
141 Ibid., article 46.

upon measures to be taken to give effect to the judgement.[142] Under article 46(5) such measures may include sanctions.

The African Union Convention on Preventing and Combating Corruption and MNCs

As noted in Chapter 4, rampant corrupt practices in the private sector have socio-economic consequences for society and may lead to violations of human rights. The AU has therefore recognised the need to have a regional strategy to combat corruption. The African Union Convention on Preventing and Combating Corruption was adopted in 2003.[143] The convention came into force in May 2006. The convention represents a consensus on what African states should do in the areas of prevention of corruption, criminalisation, international cooperation and asset recovery. The provisions of the convention are mandatory and binding. In the context of this research, the question to answer would be how the convention addresses the control of MNCs.

From the beginning, the convention signals the intention to bring the private sector within its ambit. Article 1 defines "private sector" as "the sector of a national economy under private ownership in which the allocation of productive resources is controlled by market forces, rather than public authorities and other sectors of the economy not under the public sector or government". This definition includes all kinds of private entities such as partnerships, small to medium enterprises and MNCs.[144]

Articles 4(1)(e) and (f) address the private sector and specifically provide as follows:

1   This convention is applicable to the following acts of corruption and related offences:

(e) the offering or giving, promising, solicitation or acceptance, directly or indirectly, of any undue advantage to or by any person who directs or works for, in any capacity, *a private sector entity*, for himself or herself or for anyone else, for him or her to act, or refrain from acting, in breach of his or her duties;

(f) the offering, giving, solicitation or acceptance directly or indirectly, or promising of any undue advantage to or by any person who asserts or confirms that he or she is able to exert any improper influence over the decision making of any

---

142 Ibid., article 46(4).

143 For an official copy of the convention see the African Union website, online, available at: www.africa-union.org/Official_documents/Treaties_%20Conventions_%20Protocols/Convention%20on%20Combating%20Corruption.pdf (accessed 26 September 2010).

144 I. Carr "Corruption in Africa: is the African Union Convention on Combating Corruption the Answer?" (2007) *Journal of Business Law* 111, footnote 37.

person performing functions in the public or *private sector* in consideration thereof, whether the undue advantage is for himself or herself or for anyone else, as well as the request, receipt or the acceptance of the offer or the promise of such an advantage, in consideration of that influence, whether or not the influence is exerted or whether or not the supposed influence leads to the intended result (emphasis added).

The provisions in articles 1, 4(1)(e), 4(1)(f) and 11 thus directly place responsibility on states to regulate the activities of MNCs in the areas covered by the convention.

When stipulating the legislative and other measures to be taken in the achievement of the objective of the convention, article 5(2) provides that state parties undertake to: "Strengthen national control measures *to ensure that the setting up and operations of foreign companies* in the territory of a state party shall be subject to the respect of the national legislation in force" (emphasis added). Furthermore article 11 under the title "Private Sector" provides as follows:

State parties undertake to:

1   Adopt legislative and other measures to prevent and combat acts of corruption and related offences committed in and by agents of the *private sector.*
2   Establish mechanisms to encourage participation by *the private sector* in the fight against unfair competition, respect of the tender procedures and property rights.
3   Adopt such other measures as may be necessary to prevent *companies* from paying bribes to win tenders (emphasis added).

The convention goes further by engaging with home countries of MNCs in the prevention of corruption. Article 19 on "international cooperation" provides *inter alia* as follows:

In the spirit of international cooperation, State parties shall:

1   Collaborate with *countries of origin of multi-nationals* to criminalise and punish the practice of secret commissions and other forms of corrupt practices during international trade transactions.
2   Foster regional, continental and international cooperation to prevent corrupt practices in international trade transactions (emphasis added).

The convention provides for a follow-up mechanism in article 22. The article establishes an advisory board of 11 members elected by the AU

Executive Council for a term of two years, renewable once. The board has a broad range of responsibilities. Relevant to the context of this chapter is paragraph 5(1) of the article which provides that the board shall "collect information and analyze the conduct and behaviour of multi-national corporations operating in Africa and disseminate such information to national authorities designated under article 18(1) hereof".[145] The board is required to submit a report to the executive council on a regular basis on the progress made by each state party in complying with the provisions of the convention.

The AU Convention and the OECD Convention on Combating Bribery of Foreign Public Officials in International Business Transactions (OECD Convention)

After the OECD Convention,[146] the AU Convention is arguably the most promising international convention on bribery and corruption. According to Ouzounov "the OECD Convention is probably the most powerful legislative weapon in combating corruption in international business transactions, considering its extraterritorial implications and the large number of country participants".[147] It is suggested that the AU Convention is an overdue complement to the OECD Convention in ways that will be explained presently. The OECD Convention came into force in 1999 and it is regarded as the most effective in this area.[148] The convention has been ratified by 36 countries including all 30 OECD member states.[149] The main elements of the OECD Convention are: the prohibition of bribery of foreign officials: prosecution of companies suspected of bribery of public

---

145 Article 18(1) of the AU Convention provides as follows:

> In accordance with their domestic laws and applicable treaties, state parties shall provide each other with the greatest possible technical cooperation and assistance in dealing immediately with requests from authorities that are empowered by virtue of their national laws to prevent, detect, investigate and punish acts of corruption and related offences.

146 The OECD Convention on combating bribery of foreign public officials in international business transactions was signed in December 1997 (37 ILM 1, entered into force 15 February 1999). Other major international conventions in this area but with less effectiveness and relevance include: the UN Convention against Corruption (adopted 31 October 2003 entered into force 14 December 2005); the Council of Europe Criminal Law Convention on Corruption (adopted 4 November 1998 entered into force 1 July 2002); the Council of Europe Civil Law Convention on Corruption (adopted 4 November 1999 entered into force 1 November 2003) and the Inter-American Convention against Corruption (adopted 29 March 1996 entered into force 6 March 1997).

147 N.A. Ouzounov, "Facing the Challenge: Corruption, State Capture and the Role of Multinational Business" (2004) 37 *John Marshall Law Review* 1181, 1195.

148 Ibid.

149 M. Pieth, L.A. Low and P.J. Cullen, eds., *The OECD Convention on Bribery: A Commentary* (Cambridge: Cambridge University Press, 2007), 17–18.

officials abroad by state parties: establishment of liability of legal persons on bribery by state parties: international monitoring of the implementation of the convention and a ban on tax deductibility of bribes to foreign public officials.

However, the OECD Convention has some lacunae which the AU Convention filled within the African context. First, the OECD Convention deals only with the offering of a bribe and not with the solicitation and acceptance of a bribe.[150] This is done apparently not to interfere with the jurisdiction of the country of residence of the corrupt person or entity. The AU Convention went further than the OECD Convention by dealing with both the giving and the acceptance of bribe.[151]

Second, the OECD Convention is applicable only to legal entities (including corporations) domiciled in the states that are party to the convention.[152] It would not apply to a local subsidiary unless it is proven that the local entity acted as such under direct instructions from the parent company. According to Ouzounov, the language of the OECD Convention allows for firms to circumvent its provisions and engage in bribery through their foreign subsidiaries.[153] Ouzounov suggests that this may have been due to concern over the intrusiveness of the extraterritorial application of such laws.[154] Furthermore, the OECD Convention criminalises bribery aimed at public officials but not bribery of private sector representatives.[155] However, the AU Convention is applicable to MNCs' subsidiaries in the host states and covers bribery aimed at private sector representatives.[156]

Another area on which the OECD Convention is silent is in respect of whistle blowers. The convention provides no protection for employees who expose corruption in their organisations. Protection for whistleblowers is an essential component of anti-corruption framework. Without protection, such persons would not be encouraged to expose corrupt practices. Article 5(5) and (6) of the AU Convention address this problem in the African context. It mandates state parties to:

5   Adopt legislative and other measures to protect informants and witnesses in corruption and related offences, including protection of their identities.

6   Adopt measures that ensure citizens report instances of corruption without fear of consequent reprisals.

---

150 Articles 1–3 of the OECD Convention.
151 Article 4 of the AU Convention.
152 Article 4(1) of the OECD Convention.
153 Ouzounov (note 147), 1195.
154 Ibid.
155 Pieth *et al.* (note 149), 23.
156 See article 4, AU Convention.

The major flaw of the African Convention is that there is no provision for liability of companies. While the convention recognises the need to control MNCs, it fails to go further by providing for direct liability. Instead, it focuses solely on state responsibility. However, it is suggested that by employing this approach, the convention would help state parties to do more to control MNCs.

Summary

There is an awareness of the need to strengthen host state responsibility for human rights violation by non-state actors under the African human rights system. This, it is posited, is a more realistic approach to the quest for effective control of MNCs. A rigorous and proactive application of state responsibility principles as expressed under various instruments of the African Union would ensure that states comply with their treaty obligations to regulate the activities of MNCs. It must be observed that the principle of state responsibility as enunciated under international law may be unduly restrictive. The African system may need to move further than the current position in international law. The African Commission tentatively signalled such a move in *Serac* v. *Nigeria*. It, however, did not follow through in the subsequent decision in *Zimbabwe Human Rights NGO Forum* v. *Zimbabwe*. Despite their potential, the African Court of Human and Peoples' Rights and the African Court of Justice and Human Rights may be less effective because of the problem of access to the courts. Since individuals and MNCs are the most likely candidates to employ the court system against MNCs, a lot would depend on ensuring access of individuals and NGOs to these institutions.

6 The European Union and corporate responsibility in vulnerable states

Introduction

Even though host states have the primary obligation to monitor MNCs, home countries of MNCs also have a role to play if effective control of MNCs is to be achieved. This chapter focuses on EU regional arrangements and how they interact with developing countries. This is because, as noted earlier, major MNCs domiciled in EU member states are operating in Nigeria and other major developing countries. EU member states are second only to the United States as home jurisdictions of major MNCs. The EU provides viable opportunities because of its approach to human rights, developmental issues and trade-related matters. The chapter is divided into two parts. The first examines the EU institutional approach to CSR which is a part of a broader social policy agenda. The part considers the developments within the EU that have influenced CSR practice. It considers whether these developments are relevant when it comes to the EU's relationship with the developing world. The second part examines an important aspect of the EU relationship with African, Caribbean and Pacific countries' trade agreements. These agreements are significant because the direct beneficiaries of the agreements are often EU domiciled MNCs. The part considers whether it is possible to exert influence on host states to control activities of MNCs through such trade agreements. The validity of these agreements is also considered in the context of the World Trade Organization (WTO). The discussion here is unique and significantly different from mainstream discussions in this area because it focuses on how such agreements can impact on MNCs.

The European Union, human rights and CSR

It is widely acknowledged that a core foundational principle of the European Union is the respect for human rights and fundamental freedoms in its internal and external affairs.[1] Although human rights were not

---

1 See for example P. Craig and G. De Burca, eds, *EU Law: Text, Cases and Materials* (fourth edition, Oxford: Oxford University Press, 2007), chapter 11.

expressly mentioned in the founding treaties of the EU, the concept is rooted in the EU legal order. There is an obligation on the EU to respect human rights when it acts in its area of competences.[2] The human rights obligation of the EU was initially derived from the "general principles" developed by the European Court of Justice (ECJ).[3] The obligation was also derived from article 6 of the Treaty of the European Union (TEU). The EU has lately taken steps to strengthen its human rights framework through the introduction of a Charter of Fundamental Rights of the European Union. The charter is included in the Treaty of Lisbon.[4]

The EU and developing countries

Since its creation, the European Community/European Union[5] has engaged with issues relating to developing countries.[6] Several provisions of the EU Treaties provide a basis for extending the objective of promoting respect for human rights and fundamental freedoms to all forms of cooperation with third countries, including trade.[7] In article 177 of the Treaty Establishing the EC, it is stated that community policy in the sphere of development co-operation shall foster the sustainable economic and social development of developing countries especially the most disadvantaged; the smooth and gradual integration of the developing countries into the world economy and the campaign against poverty. Subsection 2 of article 177 further states that community policy in the area of development cooperation shall contribute to a general objective of developing and consolidating

2　T. Ahmed and I. de Jesus Butler, "The European Union and Human Rights: An International Law Perspective" (2006) 17 (4) *European Journal of International Law* 771, 773.

3　Case 29/69, *Stauder* v. *Ulm* (1969) ECR 4119; Case 11/70, *Internationale Handelsgesellschaft* v. *Einfuhrund Vorratsstelle Getreide* (1970) ECR 1125; Case 4/73, *Nold* v. *Commission* (1974) ECR 491; Case 36/75, *Rutili* v. *Minister for the Interior* (1975) ECR 1219; Case 44/79, *Hauer* v. *Land Rheinland-Pfalz* (1979) ECR 3727; Case 5/88, *Wachauf* v. *Germany* (1989) ECR 2609; Case C–13/94, *P* v. *S and Cornwall CC* (1996) ECR I–2143; Case C–36/02, *Omega* (2004) ECR I–9609.

4　Treaty of Lisbon amending the Treaty on the European Union and the Treaty establishing the European Community, signed at Lisbon, 13 December 2007, OJ C 306/01.

5　Note that in strict terms, it was the European Community and not the EU that concluded agreements with third countries. See Craig and De Burca (note 1), 167–171.

6　The relationship between the EU and developing countries is more than just politics. According to Kryvoi "the European Union absorbs 20 percent of developing country exports and 40 percent of European Union imports originate in developing countries". See Y. Kryvoi, "Why European Union Trade Sanctions Do Not Work" (2008) 17 *Minnesota Journal of International Law* 209, 226.

7　These include articles 2, 3, 6, 19, 29, 49 Treaty of European Union (TEU); articles 11, 13, 177 Treaty Establishing the European Community (EC Treaty); articles 6,7, Treaty of Amsterdam (TA). See also D. Horng "The Human Rights Clause in the European Union's External Trade and Development Agreements" (2003) 9 (5) *European Law Journal* 677, 677–678.

democracy and the rule of law and respect for human rights and fundamental freedoms. For example, according to an EU policy statement this is the foundation upon which all relations between the EU and Nigeria is founded.[8] This fundamental policy generally reflects on the broader EU–Nigeria relationship including trade relationships. The question, however, is how far this underlying policy affects the EU approach to corporate responsibility and control of MNCs' activities abroad.

While it is conceded that host states bear the primary responsibility for controlling MNCs within their jurisdiction, it is argued that because of the limitations in host state control discussed in Chapter 4, home states, such as the EU member states, have an important complementary role to play in ensuring accountability. The role of the EU is important because, as stated earlier, the EU member states are second only to the United States in terms of popularity as locations for MNCs' parent companies. Furthermore, the EU has a highly developed institutional and legal framework, which has greater potential to influence issues surrounding the accountability of MNCs than either international law or laws of the host jurisdiction. Commenting on the potential of the EU legal framework for the promotion of human rights, the economic and social responsibility, Voiculescu observes that;

> At a close analysis, the EU legal framework offers the potential for a mechanism that, while more unorthodox then (sic) the usual normative approaches, can lead to an advancement of human rights and social values within an important group of less developed countries, the ACP countries. The promotion of human rights would take place through the grafting of economic and social responsibility standards on to the agenda of economic and development co-operation. The question is, of course, whether the EU offers an established legal and political mechanism through which such standards and values can become effective, and whether these mechanisms can be coupled with instruments of intergovernmental co-operation effective enough to contribute significantly to the protection and promotion of human rights.[9]

CSR as a strategy within Europe and its external dimensions

This section follows on from the discussion of CSR in Europe in Chapter 3. In 2000, the European Commission adopted its social policy agenda for

---

8 Nigerian-European Community, "Country Support Strategy and Indicative Programme for the Period 2001–2007", online, available at: www.delnga.ec.europa.eu/docs/CountryStrategy.pdf (accessed 27 September 2010).

9 A. Voiculescu, "Unorthodox Human Rights Instruments: The ACP–EU Development Co-operation from the Lomé Conventions to the Cotonou Agreement" (2006) 4 (1) *Journal of Commonwealth Law and Legal Education* 85, 86.

Europe, which emphasised the role of CSR in addressing the employment and social consequences of economics and market integration.[10] The need to integrate environmental and social concerns into business activities was also recognised in the commission's communication on sustainable development.[11] In the same year, the European Council made "a special appeal to companies' corporate sense of social responsibility regarding best practices on lifelong learning, work organisation, equal opportunities, social inclusion and sustainable development".[12] This call was in realisation of the potential of corporations to contribute to the social policies of the EU. The social responsibility of companies was linked with the EU Lisbon strategy.[13] Apart from the efforts to integrate CSR practice as part into social policy, there are legislative developments that have encouraged and bolstered a responsible approach to business within the EU. In the case of employees for example, several directives have been passed to safeguard their interests.[14] Directives have also been introduced to enhance environmental and social disclosure.[15] The position of consumers in relation to corporate actors has received significant attention in the EU.[16] Furthermore the EU

10 Communication from the Commission to the Council, the European Parliament and Social Committee, Social Policy Agenda, COM (2000) 379 final, 28 June 2000.
11 Communication from the Commission: A sustainable Europe for a Better World: An EU Strategy for Sustainable Development (Commission's proposal to the Gothenburg European Council) COM (2001) final, 15 May 2001.
12 Lisbon European Council, March 2000, "Presidency Conclusions" at paragraph 39. Online, available at: www.europarl.europa.eu/summits/lis1_en.htm (accessed 27 September 2010); G.J. Room, "Social Exclusion, Solidarity and the Challenge of Globalization" (1999) 8 *International Journal of Social Welfare* 166,167.
13 Lisbon European Council, March 2000, 'Presidency Conclusions' at paragraph 39. Online, available at: www.europarl.europa.eu/summits/lis1_en.htm (accessed 27 September 2010).
14 These include Council Directive on Redundancy 75/129 of 1975 as amended and consolidated in Council Directive 98/59/EC of 20 July 1998; Council Directive 2001/23/EC of 12 March 2001 on the approximation of the laws of the member states relating to the safeguarding of employees' rights in the event of transfers of undertakings, businesses or parts of undertakings or businesses; Council Directive 94/45/EC of 22 September 1994 on the establishment of a European works council or a procedure in community-scale undertakings and community-scale groups of undertakings for the purposes of informing and consulting employees; Council Directive 93/104/EC, of 23 November 1993, concerning certain aspects of the organisation of working time, amended by Directive 2000/34/EC of 22 June 2000 of the European Parliament and of the council.
15 Regulation (EEC) no. 761/2001 of the European Parliament and of the council of 19 March 2001 allowing voluntary participation by organisations in a community eco-management and audit scheme (EMAS).
16 Directive 99/44/EC of the European Parliament and of the Council of 25 May 1999 on certain aspects of the sale of consumer goods and associated guarantees (OJ L 171 of 7 July 1999); Council Directive 85/374/EEC of 25 July 1985 on the approximation of the laws, regulations and administrative provisions of the member states concerning liability for defective products (OJ L 210 of 7 August 1985).

has also enhanced transparency and accountability of the corporate actors within it.[17]

The approach to the social responsibility of business within the EU can be contrasted with the EU strategies in promoting CSR abroad which has not taken the same robust approach. On the external front the EU strategy for promoting CSR abroad is bifurcated. The two principal actors in this area at present within the EU institutional framework are the European Parliament and the European Commission. The European Parliament has repeatedly called for regulatory and proactive approach while the European Commission favours a voluntary approach.[18]

The European Parliament and CSR in developing countries

Since the mid-1990s, the EU Parliament has shown keen interest in the control of EU MNCs operating in developing countries. In December 1996 the Parliament's annual report on human rights called for the development of a code of conduct for European companies operating in developing countries. Such a code would oblige companies to respect human rights "in all their forms (civil, social, economic, environmental) including mechanisms of control and sanctions".[19] In December, 1997 the European Parliament passed a resolution on relocation and foreign direct investment in third countries in which it called on the commission to "draw up a code of conduct for European multinationals based on the promotion of trade union freedom, combating forced labour and child labour, the elimination of discrimination and respect for the environment".[20] It was proposed that companies that undertake to respect the provisions of such a code be recommended to be published in the official journal of the European Community.[21] The Parliament took the same approach in its 1998 report on fair trade with developing countries by calling on the commission to develop a code. The Parliament went further by suggesting that the promotion of fair trade be included as a development instrument in the conclusion of new trade agreements with African, Caribbean and Pacific

---

17 Directive 2004/109/EC of the European Parliament and of the council of 15 December 2004 on the harmonisation of transparency requirements in relation to information about issuers whose securities are admitted to trading on a regulated market and amending Directive 2001/34/EC.

18 The approaches of the European Parliament and European Commission are discussed in the following sections.

19 European Parliament Committee on Development and Cooperation "Report on EU Standards for European Enterprises Operating in Developing Countries: towards a European Code of Conduct" A4-0508/98, 17 December 1998, OJC104/176 of 14.4.1999.

20 European Parliament resolution on relocation and foreign direct investment in third countries (OJC34, 2.2.1998).

21 European Parliament Committee (note 19), 12.

states (ACP).[22] According to the European Parliament, the main reason why it took the approach was that "an EU Code could create a level playing field, reward best practice and drive up standards in underperforming companies" in developing countries.[23]

However, recognising that there was no legal basis as yet to create a binding code, the Parliament recommended, as a start, a voluntary initiative that should contribute to greater standardisation of voluntary codes of conducts based on international standards. This would involve creating a European model code of conduct supported by a European monitoring platform. According to the Parliament's 1998 report

> Such a code would aim to generate minimum standards regarding the environment, health and safety conditions in the work place, no use of forced, bonded or child labour, respect for women's and indigenous peoples' rights, and respect for basic human rights.[24]

It was suggested that the code would apply to companies whose headquarters are registered in the EU, their contractors, subcontractors, suppliers and licensees worldwide (meaning any legal or natural persons who contracted with the company and were engaged in a manufacturing process) in different sectors.[25]

The European monitoring platform suggested by the report would encompass complaint procedures and remedial actions. The monitoring system was aimed at protecting workers all over the world from oppression, abuse and exploitation where national laws are inadequate or not enforced and international conventions are not ratified. The monitoring platform was also to pay special attention to conflict areas where MNCs operate and avoidance of collusion in violations of human rights. However, the monitoring platform, it clearly stated, was not designed to determine working conditions and wages in developing countries which is to be dealt with by negotiations between workers, trade unions and employees at local level.

It must be observed that the Parliament's call for a code has precedents in the EC. In 1977, the Foreign Ministers of the European Community approved a code of conduct for community companies with subsidiary branches or representation in South Africa. The code was further revised in 1985.[26] It was designed to guide EC MNCs operations in South Africa

---

22 European Parliament "Report on Fair Trade, Committee on Development and Cooperation" A4-0198/98 of 26 May 1998, 7. Trade related issues shall be explored later in this chapter.
23 European Parliament Committee (note 19), 15.
24 Ibid., 17.
25 Ibid.
26 Code of Conduct for Community Companies with Subsidiaries, Branches or Representation in South Africa, 16 November 1985 (1985) 24 ILM 1477.

during the apartheid era. The code was abolished in 1993 after the fall of the apartheid system. Also, in 1998 the EU adopted a code of conduct for arm exports by corporate actors from the EU.[27] The code is a council declaration which contains political commitment but is not legally binding. It is designed to set common standards across the EU for the export of military equipments.

The European Commission and CSR in developing countries

In the commission's Green Paper on CSR of 2001,[28] the commission recognises both internal and external dimensions of CSR and the unique position of MNCs in the equation. The Green Paper recognises emerging issues in respect of employees, local communities, businesses, business partners, suppliers and consumers. The paper also paid special attention to the human rights dimension of CSR especially in the international context:

> Corporate social responsibility has a strong human rights dimension, particularly in relation to international operations and global supply chains ... Human rights are a very complex issue presenting political, legal and moral dilemmas. Companies face challenging questions, including how to identify where their areas of responsibility lie as distinct from those of governments, how to monitor whether their business partners are complying with their core values, and how to approach and operate in countries where human rights violations are widespread. The European Union itself has an obligation in the framework of its co-operation policy to ensure the respect of labour standards, environmental protection and human rights and is confronted with the challenge of ensuring a full coherence between its development policy, its trade policy and its strategy for the development of the private sector in the developing countries notably through the promotion of European investments.[29]

27 The European Union Code of Conduct for Arms Export, online, available at: http://consilium.europa.eu/uedocs/cmsUpload/08675r2en8.pdf (accessed 27 September 2010).

28 Commission of the European Communities, "Green Paper: Promoting a European Framework for Corporate Social Responsibility" COM(2001) 366 Final, 18.7.2001; See also Directorate-General for Employment and Social Affairs, "Promoting a European Framework for Corporate Social Responsibility: Green Paper", online, available at: http://europa.eu/legislation_summaries/employment_and_social_policy/employment_rights_and_work_organisation/n26039_en.htm (accessed 27 September 2010).

29 Commission of the European Communities (note 28).

The Green Paper thus underscores the underlying principles of article 177 of the Treaty Establishing the EC and the relationship of the principles to EU policies regarding developing countries.[30]

However, while the Green Paper, the subsequent White Paper and the setting up of the European Multi-Stakeholder Forum (discussed in Chapter 3) helped in fostering the debate on CSR within the EU, the EU largely failed to take concrete action to promote responsible business abroad.[31] As discussed in Chapter 3, the commission has decided to back a business led and completely voluntary approach to CSR.[32] In adopting its latest approach, the commission arguably failed to pay adequate attention to the social and environmental consequences of MNCs operations in developing countries. The European Parliament in its 2007 resolution on the commission's new approach expressed its disappointment as follows:

> [The Parliament] expresses disappointment that the Commission did not accord greater priority to promoting global initiatives in its communication on CSR and calls on the Commission working with Member States and stakeholders both to develop a strategic vision and to contribute to the development of CSR initiatives at a global level, as well as a major effort significantly to raise participation in such initiatives by EU companies.[33]

It is contended that while the commission's current position may work within the EU because of the institutional framework which is enhanced by robust legislative regimes and effective enforcement process, the situation in developing countries requires a much more rigorous approach.

It is observed that despite the shift in the commission's position there are still viable ways by which the EU could complement and galvanise host state's ability to control MNCs. One is through the established practice of incorporating, implementing and enforcing human rights clauses in trade

---

30 In 2001 the European Commission also introduced a communication on promoting core labour standards and improving social governance in the context of globalisation which similarly supported a voluntary approach to CSR. See Communication from the Commission to the Council, the European Parliament and the Economic and Social Committee, "Promoting Core Labour Standards and Improving Social Governance in the context of globalisation" COM (2001) 416 final, 18.7.2001.

31 See European Union Parliament, Committee on Employment and Social Affairs, "Report on Corporate Social Responsibility: A New Partnership" A6–9999/2006 of 20.12.2006, 27.

32 European Commission, "Implementing the Partnership for Growth and Jobs: Making Europe a Pole of Excellence or Corporate Responsibility" COM (2006) 136 final, online, available at http://eur-lex.europa.eu/LexUriServ/site/en/com/2006/com2006 _0136en01.pdf (accessed 27 September 2010).

33 European Parliament Resolution of 13 March 2007 on Corporate Social Responsibility P6_TA(2007)0062 (2006/2133(INI)).

arrangements with third countries. Another, is the possibility of providing remedies in home states' courts for victims of human rights abuses by MNCs abroad. These possibilities are explored in the rest of this chapter and in Chapter 7.

Trade and human rights

Legal commentators have recognised the viability of employing trade rules to control MNCs and make them amenable to positive human rights duties.[34] With the prohibition of the use of force to enforce international law under the United Nations framework, trade sanctions have emerged as one of the most coercive mechanisms available to enforce international law including international human rights norms.[35] Kinley and Tadaki have suggested that current understanding of international trade, aid and development finance, and the roles of international institutions must be re-conceptualised in order to make it possible to view MNCs as operating within the realm of international law, especially international human rights law.[36] Since corporations and especially MNCs drive free trade, commercial enterprise and are the immediate and direct beneficiaries of trade agreements, Kinley and Tadaki posit that trade sanctions would be a powerful mechanism for the control of externalities of MNCs.[37]

Another reason why trade arrangements may become significant is in regard to the emerging issue of home state responsibility for extraterritorial violations of international law by MNCs and their subsidiaries. This was argued persuasively for by McCorquodale and Simons.[38] The premise

---

34 It must be observed that even though governments do not actively trade, they make arrangements that facilitate trading activities of MNCs particularly in the international context which impact on human rights protection. See D. Kinley and J. Nolan, "Trading and Aiding Human Rights: Corporations in the Global Economy" (2007) 25 (4) *Nordic Journal of Human Rights Law* 353, 363; C. Ochoa, "Advancing the Language of Human Rights in a Global Economic Order" (2003) 23 *Boston Third World Law Journal* 57, 66–68. It should be noted that there is no consensus in the academic literature as to the extent to which there is a linkage between trade and human rights, however, most commentators agree that there is an interesting connection between the two which needs to be fully explored. For a review of literature on trade and human rights see A.T.F. Lang, "Re-thinking Trade and Human Rights" (2007) 15 (2) *Tulane Journal of International and Comparative Law* 335, 336.

35 C.M. Vazquez, "Trade Sanctions and Human Rights – Past, Present and Future" (2003) 6 (4) *Journal of International Economic Law* 797, 799–800, 803.

36 D. Kinley and J. Tadaki, "From Talk to Walk: The Emergence of Human Rights Responsibilities for Corporations at International Law" (2003–2004) 44 *Virginia Journal of International Law* 931, 936; Kinley and Nolan (note 34), 354.

37 Kinley and Tadaki (note 36), 1006.

38 R. McCorquodale and P. Simons, "Responsibility Beyond Borders: State Responsibility for Extraterritorial Violations by Corporations of International Human Rights Law" (2007) 70 (4) *Modern Law Review* 598.

of the authors' argument is that governments of industrialised states explicitly or implicitly assist their corporate nationals in their global trade and investments ventures. One of the major ways this is done is by the negotiation and ratification of bilateral investment agreements that assist extraterritorial investments by corporate nationals.[39] Based on the international principle that states have a general duty not to act in ways that cause harm outside their territory, the writers argue that where a home state of an MNC negotiates a bilateral investments treaty with a non-industrialised state and an MNC working under such framework violates human rights, the state could be deemed to have constructive knowledge of such violation and therefore held accountable for facilitating the extraterritorial harm.[40] They therefore argue that the liability of the MNC subsidiary could be attributed to the home state of the parent company in such circumstances. According to the writers:

> In these circumstances it is arguable that, although the acts of a foreign subsidiary of a corporate national cannot be directly attributed to the home state, the latter exercises sufficient control over the parent company and has constructive knowledge of the potential for the subsidiary to violate human rights law to justify the imposition of an obligation to exercise due diligence in relation to the human rights impacts of such activity. The obligation requires a state to take reasonable steps to ensure that such entities do not operate in violation of international human rights law even where such operations are conducted through a foreign subsidiary. *This obligation would include, but not limited to, a requirement that the home state enact domestic regulation, requiring human rights impact assessments, the subsequent mitigation of any such impacts, and the provision of a remedy in the home state's courts*[41] (emphasis added).

However, the argument of McCorquodale and Simons is a very radical position which this writer posits would take a long time to arrive at under the current state of international law. It is arguable that the EU would be meeting its international obligations by arranging its trade relations with developing countries in a way that ensures that MNCs play by the rules.

Can the EU pursue human rights objectives in its trade arrangements in view of World Trade Organization's rules?

Generally states are free to negotiate whatever agreements they feel best serve their interests. However, states' ability to conclude agreements are

---

39   Ibid., 599–612.
40   Ibid., 621.
41   Ibid., 623.

increasingly being constrained by norms of global governance such as international trade rules. It has been observed that since the World Trade Organization (WTO) affects state sovereignty, it is fair to say that the body shares in the balance of power among states.[42] The three core principles of GATT, which were later incorporated into the WTO agreements of 1944, are the requirement of "most-favoured-nation treatment" among member states which means that trade policies shall not discriminate on the ground of country of origin or destination (article I), the requirement of national treatment which means that imported products should not be treated less favourably than domestic products (article III) and the prohibition of quantitative restrictions under article XI.[43] These core principles seem to bar imposition of trade sanctions on WTO member states in the pursuit of non-trade issues such as human rights violations. The pertinent question here is whether in view of international trade rules the EU can use trade agreements to further human rights issues in third countries. In the context of this book, the task is to examine from a legal standpoint the extent to which member states of the WTO can legitimately pursue human rights objectives in their trade relationship without contravening WTO rules. A related enquiry is whether the ACP–EU arrangement can incorporate non trade objectives such as human rights in view of WTO rules. The position of this book is that the WTO arrangement permits member states to enter into regional arrangements which can incorporate non trade issues such as human rights.

The WTO has been described as a global governance node, "a point of intersection of a variety of regulatory networks"[44] which includes preferential trade and investments agreements and other trading arrangements. The WTO embodies the "rule of law" in world trade and its legitimacy derives from the laws establishing it.[45] It is a forum for states to negotiate rules that promote free trade, transparency and provides predictability in international business dealings. Member states are bound by its rules and the rules are enforced by an effective dispute resolution mechanism, the decision of which can lead to the imposition of sanctions against erring member states. The appellate body of the WTO, which is at the apex of the WTO dispute resolution system, has been described as an international

---

42 C.R. Kelly, "Power, Linkage and Accommodation: The WTO as an International Actor and its Influence on other Actors and Regimes" (2006) 24 *Berkeley Journal of International Law* 79, 83.

43 General Agreement on Tariffs and Trade, 1947; Marrakesh Agreement Establishing the World Trade Organization, 15 April 1994, 1867 UNTS 154, 33 I.L.M. 1144 (1994) (WTO Agreement).

44 S. Picciotto, "The WTO as a Node of Global Governance: Economic Regulation and Human Rights Discourses" 2007 (1) *Law, Social Justice and Global Development Journal* (LGD) 3.

45 Ibid., 4. See also Kelly (note 42), 81.

economic court in all but name.[46] However, the WTO trade regime is more than a mere set of rules. According to Lang, it is also:

A social environment in which ideas about the best and most appropriate trade policies are generated, legitimated, and disseminated. It is a cognitive environment in which states are taught how to interpret the international economic order and how to calculate their interests in it. It is also an institutional environment which re-shapes the mix of actors involved in trade policy-making and the avenues of influence available to them.[47]

Among scholars and commentators the relationship between the WTO and human rights has generated different positions. It has been suggested that WTO agreements stifle states' ability to achieve other objectives including human rights objectives.[48] In this connection, it has been argued that the WTO system makes it harder for states to meet their obligations under the Universal Declaration of Human Rights to respect, protect and promote human rights. A usual point of contrast (though arguable) is the fact that the WTO system has a strong and effective dispute resolution mechanism which the international system of human rights does not have.[49] It has also been argued that WTO rules give precedence to trade over human rights issues. Others have defended the WTO system, arguing that the WTO governs trade and not issues such as human rights.[50] Some WTO defenders, however, argue that the WTO system does in fact promote human rights albeit indirectly through the stimulation of trade and improved governance.[51] Eminent scholars have argued, based on

---

46   Picciotto (note 44), 5.
47   Lang (note 34), 412.
48   R. Howse and M. Mutua, *Protecting Human Rights in a Global Economy: Challenges for the World Trade Organization* (Montreal: International Centre for Human Rights and Democratic Development, 2000); F.J. Garcia, "The Universal Declaration of Human Rights at 50 and the Challenge of Global Markets: Trading away the Human Rights Principle" (1999) 25 *Brooklyn Journal of International Law* 51; J. Baghwati, "The Boundary of the WTO: Afterword: The Question of Linkage" (2002) 96 *American Journal of International Law* 126. Baghwati argues that WTO's trade regime was established for mutual benefits through trade and the attempt to link it with non-trade issues such as human rights does not promote mutual benefits and actually disadvantaged countries of the South. Similarly Jones argues that the WTO is not design for human rights and does not have the capacity or resources to monitor human rights including worker's rights. See K. Jones, *Who's Afraid of the WTO?* (Oxford: Oxford University Press, 2004).
49   S.A. Aaronson, "Seeping in Slowly: How Human Rights Concerns are penetrating the WTO" (2007) 6 (3) *World Trade Review* 413.
50   T. Eres, "The Limits of GATT Article XX: A Back Door for Human Rights" (2003–2004) 35 *Georgetown Journal of International Law* 597, 602.
51   Kinley and Nolan (note 34), 353, 354.

WTO substantive rules and practices of the organisation that the body is not simply neutral to human rights issues but is increasingly incorporating human rights issues within its framework.[52] Others have argued that the WTO should promote human rights.[53] In particular Petersmann has argued in favour of strengthening the UN human rights law by integrating it into the law of the WTO.[54]

The WTO system and human rights

The Marrakesh Agreement establishing the WTO in its preamble included not only free trade as its objective but also human rights and social issues such as raising standards of living, ensuring full employment, sustainable development and environmental protection.[55] The original agreement, the General Agreement on Tariffs and Trade (GATT) 1947, which continues to be applicable, in its article XX and article XXI provides a number of grounds upon which member states may pursue public welfare issues through trade restrictions notwithstanding that this may violate trade rules. It has been opined that "WTO members might found the foundation for a more effective approach to protecting human rights at home or responding to human rights abuses abroad in one of the GATT

---

52 S.J. Powell, "The Place of Human Rights Law in World Trade Organization Rules" (2004) 16 *Florida Journal of International Law* 219, 221; Aaronson (note 49).

53 P. Stirling, "The use of Trade Sanctions as an Enforcement Mechanism for Basic Human Rights: A Proposal for Addition to the World Trade Organization" (1996) 11 *American University Journal of International Law and Policy* 1; G.M. Zagel, "WTO and Human Rights: Examining Linkages and Suggesting Convergence" (2005) 2 (2) *International Development-Jurist Paper Series* 1.

54 E. Petersmann, "Time for a United Nations 'Global Compact' for Integrating Human Rights into the Law of Worldwide Organisations: Lessons from European Integration" (2002) 13 (3) *European Journal of International Law* 621. E. Petersmann, "The Human Rights Approach Advocated by the UN High Commissioner for Human Rights and the WTO: Is it Relevant for WTO Law and Policy?" (2004) 7 (3) *Journal of International Economic Law* 605; Ernst-Ulrich Petersmann, "The WTO Constitution and Human Rights" (2002) 3 (1) *Journal of International Economic Law* 19. See Alston's critique of Petersmann that his approach will undermine human rights promotion and protection: P. Alston, "Resisting the Merger and Acquisition of Human Rights by Trade Law: A Reply to Petersmann" (2002) 13 (4) *European Journal of International Law* 815.

55 WTO Agreement (note 43). Qureshi argues that in a sense, there is a human rights dimension to the WTO. According to him, this can be found in trade, trade related and non-trade norms of the WTO and in the manner of the implementation of these norms: A.H. Qureshi, "International Trade and Human Rights from the Perspective of the WTO" in F. Weiss, *International Economic Law with a Human Face* (The Hague/Dordrecht/London: Kluwer Law International, 1998) 159.

WTO exceptions – Article XX and XXI".[56] Article XXI will be discussed first.

Article XXI allows member states to justify breach of their obligation under GATT for national security reasons. Article XXI provides:

1   Nothing in this Agreement shall be construed:

    a   to require any contracting party to furnish any information the disclosure of which it considers contrary to its essential security interests; or

    b   to prevent any contracting party from taking any action which it considers necessary for the protection of its essential security interests

        i   relating to fissionable materials or the materials from which they are derived;

        ii   relating to the traffic in arms, ammunition and implements of war and to such traffic in other goods and materials as is carried on directly or indirectly for the purpose of supplying a military establishment;

        iii   taken in time of war or other emergency in international relations; or

    c   to prevent any contracting party from taking any action in pursuance of its obligations under the United Nations Charter for the maintenance of international peace and security.

Article XXI potentially grants wide authority because it allows member states to, among other things take "any action which it considers necessary

---

56   Aaronson (note 49), 430: Powell (note 52) argues that article XX(a) on protection of public morals opens the possibility for the application of human rights law; Lim argues that the WTO system is linked to human rights aims and outcomes through article XX, H. Lim, "Trade and Human Rights: What's at Issue?" (2001) 35 (2) *Journal of World Trade* 275; Bal also argues that article XX can be used to protect human rights. S. Bal, "International Free Trade Agreements and Human Rights: Reinterpreting Article XX of GATT" (2001) 10 *Minnesota Journal of Global Trade* 62. Note, however, that some scholars argue that article XX was not meant to incorporate human rights issues. This argument is losing ground, however. Eres argues that the drafters of article XX did not intend it as a means of incorporating human rights issues in the WTO system and that article XX cannot satisfy its "necessity" test, Eres (note 50) 597; Jarus, writing from woman's rights perspective, contends that the public moral exception under article XX(a) is a legal basis for linking trade and human rights, L.M. Jarvis, "Women's Rights and the Public Moral Exceptions of GATT Article 20" (2000) 22 *Michigan Journal of International Law* 219; see also C.T. Feddersen, "Focusing on Substantive Law and International Economic Relations: The Public Morals of GATT's XX(a) Exception and 'Conventional' Rules of Interpretation" (1998) 7 *Minnesota Journal of Global Trade* 75.

for the protection of its essential security interests ... in time of war or other emergency in international relations".[57] The member states determine what is "necessary", what is in their "essential security interests", as well as "time of war" and "emergency in international relations".[58] Interestingly, national security under article XXI has been tied to the protection of human rights abroad.[59] Goodman argues persuasively that article XXI validates member states' unilateral economic sanctions based on foreign human rights violations.[60] He contends that severe human rights violations in foreign countries may constitute a threat to national security by "heralding a threat to harmony among nations",[61] may lead to substantial destabilising effects on proximate states such as refugee-related problems and may constitute offence against humanity and therefore a threat to international peace. According to this argument, which this writer shares, a member state may justify the imposition of economic sanctions on another member state in violation of GATT/WTO provisions for human rights violations in the territory of the other member state on the ground that such violations constitute a national security threat. For example, the imposition of economic sanctions for human rights violations may be justified on the ground that such violations lead to influx of refugee/asylum seekers or that they constitute an emergency in international relations.

It has, however, recently been argued by Aaronson that a member state may only invoke article XXI to protect its own security or the security of its citizens but not that of another state or its citizens. Member states may apply the exception to other state(s) where the UN Security Council authorises such trade restrictions.[62] This writer, however, contends that from the reading of the text of article XXI, the requirement of UN Security Council's authorisation is limited to article XXI(c) and not article XXI(b) which has been tied to human rights issues. Therefore, where a member state derogates from its WTO obligations based on Article XXI(b), the UN Security Council authorisation is not required.

The invocation of XXI(c) is limited because of the difficulty in getting the authorisation of the United Nations Security Council. However, sanctions have been imposed based on article XXI and United Nations Security Council authorisation on South Africa for gross violations of human rights within her territory.[63]

---

57 Article XXI(b), GATT.
58 See P. Lindsay, "The Ambiguity of GATT Article XXI: Subtle Success or Rampant Failure?" (2003) 52 *Duke Law Journal* 1276, 1277.
59 Ibid., 1298.
60 R. Goodman, "Norms and National Security: The WTO as a Catalyst for Inquiry" (2001) 2 *Chicago Journal of International Law* 101, 106.
61 Ibid., 106.
62 Aaronson (note 49), 431–432.
63 UNSC Res. 418 (1977); UNSC Res. 569 (1985).

Article XX allows contracting states to adopt or enforce measures, including those necessary to protect public morals; to protect human, animal or plant life or health; to secure compliance with laws or regulations which are not inconsistent with GATT agreement; to restrict products of prison labour; to preserve national treasure; and to conserve exhaustible natural resources. The measures may not, however, be applied in a manner which would constitute a means of arbitrary or unjustifiable discrimination or a disguised restriction on international trade. This means essentially that member states may employ these measures but must comply strictly with the conditions set out in the section. Article XX has been significantly employed to defend measures taken to protect the environment. Some of the provisions, as will be discussed presently, have been interpreted to cover human rights issues. Article XX(a), (b), (d), (e) and (g) may potentially be construed in human rights terms. It has been argued that international human rights law is relevant in defining these exceptions.[64] It must, however, be observed that the WTO appellate body did not use international law in interpreting article XX(g) in the *Shrimp/Turtle II* case.[65]

A major significance of the *Shrimp/Turtle II* case is that it opens the door for unilateral measures in pursuit of non trade objectives. The objective in this case was to protect the environment. Furthermore the case impliedly accepted that extraterritorial measures can fall within article XX exceptions. In the *Shrimp/Turtle II* case, the United States took unilateral measures to protect the endangered species of sea turtles outside its territorial waters. The United States imposed an embargo on the import of shrimp and shrimp products from countries that fail to certify that the shrimp were caught using the turtle-excluder devices or where the turtle-excluder device employed were not up to the standard required in the United States. The appellate body ruled that the action taken by the United States fell within the scope of measures permitted under article XX.[66]

As earlier indicated, it is widely contended that article XX(a) on the protection of public morals "in particular provides a fertile source of discretion to apply human rights law".[67] It has also been observed that article

---

64 R. Howse and M. Mutua, *Protecting Human Rights in a Global Economy: Challenges for the World Trade Organization* (Montreal: International Centre for Human Rights and Democratic Development, 2000).

65 See Appellate Body Report Concerning United States – Import Prohibition of Certain Shrimp and Shrimp Products, WT/DS58/AB/R, para. 133, 12 October 1998; R. Howse, "Human Rights in the WTO: Whose Rights, What Humanity? Comment on Petersmann" (2002) 13 (3) *European Journal of International Law* 651, 656–657.

66 However, the court found that the manner by which the United States applied its measure caused arbitrary and unjustifiable discrimination. The United States was requested to bring its measures in line with its WTO obligations.

67 See generally note 52 above.

XX(a) may in fact go further than human rights of persons but may also permit measures to protect morals of persons in circumstances not implicating human rights.[68]

Charnovitz[69] rationalises that the moral exception in article XX(a) was introduced because prior to the GATT, governments were restricting imports or exports for moral or humanitarian or other non commercial reasons and they wanted to ensure that their obligations under trade treaties would not interfere with their ability to restrict trade on these grounds.[70] He attempts to interpret article XX following the directive in article 31 of the Vienna Convention to interpret a treaty according to its ordinary meaning and in the light of its scope and object. He observes that the ordinary meaning of article XX does not reveal its scope nor the extent of its applicability.[71] He then resorts to supplementary means of interpretation as provided under article 32 of the Vienna Convention. Arguing from historical antecedents to the GATT, he suggests:

> The rationale for the moral exception in trade treaties can be inferred from the contemporary trade controls that could have triggered the legal need for an exception. There were trade controls on opium, pornography, liquor, slaves, firearms, blasphemous articles, products linked to animal cruelty, prize fight films, and abortion-inducing drugs.... The various ways morality-based trade measures had been employed before the GATT was written foreshadow many of the uses to which article XX(a) might be enlisted today.[72]

Charnovitz further suggests that because of the long-standing usage of trade measures for moral and humanitarian purposes, the authors of article XX(a) might have intended it to have effect both in external relations of member states and also in the international domain.[73] Noting that leaving the determination of what is moral or immoral to individual

---

68 Vazquez (note 35), 816 (footnote 70), 818.
69 S. Charnovitz, "The Moral Exception in Trade Policy" (1998) 38 *Virginia Journal of International Law* 689.
70 Prior to GATT, there were international treaty regimes and domestic laws prohibiting trade for moral reasons. See for a discussion of some of these in Charnovitz, ibid., 710–713.
71 Ibid., 716.
72 Ibid., 717–718.
73 Interestingly the WTO's appellate body decision in the *Shrimp/Turtle* case suggests that article XX(g) could be applied in a way that impacts on external relations. The body interpreted the article in the light of the principles of international law. See Appellate Body Report Concerning United States – Import Prohibition of Certain Shrimp and Shrimp Products, WT/DS58/AB/R, para. 133, 12 October 1998; see also L. Bartels, "Article XX of GATT and the Problem of Extra-Territorial Jurisdiction: The Case of Trade Measures for the Protection of Human Rights" (2002) 36 (2) *Journal of International Trade* 353.

governments could disrupt trade and encourage imperialism by powerful states in the international market he suggests that article XX(a) should be internationalised.[74] He suggests that the WTO should employ international human rights law "to ascribe meaning to the vague terms of article XX(a)".[75]

However, it must be observed that to date, no member state has successfully invoked the provision of article XX(a) to restrict trade on the ground of human rights violations.[76]

Provisions of article XX have also been analysed in relation to labour rights. The GATT/WTO has no explicit provision permitting or requiring the use of trade restrictions against labour rights violations. However, a combined reading of article XX(a) and XX(e) may provide a legal basis in relation to labour rights. It has been suggested that article XX(a) may be employed to justify trade sanctions "against products that involve the use of child labor or denial of basic workers' rights".[77] Article XX(e) expressly permits such measures in relation to "the products of prison labour". It has further been suggested that article XX(a), article XX(e) and article XX(b) on health and safety "could be read expansively so as to include the core labour standards articulated by the ILO".[78]

The achievement of non-economic objectives such as human rights is, however, circumscribed by the "necessity" test under article XX(a), XX(b) and XX(e) which seemingly ensures that trade issues are prioritised over other objectives.[79] Article XX(a), XX(b) and XX(e) authorise only measures that are necessary to protect public morals. This has been interpreted to mean that non-economic objectives may be implemented through a measure that will be least trade-restrictive.[80] This has been the approach taken by the appellate body in the interpretation of the word "necessary" in article XX(b).[81]

The conclusion to be reached from the discussion so far is that articles XX and XXI permit member states to derogate from their WTO obligations on the ground of human rights violations in another member country. Except in the *Shrimp/Turtle II* case where the WTO appellate body considered article XX(g), the appellate body is yet to rule directly on the

74 Charnovitz (note 69), 742.
75 Ibid., 742.
76 Aaronson (note 49), 431.
77 M.J. Trebilock and R. Howse, "Trade Policy and Labour Standards" (2004–2005) 14 *Minnesota Journal of Global Trade* 261, 289.
78 E. Alben, "GATT and the Fair Wage: A Historical Perspective on the Labour–Trade Link" (2001) 101 *Columbia Law Review* 1410, 1422.
79 F.J. Garcia, "Building a Just Trade Order for a new Millennium" (2000–2001) 33 *George Washington International Law Review* 1015, 1055.
80 Powell (note 52), 229; Alben (note 78), 1410.
81 Report of the Appellate Body in European Communities – Measures Affecting Asbestos and Asbestos – Containing Products (AB-2000-11) at para. 170.

grounds provided for in the two articles. However, the majority of academics working in this area agree with this conclusion.

Some of the later WTO agreements have followed the trend of including exceptions that allow for the consideration of non-trade issues. The WTO Agreements on Sanitary Phytosanitary Measures,[82] and WTO Agreement on Technical Barriers to Trade[83] both provide that states should not be prevented from taking measures to protect human life, health or the environment at the level the concerned state considers necessary and appropriate.[84] Similarly, the WTO Agreement on Trade-Related Aspects of Intellectual Property Rights[85] allows states to provide remedies aimed at preventing patent rights from having adverse effect on the transfer of technology vital to medical care and economic development of least developed countries.

The EU, trade agreements and human rights

The European Commission recognised the challenge faced by the EU in view of its treaty obligations and its investments promotion strategy when it stated that:

> The European Union itself has an obligation in the framework of its Co-operation policy to ensure the respect of labour standards, environmental protection and human rights and *is confronted with the challenge of ensuring a full coherence between its development policy, its trade policy and its strategy for the development of the private sector in the developing countries notably through the promotion of European investment*[86] (emphasis added).

It is suggested that linking human rights issues to trade agreements is one of the more effective ways that the EU can galvanise host states into meeting their human rights commitment including their responsibility to ensure that private actors such as MNCs do not violate human rights. The EU already incorporates human rights clauses into agreements with third countries.[87] A proper approach to the implementation of human rights

---

82 WTO Agreement on Sanitary and Phytosanitary Measures, 15 April 1994.

83 WTO Agreements on Technical Barriers to Trade, 15 April 1994.

84 Powell (note 52), 222.

85 WTO Agreement on Trade-Related Aspects of Intellectual Property Rights (15 April 1994).

86 Commission of the European Communities, "Green Paper: Promoting a European Framework for Corporate Social Responsibility" COM (2001) 366 Final, 18 July 2001, 13.

87 There are arguments against this practice which we shall return to later. As of 2005 there were about 150 of such agreements containing human rights between the EU and third countries. See L. Bartels, *Human Rights Conditionality in the EU's International Agreements* (Oxford: Oxford University Press, 2005) 2.

clauses is a practical way of nudging host states in the proper direction. The implication of such a clause is that it incentivises third states to ensure compliance with international human rights standards to ensure the continuity of the trade arrangement.

Arguing for the use of trade arrangements to promote compliance with international obligations and standards in the context of labour rights, Kryvoi states:

> Unilateral sanctions such as withdrawing trade preferences because of labor rights violations can be considered a cheap way to promote compliance with international obligations in the sense that it does not require direct financial spending. Unlike multilateral sanctions, these sanctions can be implemented relatively quickly as there is no need to achieve international consensus. There is usually an aspiration that other countries would join, and that the unilateral character of sanctions might change to multilateral.[88]

The suggestion being made here is that the inclusion of a clause which demands the observance of human rights standards already signed up to by both parties and which is enforceable by the parties under the agreement will enable the EU to demand that countries comply with their human rights obligations in their territories which include ensuring that private actors do not violate human rights. The EU has concluded and is in the process of concluding a wide range of complex preferential and non-preferential trading arrangements with third countries and regional organisations.[89] The EU has insisted that all trade, cooperation, dialogue, partnership and association agreements with third parties contain a human rights clause.[90] It is important to reiterate that WTO agreements, to which the EU member states are parties, do not prevent them from incorporating international human rights principles in their own activities. Thus incorporating human rights clauses into EU trade arrangements will not infringe the obligations of member states under WTO agreements.[91]

---

88 Kryvoi (note 6), 223; see also E.M. Hafner-Burton, "Trade Human Rights: How Preferential Trade Agreements Influence Government Repression" (2005) 59 *International Organizations* 593–629.

89 See also V. Miller, "The Human Rights Clause in the EU's External Agreements" House of Commons Library, Research Paper 04133, 16 April, 2004, online, available at: www.parliament.uk/commons/lib/research/rp2004/rp04-033.pdf (accessed 17 February 2008), 9.

90 Ibid., 9. Human rights clauses are applicable in EU's treaty with around 150 countries; see Bartels (note 87), 2.

91 D. Hong, "The Human Rights Clause in the European Union's External Trade and Development Agreements" (2003) 9 (5) *European Law Journal* 677–697; Bartels (note 87), 70.

The significance of human rights clauses

Under article 60 of the Vienna Convention on the Law of Treaties (VCLT)[92] a treaty can be terminated or suspended if it is so provided in the treaty and in the case of "material breach" of the treaty. Material breach is defined to include (*a*) "a repudiation of the treaty not sanctioned by the present convention" or (*b*) "the violation of a provision essential to the accomplishment of the object or purpose of the treaty". However, in the absence of such provisions, there is no entitlement under the VCLT to terminate or suspend treaties simply on the basis of human rights violations. Therefore, a state would be entitled to terminate a treaty on the ground of human rights violations only if there is a human rights clause in the agreement and the clause is made an "essential element" of the agreement.

Human rights clauses as a strategy in EU external relations

Bartels highlights the possible reasons why the EU is taking a more active approach to human rights issues through the use of human rights clauses in trade agreements.[93] One is the possibility of the annulment of a similar scheme under the Generalised System of Preferences (GSP) programme. As will be explained later in this chapter, the GSP granted trade preferences to developing countries and there are provisions in the scheme which conditioned enjoyment of incentives under the programme on the observance of certain international standards. An arrangement under the GSP was challenged by India at the WTO in 2004.[94] The WTO appellate body held that the programme of incentives for countries combating drug and trafficking was a violation of the WTO Enabling Clause because it discriminated among developing countries.[95] The EU has since replaced this particular arrangement with the "GSP+" arrangement. Doubts have been expressed as to the compatibility of the new arrangement with WTO rules.[96] Thus a cloud of uncertainty still hovers over the GSP arrangement.[97] A second possible rationale for the EU's pro-human rights approach may be that, human rights clauses can also be used as social clauses[98] allowing the EU to discriminate

---

92 United Nations, Treaty Series, vol. 1155, 331.

93 Bartels (note 87), 40–44.

94 See WTO Appellate Body, *EC-Tariff Preferences, WT/DS246/AB/R,* adopted April 2004.

95 See Bartels (note 87), 41.

96 L. Bartels, "The WTO Legality of the EU's GSP+ Arrangement" (2007) 10 (4) *Journal of International Economic Law* 869–886.

97 Kryvoi (note 6), 225.

98 A social clause is a provision in international bilateral and multilateral trade treaties that links labour standards to liberalisation of international trade. Trading access to markets of developed countries is conditional upon compliance with international labour standards. Failure to comply results in trade sanctions and loss of market access. See R.N. Sanyal, "The Social Clause in Trade Treaties: Implication for International Firms" (2001) 29 *Journal of Business Ethics* 379, 380.

against goods that are produced in a manner that violates international labour standards.[99] Furthermore, the EU has realised that human rights clauses can be used to exert positive measure on third countries to protect human rights. This supports and encourages initiatives on the territory of the third country using trade arrangements as incentives. According to Bartels human rights clauses are "set higher than normal standards, they permit counter-measures which would not be available under customary international law, and they impose positive obligations on the treaty parties to ensure respect for human rights through their respective territories".[100]

EU competence to include human rights clauses in international agreements

The ECJ's decision in Opinion 2/94 that "no Treaty provision confers on the Community institutions any general power to enact rules on human rights or to conclude international conventions in this field"[101] would seem to suggest that the EU has no competence to include human rights clauses in its international agreements including trade agreements. However, commentators have disagreed with this reasoning, arguing that the community has competence. It is argued that the community has no need for a separate legal basis to include such clauses as the clauses establish steps in taking measures to implement existing human rights standards. It is further argued that there are express powers under EC treaties which permit the inclusion of such clauses.[102] The position that there was no need for a separate legal basis for the clauses appears to be the position of the council.[103]

The ECJ had the opportunity to consider the legality of such a clause in an EC cooperation agreement with India in the *Portuguese Republic* v. *The Council of the European Union*.[104] In that case, the government of Portugal had requested the court to annul Council Decision 94/578/EC of 18 July 1994 on the conclusion of an EC cooperation agreement with India. Portugal challenged the validity of the human rights clause and the EC's

---

99 According to Bartels (note 87), even though the EU officially opposed the use of trade sanctions in the field of labour, its incorporation of the social clause in the GSP and the commission's explicit support for social clauses, show that the EU may change its position especially if the GSP arrangement is nullified by the WTO.

100 Bartels (note 87), 238.

101 Opinion 2/94 (1996) ECR I-1759.

102 Bartels (note 87), 169–170; B. Brandtner and A. Rosas, "Human Rights and the External Relations of the European Community: An Analysis of Doctrine and Practice" (1998) 9 *European Journal of International Law* 468, 474–475.

103 Bartels (note 87), 170.

104 Case C-268/94: *The Portuguese Republic* v. *The Council of the European Union* (1996) ECJ Reports p.I 6177.

implied competence to introduce such a clause into its external agreements. Portugal contended that recourse should have been had to article 235 TEC (308EC) which requires a unanimous decision of member states. It was further argued by Portugal that the "fundamental rights" referred to in the preamble to the Single European Act (SEA) and the references to TEU were defining only general objectives and do not give rise to any specific community powers. It was further contended that article 130u(2) TEC (article 177(2) EC) made human rights a general objective of community policy and therefore agreements based on 130y (181EC) could only make general references to human rights. Therefore, human rights cannot be made an "essential element" of the agreement as this would go beyond the remit of article 130u(2) (177(2) EC) objective in the treaty.

The ECJ dismissed the application holding in favour of the commission's argument that the inclusion of the clause was valid by virtue of articles 130u (177(2) EC) and 130y (181 EC) permitting the community to "conclude agreements in the area of development cooperation with the object of promoting human rights and democracy". Thus, the ECJ conferred legal validity on the practice of inserting human rights clauses in agreements with third countries. However, the human rights clause considered here was one without a non-execution clause which, Bartels argued, is different from one with a non-execution clause.[105]

Bartels has challenged the assumption that no legal basis is required for the inclusion of such clauses, contending that this position is wrong.[106] He argues that the position is flawed for a number of reasons. One, human rights clauses do not merely restate standards under customary international law. According to him, when for example, an essential clause refers to the Universal Declaration of Human Rights; it goes beyond customary international law because not all provisions of the declaration can be regarded as such.[107] Second, both parties to the agreement have significantly enhanced rights to enforce the Norms and also corollary secondary obligations to suffer the consequence of a failure to comply. He contends that if the community has a positive obligation in this respect, it would require legislative competence to adopt appropriate measures.[108] Third, the position ignores the fact that human rights clauses imply a delegation of power to institutions created by the agreements. The decisions of such bodies can be considered to be part of the community legal order which could have direct effect thus requiring justification for the grant of such

---

105 A non-execution clause imposes positive obligations on the parties to fulfil whatever obligations are set out in the essential element clause and allow for measures to be taken against a defaulting party.
106 See generally Bartels (note 87), 172.
107 Ibid.
108 Ibid.

power under EU treaties.[109] He further argues that human rights clauses have the implication of imposing positive obligations on the community which may potentially require the enactment of legislation.[110] He also argued that there is a fundamental rule that the community needs a legal basis for every action it takes which must be ascertained having regard to the aim and content of the measure at issue.[111]

Bartels contends that human rights clauses perform three important functions which must find legal basis in EU treaties. In the first place they operate as a "sword" which gives the community a legal right to compel third countries to comply with human rights norms. The wrongful act of the third state is thus the focal point of the clause in this regard. As Bartels, correctly pointed out, the ECJ emphasised this aspect of the clause when it held in *Portugal* v. *France* that "a provision such as Article 1(1) of the Agreement may be ... an important factor for the exercise of the right to have a development cooperation agreement suspended or terminated where the non-member country has violated human rights".[112] In the second place, human rights clauses operate as a "shield" which enables the community to revoke an agreement if it contributes to violations of human rights norms in a third country. This is in keeping with the community's international obligations to protect human rights and its duty to respect fundamental rights in all of its activities under community law.[113] In the third place human rights clauses through their contents, impose positive obligations on the community to ensure respect for human rights.

Bartels also analysed in detail the express powers as provided under EU treaties to ascertain whether the clauses are justifiable by their provisions. He also considered whether the clauses can be justified as implied powers or under the doctrine of "ancillary clauses". He concluded that:

> There are express legal bases (Articles 179/181, 181a, 13, 301, and 310 EC) that can support the inclusion of human rights clauses both as a "sword" and as a "shield", though these are each subject to particular limitations. There is also an implied functional power on which human rights clauses can more generally be justified on the basis that they serve as a "shield".[114]

Bartels reached this conclusion in the light of the distribution of competences between the community and member states. That exercise,

---

109 Ibid.
110 Ibid.
111 Ibid. Craig and De Burca have, however, argued that the EU as an entity has acquired legal personality. See Craig and De Burca (note 1), 171.
112 Case-268/94, *Portugal* v. *France* (1996) ECR I-6177, para. 27.
113 Bartels (note 87), 175–176.
114 Ibid., 225.

however, is not relevant to this discussion. The important point for the purpose of this chapter is that he agreed that there is a legal basis for the inclusion of the clauses in EU trade arrangements even though he reached this conclusion in a manner different from most commentators on the subject.

The example of the ACP–EU agreements: legal issues

The developing countries played a limited role in the early development of GATT and thus had little influence in the formulation of its policies in the early days of the framework. This led many developing countries to be critical of the arrangements and suspicious of its consequences for them. In order to allay the fears of the developing countries, GATT contracting states adopted Part IV of GATT to address issues raised by the developing states. Part IV recognises that market access to products of export interest to developing countries needs to be improved. Part IV also includes a general clause on recommendations to developed states on how to promote issues of interest to developing states. Institutional arrangements to implement the Part IV provisions were also suggested.[115] However, Part IV has no legal obligation attached to it which made it ineffective in addressing the concerns of the developing countries. In 1971, two waivers were adopted allowing for two types of preferences to favour developing countries. These include the permission of a "Generalised System of Preferences" (GSPs) and permission for developing countries to exchange tariff preferences among themselves. An "enabling clause" introduced in 1979 made the waivers permanent.[116] The enabling clause established the policy of special and preferential treatment for developing countries.[117] The arrangement allows WTO members to favour certain developing countries without violating GATT's MFN requirements.[118]

It is pertinent to note that historically the EC/EU has been at the forefront of the call for the establishment of Preferential Trade Arrangements (PTAs). According to Matsushita and others, there are two main reasons for this:

---

115   See M. Matsushita, T.J. Schoenbaum and P.C. Mavroidis, *The World Trade Organization: Law, Practice, and Policy* (second edition, Oxford: Oxford University Press, 2006), 223–225; Vazquez (note 35), 819.

116   Differential and More Favourable Treatment, Reciprocity and Fuller Participation of Developing Countries, 28 November 1979, GATT BISD (26th Supp.) at 203 (1980).

117   Matsushita *et al.* (note 115), 768.

118   The WTO appellate body stated in its report on EC-tariff preferences that the enabling clause constitute an exception to article I GATT and takes precedence where there is a conflict between the two provisions. See *European Communities-Conditions for the Granting of Tariff Preferences to Developing Countries* (WTO Docs WT/DS 246/R of 1 December 2003 and WT/DS256/AB/R of 7 April 2004).

a   some of the partners were candidates for accession (and a preferential scheme was thought to be the antechamber to the European Community), or ex-colonies of the European Community members, with which, it was felt some form of preferential trade should be established;

b   trade policy was the only "genuine" common policy of the European Community in the realm of international relations: signing trade agreements with various partners carried an inherent positive externality, in that it affirmed the European *persona* as one entity in the eyes of the world.[119]

The EC/EU has thus employed the GSP in its dealings with the ACP which was later supplemented by the Cotonou Agreement.[120] The Cotonou Agreement introduced the concept of Economic Partnership Agreement, a scheme designed to redefine the relationship between the ACP and the EU.

The term "Economic Partnership Agreement" (EPA) is not commonly used in international trade. However, the arrangement is synonymous with the concept of "free-trade area" (FTA) under the WTO architecture. This point is buttressed by articles 34(4), 36(1) and 37(7) of the Cotonou Agreement requiring the establishment of WTO compatible trading arrangements. The EPAs between the EU and the ACP countries are required in particular to be compatible with article XXIV of GATT which allows for the establishment of FTAs and custom unions. FTA's are essentially preferential schemes that deviate from the obligation not to discriminate.

Article XXIV 4 GATT specifically allows for the use of Preferential Trade Arrangements (PTAs) in FTAs and custom unions. The article provides that:

> The contracting parties recognize the desirability of increasing freedom of trade by the development, through voluntary agreements, of closer integration between the economies of the countries parties to such agreements. They also recognize that the purpose of a customs union or a free-trade area should be to facilitate trade between the constituent territories and not to raise barriers to the trade of other contracting parties with such territories.

However, there are conditions that must be satisfied by the arrangement under Article XXIV. The three requirements under the article can be summarised as follows:

---

119 Matsushita *et al.* (note 115), 550.
120 Ibid., 774.

1   The obligation to notify the WTO's Committee on Regional Trade Arrangements of the scheme;
2   Obligation to liberalise among participating countries substantially all trade;
3   Obligation not to raise overall level of protection and not to make access by countries not participating in the PTA more difficult.[121]

Article XXIV:8 which states that all trade and tariff restrictions in FTAs must be liberalised expressly exempted measures under certain articles, including article XX, from the obligation and consequently such measures can be maintained.[122]

In conclusion, as long as the conditions specified under article XXIV are met, member states are free to establish FTAs among themselves. The WTO does not dictate the contents of the agreements outside the conditions specified. The WTO therefore does not preclude the inclusion of human rights issues in these agreements. The point being made in this section is that first, articles XX and XXI permit member states to derogate from their obligations under WTO rules on human rights grounds. Second, FTAs, such as the one envisaged under the EPAs, are permitted under WTO rules and can incorporate human rights issues in these arrangements. Consequently, the incorporation of human rights and social clauses in the Economic Partnership Agreements are legitimate.

ACP and the EU

The ACP group consists of 79 countries which are signatories to the Georgetown Agreement. This is the partnership agreement between the ACP and the European Union officially called "ACP–EC Partnership Agreement" and commonly known as the "Cotonou Agreement".[123] The ACP was originally created with the aim of coordinating cooperation between its members and the EU in the negotiation and implementation of cooperation agreements. The activities of the group were widened with the growth of globalisation and trade liberalisation. Since its creation cooperation between the EU and

---

121   Ibid., 555.
122   M. Matsushita and D. Ahn, eds., *WTO and East Asia: New Perspectives* (London: Cameron May Ltd, 2004), 497, 508.
123   Partnership Agreement between the Members of the African Caribbean and Pacific Group of States of the One Part and the European Community and its Member States, of the Other Part, online, available at: http://ec.europa.eu/development/geographical/cotonouintro_en.cfm (accessed 27 September 2010); A. Voiculescu, "Unorthodox Human Rights Instruments. The ACP–EU Development Co-operation from the Lomé Conventions to the Cotonou Agreement" (2006) 4 (1) *Journal of Commonwealth Law and Legal Education* 85, 85–86, 92; J. Nwobike, "The Application of Human Rights in African Caribbean and Pacific-European Union Development and Trade Partnership" (2006) 6 (10) *German Law Journal* 1381.

the group has taken place within the framework of four successive Lomé Conventions[124] (Lomé I-IV) in place since 1975 and the Cotonou Agreement. The Cotonou Agreement, which was signed in 2000 (and revised in 2005), is the latest agreement between the EU and the ACP. Under the Cotonou Agreement, new objectives for the relationship between the parties are set out as the eradication of poverty consistent with the objectives of sustainable development and the gradual integration of the ACP countries into the world economy.[125] The achievements of these goals are based on five interdependent pillars with the following objectives: fighting against poverty enhanced political dimension; increased participation; a more strategic approach to cooperation; new economic and trade partnerships; and improved financial cooperation.[126]

It may be instructive to note the main difference between the Lomé Agreements and the Cotonou Agreement. The Lomé Agreements established a privileged trade relationship between ACP and the European Community by providing non-reciprocal trade preferences. The preferences allow ACP products to benefit from more advantageous customs duties than products from other regions upon entering the European Community territory. However, ACP countries were not committed to giving the same advantages to European products. The rationale for the non-reciprocity was based on the difference in economic development between the EC and the ACP countries and the objective of article 177 EC.

The Cotonou Agreement was signed to modify EU–ACP trade relations for three main reasons: the incompatibility of Lomé IV with WTO rules;[127] the insufficiency and inefficiency of Lomé IV to integrate ACP into current international trade regimes; and the wish that Europe redefine the organisation of its trade relations with third countries. The current trade regime under the Cotonou Agreement is based on a waiver to the World Trade Organization (WTO) principles obtained in 2001.[128] The waiver was granted to allow the partnership transit from the Lomé system to new

124   Voiculescu (note 9), 89–92.
125   Article 1, Partnership Agreement between the Members of the African, Caribbean and Pacific Group of States of the One Part and the European Community and its Member states of the Other Part, signed in Cotonou on 23 June 2000 (Cotonou Agreement).
126   Ibid.
127   The preferential EU tariffs on ACP exports and the discrimination among ACP developing countries and non-ACP developing countries are deemed incompatible with the arrangement under the WTO rules.
128   The waiver includes: Most-favoured-nation (MFN) status – treating other nations equally. Reciprocity – every country has to grant equivalent trade advantages to those given by its trading partner. National treatment – treating foreigners and locals equally. Imported and locally produced goods should be treated equally at least after the foreign goods have entered the market.

international trade rules. The waiver expired on 31 December 2007 and negotiations are in progress to establish new Economic Partnership Agreements (EPAs).[129]

Storey succinctly described the shift in EU policy towards the ACP as follows:

> This shift is explained on two grounds. First, non-reciprocal arrangements are judged to be in breach of WTO rules (whereas reciprocal free-trade deals are not), and a WTO waiver allowing temporary retention of the Lomé-style provisions expires at the end of 2007. Second, there is a claimed "mutual recognition that existing non reciprocal trade preferences have not promoted the sustainable development or integration into the world economy of ACP countries" ... There is evidence for this latter claim: the ACP share of world exports fell from 3.2 per cent in 1970 to 1.3 per cent in 2003, while even the ACP share of the EU market (where they enjoyed favourable access) declined over the same period from 4.1 to 1.0 per cent ... However, whether EPAs are the best means to reverse this trend towards marginalisation is not as widely agreed upon.[130]

A major consequence of the Cotonou agreement is that the non-reciprocal trade preferences under Lomé IV will be replaced by new schemes (the Economic Partnership Agreements (EPA)) originally scheduled to commence in 2008 but there have been delays in the negotiations. To date only one out of six proposed new agreements has been concluded. However, interim agreements have also been concluded with other ACP member states. The arrangement will provide for reciprocal trade agreements whereby ACP countries will also provide duty-free access to their markets for EU exports. However, countries in the ACP designated as least developed countries (LDCs) may be able to either continue with the arrangements under Lomé IV or the "Everything But Arms" regulation.[131]

---

129 C.M.O. Ochieng, "The EU–ACP Economic Partnership Agreements and the 'Development Question': Constraints and Opportunities posed by Article XXIV and Special and Differential Treatment Provisions of the WTO" (2007) 10 (2) *Journal of International Economic Law* 365, 367.

130 A. Storey, "Normative Power Europe? Economic Partnership Agreements and Africa" (2006) 24 (3) *Journal of Contemporary African Studies* 331, 335.

131 Everything but arms (EBA) is an initiative of the EU under which all imports to the EU from designated LDCs (least developed countries) are duty free and quota free with the exception of armaments. The initiative is part of the EU Generalised System of Preferences (GSP) which will be elaborated upon later in this chapter. It should be observed that GSP is currently one of the few methods available for going beyond state sovereignty to ensure compliance with international labour standards. See Kryvoi (note 6), 209.

Furthermore other ACP countries who decide that they are not in a position to enter into the new regime under EPAs may enter into other available cooperation mechanisms such as the EU's Generalised System of Preferences (GSP) subject to compatibility with WTO rules.[132]

Lomé IV: human rights clauses and "essential elements"

In its agreements with the ACP, the EU first introduced general references to human rights in the preamble of Lomé III.[133] The subsequent 1989 Lomé IV Convention included a specific human rights element in article 5(2) but the human rights element was not included as an "essential element". Thus human rights standards could not be used under Lomé IV as a justification for terminating or suspending the trade arrangement. However, in the 1990s the agreement between the EU and third countries started incorporating human rights clauses as important elements of the agreement but not in the terms of "essential elements" under the VCLT.[134] In November 1991, the Council of Ministers adopted a resolution recognising human rights as an aim of community development policy which included provisions for sanctions against violating states as a last resort.[135] Thereafter EU agreements with third countries started featuring human rights clauses as an essential clause of the agreements.[136]

132 It should be noted that a GSP arrangement is not negotiated. The EU designs it and offers it on its own terms. The EU could amend or suspend it whenever it deems fit. There are doubts whether the GSP and the EBA are actually alternatives to EPA as they can be rescinded at any time by the EU. See House of Commons, International Development Committee, "Fair Trade? The European Union's Trade Agreements with African, Caribbean and Pacific Countries" Sixth Report of Session 2004–2005, 23 March 2005.

133 Lomé III Convention (1980) OJ L86/3.

134 See for example: The Framework Treaty signed with Argentina, April 1990 OJL 295/90, 26 October 1990, 67–73; Chile 1990, OJL 79/91, 26 March 1991 2–11; Uruguay 1992, OJL 94/92, 8 April 1992, 2–11; Paraguay 1992, OJL 313/92, 30 October 1992 72–81 See also D. Horng, "The Human Rights Clause in the European Union's External Trade and Development Agreements" (2003) 9 (5) *European Law Journal* 677, 678.

135 See Doc. no. 10107/9; see EU Annual Report on Human Rights, 10 October 2003, COHOM 29.

136 See for example, Agreement between the European Economic Community and the Republic of Albania, on Trade and Commercial and Economic Cooperation, OJL 343, article 1 of the agreement provides that

> Respect for democratic principles and human rights established by the Helsinki Final Act and the Charter of Paris for a new Europe inspires the domestic and external policies of the Community and Albania and constitutes an essential element of the present agreement;

See also The Bulgaria's Europe Agreement signed on 8 March 1993 and came into force on 1 February 1995 (OJ 1994 L358/3); Romania, OJ1994 L357/2; see also L. Bartels, "The Trade and Development Policy of the European Union" (2007) 18 (4) *The European Journal of International Law* 715, 738.

In response to an EC communication for the inclusion of respect of democratic principles and human rights in agreements between the community and third parties, the Council of Ministers in 1995 decided to include suspension mechanisms in all community agreements with third parties which would enable the community to react immediately in the event of violations of human rights or any other essential aspects of the agreements.[137] The suspension clauses are referred to in the literature as "non-execution clauses". In the communication leading up to the decision, the commission recommended model clauses to be included in all community agreements.[138] It was stated that the preamble should contain "general references to human rights and democratic values" and "references to universal and regional instruments common to both parties". The agreement should also contain an article X, defining the essential elements of the agreement as follows:

> Respect for the democratic principles and fundamental human rights established by [the Universal Declaration of Human Rights/the Helsinki Final Act and the Charter of Paris for a New Europe] inspires the domestic and external policies of the Community and of [the country or group of countries concerned] and constitutes an essential element of this agreement.

The commission further stated that the agreement should include an article Y on non execution which entitles parties to take appropriate measures in the event of breach of article X, respecting the principle of proportionality between the breach and the reaction. The draft clause further provides that before either party take measures against a breach, it shall supply the relevant body under the agreement with any information required for a thorough examination of the situation with a view to seeking a solution acceptable to the parties. However, this shall not be applicable in cases of special urgency. The commission also required that an interpretative declaration should be included in the agreement clarifying "cases of urgency" under article Y and "material breach" under article X.

The community subsequently revised the human rights clause in Lomé IV in 1995 to make the clause an essential element of the agreement. The revision also permits the suspension of the convention, including trade

---

137 See Commission's Communication on the Inclusion of Respect for Democratic Principles and Human Rights in Agreements between the Community and Third Countries COM(95) 216 of 23 May 1995; Commission's Communication on the European Union and External Dimension of Human Rights Policy: From Rome to Maastricht and Beyond, Com(95) 567.

138 Ibid.

rights, in the event of contravention of the essential element clause.[139] Article 5 of the convention provides *inter alia* that:

> Respect for human rights, democratic principles and the rule of law, which underpins relations between the ACP states and the Community and all provisions of the Convention, and governs the domestic and international policies of the contracting parties, shall constitute an essential element of this convention.

Article 366a(2) of the convention states:

> If one Party considers that another Party has failed to fulfil an obligation in respect of one of the essential elements referred to in Article 5, it shall invite the Party concerned, unless there is special urgency, to hold consultations with a view to assessing the situation in detail and, if necessary, remedying it.

The Cotonou Agreement in 2000 introduced a new version of the "essential element" clause and this version became the standard model for subsequent agreements with third countries. The EU's 2003 Annual Human Rights Report described the clause in the Cotonou Agreement as a "state of the art" version of the essential element clause. The clause is very extensive and contains an elaborate procedure for implementation. Article 9 of the Cotonou Agreement titled "Essential Elements and Fundamental Element" provides *inter alia*:

> The parties undertake to promote and protect all fundamental freedoms and human rights, be they civil and political, or economic, social and cultural ... Respect for human rights, democratic principles and the rule of law, which underpin the ACP–EU Partnership, shall underpin the domestic and international policies of the parties and constitute the essential elements of this Agreement.[140]

The agreement contains a non-execution clause in article 96. A system of sanction is provided for failure of a state party to fulfil an obligation stemming from respect for human rights, democratic principles and the rule of law.[141] In such circumstances consultations are to be held and if the

---

139 See article 5(1)(3) and article 336a of Lomé IV, introduced in the Agreement Amending the Fourth ACP–EC Convention of Lomé IV signed in Mauritius on 4 November 1995 (1998) OJ L156/3. See also L. Bartels, "The Trade and Development Policy of the European Union" (2007) 18 (4) *The European Journal of International Law* 715, 738.

140 Article 9, Cotonou Agreement (note 125).

141 Section 96(2) Cotonou Agreement (note 125).

consultation does not yield an acceptable solution, or if consultation is refused or where there is a special urgency, appropriate measures may be taken in accordance with international law and proportionate to the violation.[142]

A slight amendment was made to the provisions in 2005 placing emphasis on political dialogue before the imposition of sanctions in case of contravention of the essential element clause.[143]

The desirability of human rights clauses in EU–ACP agreements

Both within and outside academic circles, there are divergent views as to the use of human rights clauses in trade agreements. Some argue that human rights clauses do not go far enough and some think they go too far. For some commentators human rights conditionality is legally unacceptable and morally unjustifiable. Some argue that it goes outside the competence of the EC while others question its effectiveness.[144] Third world countries have viewed the clauses as an intrusion on national sovereignty. There have been objections to the clauses from ACP countries. The introduction of human rights clauses in the Lomé Convention was regarded as an attack on national sovereignty and hypocritical on the part of the EU. Furthermore, the clauses were considered to take a narrow interpretation of human rights as only civil and political rights, ignoring economic, social and cultural rights.[145]

It is, however, contended that these arguments are overstated. Clearly, there is a legal basis for the inclusion of these clauses (as has been shown in this chapter). Furthermore, the clauses do not create new norms but only seek to enforce existing norms that have been ratified by the parties to the agreements. In fact, the EU could not act otherwise as it is obligated under its laws to adhere to these principles both in its domestic and external relations. What would thus be hypocritical is for it to maintain a domestic system which respects human rights within Europe without doing the same in its external relations. The argument that the clauses are intrusions into national sovereignty is equally misconceived as it ignores the fact that the clauses give similar rights to all parties under the agreement.

---

142 Section 96(2)(a), Cotonou Agreement (note 125). Since the signing of the Cotonou Agreement, its provisions have been invoked to impose sanctions on Haiti, Zimbabwe and Republic of Guinea. J. Nwobike, "The Application of Human Rights in African Caribbean and Pacific-European Union Development and Trade Partnership" (2005) 6 (10) *German Law Journal* 1382, 1391–1392.

143 Agreement amending the Cotonou Agreement (2005) OJ L209/27, amending articles 8, 9 and 96 and introducing a new Annex VII.

144 Miller (note 89), 30.

145 Miller (note 89), 40.

It is not suggested here that there is equality of partnership between the EU and the ACP. The House of Commons in England succinctly describes the scenario when considering the ongoing negotiations of EPAs between the two blocs as follows:

> The relationship between the EU and the ACP has never been an equal one. This has not changed in the negotiations for the Economic Partnership Agreements. There appears to be an assumption within the UK Government and the European Commission that the ACP can sign up to, or reject, whatever they wish. This is not the case. The ACP states remain recipients of EU aid, some of which funds ACP negotiating capacity. The ACP nevertheless lacks the negotiating capacity of the EU and is stretched to negotiate simultaneously in the WTO and other regional negotiations. The ACP is also economically weak compared to the EU: it has very little to offer the EU and potentially much to gain from the negotiations. The collective ACP stake in the partnership negotiations is therefore significant. The negotiating process should be undertaken with this disparity in power in mind.[146]

This situation thus put responsibility on the EU to negotiate an agreement consistent with its standards and its obligation under international law.

The application of the human rights clauses and multinational corporations

Despite the lofty ideals espoused in human rights clauses, their invocation in actual practice in EU external relations has been very modest.[147] The interesting point, however, is that these clauses have the potential of being invoked in many areas. Some of the areas in which EU institutions have made reference to the applicability of the clauses include violations of minority rights, women's rights, the right to travel, freedom of speech and political activities, child sex tourism, women trafficking, violations of impunity from prosecution for human rights violations, treatment of detainees and dissidents and core labour standards.[148] Their application has been more rigorous under Lomé IV and the Cotonou Agreements. However, under the later agreements, the targets have generally been the poorest ACP countries and it has been applied mostly in cases of unlawful change

---

146 House of Commons, International Development Committee, "Fair Trade? The European Union's Trade Agreements with African, Caribbean and Pacific Countries" Sixth Report of Session 2004–2005 para. 6, 6.
147 Bartels (note 87), 37.
148 Ibid., 36.

of government.[149] In most cases the measures taken have been the suspension of financial and other cooperation but not trade benefits.[150]

The invocation of the human rights clauses in these limited circumstances is a drawback of the practice. There is a need for a comprehensive approach to accommodate other human rights violations such as the violation of human rights by MNCs. Where there is clear evidence that MNCs are violating human rights and the state concerned is not taking steps to remedy the situation, the non-execution clause should be triggered in order to check the situation. For example in 1995, Shell was implicated in the supply of arms to Nigerian security forces which was used for widespread violations of human rights in the country.[151] The issue was debated both at the EU level and in member states.[152] The EU resorted to measures by which military cooperation and training courses for all Nigerian military personnel were suspended and an embargo was placed on the sale of arms, munitions and military equipment.[153] This step proved to be ineffective. It is suggested that if similar circumstances should occur today, the EU should be bold enough to invoke the human rights clause and the

---

149 Some examples of the invocation of the clauses under the agreement between the EU and ACP: In 1999, following a *coup d'état* in Niger, the EU held consultations with the Niger government and the ACP states under article 366a of Lomé IV. The same procedure was used when there was a violence outbreak in Guinea-Bissau, May 1999; Togo in 1998 and Comoros, following a *coup d'état* in 1999 (See EU Annual Report on Human Rights 1998/1999). The EU has also used the unilateral suspension of benefits under Lomé IV for failure to move towards democracy or observe human rights. The case of Haiti is an example. After a general election in 2000, which was marred with various irregularities and fraud, the EU invited the Haiti government to enter into consultations under article 96 of the Cotonou Agreement. Haiti did not respond and the EU adopted a decision on 29 January 2001 under article 96(2) to take proportionate measures against Haiti which included suspending direct budgetary aid and withholding future aid from the European Development Fund. The measures were renewed in 2001, 2002 and 2003. See Miller (note 98), 29. The human rights clause was used in a comprehensive way in the case of human rights violations in Zimbabwe. In March 2001, the EU called for political dialogue under article 8 of the Cotonou Agreement and because there was no meaningful progress from the talk, in July 2001, the Commission invoked article 96 against Zimbabwe and suspended the application of the Cotonou Agreement to Zimbabwe. The EU thereafter based on a finding that the essential elements in article 9 were not being respected and because article 96 consultations had failed to remedy the situation decided to impose sanctions on Zimbabwe. See Bartels (note 87), 37.
150 L. Bartels, "The Trade and Development Policy of the European Union" (2007) 18 (4) The *European Journal of International Law* 715, 739.
151 See O. Owolabi, "Oil and Security in Nigeria: The Niger Delta Crises" (2007) 1 *Africa Development* 1; J.G. Frynas, "Shell in Nigeria: A Further Contribution" (2000) 21 (1) *Third World Quarterly* 157,160.
152 See for example, Debate in the Irish Parliament: Dail Eireann-Volume 461-06 February, 1996, Ceisteanna-Questions. Oral Answers. – EU Sanctions against Nigeria.
153 See Common Position 95/515/CFSP.

non-execution clause in the Cotonou Agreement to ensure that the state end the abuse by the MNC.

Economic Partnership Agreements and human rights clauses

The next issue to consider is the implication of the human rights clauses for the EPAs. However, first, it is necessary to examine the significance of the EU GSP system which predates the EPAs.

The EU GSP system and human and labour rights

The GSPs are unilateral acts between EU and third countries which grant trade preferences to beneficiary countries upon the fulfilment of specific criteria. There are three arrangements under the GSP.[154] The first, which is the default rule, is to the effect that all beneficiary countries enjoy the benefit of a general arrangement. The second is the special incentive arrangement (GSP+). This provides additional benefits for countries which agree to implement certain international standards relating to human rights, labour rights, environmental protection, combating illegal drug trafficking and good governance.[155] The third is a scheme of special arrangements for least developed ACP countries. An interesting provision from the perspective of this chapter is the special incentive arrangement contained in the GSP scheme. Under the council regulation[156] on GSP schemes in the EU, additional preferences are granted to some countries based on ratification and effective implementation of all core human and labour rights UN/ILO conventions under the special incentive clause.[157] Furthermore, such a country must have ratified and effectively implemented at least seven of the conventions relating to the environment and governance principles listed in Part B of Annex III of the regulation. Beneficiaries must also give an undertaking to maintain the ratification of the conventions and domestic implementing legislation and also to review the mechanisms under appropriate conventions.

Under article 16 of the regulation, the grounds upon which the preferential arrangement under the GSP could be suspended include among others: serious and systematic violations of core human and labour rights conventions listed in Part A of Annex III of the regulation, exportation of

---

154   Article 1, Council Regulation (EC) no. 980/2005 of 27 June 2005, Applying a scheme of Generalized Tariff Preferences, 2005 OJ (L169).

155   Commission's Decision 2005/924/EC listing beneficiary countries.

156   Council Regulation (EC) no. 980/2005 of 27 June 2005, Applying a Scheme of Generalised Tariff Preferences, 2005 OJ (L169).

157   Part A of Annex III to Council Regulation (EC) no. 980/2005 of 27 June 2005.

goods made by prison labour, failure to implement or withdrawing from the implementation of core human and labour rights and conventions relating to environment and governance principles as stated under the Act. The EU GSP mechanism was invoked against Myanmar in 1997[158] because of the use of forced labour in the country and against Belarus in 2006[159] because of the violation of freedom of association. These provisions can have direct impact on the operations of MNCs as they are aimed at ensuring that countries under the scheme are made to comply with international standards in their domestic law and policy. This would discourage the tendency in the ACP countries to lower human rights, labour and environmental standards to attract or maintain foreign investments. The scheme may thus act as leverage on host governments to adequately regulate these areas and ensure that all companies comply with them. The design of the GSP and the special incentive clause demonstrates the capacity of trade agreements to influence human rights, labour and environmental issues.

Economic Partnership Agreements (EPAs)

The EPAs which are being negotiated with sub regional groupings within ACP are designed to regulate the trade aspects of the ACP–EU partnership. Under the Cotonou Agreement the EPAs are to be negotiated "in full conformity with the provisions of the WTO, including special and differential treatment, taking account of the parties' mutual interests and their respective levels of development".[160] Furthermore article 35 stipulates that special consideration be given to ACP LDCs (least developed countries).The European Commission has the mandate to negotiate EPAs with ACP countries on behalf of the EU.[161] The objectives of the EU negotiations strategy include: stimulation of the economic growth of ACP developing countries by making them more competitive; support for regional integration process within the ACP group; the encouragement of the

---

158 Council Regulation (EC) no. 552/97 of March 1997, Temporary Withdrawing Access to Generalised Tariff of Preferences from the Union of Myanmar. Official Journal 85, 27 March 1997, at 8–9.

159 Council Regulation (EC) no. 1933/2006 of 21 December 2006, Temporarily Withdrawing Access to the Generalised Tariff Preferences from the Republic of Belarus. OJ C, 14 February, 2004.

160 Article 34(4) Cotonou Agreement.

161 Directives for the Negotiations of Economic Partnership with ACP Countries and Regions adopted by the European Union, 17 June 2002, EU Council 9930/02,dd, 12 June 2002. Exclusive competence for trade and trade-related matters is vested in the European Community. By virtue of article 133 TEC on Common Commercial Policy (CCP), the commission rather than individual member states generally negotiates trade agreements with third countries and signs them on their behalf.

integration of ACP regional groups into the world economy; and the establishment of a trade agreement respectful of WTO rules.[162]

Potential implications of EPAs for the operations of MNCs

As major exporters of goods and services and international investments around the world, the EU MNCs need to expand beyond the European market to continue their profitability. EPAs are thus part of the strategies through which the EU is expanding the market for its MNCs. The EPAs are currently under negotiation and there are worries being raised as to the potential implications of the agreements for human rights, labour and social issues.[163] The EPAs would liberalise the ACP market, which has been undergoing liberalisation in the past decade, thus making it more accessible to MNCs from Europe. This would further widen the scope of MNCs' operations. The South African experience is instructive here, where in the expectation of the signing of the Trade Development and Cooperation Agreement (TDCA) with the EU, two-thirds of the South African dairy processing sector were taken over by or passed into partnership with EU companies in a period of 18 months in the 1990s.[164] The challenge is

---

162 Ibid.

163 Gumisai Matume "Africans Fear 'Ruin' in Europe Trade Talks: Opposition Grows to more Inequitable Trade Liberalization" (July 2007) 21 (2) *Africa Renewal*; It has been predicted that the EPAs would open up the local market to a lot more pressure and competition which the local economy might find difficult to withstand. Furthermore, the requirement of tariff removal in the process of liberalisation would lead to revenue loss for ACP countries. It is observed that such changes may have consequences for government budgetary structure and consequently the ability to fund social policies. Furthermore, stiff competition from Europe may lead to massive loss of jobs and have adverse impact on general standard of living. Stiff competition, it is predicted, would have a major impact in the area of agricultural products from the EU which has higher productivity rates and high public subsidies. Such development would threaten the work and income of a large proportion of the population in ACP countries which depend on subsistence agriculture thereby endangering the right to work and the right to adequate standard of living including the right to food as guaranteed by the International Covenant on Economic, Social and Cultural Rights and the African Charter. These potential implications have been pointed out by impact assessments commissioned by the EU Commission. See PricewaterhouseCoopers, "Sustainability Impact Assessment (SIA) of the EU–ACP Economic Partnership Agreements" 1 October 2003, 125–127 which predicted that the agreement could lead to the collapse of the manufacturing sector in West Africa. See also PricewaterhouseCoopers, "Sustainable Impact Assessment (SIA) of the EU–ACP Economic Partnership Agreements" 11 September 2006 which predicted that EPAs could lead to a strong decrease in public revenues in Central Africa. See also A. Storey, "Normative Power Europe? Economic Partnership Agreements and Africa" (2006) 24 (3) *Journal of Contemporary African Studies* 331, 336–337.

164 P. Goodison "The Future of Africa's Trade with Europe: 'New' EU Trade Policy" (2007) 34 *Review of African Political Economy* 139, 150.

therefore to ensure that the expansion of MNCs' activities pursuant to these trade agreements is consistent with EU human rights policies. The question to ask is how much social and human rights issues would form part of the EPAs and if this could have any bearing on the control of MNCs?

Another worrisome aspect of the EPA regime is the underlying rationale for the aggressive promotion of the agreements by the EU. Commentators have shown that in the recent past, the EU has resorted to a bilateral strategy through trade agreements to achieve aims that it failed to get through the WTO framework.[165] Goodison suggested that the failure of a range of trade-related issues at Cancun (September 2003) and Hong Kong (December 2005) WTO ministerial meetings precipitated the EC's resort to advocating similar issues that failed at those talks within the EPA's framework.[166] It may thus be that in the end trade considerations may trump other considerations such as human rights.

The direct beneficiaries of the EPAs on the EU side are MNCs from the EU who will have a freer access to the ACP market. This development, coupled with the ongoing privatisation and commercialisation programmes in many ACP countries, is set to increase the sphere of operation of MNCs significantly. Most of the fears expressed such as harsh competition, loss of jobs and income, social, environmental and human rights concerns could emanate from the activities of MNCs. As discussed in Chapter 4, currently most of the MNCs that operate in Nigeria are embroiled in disputes about human rights violations. With the expansion of the market, these issues are likely to become more complex especially because of the gaps within host jurisdictions' regulatory framework. There is thus an onus on the EU to ensure that its trading arrangements do not facilitate the violation of human rights.

Looking to the future

In order to enhance the ability of host states to ensure that the business activities of MNCs do not lead to the violation of human rights, is a need to expressly incorporate the essential element clause and the non-execution clause in the EPAs. The inclusion of the clauses would signal to the host state that they stand to lose the benefits of the arrangement if they fail to prevent human rights violations on their territory. Furthermore, there is an indirect consequence to MNCs who are the beneficiaries under the arrangement. They will realise that it is in their best interests

---

165 Ibid., 141.
166 Talks on the Doha round of the WTO talks also collapsed partly because of the reluctance of richer nations to liberalise their agricultural sectors while insisting that developing nations open their economies further to products from the richer nations. See Goodison (note 164).

not to engage in activities that violate human rights as this can lead to the suspension of the terms under which they benefit.

In addition, there is the need for a more robust application of human rights clauses beyond the present limited use in cases of unlawful change of governments. For example, the situation in the Niger Delta area of Nigeria where many MNCs operate has shown that the operation of MNCs can lead to the denial of rights. Therefore, the EU should be willing to utilise the human rights clauses where a host state is not doing its duty to prevent private actors from violating human rights.

There will be the need, of course, to maintain transparency in the use of the human rights clause. The EU has a relatively good track record in using similar clauses under the GSP when compared with the United States which is the only country apart from the EU to have such clauses in its GSP arrangement.[167] Whereas the United States has been accused of engaging in "aggressive liberalism" in its use of the provision for political and foreign policy ends, the EU has been adjudged to be more transparent.[168] The EU has been adjudged to apply the scheme strictly within the confines of international law.[169]

There are reasons to be optimistic. In January 2008, the CARIFORUM states[170] and the Dominican Republic became the first of the six sub-groupings of the ACP to conclude an Economic Partnership Agreement with the EU. The agreement contains strong wording on human rights, labour and environmental issues, unique in EU's practice.[171] The preamble to the agreement provides *inter alia* that the parties reaffirm "their commitment to the respect for human rights, democratic principles and the rule of law, which constitute the essential elements of the Cotonou Agreement, and to good governance, which constitutes the fundamental element of the Cotonou Agreement".[172] This reaffirmation of the commitment to the respect for human rights and the reference to the fact that the commitment is an essential element of the Cotonou Agreement suggests that the provisions would be applicable under the EPAs. Any doubt as to the incorporation

---

167 Kryvoi (note 6), 226.
168 L. Compa and J. Vogt, "Labour Rights in the Generalised System of Preferences: A 20-Year Review" (2002) 22 (2/3) *Comparative Labor Law and Policy Journal*, 199, 235.
169 G. Tsogas, "Labour Standards in the Generalised Systems of Preferences of the European Union and the United States" (2000) 6 *European Journal of Industrial Relations* 349.
170 CARIFORUM comprises the Caribbean countries of Antigua and Barbuda, Bahamas, Barbados, Belize, Dominica, Grenada, Guyana, Haiti, Jamaica, Saint Lucia, Saint Vincent and the Grenadiers, Saint Christopher and Nevis, Surinam, and Trinidad and Tobago.
171 Bartels recently voiced similar opinion. See L. Bartels, "Cariforum–EU Economic Partnership Agreement, Comments by Dr Lorand Bartels" Paper presented to the European Commission, 13 February 2008.
172 Economic Partnership Agreement between the CARIFORUM States and the European Community and its Member States OJL 289/1/3.

of human rights clauses into the EPAs is dispelled by article 2 of part I of the agreement which provides that,

1 This Agreement is based on the Fundamental Principles as well as the Essential and Fundamental Elements of the Cotonou Agreement, as set out in Articles 2 and 9, respectively, of the Cotonou Agreement. This Agreement shall build on the provisions of the Cotonou Agreement and the previous ACP–EC Partnership Agreements in the area of regional cooperation and integration as well as economic and trade cooperation.

2 The parties agree that the Cotonou Agreement and this Agreement shall be implemented in a complementary and mutually reinforcing manner.

The agreement also expressly allows for the non-execution clause under the Cotonou Agreement by providing in article 9(2) of part VI that:

2 Nothing in this Agreement shall be construed so as to prevent the adoption by the EC Party or a Signatory CARIFORUM state of any measures, including trade-related measures under this Agreement, deemed appropriate, as provided for under Articles 11b, 96 and 97 of the Cotonou Agreement and according to procedures set by these Articles.

Title II of the agreement covers investors, among other matters. Article 11, chapter 2 of title II specifically addresses behaviour of investors. Under the article contracting parties are required to take measures within their territories to ensure that investors do not engage in corrupt practices in their operations, that they comply with ILO defined core labour standards and that they do not operate in manners that circumvent international labour or environmental obligations. This provision, it is argued, covers home and host states regulation. Article 12 of the chapter goes further to provide that contracting parties shall "ensure that foreign direct investment is not encouraged by lowering domestic environmental, labour or occupational health and safety legislation and standards or by relaxing core labour standards or laws aimed at protecting and promoting cultural diversity".

The EPA contains further regulation of labour practices and the environment in title IV chapters 4 and 5. The contracting parties have the obligation to ensure a high level of labour and environmental standards. Chapter 5 contains stipulations to prevent the lowering of labour standards.[173] The parties commit themselves to core labour standards as defined

---

173 Chapter 5 of Part IV. Similar stipulations in respect of the environment are covered in chapter 4 of part V.

by ILO conventions in particular the freedom of association and the right to collective bargaining, the abolition of forced labour, the elimination of worst form of child labour and non discrimination in employment matters.[174] The parties explicitly reaffirm their obligations as members of the ILO and their commitments under the ILO Declaration on Fundamental Principles and Rights and its Follow-Up (1998).[175] The agreement expressly prohibits lowering of standards to enhance or maintain competitive advantage.[176] It also prohibits using labour standards for protectionist trade purposes.[177] Article 237 of the agreement also reiterates the parties' commitment to fight against corruption.

It is opined that there are provisions under the agreement that can be utilised to ensure that human rights are not violated by all parties including MNCs. There is no doubt that the human rights clause and the non-execution clause under the Cotonou Agreement are applicable under this agreement. The question, however, is how far the EU will be willing to go in utilising the clauses to prevent human rights abuses especially when violations of human rights by MNCs are involved.

Summary

This chapter has explored current EU strategies aimed at ensuring that its MNCs behave responsibly while operating abroad. The chapter noted that the EU has a broad underlying objective of promoting human rights, economic and social responsibility abroad as stated in article 177 of the Treaty Establishing the EC. The chapter examined the major approaches that have been taken within the EU to encourage responsible behaviour by EU MNCs while operating abroad: the promotion of the CSR concept and the incorporation of human rights and social issues into trade arrangements. In respect of the promotion of the CSR concept the chapter observed that the EU approach has been bifurcated. The chapter further noted that there is more talk and less action in the promotion of CSR as a strategy for the promotion of responsible behaviour abroad. In the case of trade arrangements, the chapter posits that the ongoing negotiations of Economic Partnership Agreements (EPA) with ACP countries have to take into account issues relating to the externalities of the operations of MNCs. It is suggested that a more proactive approach is necessary to ensure a responsible approach to business by MNCs while operating abroad. Such an approach would include emphasising issues of labour standards, human rights and environmental standards within the EPA framework.

174 Article 1(1), chapter 5 of part IV.
175 Article 1, chapter 5 of part IV.
176 Article 3, chapter 5 of part IV.
177 Article 1(4), chapter 5 of part IV.

7 Judicial process as a means of promoting corporate responsibility abroad

Extraterritoriality

This chapter considers the possibility of a more effective judicial oversight of MNC operations by home states of MNCs. This possibility is explored in the light of the concept of extraterritoriality, the EU regulatory framework and the Alien Torts Claim Act (ATCA)[1] jurisprudence in the United States.

The concept of extraterritoriality

Extraterritoriality sometimes referred to as prescriptive or legislative jurisdiction, exists where a court applies domestic law or international law to conduct that took place beyond the country's borders and to foreigners.[2] The concept negates the traditional concept of jurisdiction which limits the exercise of the jurisdiction of the state to its borders and in exceptional circumstances to its nationals who are beyond its borders. The traditional view is tied to state sovereignty and territorial integrity. However, over the years, a body of law has developed which applies extraterritorially, especially in the enforcement of international law. This development has led to a divergence of opinion among international law scholars as to whether it is to be welcomed and encouraged or not. The sovereignists consider the increased application of domestic jurisdiction extraterritorially as incompatible with the traditional view of the territorial limit of exercise of jurisdiction. The sovereignists focus on state level interaction and are less interested in sub-state entities such as domestic courts. On the other side are the new internationalists who favour extraterritorial application of domestic jurisdiction as a viable way of implementing and enforcing international law. The new internationalists differ from the classical internationalists who despite their faith in the efficacy of international law

---

1 Alien Tort Claims Act (ATCA), 28 USC §1350.
2 A.F. Lowenfield, *International Litigation and Arbitration* (second edition, Minnesota: West Group, St. Paul, 2002) 39 discussing extraterritoriality from the American perspective.

would not go as far as involving domestic non-state actors such as the courts in the implementation and enforcement of international law.[3]

It must be observed from the onset that extraterritorial application of home state law to activities that took place abroad is not as strange as it would appear. It is generally recognised in international law that states can exercise extraterritorial jurisdiction over wrongs committed abroad by their own nationals and this would include corporations incorporated in such states.[4] Within the EU, extraterritorial jurisdiction is well entrenched in EU competition policy based on the effect doctrine.[5] Furthermore, the EU's "Joint Action to Combat Trafficking in Human Beings and Sexual Exploitation of Children" of 24 February, 1997 affirms the principle of extraterritorial jurisdiction.[6] Member states of the EU also, in different ways, allow for the operation of the principle of extraterritoriality in their domestic spheres. In the United Kingdom for example, a person can be tried for capital offences committed abroad. The UK courts have assumed jurisdiction on a number of cases pertaining to activities that took place abroad.[7] Some of these cases shall be discussed later in this chapter. In France, claims for torts in violation of the laws of nations can be brought before a court of general jurisdiction (*Tribunal de Grande Instance*) because the court regards treaty law and customary international law as an integral part of the French domestic legal order. This is achieved by joining a civil claim (*action civile*) to a criminal prosecution in respect of a crime under customary international law. The victim of the crime may initiate the *action civile* and it is instituted to claim compensation for the damages resulting from the crime. The judgement resulting from the process may be enforced anywhere the defendant's assets are located.[8] Interestingly and significantly, article 689 of the French Code of Criminal Procedure grants the French courts universal jurisdiction for offences committed abroad where "an international convention grants jurisdiction to the French".

---

3 See generally L.A. Parrish, "Reclaiming International Law from Extraterritoriality" (September 2007). Online, available at: http://ssrn.com/abstract=1013740 (accessed 29 September 2008).

4 S. Joseph, *Corporations and Transnational Human Rights Litigation* (Oxford and Portland, OR: Hart Publishing, 2004) 11–12.

5 See *Gencor Ltd* v. *Commission* (1999) ECR, Page II – 0753 at paras 89–92.

6 Joint Action 97/154/JHA of 24 February 1997 adopted by the European Council on the Basis of Article K3 of the Treaty on European Union Concerning Action to Combat Trafficking in Human Beings and Sexual Exploitation Of Children (Official Journal L 63 of 4 March 1997) as Amended by Council Outline Decision 2002/629/JHA of 19 July 2002 Concerning Trafficking in Human Beings.

7 Joseph (note 4), 113–122.

8 E.A. Engle, "Alien Torts in Europe? Human Rights and Tort in European Law?" *ZERP-Diskussionspapier no. 1/20.*1/20 (2005) 1; J. Wouters and L. Chanet, "Corporate Human Rights Responsibility: A European Perspective" (2008) 6 (2) *Northwestern Journal of International Human Rights* 262.

However, French courts have been very hesitant to apply universal jurisdiction.[9] Prior to 2003, Belgium had offered universal jurisdiction *in absentia* regardless of the nationality of the victims or perpetrator. However, the ICJ ruling in *Congo* v. *Belgium*[10] invalidating a case prosecuted under the statute and also pressure from the United States caused Belgium to amend its universal jurisdiction law. Under the new law, for the universal jurisdiction to be invoked, the victim must be Belgian or legal residents of Belgium as at the time of the crime. Under article 12 of the Belgian penal code, not only international conventions but also international custom could be the basis of a claim.

The European Court of Human Rights (ECtHR) which monitors compliance with the European Convention on Human Rights (ECHR) of which all EU members are signatories to have also accepted the extraterritorial application of the convention. The ECtHR has held in a long line of cases that the scope of the ECHR is not to be confined within the contracting parties' boundaries.[11]

The example of the US Alien Torts Act (ATCA)

At present, ATCA is by far the most robust civil legal mechanism, which offers the possibility of holding corporate entities accountable for their egregious activities committed abroad. In the past two and a half decades, human rights advocates have found the use of the US Alien Torts Act very attractive in the struggle to hold corporate human rights violators accountable under international law in US courts.[12] Legal experts and major organisations like Amnesty International and Oxfam are increasingly becoming more disposed towards the litigation option under the ATCA as the most effective way for controlling MNCs.[13] Colliver and others have opined that the recourse to ATCA litigation can be seen as filling the prevailing accountability vacuum created by the absence of comprehensive international regulation. They also correctly noted that the ATCA litigation may act as a catalyst for future reform efforts.[14] However, this

---

9 Engle (note 8).

10 Judgement, online, available at: www.icj-cij.org/icjwww/idocket/iCOBE/icobejudgment/icobe_ijudgment_20020214.PDF (accessed 31 October 2007).

11 For examples see *Bankovic and Others* v. *Belgium and 16 Other Contracting States*, Application no. 52207/99, Admissibility Decision of 12 December 2001, 41 ILM (2002), 517, *Soering* v. *UK* (1989) 11 EHRR 439 – This is a key decision in which the principle was established by the ECtHR.

12 S. Colliver *et al.*, "Holding Human Rights Violators Accountable by Using International Law in US Courts: Advocacy Efforts and Complementary Strategies" (2005) 19 *Emory International Law Review* 169.

13 J. Kurlantzick, "Taking Multinationals to Court: How the Alien Tort Act Promotes Human Rights" (2002) *World Policy Journal* 60.

14 Colliver *et al.* (note 12).

potential must not be overstated, as most of the few successful cases under ATCA to date have largely been symbolic actions against defendants with no assets in the United States and in some cases defendants whose assets are beyond the reach of the United States.[15] In the case of MNCs however, the situation may be different because of their presence in many jurisdictions at the same time, thereby making their assets vulnerable. The eventual settlement of the Unocal case is a step in this direction.[16]

Described in 1975 by Judge Friendly as "a kind of legal Lohengrin", with an uncertain origin, the United States Alien Tort statute,[17] originally appeared in Section 9 of the first Judiciary Act of 1789.[18] The one sentence law provides as follows: "The district courts shall have original jurisdiction of any civil action by an alien for a tort only, committed in violation of the law of nations or a treaty of the United States."[19] The Act thus confers jurisdiction on the federal courts in the United States in respect of all causes where an alien sues for a tort in violation of the law of nations or a treaty of the United States[20] against defendants who have minimum contact with the jurisdiction of the US courts.[21]

The reason for the enactment of the legislation has largely remained a mystery. It has been suggested that the law was promulgated by the then newly-created United States following the assault on two foreign ambassadors or merchants in the United States.[22] Sweeney also suggested that the Act was intended to address torts committed by the crews of vessels in the course of stopping and boarding ships suspected of aiding the enemy in time of war.[23] The US legislature thus probably passed the legislation to show US commitment to defending international standard of good behaviour.[24]

15 I. Fuks, "Sosa v. Alvarez-Machain and the Future of ATCA Litigation: Examining Bonded Labor Claims and Corporate Liability" (2006) 106 *Columbia Law Review* 112.
16 110 F. Supp. 2d 1294 (CD Cal. 2000), affirmed in part reversed in part, 2002 WL 31063976 (9th Cir. 18 September 2002) Re hearing en blanc granted, vacated, 2003 WL 359787 (9th Cir. 14 February 2003) (discussed below).
17 *IIT* v. *Vencap, Ltd.,* 519 F.2d 1001. 1015 (2d Cir.1975).
18 The Act created the US judicial court system.
19 Judiciary Act of 1789 28 USC 1750.
20 Lowenfield (note 2) 705.
21 Colliver *et al.* (note 12).
22 G.C. Hufbauer and N.K. Mitrokostas, *Awakening Monster: The Alien Tort Statute of 1789* (Washington, DC: Institute for International Economics, 2003).
23 J.M. Sweeney, "A Tort in Violation of the Law of Nations" (1995) 18 *Hastings International and Comparative Law Review* 445.
24 Hufbauer and Mitrokostas (note 22).

The development of the ATCA jurisprudence

The Act was largely dormant until 1982, when the US second circuit court decided *Filartiga* v. *Pena-Irala*.[25] According to Randall[26] in the 199 years preceding the *Filartiga* decision, the statute was invoked in around 21 cases and jurisdiction was found only twice. However, in about three decades following the *Filartiga* decision, it was invoked and ruled upon in about 88 cases.[27] Jurisdiction was sustained wholly and in part in about half of the cases filed as at 2004. The rate at which cases brought under the ATCA were dismissed casts some doubts on the effectiveness of using the procedure as a means of holding MNCs accountable. Furthermore, before the *Filartiga* decision, the statute was generally perceived as a jurisdiction statute only, which does not create a cause of action.[28] The statute conferred jurisdiction on the federal district court to adjudicate on tort cases brought by foreigners but did not list the torts that could be the basis of the suit beyond those recognised in 1789 and those enacted by Congress including those created under the later Tort Victim Protection Act of 1991.[29]

In the *Filartiga* decision, the second circuit court expanded the scope of the ATCA when it held that the statute itself conferred jurisdiction over violation of human rights in the light of evolving jurisprudence. The court further held that the statute enabled foreigners to sue in the US courts for any tort committed in violation of international law (as international law may be contemporaneously interpreted). The court listed the conditions for establishing subject matter jurisdiction as the initiation of action by a foreigner, for any tort, committed in violation of international law. Other courts in the United States, proceeding from this point of view, have further expanded the reach of the statute by holding that it not only confers jurisdiction but also empowers the court to infer cause of action under international law.[30]

The decision in *Kadic* v. *Karadzic*[31] extended the application of the ATCA to private parties. It was held in the case that the ATCA is

25 *Filartiga* v. *Pena-Irala* 630 F.2d 876. See also C.A. D'Amore, "Note: Sosa v. Alvarez-Machain and the Alien Tort Statute: How Wide Has the Door to Human Rights Litigation Been Left Open?" (2006) 39 *Akron Law Review* 593.

26 K.C. Randall, "Federal Jurisdiction over International Claims: Inquiries into the Alien Tort Statute" (1985) 18 *New York University Journal of International Law and Politics* 1.

27 L. Londis, "The Corporate Face of the Alien Tort Claims Act: How an Old Statute Mandates a New Understanding of Global Interdependence" (2005) 57 *Maine Law Review* 141.

28 D'Amore (note 25), 593.

29 Hufbauer and Mitrokostas (note 22), Tort Victims Protection Act of 1991, 106 Stat.73 (1992).

30 Ibid.

31 *Doe* v. *Karadzic and Kadic* v. *Karadzic* 2001 US Dist LEXIS 12928; 2000 WL 763851 (SDNY 2000); 70 f.3D 232 (2nd Cir.1995).

applicable to private parties provided that their conduct is undertaken under the colour of state authority or violates a norm of international law that is recognised as extending to the conduct of parties. *Kadic* v. *Karadzic* laid the groundwork for lawsuits against MNCs. In *Kadic* v. *Karadzic*, it was affirmed that international law is applicable to private actors under ATCA and thus private actors can be held liable for their violations. It was further held in *The Presbyterian Church of Sudan et al.* v. *Talisman Energy, Inc*[32] that business entities have no immunity against lawsuits alleging grave violations of international law. The court also held that the statute, as interpreted by the Supreme Court in *Sosa* v. *Alvarez Machain* (discussed below), explicitly contemplated the existence of corporate liability under customary international law.[33]

To a significant extent, the US Supreme Court has affirmed the reasoning in *Filartiga* and cases following it in *Sosa* v. *Alvarez Machain*.[34] The court said that ATCA must be founded upon "norms of international character accepted by the civilized world and defined with specificity comparable to the features of the eighteenth-century paradigms we have recognized".[35] The norm or standard is a task for the lower courts to work out as cases come before them based on the statute.

There are three major ways in which the courts have extended the scope of the ATCA. The courts have held that jurisdiction is conferred under the statute for all torts, which are in violation of international law. Second, the courts have held that MNCs can be made defendants when they act in concert with a foreign state and third, the plaintiffs are not required to exhaust remedies in their own country before resorting to US courts.[36] In *Sarei* v. *Rio Tinto*[37] the court rejected the exhaustion of local remedies requirement in ATCA cases.

Three strands of cases have emerged from the application of the statute. The first sets of cases involve the institution of ATCA cases against state actors such as foreign governments, state officials and state entities. The second strand involves aliens suing private individuals. The third involves alien instituting actions against MNCs. According to Hufbauer and Mitrokostas, in the third strand of cases plaintiffs usually allege that the MNCs aided and abetted foreign governments or were acting "under colour of law" or were "joint actors".[38]

---

32 244 F. Supp. 2d 289 (SDNY, 2003).
33 124 S.Ct.2739 (2004).
34 *Sosa* v. *Alvarez Machain* (03-339) 542 US 692 (2004) 331 F.3d 604.
35 Ibid.
36 Hufbauer and Mitrokostas (note 22).
37 *Sarei* v. *Rio Tinto* 221 F. Supp. 2d. 1116, 1207 (CD Cal. 2002). (The facts of this case are discussed below.)
38 Hufbauer and Mitrokostas (note 22).

The reasons why the ATCA approach is attractive are many. In the first place because it is targeted at the financial resources of MNCs, it is reasoned that it will create an incentive for corporations to desist from acting in ways, which may lead to judicial proceedings. Second, since it is privately initiated, it reduces the cost of the state on litigation. Proceedings under the ATCA thus remove the necessity of reliance on the state for the institution of proceedings. States may, and often do, lack the incentive to sue. Third, the evidentiary burden required to establish a claim is not as high as in cases of international crime and the burden of proof is also lower. Furthermore, finding corporations liable for the acts of their subsidiary or agents is also potentially easier in tort than in criminal law. According to Davidson, proponents of the ATCA have argued that because international criminal prosecutions are not very common, civil remedies become more important and even where criminal prosecutions are available, international tort remedies may complement such proceedings by giving victims a forum that they can control.[39] She further notes that these cases give satisfaction to victims and also hold out the possibility of compensation. The statute also affirms the US commitment to respect for life in other countries. It gives a human face to US corporations' activities in other parts of the world especially in the developing countries, by showing that MNCs can be held accountable in their home countries.

However, there are significant limitations to the ATCA procedure that must be taken into consideration in this discussion. These include accessibility of the forum to litigants (the courts are reluctant to assume jurisdiction where the plaintiffs are not resident in the United States), prohibitive costs and time in filing suits, the limitation on the types of cases that can be brought and the barring of proceedings against sovereign nations under ATCA by the Foreign Sovereign Immunities Act.[40] It has been suggested, however, that the potential of the procedure may outweigh its limitations.[41]

Applying international law in the domestic forum

The application of international law by domestic courts in the United States has aided the ATCA jurisprudence. When the ATCA was passed, international law contemplated private liability for piracy.[42] However, since

---

39 C. Davidson, "Tort au Canadien: A Proposal for Canadian Tort Legislation on Gross Violations of Human Rights and Humanitarian Law" (2005) 38 *Vanderbilt Journal of Transnational Law* 1403.

40 D. Kinley and J. Tadaki, "From Talk to Walk: The Emergence of Human Rights Responsibilities for Corporations at International Law" (2004) 44 *Virginia Journal of International Law* 931, 940–942 discussing some of these limitations.

41 J.M. Chanin, "The Regulatory Grass is Greener: A Comparative Analysis of the Alien Tort Claims Act and the European Union's Green Paper on Corporate Social Responsibility" (2005) 12 *Indiana Journal of Global Legal Studies* 745.

42 Hufbauer and Mitrokostas (note 22).

then international offences have grown to include slave trading, war crimes and genocide. The courts in the United States have held that the mere fact that the United States has not ratified an international treaty does not bar a claim based on such treaty as a violation law of nations. In *Sarei* v. *Rio Tinto*[43] the court held that the defendant MNC could be held liable at the suit of a foreigner for the violation of the United Nations Convention of the Law of the Sea (UNCLOS) despite the fact that the United States has refused to ratify the treaty. This is a case relating to events that occurred in Papua New Guinea. Rio Tinto was an international mining group with its headquarters in London. The plaintiffs were former and current residents of Papua New Guinea. They brought an action against Rio Tinto under ATCA alleging that Rio Tinto's operation of a copper mine in Papua New Guinea violated international law and that the operation violated their human rights. They alleged that the company's operation polluted waterways and atmosphere thereby undermining the physical and mental health of the island's residents. In addition, the black natives of the island who worked for the company were paid lower wages than white workers recruited from other places and were made to live in slave-like conditions. Earlier in 1988, the natives took action to sabotage the mines, which led to their closure. It was the plaintiffs' case that the company sought and received assistance from the government, which led to the state army committing human rights abuses and war crimes, including blockade, area bombardment of civilian targets, arson, rape and pillage. The US State Department filed a statement of interest stating that the adjudication by the US courts was risking the conduct of foreign relations by the state and the court should therefore decline jurisdiction.[44] The district court dismissed the plaintiff's claim under the political question doctrine. On 7 August 2006, the US Court of Appeal, ninth circuit, reversed the decision by a 2–1 majority and held *inter alia* that the plaintiffs' claims, except the one based on the UNCLOS, assert *jus cogens* violation actionable under the *Sosa* decision. Second and most importantly in this connection, the court held that even though UNCLOS is not *jus cogens*, it can provide the basis for an ATCA claim because of the widespread ratification of the treaty. The case was sent back to the lower court for further proceedings.

In the *Filartiga* decision the court defined law of nations under ATCA to mean "international law as it has evolved and exists among the nations of the world today".[45] According to the court, international law is evolving and courts have the duty of interpreting the law as it has evolved among

---

43 *Sarei* v. *Rio Tinto* (221 F. Supp. 2d 1116 (CD Cal. 2002). The latest pronouncement: no. 02-56256; DC NO CV-00-11695-MMM.

44 This is a ruling that the matter in controversy is a political question.

45 *Filartiga* v. *Pena-Irala* 630 F.2d 876.

the nations of the world.[46] Evidence of such law can be found in "works of jurists, writing professedly on public law; or by the general usage and practice of nations; or by judicial decisions recognizing and enforcing the law". In *Sosa* v. *Alvarez Machain*[47] it was held that a law must be specific, universal and obligatory before it can qualify as law of nations. In *Doe* v. *Unocal*[48] it was held that MNCs could be liable for "aiding and abetting" a state in the violation of the law of nations. According to the court, proof that the corporation knowingly gives practical assistance or encouragement, which had a substantial effect on the perpetration of the crime, is sufficient proof of aiding and abetting the state actor. Knowledge in this regard was interpreted by the court to mean actual or constructive knowledge. The court further suggested that moral support alone might establish private liability.[49]

To date, courts in the United States have allowed cases alleging the following violation of international law to proceed: slavery, forced labour, genocide, crimes against humanity, summary execution, torture, cruelty, inhuman or degrading treatment, forced exile, arbitrary detention, denial of freedom of association and right to life.[50]

Opposition to ATCA

The business community in the United States and the government are very much opposed to litigation under the ATCA. It is the argument of business that enforcing human rights laws is within the domain of governments and not corporations (private litigants). Furthermore, it is argued that the broad application of the ATCA would undermine all efforts being made by companies through the adoption of voluntary company codes.[51] It has further been argued that the broad application of the ATCA would adversely affect US global commerce. According to a study conducted in 2003, possibility of judgements in ATCA cases as of then was a threat to about \$300 billion worth of global investment.[52] It is further argued that if the threat of ATCA forced western countries to leave countries with bad human rights records they would simply be replaced by companies from countries like China who are less scrupulous about issues of human rights.[53] The business community has thus, persistently lobbied the US

---

46 Ibid.
47 *Sosa* v. *Alvarez Machain* (03-339) 542 US 692 (2004) 331 F.3d 604.
48 110 F. Supp. 2d 1294 (CD Cal. 2000), affirmed in part reversed in part, 2002 WL 31063976 (9th Cir. 18 September 2002) Re hearing en blanc granted, vacated, 2003 WL 359787 (9th Cir. 14 February 2003).
49 Hufbauer and Mitrokostas (note 22).
50 Colliver *et al.* (note 12).
51 Kurlantzick (note 13).
52 Hufbauer and Mitrokostas (note 22).
53 Kurlantzick (note 13).

government to intervene to curb the expansion of the ATCA to corporations.

From a political perspective, it has been argued that cases under ATCA involve the court in making decisions in respect of foreign policy that are best left to government.[54] Furthermore it is argued that it shifts official condemnation of foreign governments from elected officials to private plaintiffs and their representatives.[55] It has similarly been criticised as capable of costing the US government dearly in term of its foreign policy.[56] It has also been argued that the application of US law to events that happened in other places unconnected with the United States may constitute judicial imperialism.[57] Another problem identified is how to delimit the boundaries of what constitute international law or "law of nations" under the statute.[58]

The US government has filed a number of briefs in some of the ATCA cases arguing that such cases could obstruct foreign policy making especially in the post 9/11 era as the US government needs the cooperation of the governments that are often the targets of ATCA litigation.[59] It is also argued that such decisions may constitute imposition of American views on legality and morality, which may enrage other nations and turn them against the United States.[60] The government further argued that the statute grants federal courts jurisdiction but does not grant a private cause of action to plaintiffs.[61]

These complaints are, however, overstated. According to Kurlantzick in the first place corporations are not simply held accountable for operating in an environment with poor human rights records but in cases of direct complicity in acts involving "specific, universal, and obligatory" international norms.[62] Second the fear of the abuse of process is most unlikely as US judges have been very strict in the application of the statute. As Ruggie noted in his interim Report "of the 36 ATCA cases to date involving companies, 20 have been dismissed, 3 settled and none decided in favour of the plaintiffs: the rest are ongoing".[63] The US courts have refused about

---

54 "Department of Justice Position on 'Unocal' case" (2003) 97 *American Journal of International Law* 703.
55 Ibid.
56 Ibid.
57 Ibid.
58 Davidson (note 39).
59 Brief for the United States of America, as Amicus Curiae at 2–4 (filed 8 May 2003), *Doe v. Unocal*, Nos. 00-56603&00-56628 (9th Cir.).
60 Ibid.
61 Ibid.
62 Kurlantzick (note 13).
63 Promotion and Protection of all Human Rights, Civil, Political, Economic, Social and Cultural Rights, including the Right to Development; Protect, Respect and Remedy: A Framework for Business and Human Rights; Report of the Special Representative of the Secretary General on the Issue of Human Rights and Transnational Corporations and other Business Enterprises, John Ruggie. A/HRC/8/5, 7 April 2008.

half of the ATCA claims on several grounds including no cause of action, non-justiciable political question and forum non conveniens.[64]

However, it must be noted that some lower courts in the United States have recently ruled that corporations cannot be sued under ATCA. This position appears to conflict with earlier decisions. It is likely that the Supreme Court will make a definitive pronouncement on this in the near future.[65]

The possibility of judicial oversight of MNCs in the EU

Most victims of the violation of rights by corporations are in developing countries. Many of these countries suffer from corrupt governments and overburdened judicial systems. Most of the judicial systems are also weak and corrupt. It has been suggested that

> The economic and political inequalities between, say, poor peasants on the one hand and wealthy multinational companies and/or governments on the other explain why, practically speaking, there is no remedy for basic violations of human rights in the third world.[66]

Justifying why home jurisdiction may be best in the circumstances Engle observed that:

> Even if there were no corruption in any third world country the fact that systematic violations of human rights can be very profitable explains why such rights must be protected in the first world. After all, it is the first world which profits from unfair and in fact predatory labour practices in the third world.[67]

This position further finds support in the principle laid down in the influential judgement of the International Court of Justice in *Barcelona Traction, Light and Power Company, Ltd (Spain v. Belgium)*[68] where the ICJ affirmed the nationality principle to the effect that home states have jurisdiction over MNCs incorporated under their jurisdiction in respect of their activities abroad.

The fact that EU MNCs are potentially exposed to litigation under the ATCA in the United States also poses a challenge. In *Wiwa v. Royal Dutch*

---

64 Londis (note 27).
65 See *Kiobel v. Royal Dutch Petroleum*, no. 06-4800-cv, 06-4876-cv, 2010 WL 3611392 (2d Cir. 17 September 2010); Doe I v. Nestle, no. 2:05-cv-05133, at 121–160 (CD Cal. 8 September 2010).
66 Engle (note 8), 2.
67 Ibid.
68 *Barcelona Traction, Light and Power Company, Ltd (Spain v. Belgium)* 16 ICJ Rep. 1970, 3.

Petroleum Co.[69] an ATCA case was filed by three Nigerian émigrés and an anonymous plaintiff against two European-based companies, Royal Dutch Shell, incorporated and headquartered in Netherlands and Shell Transport and Trading Corporation, incorporated and headquartered in England. The two companies control the Royal Dutch Shell Group, an MNC with a wholly owned subsidiary, Shell Nigeria. Shell Nigeria is the biggest oil exploration and extraction corporation in Nigeria. The plaintiffs alleged that the company had participated in grave human rights abuses against them and/or their relations in Nigeria. On a motion for the case to be dismissed on the ground of *forum non-conveniens*, the lawyers to the MNCs argued that the case would be more properly litigated either in the Netherlands or England. The court was not persuaded because in the first place, it held, the European forum might not categorise the tort as a violation of international law. Second, the courts of England or the Netherlands may apply a choice of law rule that would point to the location where the abuse took place (in this case Nigeria), which may deny the assertion of such claim. Third, under the double actionability rule in England, extraterritorial tort claims would not be permitted unless it is shown that the torts complained of are actionable in the place where they occurred.

Thus the provision of an alternative forum in the EU may potentially have the added advantage of lessening the risk of European corporations' exposure to litigation in the United States under ATCA. Furthermore, such an approach would underscore the EU's commitment to controlling corporate abuses committed abroad. It is important to emphasise that even though competitiveness is good for business, human rights and human dignity must not be subject simply to a cost–benefit analysis. It has also been observed that corporations would be less inclined to increase their costs by complying with voluntary codes that they adopt unless there are heavy enforceable penalties that shift the cost–benefit analysis in favour of doing so.[70]

The viability of extraterritorial jurisdiction in the EU: the example of the English jurisdiction

A study was carried out in 2001 to explore the possibility of employing civil actions in the English courts under the common law system against corporations for serious human rights violations abroad.[71] The report examines the obstacles posed by the doctrine of sovereign immunity, the act of state

---

69 226 F.3d 88 (2d Cir.2000), 532 US 941 (2001); see also A.X. Fellmeth, "*Wiwa* v. *Royal Dutch Petroleum Co.*: A New Standard for the Enforcement of International Law in US Courts?" (2002) 5 *Yale Human Rights and Development Law Journal* 241.

70 Chanin (note 41).

71 International Law Association Human Rights Committee, "Report on Civil Actions in the English Courts for Serious Human Rights Violations Abroad" (2001) 2 *European Human Rights Law Review* 129.

doctrine and the problem of establishing the connection of the dispute to the jurisdiction. The major conclusion of the report is that there are significant hurdles to surmount before such a challenge can be successfully pursued in England. Therefore, the group concluded that the likelihood of such litigation in England was slim.[72]

An examination of the English jurisprudence and MNCs

The development in England in respect of the extraterritorial jurisdiction over MNC activities abroad is instructive. Several cases have come before the English courts in respect of the England-/UK-based MNCs' operations abroad. One major hurdle against these claims is the common law doctrine of forum non conveniens. The doctrine as developed in the *Spilada Maritime Corporation* v. *Cansulex Ltd* case[73] is to the effect that a judge may decline to take a case where it is established that there is another and more appropriate forum where the case should be heard.[74] The consequence of this doctrine for cases alleging misconduct by MNCs is that since the conduct complained of took place in another jurisdiction and the MNC's subsidiary is also in that jurisdiction, the most suitable forum will be the foreign jurisdiction.

The courts in England have, however, tried to find ways around the doctrine. In *Connelly* v. *RTZ*[75] the plaintiff, a Scottish man, while working

---

72 Engle (note 8) reached a different conclusion from the ILA report in respect of the English common law. He compared US law, which has made possible the application of the ATCA to English common law. He was of the opinion that major doctrines in the United States that facilitated ATCA litigation have equivalents under English common law. These include the doctrine of sovereign immunity, act of state doctrine, comity and forum non-conveniens. More importantly he noted that like in the United States, customary international law is an integral part of English common law. The common law jurisdiction operates a dualist approach to treaty law requiring that treaty be incorporated into domestic law through enabling act.

73 *Spiliada Maritime Corporation* v. *Cansulex Ltd* (1987) AC 460.

74 The ECJ succinctly explained the doctrine in *Owusu* v. *Jackson* (2005) EUECJ C-281/02 (1 March 2005) paragraphs 8 and 9 as follows:

> According to the doctrine of forum non conveniens, as understood in English law, a national court may decline to exercise jurisdiction on the ground that a court in another state, which also has jurisdiction, would objectively be a more appropriate forum for the trial of the action, that is to say, a forum in which the case may be tried more suitably for the interests of all the parties and the ends of justice (1986 judgement of the House of Lords, in Spiliada *Maritime Corporation* v. *Cansulex Ltd* (1987), AC 460, particularly at p. 476). An English court which decides to decline jurisdiction under the doctrine of forum non conveniens stays proceedings so that the proceedings which are thus provisionally suspended can be resumed should it prove, in particular, that the foreign forum has no jurisdiction to hear the case or that the claimant has no access to effective justice in that forum.

75 *Connelly* v. *RTZ Corporation Plc* (1998) AC 854.

for a subsidiary of the defendant at their uranium mine in Namibia contracted laryngeal cancer at the age of 32 and underwent a laryngectomy. The defendant company was domiciled in England. The plaintiff brought an action for a compensation of £400,000 before a court in England. The lower English courts refused his action on the basis that it should be heard in Namibia and not the English courts. The case went to the House of Lords, which held that despite the fact that Namibia was a more appropriate forum, it would not be in the interests of justice to make the plaintiff litigate in Namibia because the funding for a legal action was not available to the plaintiff in Namibia.[76] It must be noted that a majority of the House of Lords felt that the case was an exceptional one which required experts' legal representations and scientific assistance available in England but not in Namibia.

In the *Thor Chemicals Holdings Ltd* cases,[77] Thor Chemicals Holding Ltd was an England-based MNC which had a manufacturing subsidiary in South Africa. The company relocated its manufacturing operation to South Africa because there were complaints against its operations in England and environmental and labour legislation was lax in apartheid South Africa. In South Africa, the company was able to use untrained temporary workers to do hazardous work which led to the death of some workers and the poisoning of others. The plaintiffs, which included representatives of three dead workers and 17 other workers who suffered injury, brought two lawsuits against Thor Chemicals Holdings Ltd and its chairman in the English courts. The plaintiffs contended, *inter alia*, that the parent company should be liable to compensate them because it was responsible for setting up and maintaining the South African factories which they knew or ought to know were not safe for workers to work in. The company applied for a stay of proceedings arguing that the case should be heard in South Africa as it is a more convenient and appropriate forum. The court ruled in favour of the plaintiffs and the defendant's application was refused. The defendant subsequently settled the matter out of court.

Another case brought before the English courts is *Lubbe* v. *Cape Plc*.[78] The company concerned, Cape Plc, was based in England. During the apartheid era in South Africa, the company had a wholly owned subsidiary in South Africa. Between 1997 and 2000, over 3,000 people, who had been afflicted with asbestos-related lung cancer while working in the subsidiaries of the company in South Africa, issued claims against the England-

---

76 Note that the case later failed because it was instituted after the limitation period.
77 *Ngcbo and Others* v. *Thor Chemicals Holdings Ltd. And Others* (10 November 1995), *Times Law Reports*.
78 Note that there are several cases on related issues filed by different defendants. See *Lubbe and Others* v. *Cape Plc*, 2000 All ER 268.

based parent company. Some of the claimants died before the case was concluded. A major issue that arose in the case was whether an action brought by the South African plaintiffs against the company incorporated and domiciled in England should be stayed on grounds of forum non conveniens. At the High Court, the judge held that the defendant succeeded in establishing that South Africa is an available forum which is more appropriate than the English forum. The Court of Appeal reversed the decision of the High Court on several grounds. In the first place, the court was of the view that the plaintiffs' case was that the defendant company "controlled" the operations of the South African subsidiaries. This meant that the decisions that led to the injuries suffered by the plaintiffs were taken in England. According to the court "the alleged breaches of duty occurred essentially in England, although their effects were felt by the plaintiffs in South Africa where the decisions were implemented".[79] Second, the court also said that the South African forum was not available to the plaintiffs as they could not bring an action in South Africa against a foreign based company without the consent of the company.

The House of Lords, held that there are two stages to the application of doctrine of forum non conveniens. At the first stage, the court will consider whether the defendant who is seeking for a stay of the action has discharged the burden on him to show prima facie that there is another available forum which is clearly or distinctly more appropriate than the English forum. At the second stage the court will grant a stay unless the plaintiff can show that there are circumstances by reason of which justice requires that the matter be heard in England *i.e.* that substantial justice will not be done in the appropriate forum. The House of Lords held that the *Lubbe* case should be heard in England and not South Africa because legal aid would not be available to retain services of expert legal counsel for such litigation in South Africa. This, the court concluded, would amount to a denial of justice. According to the court

> If these proceedings were stayed in favour of the more appropriate forum in South Africa the probability is that the plaintiffs would have no means of obtaining the professional representation and the expert evidence which would be essential if these claims were to be justly decided. This would amount to a denial of justice. In the special and unusual circumstances of these proceedings, lack of the means, in South Africa, to prosecute these claims to a conclusion provides a compelling ground, at the second stage of the Spiliada test, for refusing to stay the proceedings here.[80]

---

79 *Lubbe and Ors* v. *Cape Plc* (1998) EWCA CIV 1351 (30 July 1998).
80 *Lubbe and Ors* v. *Cape Plc* (1998) EWCA CIV 1351 (30 July 1998).

The House of Lords was of the view that its decision is supported by article 6 of the European Convention on Human Rights which guarantees a right to a fair hearing.

The conclusion to be reached from these cases is that English jurisdiction has yielded to entertaining cases involving activities of MNCs abroad despite the obstacle placed by the doctrine of forum non conveniens. The compatibility of the doctrine of forum non conveniens with the Brussels Convention has also come before the English courts and the European Court of Justice (ECJ). The decisions of the courts have had important consequences for the availability of home jurisdiction for MNCs operations abroad. We now examine this issue.

The Brussels Convention on Jurisdiction and the Enforcement of Judgement

The Brussels Convention is applicable in determining jurisdiction where the defendant is domiciled in a member state of the European Union. A useful starting point for a discussion of the Brussels Convention is the arguments of the parties before the House of Lords in *Lubbe and Ors* v. *Cape Plc* regarding article 2 of the convention.[81] The plaintiffs argued that article 2 allows victims to bring actions in English courts where the defendant is domiciled in England. The court is therefore precluded from applying the doctrine of forum non conveniens to grant a stay in favour of another jurisdiction. The defendant contended that the jurisdiction of the court to grant a stay in favour of a forum in a non-contracting state is unaffected by article 2. In his judgement, Lord Bingham observed that the parties' argument was anchored on the Court of Appeal decision in *In re Harrods (Buenos Aires) Ltd.*[82] The plaintiffs requested that if the court was not satisfied by its argument in this respect, it should refer the issue to the European Court of Justice. However, the court was of the opinion that the answer to the question whether the effect of article 2 of the Brussels Convention is to deprive the English courts of the jurisdiction to stay proceedings was not relevant in this case.

In *In re Harrods (Buenos Aires) Ltd* the Court of Appeal held that in view of the Brussels Convention, a stay of proceedings on the ground of forum non conveniens was not available in cases involving competing jurisdiction between contracting member states. However, this would not be the case in respect of a court of a non contracting state. The court held that the

---

81   The Brussels Convention on Jurisdiction and the Enforcement of Judgements in Civil and Commercial Matters (1968) provides mandatory rules of determining jurisdiction among member states of the European Union in matters that come within the scope of the convention. A general rule under the convention is that the courts of the defendant's domicile are to have jurisdiction subject to the exceptions under the convention.

82   *In re Harrods (Buenos Aires) Ltd* (1992) ch. 72.

English courts have the discretion under the doctrine to grant a stay in favour of the forum of a non-contracting state because the convention is not applicable in such situations.

Similar issue arose in a reference to the ECJ in *Group Josi Reinsurance Company SA* v. *Universal General Insurance Company.*[83] This case involved a Canadian company which sought to bring proceedings against a Belgium-based company in France. The Belgian company argued that in virtue of the Brussels Convention the courts in Belgium had jurisdiction and not the French courts. The ECJ considered the following question:

> Does the Brussels Convention apply not only to intra-Community disputes but also to disputes which are integrated into the Community? More particularly, can a defendant established in a contracting state rely on the specific rules on jurisdiction set out in that Convention against a plaintiff domiciled in Canada?

The ECJ held that in determining jurisdiction, the rules in the convention may be applied to a dispute between a defendant domiciled in the contracting state and a plaintiff domiciled in a non-member state. It must be noted, however, that the competing jurisdictions in this case are both within the EU and the ECJ did not clearly address the circumstance where the competing jurisdictions involved an EU jurisdiction and a non contracting state.

Owusu v. *Jackson and Ors*[84] resolved this question to a large extent. The competing jurisdictions in this case were England and Jamaica – one contracting state and one non contracting state. One of the defendants, Jackson, was domiciled in England but the harmful event in issue in the case occurred in Jamaica. The question referred to the ECJ was whether the forum non conveniens doctrine is available in favour of the courts of a non-contracting state, when the defendant is domiciled in the contracting member state. The question was posed as follows:

> Is it inconsistent with the Brussels Convention –, where a claimant contends that jurisdiction is founded on Article 2, for a court of a contracting state to exercise a discretionary power, available under its national law, to decline to hear proceedings brought against a person domiciled in that state in favour of the courts of a non-contracting state:
>
> a   if the jurisdiction of no other contracting state under the 1968 Convention is in issue;

---

83 *Group Josi Reinsurance Company SA* v. *Universal General Insurance Company* (2000) ILPr 549 (ECJ); (2001) QB 68.
84 Case C-281/02 (2005) 2 WLR 942 (2005) EUECJ C-281/02.

b   if the proceedings have no connecting factors to any other contracting state?

2   If the answer to question 1(a) or (b) is yes, is it inconsistent in all
circumstances or only in some and if so which?

The ECJ held that article 2 of the Brussels Convention applies to circumstances "involving relationships between the courts of a single contracting
state and those of a non-contracting state rather than relationships
between the courts of a number of contracting states".[85] In answering the
first question formulated in the reference it held that

> The Brussels Convention precludes a court of a contracting state from
> declining the jurisdiction conferred on it by Article 2 of that conven-
> tion on the ground that a court of a non-contracting state would be a
> more appropriate forum for the trial of the action even if the jurisdic-
> tion of no other contracting state is in issue or the proceedings have
> no connecting factors to any other contracting state.[86]

However, the court refused to answer the second question seeking essentially to know whether the Brussels Convention precludes the application
of the doctrine of forum non conveniens in all circumstances or only in
certain circumstances. The court was of the opinion that the question
raised factual circumstances different from the main questions and according to the court "the justification for a reference for a preliminary ruling is
not that it enables advisory opinions on general or hypothetical questions
to be delivered but rather that it is necessary for the effective resolution of
a dispute".[87] In the final paragraph of the judgement, however, the court
stated categorically that the convention:

> Precludes a court of a contracting state from declining the jurisdiction
> conferred on it by Article 2 of that Convention on the ground that a
> court of a non-contracting state would be a more appropriate forum
> for the trial of the action even if the jurisdiction of no other contract-
> ing state is in issue or the proceedings have no connecting factors to
> any other contracting state.[88]

It is submitted that the ECJ has effectively put an end to the application of
the forum non conveniens by its ruling in *Owusu* v. *Jackson.*

---

85   Para. 35.
86   Para. 46.
87   Para. 50.
88   Para. 53.

Applicable law in England

Even, if as it is suggested, the English forum is available, the next question to consider is the law to be applied by the court. As noted earlier, in the case of the ATCA, international law is applicable to cases brought under that statute. However, in England, it is more likely that the English courts will refer to the law of the place where the injury took place and where due to a weak legal framework such a claim might not be cognisable. Apart from the law of the state where the injury occurred, the other possibilities in England are:

1 Customary international law
2 Ordinary rule of English domestic tort law
3 Human Rights Act, 1998.

Reliance on customary international law may be possible in theory because there exists a corresponding tort for each of the customary crimes under international law and thus it is possible to make a claim in tort such as torture under the common law without resort to a statute similar to the Alien Torts Claim Act.[89] All EU countries have ratified the Rome Statute of the International Criminal Court and revised (or are in the process of revising) their domestic criminal law to incorporate international crimes of genocide, war crimes and crimes against humanity. Therefore the EU states would appear to have provided a forum to bring suit against legal and natural persons for the aforementioned crimes under the ICC principles of complementarity. Most of the crimes that have been incorporated into domestic law can also constitute tort. Here universal jurisdiction would apply because:

> It is logical to presume that if universal jurisdiction exists as to the substantive crime which is the basis of the international tort claim then it would logically also exist as to the corresponding common law tort. If the law permits the greater punishments of imprisonment or execution it also permits a lesser punishment of restitution.[90]

89 Ibid. This was, to some extent the reasoning in *Regina* v. *Bartle* and the *Commissioner of Police for the Metropolis and Others Ex Parte Pinochet Regina* v. *Evans and Another* and the *Commissioner of Police for the Metropolis and Others Ex Parte Pinochet (On Appeal from a Divisional Court of the Queen's Bench Division)* (1998) 3 WLR 1456 (HL) (1999) 2 WLR 272 (HL) (1999) 2 WLR 827 (HL). However, the House of Lords looked at the implementing legislation of the Convention against Torture, the domestic law, to ground its jurisdiction over Pinochet. The House of Lords looked at the domestic definitions of the relevant crime and not its international dimensions. According to Professor Roht-Arriaza, "It was the incorporation of Torture Convention into UK law that gave the Court jurisdiction not the underlying customary law norms". See N. Roht-Arriaza, "The Pinochet Precedent and Universal Jurisdiction" (2001) 35 (2) *New England Law Review* 311.
90 Engle (note 8), 16.

However, as Stephens and the ILA report note, in England proof of a right to sue under customary international law requires a development of extensive record that is likely to be time consuming, expensive and difficult to achieve.[91] Furthermore, Engle argues that torts claims for wrongs committed abroad can be brought as ordinary torts under customary common law torts such as wrongful imprisonment, battery, conversion or action on the case subject to ordinary rules of conflicts of law and without benefit of universal jurisdiction. This approach, however, is unlikely to be attractive because of hurdles such as doctrine of immunity, jurisdiction and until recently forum non conveniens.[92]

Controlling MNCs through the judicial process under a European framework

It is noted that there is no law (except the OECD Convention on Bribery) that imposes an obligation on home states of MNCs to control their activities abroad.[93] However, given the EU's commitment to social justice and human rights and given that a large number of MNCs from Europe operate in the countries of the South and against the backdrop of the lack of institutional framework for controlling MNCs in the countries of the South, there is a necessity for the EU to take more proactive steps.

There have been suggestions within the EU to allow access to the EU jurisdiction for foreigners in case of complaint of corporate abuse by EU MNCs abroad. In a motion for a resolution presented to the European Parliament in 1999, it was initially requested that:

> The European Council confirm the interpretation in the 1968 Brussels Convention that, for cases of basic duty of care, legal action may be taken against a company in the EU country where its registered office is, in respect of any third country throughout the world, and call on Commission to study the possibility of enacting legislation, which open European courts to lawsuits involving damage done by

---

91 B. Stephens, "The Amorality of Profit: Transnational Corporations and Human Rights" (2002) 20 *Berkeley Journal of International Law* 45; See also S. Chesterman, "Oil and Water: Regulating the Behaviour of Multinational Corporations through Law" (2004) 36 *International Law and Politics* 307; see also International Law Association Human Rights Committee, "Report on Civil Actions in the English Courts for Serious Human Rights Violations Abroad" (2001) 2 *European Human Rights Law Review* 129.

92 The European Court of Justice decision in *Owusu* v. *Jackson* (2005) 2 WLR 942 has put an end to the use of *forum non conveniens* by UK courts on the ground that it was incompatible with article 2 of the Brussels regulation. The decision removed one of the significant hurdles for claimants seeking to use the UK courts.

93 Article 2 of the OECD Convention on Bribery of Foreign Public Officials in International Business Transactions of 1997.

MNEs, thus creating a precedent for developing customary international law in the field of corporate abuse. [94]

However, this passage was not included in the final adopted text the "Resolution on EU Standards for European Enterprises Operating in Developing Countries: Towards a European Code of Conduct".[95]

Again in 2002, the European Parliament's Committee on Employment and Social Affairs in their report on the commission Green Paper on promoting a European framework for corporate social responsibility[96] stated that it:

> Draws attention to the fact that the 1968 Brussels Convention as consolidated in Regulation 44/2001 enables jurisdiction within the courts of EU member states for cases against companies registered or domiciled in the EU in respect of damage sustained in third countries; calls on the Commission to compile a study of the application of this extraterritoriality principle by courts in the member states of the Union; calls on the member states to incorporate this extraterritoriality principle in legislation.

According to Wouters and others,[97] this shows the thinking on the part of the committee that enacting a European framework similar to ATCA is a viable possibility. As the report indicated and Wouters and others have also opined, article 2 of Regulation (EC) NR 44/2001 on Jurisdiction and Enforcement of Judgements in Civil and Commercial Matters already grants the courts of EU member states the jurisdiction to hear tort claims against MNCs that have their registered office, principal place of business or centre of operation in the EU, even where damages has occurred abroad. Article 2(1) provides that: "Subject to this regulation, persons domiciled in a member state shall, whatever their nationality, be sued in the court of that member state." In the case of companies, domicile is determined by the country where they have their statutory seat, central administration or principal place of business.[98] By virtue of article 60(2),

---

94 O. De Schutter, "The Accountability of Multinationals for Human Rights Violations in European Law" in P. Alston, ed., *Non-State Actors and Human Rights* (Oxford: Oxford University Press, 2005), 263.

95 A4-058/1998, OJ 1999 c 104/176.

96 "Report on the Commission Green Paper on Promoting a European Framework for Corporate Social Responsibility" (A5-159/2002, April 2002).

97 J. Wouters *et al.*, "Tort Claims Against Multinational Companies for Foreign Human Rights Violations Committed Abroad: Lessons from the Alien Tort Claims Act?" (K.U. Leuven Faculty of Law, Institute for International Affairs, Working Paper no. 46, November 2003).

98 Article 60 Regulation 44/2001.

in respect of the United Kingdom and Ireland statutory seat is defined to mean the registered office or, where there is no such office anywhere, the place of incorporation or, where there is no such place anywhere, the place under the law of which the formation took place.

While most EU member states interpret article 2 of the convention as conferring jurisdiction on cases brought from any country throughout the world, some European member states such as the United Kingdom are reluctant to interpret the article the same way.[99] One of the reasons for this approach in the United Kingdom is the application of the doctrine of forum non conveniens. Happily, the European Court of Justice in *Owusu* v. *Jackson*[100] has put an end to the use of forum non conveniens on the ground that it was incompatible with article 2 of the convention. The decision removed one of the significant hurdles for claimants seeking to use the UK courts. It is suggested that the answer to the ATCA in Europe lies in the proactive application of Regulation 44/2001.

After reviewing article 2 and article 5(b) of the regulation and the decision of the ECJ in *Reunion Europeenne SA and others*[101] De Schutter concluded that,

> These provisions therefore recognize that the jurisdictions of the member states are competent to hear tort actions based on the damage suffered by victims, wherever these are domiciled and whatever their nationality, caused by the activities of a multinational enterprise domiciled in a member state or by any of its branches. The action will be lodged either in the state where the parent company is domiciled or, where a branch of that company has actually been at the basis of the act causing the damage, in the state where the branch is located.[102]

De Schutter also opined that such an interpretation is analogous to a European version of ATCA. He observed that the jurisdiction provided from this perspective may even be wider than the one provided under the ATCA as it is not restricted only to aliens but also allows nationals of the EU to use it.

It must be noted that the regulation rejects jurisdiction based on transitory presence and bars such exercise between domiciliaries of member states. However, member states can rely on such litigation involving non-member states. Thus, for example, while the convention prohibits jurisdiction based

---

99 N. Jagers, *Corporate Human Rights Obligations: in Search of Accountability* (New York: Intersentia, 2002).

100 *Owusu* v. *Jackson* (2005) 2 WLR 942.

101 (1998) ECR I-6511.

102 De Schutter (note 94), 265.

on transitory presence, it is permitted in England and Ireland.[103] This is different from the ATCA position which permits the exercise of jurisdiction over foreign actors for abuses committed in foreign countries based on transitory presence. There is no suggestion here that the EU should shift its stance in this regard as the focus is on corporations properly domiciled in the region.

An important gap within the EU framework based on Regulation 44/2001 is the question of the applicable law. While the ATCA expressly resolves the question of applicable law by reference to the law of nations, the Brussels Regulation has no such provision.[104] The determination of the applicable law is thus left to member states which choice may invariably point to the law of the place where the tort took place.

The next step, therefore, would be the need to recognise tort in violation of international law within the EU legal scheme. In the first place, as we have noted earlier, with the exception of ATCA, no other jurisdiction expressly recognises the violation of international law as a tort. As we have also noted above, all EU member states have signed up to the Rome Convention. The international crimes codified therein, which are incorporated into member states' law, also constitute torts, which may give rise to claims for damages by victims. As a first step, it would be necessary to recognise the tort dimension of international crime and the extension of member states' jurisdiction to cover adjudication of torts committed in violation of international law. Second according to the ILA study, it is possible to establish a core of the most serious violations of international human rights that will be generally applicable as a matter of customary international law.[105] These would include the principle of equality before the law, rules prohibiting pervasive racial discrimination, arbitrary deprivation of life, slavery, torture and genocide.[106] Third, all customary international law rights, which are already recognised as *jus cogens*, would also form the basis of the recognised international law constituting torts.[107]

The EU could have addressed the issue in Regulation (EC) 864/2007 on the Law Applicable to Non-Contractual Obligation which took effect in January 2009 (Rome II).[108] Rome II governs the choice of law rules of EU member states on non-contractual obligations arising from torts or delicts

---

103 Stephens (note 91) also cites the examples of other prohibited jurisdictional practices under the convention but permitted against non member states: ownership of property within jurisdiction which is not the basis of litigation, permitted in Sweden; jurisdiction based on the French nationality of plaintiff or defendant permitted in France. Similar provisions exist in Luxembourg and The Netherlands.

104 De Schutter (note 94), 274.

105 International Law Association Human Rights Committee (note 91).

106 Ibid.

107 Ibid.

108 2007 O.J. (L199)40.

and from other acts or facts. By virtue of paragraph 7 of the preamble to the regulation, the substantive scope and the provisions of the regulation should be consistent with Regulation 44/2001. Under article 3, the regulation has universal application because it covers torts occurring both within and outside the EU and may lead to the application of the law of a third state.[109] Article 3 provides that "any law specified by this regulation shall be applied whether or not it is the law of a member state". It would have been interesting if article 3 had gone further to include international law. It is, however, opined that, to the extent that international law is part of a relevant country's law, it should form part of the applicable law.

Rome II did not go as far as ATCA because its central provision (the general rule), article 4, provides that the applicable law "shall be the law of the country in which the damage occurs irrespective of the country or countries in which the indirect consequences of that event occur". This is a restatement of the *lex loci delicti* rule. Symeonides illustrates the effect of the general rule with the following hypothetical case:

> Blasting operations by a Swiss mining company in the Swiss Alps cause a snow avalanche in the French Alps injuring a group of English tourists. Although there is some room for contrary argument, it seems that Article 4(1) views Switzerland as the country of the "event giving rise to the damage", France as the country in which "the damage occurs", and England as the country in which "the indirect consequences of that event occur". Translated into simpler English, Article 4(1) provides that the applicable law is the law of the country in which the injury occurs, and more precisely the harmful physical impact (France), irrespective of the country in which the injurious conduct occurred (Switzerland), and irrespective of the country in which the indirect consequences of the injury are felt (England).

The convention thus favours domestic law as opposed to international law as it is applicable under the ATCA.

It is important to note the special provision in respect of environmental torts. The regulation allows the victim to make a choice between the law of the place of injury or the law of the place of conduct leading to the injury. The choice is meaningful in a situation where the country of conduct and the country of injury have different standards or financial protection for victims.[110] According to Symeonides, the choice is given not to benefit the victim as such but to protect the interests of member countries and the community as a whole in deterring pollution.[111] It is argued that if the

---

109　S.C. Symeonides, "Rome II and Tort Conflicts: A Missed Opportunity" (2008) 56 *American Journal of Comparative Law* 173.
110　Ibid.
111　Ibid.

court of a member state assumes jurisdiction in a case of environmental pollution involving a victim in a non contracting state this choice may also be available.

Summary

This chapter has argued that there is an important role for the home jurisdiction to play in the promotion of corporate responsibility abroad. It has explored the possibility of controlling EU based corporations' activities abroad through the judicial process of the EU. This is important because of the need to demonstrate in a practical and proactive way the EU's commitment to human rights standards in relation to their companies' operations in the countries of the South. It is the opined that through the proper application of Regulation 44 and the application of international law by domestic courts, an effective mechanism could be evolved within the home jurisdiction to promote corporate responsibility abroad.

8 The foundation for a global company law for multinational corporations

The complementary role at the international level

The modern world has been transformed by globalisation and national boundaries are increasingly disappearing. There are institutional elements resembling a world government: the United Nations; world banking institutions: the World Bank and the International Monetary Fund and international courts: the International Court of Justice and the International Criminal Court. Also, interestingly, international legal personality is expanding. Over the years, it has expanded to include non state actors: intergovernmental organisations and individuals. Multinational corporations (MNCs) are recognised as major actors in the globalisation process. However, the international regulatory agenda has not paid sufficient attentions to MNCs. Their regulation has remained largely confined to the domestic forums. The inadequacies of domestic law to grapple with the concept of MNCs and the failure at international law to deal effectively with it have led to regulatory problems and the attempts to fill these gaps with corporate social responsibility initiatives.

This chapter argues that part of the solution may lie in establishing the locus for the international regulation of the company as a method of doing business. This will involve developing the concept of international company (IC) with an international corporate personality (analogous to corporate personality under domestic law) under an international company law framework to fill the regulatory gaps. This approach will facilitate the effective regulation of MNCs.

MNCs and domestic company law paradigm

It has been strongly and correctly argued that the key elements of domestic corporate law i.e. "legal personality, limited liability, transferable shares, delegated management and shareholder primacy"[1] have encouraged companies at the domestic level to avoid responsibilities despite the

---

1 P. Ireland, "Limited Liability, Shareholder Rights and the Problem of Corporate Irresponsibility" *Cambridge Journal of Economics Advance Access* (2008) 1.

fact that they owe their existence to the domestic regulatory framework.[2] These elements of domestic corporate law have been extended to the global level where there is no law regulating the "global corporation". Strikwerda opined that because there is no international company law for MNCs, they are "forced" to operate through national subsidiaries.[3] However, this observation failed to take into account the possibility that it may be more convenient for MNCs to operate through subsidiaries because of the possibility of regulatory arbitrage.

The domestic corporate law governance paradigm today allows for *rentier* investors with limited liability who may take no part in the running of the company. They can choose to ignore what the company does knowing full well that their liabilities are limited to their shareholding. Liabilities rest with the company for what is done by it. Perhaps it is arguable that a company (and in some cases its management) should be held responsible for the company's acts but not shareholders who took no active part in the running of the company. Shareholders may choose to be active, but they are not required to be. However, in the multinational context, the shareholder is usually a parent company and in most cases, not a passive participant like individual shareholders but usually exercises control over the subsidiary. According to Strikwerda:

> The subsidiaries legally are independent firms and the formal relationship between the parent board and the subsidiary is that of shareholder. This statutory approach enables parent boards to co-ordinate the activities of subsidiary firms as if the parent is the direct owner of the assets contained in the subsidiaries.[4]

The *Salomon* principles[5] separate the MNC from the subsidiary, while the limited liability concept shields the MNC from liabilities arising out of the subsidiary's activities. According to Ireland:

> At present, corporate shareholders (including parent companies) enjoy the best of all possible legal worlds. On the one hand they are, for some purposes, treated as "completely separate" from the companies in which they hold shares and draw dividends, in that they are not personally responsible for the latter's debts or liabilities (or behaviour). On the other hand the companies in which they hold shares must be run exclusively in their interests: for these purposes

---

2 Ibid.
3 J. Strikwerda, "An Entrepreneurial Model of Corporate Governance: Devolving Powers to Subsidiary Boards" 3 (2) *Corporate Governance* (2003) 38, 40.
4 Ibid., 49.
5 *Salomon* v. *A. Salomon and Co Ltd* (1897) AC 22.

the interests of the "company" (formally a separate entity) are synonymous with those of its shareholders.[6]

Ireland and others have noted the concerted effort in extending this Anglo-American model to the international level.[7]

Delineating regulatory space at the international level

The question to be addressed is whether there is an identifiable entity at the global level that should be subject to a different type of regulatory framework different from domestic company law?

Professor Backer's insightful article in 2006 shed light on this question.[8] Building on earlier works by Hansmann and Kraakman and Iwai, he argues that "the nexus of multinational enterprises and globalization provides a foundation for the emergence of self-conscious, autonomous, self-regulating economic enterprises".[9] As he rightly notes, the idea is not entirely new in the literature. The idea of a corporation with an interest in itself separate from others with interest in it has been persuasively canvassed in the past. However, the concept has been discussed in the context of territorial companies and not in the global context.[10] Backer's argument is apposite because it took the idea of the autonomy of the corporation to the international level where it is more relevant.

Corporate autonomy: Hansmann and Kraakman, and Iwai's propositions and Backer's analysis

Hansmann and Kraakman's asset partitioning proposition contends that law of business organisation is essentially property law and not contract law as widely canvassed.[11] According to them, the popular nexus of contract proposition[12] does not reflect reality of organisational behaviour as the ability to "define the property rights over which participants in a firm can contract"

---

6 Ireland (note 1), 12.

7 Ireland (note 1); S. Soederberg, *The Politics of the New Financial Architecture: Reimposing Neoliberal Domination in the Global South* (London: Zedbooks, 2004).

8 L.C. Backer, "The Autonomous Global Corporation: On the Role of Organizational Law Beyond Asset Partitioning and Legal Personality" 41 *Tulsa Law Journal* (2006) 541.

9 Ibid., 545.

10 See Chapter 3.

11 H. Hansmann and R. Kraakman, "The Essential Role of Organizational Law" 110 *Yale Law Journal* (2000) 287.

12 The nexus of contract proposition conceives the company as a vehicle for contracting where each constituency is placed within a contractual paradigm that only recognises bargained rights. O Amao, "Reconstructing the Role of the Corporation: Multinational Corporations as Public Actors in Nigeria" 29 *Dublin University Law Journal* (2007) 312, 313.

does.[13] The two essential components of asset partitioning are the creation of a pool of assets distinct from the personal assets of the firm's owners and managers and the assignment of priority of creditors within the created pools of assets. Hansmann and Kraakman, added a significant component to the concept of autonomy of the enterprise in itself. According to Backer:

> It suggests, first, that a self-contained (or containing) vessel must exist into which assets can be segregated and, second, that assets and other things of value can be segregated within and placed beyond the direct reach of people with an interest in the entity … [S]trengthening asset partitioning also strengthened the possibility of entity autonomy at the expense of direct control by the shareholder. More importantly, it provided a single institutional shield for assets aggregated by the collective. When combined with the idea of the independence of juridical personhood, it provided a means to disperse assets in a way that protected them from creditor and owner alike. An entity that can disperse assets and other things of value among other entities it owns or controls can significantly enhance its operation as a unit independent of its owners or those with interests in its assets, such as creditors and other stakeholders.[14]

Backer correctly identifies the limitations of Hansmann and Kraakman's analysis. The authors' focus is on corporations within the same territorial border. The concept thus persuasively analyses the autonomy of national corporations. It is thus unclear, from their writing, how asset partitioning may be applied to assets dispersed across jurisdictions and among actors in different jurisdictions.[15]

Backer also analysed the proposition of Iwai in the light of enterprise autonomy. Like Hansmann and Kraakman, Iwai explores the relationship between the corporate entity and its owners. He argues that a corporation is neither a person nor a thing but an amalgamation of the two because of its capacity to be owned and to own itself. On the one hand the corporation is owned by its shareholders; on the other hand the corporation owns all of the assets of the corporation. The corporation thus has a dual nature: a person and a thing. However, Iwai's analysis is also limited by the territorial principle.[16]

Nonetheless, while the extent of the ownership of shareholders of the modern corporation is debatable,[17] the corporation ownership of its own assets is settled in law.

---

13 Backer (note 8), 550.
14 Ibid., 551.
15 Ibid., 551–552.
16 Ibid., 554.
17 For example while shareholders are widely perceived as the owners of the company, they do not own the assets of the company.

These writers' arguments have demonstrated that the modern corporation in the sense that we know it has emerged as an autonomous entity, that autonomy is, however, limited by the political will of the state under which an enterprise is organised at the domestic level.

The question then is: if the autonomous enterprise is constrained by the political will of the state under which it is organised at the domestic level, what constrains or what should constrain the enterprise when it operates globally? One might argue that it is the various laws of the countries where it operates through subsidiaries, affiliates or the like. However, this will not address the complexity of MNCs, as often is the case, where the act of the corporation is not about what is done in a particular local situation but what is brought about by the nexus of the MNCs' global operations. Since there is no international company law comparable to domestic company law, MNCs appear at the moment to be organised by no law and constrained by no law.

The consequences of this situation were succinctly put by Backer:

> The nature of the perversities is well-known. They range from the benign to the disturbing. Enterprises can exploit the territorial principle, the principles of limited liability, and that of independent juridical personality to minimize risks to assets partitioned to the entity. This risk minimization is accomplished by distributing assets among widely dispersed subsidiaries incorporated in different jurisdictions and by engaging in enterprise activities indirectly through joint ventures, distributorships, franchises, local agents, or other indirect forms of operation. Multinational enterprises have been able to exploit their economic power to negotiate with states for the enactment of regulations favourable to the enterprise and to avoid liability for local actions, local taxes, and other impositions charged by the state to others similarly situated. Multinational enterprises have also used their power to intervene directly or indirectly in the politics of political jurisdictions. The involvement of large enterprises in local civil wars, coups, and other changes of government, and the willingness of enterprises to engage local corruption are well documented.[18]

Backer went on to argue that through its autonomy, the corporation has evolved to an entity that can regulate itself independent of the state. The task of this chapter is not to test the veracity of this assertion but to demonstrate the need for a global law to regulate MNCs.

18 Backer (note 8), 556–557.

The Norms: a disguise for an "international company law"?

There is a perception that there is slowly emerging a new regulatory node for the governance of corporations at the international level. Generally, this regulatory node is hardly acknowledged. In another work, Backer recognised the emergence of this separate field of law which he describes as "transnational law".[19] Various attempts that have been made in the past to devise a framework for the regulation of MNCs' activities at the international level (discussed in Chapter 2) support this notion. However, the Norms on Responsibility of Transnational Corporations and other Business Enterprises with Regard to Human Rights are unique because they took an approach that theoretically has the potential to address the peculiar structure of global corporations.

The Norms and the regulatory space at the international level

In his analysis of the Norms, Backer posited that the Norms are important because of two interconnected reasons. First, they indicate the "evolution of significant changes in global thinking about corporations and character and source of their regulation".[20] Second, they "illustrate the development *in fact* of a mechanics of interplay between national, international, public, and private law systems in allocating and competing for regulatory power" which is evidence of transnational law emerging as a separate field of law.[21] What the Norms did according to Backer include:

1 Altering considerably the debate on corporate social responsibility by conceiving the corporations as social, political and economic actors which should serve a broader set of stakeholders including traditional stakeholders, the state and international community;[22]
2 Disregarding traditional constraints on action against shareholders virtually for all purposes;
3 Altering the balance of power over corporate governance between inside stakeholders and outside stakeholders by the provision of a substantial role for NGOs to monitor the compliance of MNCs with the Norms.[23]

As Backer correctly notes, the Norms introduced standards that are in conflict with domestic corporate law of many states with little effort to

---

19 Backer (note 8).
20 Ibid., 288.
21 Ibid.
22 Ibid., 292.
23 Ibid., 293.

recognise or resolve the conflict.[24] Backer is of the opinion that the approach reflects a clever idea that asserts the autonomy and supremacy of international law over domestic law by imposing international law standards through private law. The approach makes state acceptance of the standards less relevant to implementation. According to Backer, the Norms seek to achieve the objective by putting forward the norms-grounded private and contractually binding behaviour of MNCs as the basis for the recognition of new customary international law applicable to companies in the international context. As Backer pointed out, the drafters of the Norms while recognising these conflicts aim to circumvent them by employing the Norms as a vehicle for creating what may be called "customary international company law" in this area which will pre-empt state corporate law to the extent of their inconsistency.[25]

A striking example of the Norms' approach is its treatment of the conflict between shareholder primacy and stakeholder model. In most domestic law, shareholder primacy holds sway in varying degrees. The Norms moved away from this position to a broader approach that sees diverse stakeholders in the territory which the company operates as stakeholders of the corporation. They thus suggest a stakeholder primacy model.[26] The concept of stakeholder was expanded to include virtually all elements of society.[27] Stakeholders according to the Norms, include any individual or entity who is "substantially affected by the activities" of the MNC.[28] It may therefore include consumer groups, customers, governments, neighbouring communities, indigenous peoples and communities, non-governmental organisations, public and private lending institutions, suppliers, trade associations and others.[29] Since the Norms are an international law instrument designed to be binding in all states, assuming that it came into force, it would have overridden any conflicting corporate governance models at the state level. For example, to the extent that the Norms are applicable, the shareholder primacy model prevalent in the United States could have been supplanted.[30]

Another example is the treatment of labour/employees under paragraph 9 of the Norms which requires that MNCs should incorporate the terms of the Norms into labour contracts and the right to go to arbitration. This according to Backer will have the effect of treating labour as a

24 Ibid., 357.
25 Ibid. Examples of the Norms' attempt to introduce a different conception at the international level include its treatment of shareholders interest, directors' duties to incorporate the Norms, treatment of employees and enterprise liability.
26 Ibid., 358.
27 Ibid.
28 The Norms, para. 22.
29 Ibid.
30 Backer (note 8), 356; the Norms, para. 16.

direct constituency of the corporation.[31] This position again conflicts with the corporate law tradition of most states. Only few states like Germany have some degree of labour participation in corporate governance.

A further example is the internationalisation of the widely debated concept of enterprise liability. The Norms attempted to internationalise the enterprises liability model in determining the scope of liability of MNCs. This runs against the tradition of the autonomous legal personality of the corporation. States, of course, can lift the veil of incorporation of corporate groups where the parents and the affiliates are in the same territory but this is hardly ever extended to groups in different territories. The Norms will thus appear to have disregarded the domestic limitations here and impose enterprise liability as a matter of international law adopted by states.

In domestic jurisdictions where enterprise theory has been considered as a means of making parent companies responsible for the activities of their subsidiary, it has been rejected.[32] This is hardly surprising as such unilateral action by one country may put its corporations at a disadvantage when compared with other countries which have not taken the approach. According to Muchlinski, "enterprise entity" doctrine "deduces parent company liability from the fact of economic integration between itself and the subsidiary".[33] The theory recognises the corporate group as a distinct form of business organisation. This recognition "opens the way for the evolution of a specialised legal regime going beyond the paradigm of the single unit limited liability joint stock company".[34]

Muchlinski suggests two ways by which the concept could be adopted which include: the introduction of a new type of supranational incorporation for corporate groups which assumes group liability as one of its consequences. In this regard, he made reference to the original European Company (Societas Europaea (SE)) proposal which contains provisions that will permit the management of the company as a single entity.[35] He did not, however, elaborate on this point. Second is the proposal for a presumption of control by the parent over the subsidiary which gives advance notice of liability to the parent company. The onus is on the parent company to rebut the presumption by proving the independence of the subsidiary. Muchlinski discussed the limitation of the second approach which renders its practicality doubtful. The supranational incorporation idea, however, is relevant to the core arguments of this chapter.

---

31 Ibid.
32 P.T. Muchlinski, *Multinational Enterprises and the Law* (second edition, Oxford: Oxford University Press, Oxford, 2007), 319; for a discussion of enterprise liability see P.I. Blumberg, *The Multinational Challenge to Corporation Law* (New York: Oxford University Press, 1993).
33 Muchlinski (note 32), 317.
34 Ibid.
35 Commission Proposal for a Council Regulation on the Statute for a European Company, COM (89) 268 final – SYN 218.

Having delineated the regulatory space at the international level, the next task is to consider how to regulate this unique space.

An innovative framework for regulating the global corporations: a proposal

Because of the transborder nature of MNCs' activities and the lack of consensus on how MNCs should be controlled, regulating MNCs requires institutional innovation at the international level. Recently the UN Human Rights Council in extending the mandate of the UN special representative underscored the need to act at the international level when it observed that:

> Weak national legislation and implementation cannot effectively mitigate the negative impact of globalization on vulnerable economies, fully realize the benefits of globalization or derive maximally the benefits of activities of transnational corporations and other business enterprises and that therefore efforts to bridge governance gaps at the national, regional and international levels are necessary.[36]

In his report to the Human Rights Council, Ruggie suggests the creation of a well-resourced global ombudsman office that could receive and handle complaints.[37]

This writer posits that the prerequisite task is to facilitate the recognition of international corporate personality for international companies (IC) and the scope of responsibility and liability attached to the concept.[38]

---

36 Human Rights Council, Preamble to Resolution 8/7, Mandate of the Special Representative of the Secretary General on the Issue of Human Rights and Transnational Corporations and other Business Enterprises.

37 Promotion and Protection of all Human Rights, Civil, Political, Economic, Social and Cultural Rights, Including the Right to Development; Protect, Respect and Remedy: A Framework for Business and Human Rights; Report of the Special Representative of the Secretary General on the Issue of Human Rights and Transnational Corporations and other Business Enterprises, John Ruggie, A/HRC/8/5, 7 April 2008.

38 This will be similar to the provisions of the European Company (Societas Europaea or SE) Regulation, 2004. The EU statute intervenes in areas which are essential to enable companies to maximise their potentials and left other matters within national remit as they were before the statute. The aim was to create a single European structure that companies may choose to use in doing business in the European Union. The statute gives firms operating in two or more member states the option of forming a European company. Under article 2 and title II of the regulation, generally, the SE can be formed by the consequence of first, the merger of two or more existing companies originating from at least two member states, second, the formation of a holding company promoted by public or private limited companies, third, the formation of jointly held subsidiary and fourth, the conversion of an existing public limited company. Under article 38(b) of the regulation, it is provided that the European Company shall be regulated by the domestic law of the place where the company is registered.

The UN is best placed to develop a model framework in this area. This, potentially, will be more fruitful than the past attempts by the UN discussed earlier.

The IC will be a distinct and separate personality from other ICs and companies but not from its subsidiaries. The framework shall also define the concept of MNCs. It shall define the scope of the liability relating to shareholding by a parent company in a subsidiary in the multinational context different from the liability of individual (human) shareholding. Furthermore, the framework will address the need to establish a common disclosure regime for MNCs at the international level. Member states should be encouraged but not mandated to incorporate the provisions of the framework into domestic law. Once incorporated into domestic law, companies that met the criteria of MNCs wishing to operate within the domestic jurisdiction will be obliged to obtain the "international company (IC)" status before commencing operation.

The UN shall provide supporting mechanisms by maintaining a global registry for ICs. The registry will issue IC certificates and keep record of the international network of operations of registered ICs.

Laws relating to ICs will be primarily enforced at the domestic level but domestic courts will be able to refer disputes as to the interpretation and application of the UN framework to a panel of experts to be established under the framework. The framework law will not address issues relating to internal regulations of companies but to the regulatory gaps which are created by the global operation of companies as they arise.

Perhaps the European endeavour to create a pan European Regulatory framework for MNCs operating within the EU may serve as a useful guide for the international community. Tudway has described the European activities in this area as the most developed response to the issue of MNCs.[39] Starting from 1968, the European Community embarked on creating a pan European company law. In its early days the ambition was to harmonise European company law in totality.[40] One of the two main aims of the harmonisation is dealing with externalities arising from cross border activities. These externalities occur because of the focus of national legislation on the internal governance of the company and from competition between jurisdictions.[41] However, this ambition was not followed through. The European Community shied away from the initial move to include substantive provisions on corporate groups in its European Company

---

39 R. Tudway, "The Juridical Paradox of the Corporation" in F Macmillan (ed.,) *International Corporate Law Annual* (Oxford and Portland, OR: Hart Publishing, 2003), 82.

40 T. Baums and P.K. Andersen, "The European Model Company Law Act Project", ECGI – Law Working Paper no. 97/2008.

41 J. Wouters, "European Company Law: Quo Vadis?" (2000) 37 *Common Market Law Review* 257, 294.

Statute.[42] However, there are developments in the evolution of the EU regulation of companies which may be instructive for the international community. The European endeavour can be useful for example in identifying
corporate groups and determining parents' liability for subsidiary
activities.

The Draft for a European Company Statute of 1970 dealt with the identification of corporate groups and determining parents' liability for subsidiaries. The provisions of this draft were to be applicable to companies
created under the statute. The draft has specific provisions concerning
corporate groups. Article 239 of the statute provides that:

1   The controlling company of a concern shall be liable for the debts
    and liabilities of its dependent subsidiary companies.
2   Proceedings may be bought against the controlling company only
    after the creditor has first made a written demand for payment on
    the dependent subsidiary company and failed to obtain
    satisfaction.

There is a rebuttable presumption that if a parent owns a majority stake in
the subsidiary, it is in control of it. This presumption can be rebutted if
the parent provides evidence that it is a mere passive shareholder.[43] Under
article 225, the European Court of Justice can entertain a request to determine whether a parent is considered to be in control of a subsidiary or
not.

Another relevant development in the EU was the draft proposal for a
ninth directive on corporate groups/affiliated undertakings which also
had as one of its aims, the harmonisation of corporate group law in the
community. There are four categories of corporate groups identified
under the directive: de facto groups, contract concerns, declaration concerns and concerns under national laws. Owning shares in a subsidiary
establishes a de facto type group and where the parent in such a group is
involved in the management of the subsidiary, the parent is liable for all
violations of the subsidiary's fiduciary duties.[44] Contract groups are those
connected by control agreements.[45] Minority shareholders of the subsidiary are entitled to sue the parent company in case of violation of the
control agreements.[46] The parent is jointly liable for all subsidiary obligations to third party creditors.[47] Declaration concerns involves where a

42 1989 Proposal, KOM (1989) 268 endg.
43 Articles 6(3) and 223(2), European Company Statute of 1970.
44 Ibid., articles 6–12.
45 Ibid., article 13–32.
46 Ibid., article 26.
47 Ibid., article 29.

parent company owns 90 per cent or more of the shares of the subsidiary. In this scenario, the subsidiary can be formally declared as part of the parent company and the companies will be subject to similar liabilities as in the case of contract concerns.[48] National concerns are established in accordance with national laws and are required to have safeguards similar to contract concerns.[49]

Summary

The contention of this chapter is that the global corporation is a distinct entity different from the corporation as recognised under domestic law. The global corporations hitherto have been operating in regulatory vacuum employing elements of domestic company law where it favours them. This state of affairs has led to negative consequences especially in the human rights sphere. The chapter argued that the global corporation operates in a different regulatory space which requires a different regulatory approach. The chapter suggested an innovative approach to the regulation of the global corporations which will bypass the lack of consensus at the international level. The chapter suggests that the United Nations should direct its effort and resources towards the creation of a framework that will recognise the international company with international corporate personality. This will set out the requirement for and the consequences of international corporate personality. Supporting mechanisms shall also be provided at the UN level. A state will have the discretion to incorporate the framework into domestic law if it so desires. This approach will be beneficial to host states especially in developing countries with weak institutions.

48 Ibid., articles 33–37a.
49 Ibid., article 38.

Conclusions

CSR as practised by corporations is vague, its boundaries are fluid and it is difficult to evaluate. While the CSR concept has its advantages, it is opined that it is not adequate to remedy many of the issues arising out of MNCs' operations, particularly as they relate to human rights. While this book recognised the opportunities presented by international law, it concluded that because of its limitations it is better to focus on the domestic forum and employ international law as a supporting mechanism.

The main arguments of this book are grouped into five. First, attempts at the international level to find solutions to the challenges posed by MNCs have proved unsuccessful to date. International law has inherent limitations that are hindering the achievement of a global consensus on the control of MNCs. The political will to control MNCs is not present and the prospect of having that will in the near future is not likely. Home and host countries have jurisdiction over companies in their territories. Practical solutions lie in exploring home and host states' control, complemented by regional-treaty based arrangements and international law.

Second, the CSR concept originated within legal discourse. However, it has since moved from that starting point to becoming a business-led public relation strategy adopted on a voluntary basis. The book argued that the embracing of the CSR concept by corporations indicates responsiveness to responsibility which companies would have otherwise denied such as the promotion and protection of human rights. It is argued that with the accordance of "human rights" to corporations as "persons" in many jurisdictions, corporations should also have human rights obligations under both domestic and international law as is the case of individuals. It is noted that given the move towards regulating aspects of CSR in some jurisdictions, the law might do more in the future to regulate issues raised in the CSR debate.

Third, the book concluded that there are viable opportunities at the domestic level which have not hitherto been fully explored. It identified the limitations within the domestic forum focusing on Nigeria as a case study and made recommendations for regulatory reforms. It also highlighted areas of opportunity and the need to tap into these areas. In the field of human rights, it showed the emerging judicial readiness to apply human rights law to MNCs' activities. This is a novel development that has no precedent in the country. The decision of the federal High Court in Nigeria in the case of *Gbemre* v. *Shell* opens a vista which it is recommended should be explored further. The book also pointed to the need for a shift to the corporate governance paradigm in order to properly situate the company within the local context. It is argued that corporate law should reflect the true role of the corporation within a society.

Fourth, based on the principle of state responsibility and the provisions of the African Charter, it is concluded that the African regional system has the potential to ensure that states comply with their obligations to prevent human rights abuses by MNCs. While the book noted the promising jurisprudence of the African Commission on Human and Peoples' Rights in this regard, it is cautious because of the problem of access to the institutions of the African Union. The book also noted the approach of the African Union Convention on Preventing and Combating Corruption to private parties which it is argued is robust and a welcome complement to the OECD Convention. It, however, finds that the mechanisms for enforcement under the convention are weak and inadequate.

Fifth, the work identified ways through which home states of MNCs, can influence the host state's capacity to control MNCs. First, through a broader implementation and enforcement of human rights clauses in trade agreements. Second, through the provision of freer access to member state's courts for victims of abuse by MNCs.

Finally, the book proposed a meaningful role at the international level to complement developments at the domestic level. This will involve developing a concept of international company under an international company law framework. It is suggested that the United Nations is best placed to develop and facilitate such a framework. The framework should not be imposed on states but may be adopted voluntarily. The advantages of such a framework include formal recognition of the global nexus points of MNCs and the establishment of a uniform standard for ascertaining liability of MNCs for the operations of their subsidiaries.

Selected bibliography

Addo, M. (ed.), *Human Rights Standards and the Responsibility of Transnational Corporations* (The Hague: Kluwer Law International, 1999).

Alston, P. (ed.), *Non-State Actors and Human Rights* (Oxford: Oxford University Press 2005).

Barnet, R.J. and Muller, R.E., *Global Reach: The Power of Multinational Corporations* (New York: Simon and Schuster, 1974).

Bartels, L., *Human Rights Conditionality in the EU's International Agreements* (Oxford: Oxford University Press, 2005).

Berle, A.A. and Means, G.C., *The Modern Corporation and Private Property* (New York: Commerce Clearing House, 1932).

Berle, Jr., A.A., *The 20th Century Capitalist Revolution* (New York: Harcourt, Brace and Co., 1954).

Black, E., *IBM and the Holocaust* (London: Time Warner, 2002).

Blumberg, P., *The Multinational Challenge to Corporate Law* (Oxford: Oxford University Press 1993).

Boeger, N., Murray, R. and Villiers, C. eds, *Perspectives on Corporate Social Responsibility* (Cheltenham: Edward Elgar, 2008).

Campbell, T. and Miller, S. *Human Rights and the Moral Responsibilities of Corporate and Public Sector Organizations* (The Netherlands: Kluwer Academic Publishers, 2004) 63.

Cohen, J.L., *Regulating Intimacy* (New Jersey: Princeton University Press, 2002).

Cook, A.N., *British Enterprise in Nigeria* (London: Frank Cass & Co. 1964).

Crawford, J., *The International Law Commission's Articles on State Responsibility: Introduction Text and Commentary* (Cambridge: Cambridge University Press, 2002).

Curtin, P.D., *Cross Cultural Trade in World History* (Cambridge: Cambridge University Press, 1984).

Dan-Cohen, M., *Rights, Persons, and Organizations* (Berkeley: University of California Press, 1986).

Dine, J., *Companies, International Trade and Human Rights* (Cambridge: Cambridge University Press, 2005).

Donaldson, T., *Corporations and Morality* (New Jersey: Prentice Hall, 1982).

Easterbrook, F.H. and Fischel, D.R., *The Economic Structure of Corporate Law* (Cambridge: Harvard University Press, 1991).

Ekelund, R.B. and Tollison, R.D., *Mercantilism as a Rent-Seeking Society: Economic Regulation in Historical Perspective* (Texas, College Station: Texas A&M University Press Texas, 1981).

Emberland, M., *The Human Rights of Companies: Exploring the structure of ECHR Protection* (Oxford: Oxford University Press, 2006).

French, P., *Collective and Corporate Responsibility* (New York: Columbia University Press 1984).

Freund, E., *The Legal Nature of Corporations* (Chicago: University of Chicago Press, 1897).

Friedman, M., *Capitalism and Freedom* (Chicago: University of Chicago Press,1962).

Friedman, M., "The Social Responsibility of Business is to Increase its Profits" in M.W. Hoffman and R.E. Frederick (eds), *Business Ethics, Readings and Cases in Corporate Morality* (New York: McGraw Hill, 1995), 133.

Gierke, O., *Political Theories of the Middle Age* (Translated by Frederic W. Maitland) (Cambridge: Cambridge University Press 1990).

Henderson, D., *Misguided Virtue: False Notions of Corporate Social Responsibility* (New Zealand: Business Roundtable, 2001).

Howse, R. and Mutua, M., *Protecting Human Rights in a Global Economy: Challenges for the World Trade Organization* (Montreal: International Centre for Human Rights and Democratic Development, 2000).

Hufbauer, G.C. and Mitrokostas, N.K., *Awakening Monster: The Alien Tort Statute of 1789* (Washington, DC: Institute for International Economics, 2003).

International Law Association Human Rights Committee, "Report on Civil Actions in the English Courts for Serious Human Rights Violations Abroad" (2001) 2 *European Human Rights Law Review* 129.

Jagers, N., *Corporate Human Rights Obligations: in Search of Accountability* (Antwerp: Intersentia, 2002).

Joseph, S., *Corporations and Transnational Human Rights Litigation* (Oxford and Portland: Hart Publishing, 2004).

Lynch Fannon, I., "The European Model of Corporate Governance: Prospects for Success in an Enlarged Europe" in P. Ali and G. Gregoriou (eds), *International Corporate Governance after Sarbanes-Oxley* (New Jersey: John Wiley & Sons, 2006), 423.

Lynch Fannon, I., *Working within Two Kind of Capitalism: Corporate Governance and Employee Stakeholding: US and EU Perspectives* (Oxford and Portland, OR: Hart Publishing, 2003).

McBarnet, D., A. Voiculescu and T. Campbell (eds), *The New Corporate Accountability: Corporate Social Responsibility and the Law* (Cambridge: Cambridge University Press, 2007), 241.

Manby, B., *The Price of Oil: Corporate Responsibility and Human Rights Violations in Nigeria's Oil Producing Communities* (New York: Human Rights Watch, 1999).

Mason, E.S. (ed.), *The Corporation in Modern Society* (Cambridge, MA: Harvard University Press, 1959).

Matsushita, M. and Ahn, D. eds, *WTO and East Asia: New Perspectives* (London: Cameron May Ltd, 2004).

Matsushita, M., Schoenbaum, T.J. and Mavroidis, P.C., *The World Trade Organization: Law, Practice, and Policy* (second edition, Oxford: Oxford University Press, 2006).

Meredith, M., *The State of Africa: A History of Fifty Years of Independence* (London: Free Press, 2005).

Micklethwait, J. and Wooldridge, A., *The Company: A Short History of a Revolutionary Idea* (London: Phoenix, 2005).

Mitchell, L., *Corporate Irresponsibility: America's Newest Export* (New Haven and London: Yale University Press, 2001).

Muchlinski, P.T., *Multinational Enterprises and the Law* (second edition, Oxford: Oxford University Press, 2007).

Mullerat, R. ed., *Corporate Social Responsibility: The Corporate Governance of the 21st Century* (The Netherlands: Kluwer Law International and International Bar Association, 2005).

Murray, R., *The African Commission on Human and Peoples' Rights and International Law* (Oxford, Portland, OR: Hart Publishing, 2000).

Okonta, I. and Douglas, O., *Where Vultures Feast: Shell, Human Rights, And Oil* (London and New York: Verso, 2003).

Omeje, K., *High Stakes and Stakeholders: Oil Conflict and Security in Nigeria* (England: Ashgate, 2006).

Orojo, J.O., *Company Law and Practice in Nigeria* (third edition, Lagos: Mbeyi & Associates Nigeria Ltd, 1992).

Parker, C., *The Open Corporation: Effective Self-regulation and Democracy* (Cambridge: Cambridge University Press, 2002).

Parkinson, J.E., *Corporate Power and Responsibility: Issue in Theory of Company Law* (Oxford: Clarendon Press, 1993).

Pieth, M., Low, L.A. and Cullen, P.J. eds, *The OECD Convention on Bribery: A Commentary* (Cambridge: Cambridge University Press, 2007).

Posner, R.A., *Economic Analysis of Law* (fifth edition, New York: Aspen Publishers Inc, 1989).

Rawls, J., *A Theory of Justice* (revised edition, Cambridge, MA: Harvard University Press, 1971, 1999).

Rogowski, R. and Wilthagen, T. eds, *Reflexive Labour Law* (Deventer and Boston: Kluwer Law and Taxation Publishers, 1994).

Villiers, C., *Corporate Reporting and Company Law* (Cambridge: Cambridge University Press, 2006), 229.

Wallace, C.D., *The Multinational Enterprise and Legal Control: Host State Sovereignty in an Era of Economic Globalization* (The Hague: Martinus Nijhoff Publishers, 2002).

Wheeler, S., *Corporations and the Third Way* (Oxford and Portland, OR: Hart Publishing, 2002).

Wilson, I., *The New Rules of Corporate Conduct: Rewriting the Social Charter* (Westport, CT: Quorum Books, 2000).

Wolgast, E., *Ethics of an Artificial Person: Lost Responsibility in Professions and Organizations* (Stanford: Stanford University Press, 1992).

Zerk, J.A., *Multinationals and Corporate Social Responsibility: Limitations and Opportunities in International Law* (Cambridge: Cambridge University Press 2006).

Index